THOREAU ON BIRDS

Books by Helen Cruickshank

Wonders of the Bird World

Wonders of the Reptile World

John and William Bartram's America

With Allan Cruickshank

1001 Questions Answered about Birds

THOREAU
ON BIRDS

Compiled and with Commentary by HELEN CRUICKSHANK

Thoreau

Foreword by
Roger Tory Peterson

598.2
T 39 t

New York · Toronto · London McGRAW-HILL BOOK COMPANY

Dedicated to Allan,
who devotes his life to advancing the cause of
conservation of our natural resources and the
greater enjoyment of the out-of-doors

ACKNOWLEDGMENTS

There are many research problems when a book about Thoreau is prepared far from the great libraries. Therefore my gratitude to all those who assisted in the preparation of *Thoreau on Birds* is very deep. I am particularly grateful to Mrs. Samuel A. Harper and the late Judge Harper for the privilege of borrowing whatever I wished from their fine library. The staff of the Cocoa Library went far beyond the call of duty to locate and borrow rare, out-of-print publications for me. The help of my sisters, Florence and Clare Elizabeth, was invaluable in obtaining photostats of material which could not be borrowed. I appreciate the help of Luther Goldman of the United States Fish and Wildlife Service and of Richard Borden of Concord whose ponds supply water when needed to maintain the level of the Great Meadows National Wildlife Refuge.

Less tangible, but no less appreciated help was given by Ward L. Johnson, the educator, who generously enriched my knowledge and appreciation of Thoreau's Concord. When very young, Mr. Johnson became acquainted with every part of Concord under the guidance of Adams Tolman who was once a member of the Thoreau household. The geographer, Dr. Millicent Todd Bingham, whose grandfather knew Thoreau well, aroused in me over the years a deep respect and admiration for Thoreau as a naturalist and conservationist.

As never before, I join the host of people around the world who enjoy reading Thoreau in recognizing our debt to Bradford Torrey and Francis H. Allen for having edited the major parts of Thoreau's *Journal*, enabling us to read it.

In addition, grateful appreciation goes to the many, many people who have published Thoreau's works, or have added to our knowledge of the man and his writing by their thoughtful studies.

Many delightful hours spent with Mr. and Mrs. Edwin Way Teale were to a great degree responsible for my enthusiasm in undertaking the task of selecting some of the best of the birds of Thoreau's *Journal*, together with bird material from his other books. Edwin Way Teale, editor and illustrator of the finest edition of *Walden* now in print has also edited *The Thoughts of Thoreau* (Dodd, Mead and Co., New York, 1962). He is a past president of the Thoreau Society and was one of the leaders in the battle, which had to be carried to the highest court in the state, to preserve Walden Pond in accordance with the wishes of Edith Emerson when she gave Walden to the state of Massachusetts. It is with the most profound appreciation that I thank Edwin Way Teale, the distinguished student of Thoreau and himself a great nature writer, for taking time in spite of a heavy work schedule to read the manuscript and offer constructive suggestions. Only those who have seen his unerring judgement at work can fully grasp the tremendous contribution his reading of the manuscript has made to the finished work.

Helen Gere Cruickshank
Rockledge, Florida

FOREWORD

The measure of a man is his durability. David Henry (Henry D.) Thoreau, more than any other naturist (as distinct from naturalist), has survived the changing thought patterns of the past century. Today he is actually read more, analyzed more, and discussed more than at any other time since he put his thoughts to paper with his own homemade pencils.

There have been many books written by and about this articulate man, and a number of collections have been extracted from his writings—books about his Concord neighbors, his New England travels, his aphorisms. This book, edited by Helen Cruickshank, gathers together his birds.

It may be argued that the hermit of Concord made no great contribution to the science of ornithology, but he is significant, if only because he was the first of a long succession of observers to make notes on the avian residents and visitors of the Concord River Valley in Massachusetts. He was followed, with but a short break, by Brewster, father of the American Ornithologists' Union, and later by the incomparable Griscom and more recently by Drury and his associates. One hundred and thirty years of almost continuous observation gives Concord a history of bird watching unmatched anywhere in the New World.

Although Thoreau's interest in birds may not have been particularly scientific, his writings about them have had more than ordinary influence, for he saw them through the eyes of a philosopher. The reason a Phoebe interested him was not because it mirrored human traits, but because it was completely dedicated to "phoebe-ism"—being a Phoebe. This view of life could not help but bring his fellow man into better focus.

That Walden Pond should have been the focal point of his studies is but an accident. There are a score of other ponds in Massachusetts—perhaps a hundred in New England—that have a more varied avifauna. But that is irrelevant. It just so happened that this deeply aware man lived handy by in Concord, a prophet who even in those less complicated days sensed man's maladjustment to his environment, his estrangement from the natural world that nurtured him.

Thoreauvians attack like a swarm of angry bees when Walden's woods and waters are threatened with modern development. It is not the few hundred pairs of woodland birds that are their principal concern: there are scores of millions of Ovenbirds and Towhees elsewhere in North America and millions of Crested Flycatchers, Blue Jays, and other Walden species. Their anger rises because a shrine has been threatened.

Helen Cruickshank, who edited and arranged this collection, is the wife of one of America's finest wildlife photographers, Allan Cruickshank. An accomplished ornithologist, conservationist, and photographer in her own right, she knows New England well, from lower Connecticut to the coast of Maine. The birds that Thoreau watched and wrote about are the birds she grew up with in the Appalachian hills.

Roger Tory Peterson

CONTENTS

(*Following page 207 is a section of illustrations taken from some of Thoreau's ornithological reference books.*)

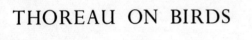

THOREAU ON BIRDS

Introduction: *Thoreau's Birds*

Long before he began observing birds in Concord, Henry David Thoreau saw the need of man to know and enjoy the world around him. On August 30, 1837, at the age of twenty, he was one of ten in the Harvard graduating class to take part in the commencement program. His subject was "The Commercial Spirit of Modern Times, Considered in its Influences on the Political, Moral, and Literary Character of a Nation", and he said:

This curious world which we inhabit is more wonderful than it is convenient; more beautiful than it is useful; it is more to be admired and enjoyed than used. The order of things should be somewhat reversed; the seventh should be man's day of toil, wherein to earn his living by the sweat of his brow; and the other six his Sabbath of the affections and the soul,—in which to range this widespread garden, and drink in the soft influence and sublime revelations of Nature.

This short paragraph foreshadows the plan for his life that Thoreau later evolved for himself. The plan, set forth in some detail in *Walden*, enabled him to achieve complete independence and to take care of his obligations to the last fraction of a cent. Through simplification he supplied his needs with a minimum expenditure of time and was free to spend the major part of his life in observation, thought, and writing.

After his college days Thoreau taught briefly, lived for some time in the home of Ralph Waldo Emerson, edited, wrote, and lectured, and spent several months as tutor for Emerson's nephew, William Emerson, Jr., on Staten Island. There his determination to return to Concord to stay crys-

3

tallized. Late in 1843 he went back to the town where he was born, and there he lived for the rest of his life except for occasional short excursions elsewhere.

He believed that Concord was a microcosm representative of the world. Frequently he read about a plant or animal found in some distant place and then, either found the same species or one closely related to it in Concord. He read about red snow in the Arctic and rejoiced when he found red algae in the snows of Concord. He was convinced that if he knew one small area well, he would understand the world and himself far better than if he traveled widely and therefore superficially. It was not necessary, he believed, to go around the world to count the cats in Zanzibar.

To learn the truth about life became Thoreau's guiding principle, once he had solved to his satisfaction the necessary economics for a free and independent existence. In everything he wrote, with pencils he made himself, he sought to record some kernel of truth. This is the link which binds together all of his work.

Thoreau's desire to understand the world through a study of one Massachusetts township required him to learn about all facets of his environment from the people to the most insignificant lichen and the relation of each to the other and to the land, waters, air, and rocks. He must know domestic plants and animals, but it was more important to know the wild ones. Though his ideas matured slowly, they began to flower during his stay at Walden Pond.

As he grew more familiar with Concord and its miles of rivers, its lakes, farms, and woods, it became for him a friendly and deeply loved universe. He devoted a prodigious amount of time and energy to its study. He seldom missed the dawn, and for half of most of his days, most often in the afternoon, he tramped the fields and woods or rowed on the Concord waters. He occasionally walked throughout fine, moonlit summer nights.

He preferred to spend those hours alone but occasionally a special friend—William Ellery Channing, Bronson Alcott, Harrison G. O. Blake of Worcester, or Daniel Ricketson of New Bedford—accompanied him. But even the most congenial of companions distracted his thoughts and hampered his observations. He made notes as he advanced along favorite trails. Then, after long hours of intense concentration, he returned home to distill for his *Journal* some truth or observation which he considered important.

Thoreau, with a college education, outraged local opinion by failing to settle down to a well-paying job. Even his clothes were severely criticized. He insisted that the reluctant Concord seamstress make large pockets adequate for his field equipment. He habitually carried a sharp knife, some string which he used in any of a dozen ways from tying a flying squirrel in his handkerchief to measuring the girth of an ancient elm, and a notched stick used to make fairly precise small measurements. After March, 1854, he carried his telescope. A paper and pencil for making field notes helped give accuracy to his subsequent reports. He often carried an old book in which plants could be pressed. More often plant specimens were carried home in his hat. This "botany-box" was formed by pulling the lining of his hat part way down the crown to make a small shelf. He felt plants kept particularly well in the warm, damp, darkness above his head.

In the woods his dull-colored clothes were not only serviceable but they enabled him to walk through farmers' fields and pastures unnoticed. He always perferred to travel the paths of foxes and woodchucks and made a game of approaching a house by keeping some tree or other object between himself and the owners so no one was aware of his passing. On May 8, 1857 he wrote:

Within a week I have had made a pair of corduroy pants, which cost when done $1.60. They are of that peculiar clay-color, reflecting the light from portions of their surface. They have this advantage, that, beside being very strong, they will look about as well three months hence as now,—or ill, some would say.... I like the color on other accounts.... The birds and beasts are not afraid of me now. A mink came within twenty feet of me the other day as soon as my companion left me, and if I had had my gray sack on as well as my corduroys, it would perhaps have come right up to me.

It was the custom in Concord to use a particular brand of shoe polish, but Thoreau again went against convention. Not the color but the softness of the leather and its waterproof qualities were important to him. Therefore he never blackened his shoes but kept them pliable and assured himself of dry feet by rubbing his footwear with tallow.

Thoreau rejoiced when spring days permitted the laying aside of heavy boots and overcoat which hampered his movements. One day while boating on Fair Haven he was caught in a rainstorm. He wore his umbrella like an ungainly cap. But this made it difficult for him to see, and his arms and legs were exposed to the rain. At length he began to enjoy the adventure, but he wrote, on April 22, 1856:

It is highly important to invent a dress which will enable us to go abroad with impunity in the severest storms. We cannot be said to have fully invented clothing yet.

Since this observation, tremendous effort has been expended in the development of proper clothing for extreme conditions encountered by explorers, astronauts, and field men engaged in less spectacular activities, yet the perfect answer to all situations has not yet been found. In spite of the shortcomings of his clothing, it was quite impervious to the thorniest brambles and its dun color blended almost invisibly into the background. We can almost see him, a faint shadow, moving across the Concord fields in search of birds. He felt himself one with the muskrats, the rabbits, and the birds, and as able as those creatures to avoid the attention of farmers, lumbermen, and fishermen. Birds, having the keenest eyesight of any animal in the world, did not overlook Thoreau. But he was willing to sit quietly. Therefore they often approached him, for quick movements rather than conspicuous colors alarm birds.

In making himself as inconspicuous as the native life he observed, Thoreau saw himself as part of nature, and the birds and mammals as natives of Concord, who, far from being his inferiors, were well adjusted to life there. They were natives of different nations, but nations with whom he was not at war.

This attitude toward his fellow beings is found only in slight glimpses before in human history. Centuries ago an early Christian book written, perhaps, by St. Augustine, contained a germ of Thoreau's thought when it says that God created angels in Heaven, and worms in the earth. He was not superior in one creation, nor inferior in the other; only His hands could create angels and only His hands could create worms.

Thoreau set in motion a whole new attitude toward nature. His strong vigorous prose related his observations and his relationship to the plants and animals of Concord so delightfully that they have given pleasure for more than a century to readers around the world. His prose has also had a profound influence on nature writers during the century since his death.

The Concord valley Thoreau knew had been farmed for two centuries. Most of his great woods were scarcely more than fifty year old, though many individual ancient trees and some primeval stands had escaped the lumberman's ax. Already some of the old fields cleared by the first settlers were growing up to brush or trees, chiefly white pine.

The woodlands, which deteriorated sharply after the arrival of the English settlers, continued this downward trend during Thoreau's time. In April, 1844, he set out to explore the source of the gently flowing Concord with his friend Edward Hoar. They borrowed a match from a shoemaker to build a fire for cooking the fish they had caught. Accidently they lost control of the blaze which burned more than a hundred acres of woodland near Fairhaven. For this, Thoreau was called a "damned rascal," and for decades he was condemned in Concord for that forest fire far more than he was appreciated there for the great thoughts he put in writing. Later, in 1850, he wrote about the fire and added:

When lightning burns the forest its Director makes no apology to man, and I was but His agent. Perhaps we owe to this accident partly some of the noblest natural parks. It is inspiriting to walk amid the fresh green sprouts of grass and shrubbery pushing upward through the charred surface with more vigorous growth.

Today Dr. Herbert Stoddard and many other scientists see the value of fire to the land even more clearly than Thoreau did more than a century ago. They believe it is a vital natural element in the wilderness and essential to the constant regeneration of forests. Research shows that good Bobwhite and Turkey habitat can only be maintained through periodic, properly controlled burning. But uncontrolled fires—and there have been many since Thoreau accidentally set fire to some Concord woods—have severely damaged the woodlands there. Added to fires, storms such as the hurricane of September 21, 1938, have caused further devastation.

Thoreau's Concord seems wild and primitive to his readers, but he well knew that interesting plants and animals had already vanished from it. He wrote on March 23, 1856:

I spend a considerable portion of my time observing the habits of wild animals, my brute neighbors. By their various movements and migrations they fetch the year about for me. Very significant are the flight of geese and the migration of suckers, etc., etc. But when I consider that the nobler animals have been exterminated here,—the couger, panther, lynx, wolverene, wolf, bear, moose, deer, the beaver, the turkey, etc., etc.—I cannot but feel as if I lived in a tamed, and, as it were emasculated country. Would not the motions of those larger and wilder animals have been more significant still? Is it not a maimed and imperfect nature that I am conversant with? As if I were to study a tribe of Indians that had lost all its warriors. Do not the forest and the meadow now lack expression, now that I never see nor think of the moose with a lesser forest on his head in the one, nor of the beaver in the other? When I think what were the various sounds and notes, the migrations and works, and changes of fur and plumage which ushered in the spring and marked the other seasons of the year, I am reminded that this my life in nature, this particular round of natural phenomena which I call a year is lamentably incomplete. I listen to [a] concert in which so many parts are wanting. . . . I take infinite pains to know all the phenomena of the spring, for instance, thinking that I have here the entire poem, and then, to my chagrin, I hear that it is but an imperfect copy that I possess and have read, that my ancestors have torn out many of the first pages and grandest passages, and mutilated it in many places.

Though nature in Concord had been mutilated, the fact that Thoreau recorded with infinite care, details about the soil and waters, the plant and animal life in various parts of the township, is of immense importance today. In all America there is no area where birds have been studied as long and as thoroughly by so many qualified observers as in Concord. Thoreau laid a firm foundation for understanding the changes in the bird life of that area brought about by time and man. His foremost contribution to the science of ornithology lies in the picture he created of the Concord bird life in his day, and the habitats in which various birds were found. His studies form the base for a continuous study which has progressed unbroken for more than a century since Thoreau left the scene. The Concord environment has changed, but the picture of the changes has been recorded decade after decade. Without doubt, it will be continued through decades to come.

Thoreau's interest in birds was slow to develop, though some of his notes, according to Ludlow Griscom in *Birds of Concord,* go back as far as 1832. He began placing charming notes about birds in his *Journal* as early as October 20, 1837. From childhood he was able to recognize a few very conspicuous or very common birds of Concord such as Robins, bluebirds, and crows. Then his brother John was far more interested in them than Henry who regarded them as little more than pleasant elements in the landscape. During and after his college days he wrote about birds chiefly as winged vehicles for his thoughts or to give color to a philosophical concept.

It was not until he began to clear land for his Walden cabin late in March, 1845, that he began to observe them closely. From that time onward he spent much time watching birds, reading about them, inspecting those shot by sportsmen and farmers, and from time to time studying skins, eggs, and nests in the Natural History Museum. Based on his studies, he wrote voluminously about the birds he observed.

There is little doubt that Thoreau would have gained much and learned faster had he had closer ties with the ornithological studies then being carried on in Massachusetts and elsewhere in the country. But the emphasis on the study of collected birds and their feeding habits as revealed by the examination of their crops repelled him. He believed the intrinsic values of birds lay in their beauty, their interesting behavior, their freedom in the air, and their songs. Part of their appeal to Thoreau, and to many who have lived after him, lay in the mystery of fleeting glimpses and brief snatches of song which were infinitely lovely but unknown to him.

Thoreau's readers are frequently surprised by the gaps in his knowledge. Today, bird identification is made easy even for beginners and it is sometimes forgotten that Thoreau was a pioneer in field identification. His contemporaries restricted their identification of birds to collected specimens. Since his time, field identification has progressed from infancy to highly skilled proficiency. A stranger wishing to look for birds in Concord may obtain a list of all the species he may expect to see there at any time of year as well as information about rarities and species only occasionally seen. Habitat preferences for all species are well known. Easily used field guides point out the differences between species that look somewhat alike. Excellent optical equipment enables the observer to see a brilliant image of the birds. Accurate recordings of bird songs and calls train the bird watcher's ears so the songs heard can be carefully analyzed. In order to place Thoreau's birds in correct perspective it is essential to understand the state of ornithological development during his lifetime.

The seventeenth century saw a great upsurge of interest in plants and animals not only in western Europe but in America. Collectors in far off parts of the earth sent specimens to scientists and interested laymen. The more curious they were, the greater interest they aroused. Those receiving collections proceeded to describe and name the specimens, and as a result so many names were given to a single species that chaos resulted and names became meaningless.

In the eighteenth century the great Swedish scientist Carl Linnaeus (1707–1778) set about the tremendous task of bringing order to the names of plants and animals. He set up clear principles for defining genera and species. He originated the binominal system in Latin, a language in world-wide use among scientists, under which all members of a genus had the same name plus an individual species name for each member. This system was quickly adopted by American scientists, but communication between them was slow and two or more often described and named a single species. There was often disagreement about genera. Though great strides had been made by the middle of the nineteenth century, Thoreau often found contradictory names and information in the books available to him.

Fragmentary notice of American birds had been made from the time Columbus noted migrating land birds and changed the course of his ships toward the direction from which they came. Birds, then, guided him to his landfall. Early explorers such as Captain John Smith, Cabot, and Weymouth took casual note of the conspicuous birds they saw. During early colonial days, Wood's *New England's Prospect* included some notes about birds which Thoreau found most interesting.

Between 1730 and 1748, Mark Catesby's *The Natural History of Carolinas, Florida,* etc., published in installments, was the first really great work about American birds. This had a hundred colored plates of birds and as many pages of text about them. The illustrations were recognizable and most species were for the first time described in this publication.

For several decades after Catesby's work was published, various individuals, among them John and William Bartram, John Reingold Forster, and the Swedish scientist Peter Kalm, contributed more information about American birds. Thomas Jefferson appeared in the role of ornithologist when his *Notes on the State of Virginia* was published.

In the early years of the nineteenth century, exploration of the North

American continent, spurred by Jefferson and the Louisiana Purchase, moved forward. So vast was the area to explore, scientists on expeditions seldom had time or opportunity for studies beyond the mere collection and preparation of specimens.

During this period two brilliant ornithologists appeared on the American scene. Alexander Wilson (1766–1813) and John James Audubon (1785–1851) began painting and describing birds. Both men roamed the eastern part of the continent in search of subjects. Each added unknown species to the growing list of American birds. Wilson's contribution to American ornithology was tremendous. He wrote careful descriptions of about two hundred and eight species of birds and made colored illustrations of most of them. His work, far overshadowing anything that had been done before, formed a sound basis for the study of ornithology in future years. The first volume of his *Ornithology* was published in 1808. When he died in 1813, seven volumes had been printed. He is referred to as the Father of American ornithology.

Audubon surpassed Wilson because he was a more dramatic personality and his genius as a painter was incomparably greater. Moreover, he painted almost twice as many species of birds as Wilson. Audubon's original *Elephant Folio* contained four hundred and thirty-five species painted life size against their natural habitat. The final work, as it left the author's hands, had a total of five hundred and six species represented. Though many people helped Audubon in the accomplishment of his Herculean task, it represents an achievement greater than that of any other pioneer work in American natural science.

Wilson and Audubon aroused a tremendous interest in American birds. They painted and described the majority of bird species found east of the Mississippi River. Sometimes they described immature birds as separate species. Often they confused the names of birds. Many other errors could be charged against them. But those pioneers, through their painting and writing, gave an impetus to the study of ornithology that has never subsided.

In the meantime, Thomas Nuttall (1786–1859), though primarily a botanist but deeply interested in birds, produced his *Manual of Ornithology of the United States and Canada.* The first volume of this work appeared in 1832, the year when Thoreau wrote his first known bird note. Nuttall's *Manual,* called the first handbook of birds, was priced within the means of many people and contained much sound information charmingly written in spite of numerous errors. Thoreau often referred to this manual. While it sometimes led him astray, it was a useful tool in identifying the birds of Concord.

By the end of Thoreau's life, most eastern species of birds had been collected, described, named, and their skins placed in museums and university collections. Many of the birds had been painted or drawn. Nests and eggs of many species had been found and collected, yet little or nothing was known about the habits of many of them. Plumage changes from juvenile to adult were often unknown as were seasonal changes. Information about nesting and wintering ranges was sketchy or lacking altogether. Many errors had been incorporated in books by distinguished scientists, but this in no way belittles their achievements. Most of the work done by the early ornithologists was sound though admittedly limited in scope.

Illustrations of birds which not only showed correct patterns and colors but reflected their individuality were a half-century or more in the future when Thoreau died. There was only confused bird banding until 1909 when the American Bird Banding Society was formed. Bird photography, study of birds from blinds, recordings of songs, field guides to the birds, local bird lists, and behavior studies now taken for granted belonged to a time long after Thoreau watched the birds of Concord.

Today's bird watchers not only have the advantage of fine optical equipment. The combined results of scientific research over the years, lifelike illustrations, still and moving pictures of birds in natural color, and other developments are all available to them. Moreover, by telephone bird watchers can learn where the largest concentrations of birds, or the most interesting species, may be found, and in a single day they may study the birds on mud flats behind falling tides, search conifer woods and deciduous forests, scan marshes and fields, and perhaps end the day high on a mountain slope. The swift mobility of people now makes distance relatively unimportant.

Thoreau's walks were leisurely. He called them sauntering trips, and while he often covered in a single day twenty miles or more, a trifling distance by present standards, he went by foot or by boat and always took time to observe natural phenomena. He recorded details, checked his first impressions for accuracy, and made careful notes. Later he compared his new observations with those made on previous occasions. The observations he found most interesting or which contributed to a particular study he was making, were entered in his *Journal* in vivid words which recreated the episode.

He proceeded cautiously with the naming of Concord birds. His references were Wilson, Audubon, Nuttall, and Brewer. He carefully checked and rechecked his observations against those inadequate references. Over the years he built up a good list of the birds in the area at that time. This list gains in value when compared with the present bird population of Concord, and during the intervening years. Thoreau initiated the most complete study ever made of any area of the United States. Following him came William Brewster, Dr. Herbert Ernest Maynard, and Ludlow Griscom. Today Virginia Armstrong, Mr. and Mrs. William Cottrell, Allen Morgan, Richard

Borden, and many others carry on studies of Concord birds—studies which have continued unbroken since Thoreau watched wood ducks merrily dabbling in the Concord River.

The fact that Thoreau frequently applied the blanket term "wood thrush" to all thrushes has been repeated through the years by his casual readers as evidence that he could not distinguish between the species. Entries in the *Journal* belie this. On occasion he placed notes in his *Journal* that prove he was able to identify the Wood Thrush, the Hermit Thrush, and the Veery if the situation permitted him to study the bird with care. He had trouble with sparrows, but bird watchers today, using the best binoculars and the finest field guide, experience difficulties and uncertainty at times in the field identification of sparrows in immature plumages or when but a brief glimpse of the bird is possible. Hawks and "beach-birds" also presented Thoreau with puzzles. But he continued to study each new bird with care, note its colors as precisely as possible, assign a name to it, and then reexamine his reference books in the light of his newest observations. Repeatedly he rechecked his own notes for accuracy.

Probably no nature writer in all history ever worked as diligently or spent as long hours in careful observation as did Thoreau. He took time to learn as much as possible from each episode. He squeezed the marrow from it. All of his senses were exceptionally keen, and he took pains to preserve their excellence. His ability to concentrate his attention was another valuable factor. This habit undoubtedly played a significant part in his work. His concentrated attention on subjects which interested him to the exclusion of others sometimes annoyed his friends and family. For instance, on March 28, 1853, he wrote:

My Aunt Maria asked me to read the life of Dr. Chalmers [Memoirs of Thomas Chalmers (in four volumes), a Scottish minister] *which, however, I did not promise to do. Yesterday, Sunday, she was heard through the partition shouting to my Aunt Jane, who is deaf, "Think of it! He stood half an hour to-day to hear the frogs croak, and he wouldn't read the life of Chalmers."*

At the present period in history when travel by car and hurried walking from one point to another are characteristic of field trips, Thoreau teaches a leisurely way of going afield with relaxed and intent attention. He found joy in the sounds of birds, and took time to go beyond the mere identification of them to really appreciate them, their wildness or delicacy or mystery, and his art of writing communicates his delight to his readers.

When contemporary ornithologists concentrated on the study of specimens and knew little about living birds and their habits, and when amateurs were largely egg collectors, Thoreau was learning the place of birds in their environment. Well in advance of his time, he realized that the study of dead birds left out the most important things about them. He preferred to learn about their food habits by watching the birds obtain and eat their food. He observed the birds as they collected materials for their nests and sometimes found their choice led him to a plant having unique strength in its fibers. He recorded the arrival and departure of the birds on their annual migrations. He paid particular attention to the place of birds in the landscape. One day while setting pines at Walden he enjoyed the singing of field sparrows and observed (April 22, 1859):

By a beautiful law of distribution, one creature does not much interfere with another. I do not hear the song sparrow here. As the pines gradually increase, and a wood-lot is formed, these birds will withdraw to new pastures and the thrushes, etc., will take their place.

Thoreau watched the manner in which many species of birds distributed the seeds of wild plants and domestic cherries. Not until the twentieth century was well advanced did scientists generally begin to understand the complex interrelationship of all forms of life in a healthy natural situation.

It is interesting to note that today many leading scientists are reluctant to use their collectors' permits to obtain laboratory specimens. Instead of shooting the birds they need for their studies, they use whenever possible birds that have been killed at windows, on highways, and so on. Tall Timbers Research Station in north Florida was established because of the great numbers of birds killed by flying into the TV tower. The dead birds are collected daily and sent to various institutions where they are studied by scientists engaged in dozens of research projects. Thoreau did not care for any laboratory, but he would have approved of making scientific use of the victims of accidents.

Thoreau listened with lively interest to the accounts of observations by his neighbors. Rarely does he comment on such observations. One exception to his silence came on January 14, 1858, after he had been told of a sea serpent off Swampscott and Little Nahant according to one Buffum. Thoreau then commented at the end of the tale that Buffum (as affecting the value of his evidence) was a firm believer in Spiritualism. Another time his delightful sense of humor emerged in a footnote after he told of the brave hunters who pursued a lynx, reported to be ten feet long, into an Andover swamp where it was shot by a young boy. The average length of a lynx is about three feet. Thoreau's footnote informs the reader that the lynx weighed nineteen pounds, which is about an average weight for the species. In the *Journal* notes here included are a few tales about birds told Thoreau by his neighbors.

By simplifying his life, Thoreau gained for himself the kind of leisure available to the great thinkers of ancient Greece. His leisure time was not simply time off from a job such as the vast majority of people have today. Most people fill their time off with play, household duties, or any of a thousand activities. Thoreau's leisure was filled with intense observation and deep thought. He had extraordinary vitality, and in all history few men have worked harder than Thoreau. He spent his enormous energy in thought, in observation, and in other ways which he believed were important.

There is much repetition in the material Thoreau wrote about birds. Each year he checked again his notes on the arrival of birds, on song period, and on nest building. Each year he added some new discoveries. Had he lived long enough to make use of the *Journal* material, he would probably have pruned and condensed his bird notes, distilling them to a fifth or even a tenth of their present volume.

The fact that Thoreau recorded in such infinite detail information about the plants, trees, and birds of various areas in Concord increases in importance as changes occur there. His *Journal* laid a foundation for understanding the changes in bird life that accompany changes in habitat, whether caused by time or, as is happening with such speed today, because of man's activities. Some of the birds that nested in Concord are now found there only on migration. Passenger Pigeons are extinct. The Prairie Warbler, unknown there a century ago, has established nesting colonies in fire-created scrub-oak barrens. Because of Thoreau's *Journal* we know of these and many more changes in Concord birds.

There is little doubt that Thoreau was a genius. His writing never lost the keen, joyful freshness of youth. It revives in his readers that same sense of exploration into the unknown that Thoreau experienced in the Concord woods. He was already mature when he first gave full attention to nature. He employed all his senses in the appreciation of each experience. His penetrating observations, written in powerful, living prose, arouse a determination in his readers to enjoy firsthand the same pleasure he brings alive in his books. Because of this, Thoreau's observations will continue to be important to bird watchers as long as books are read.

Walden, of course, is Thoreau's most famous book. During his two years beside that pond, birds for the first time became an important part of his life and the pages of that book contain some of his finest writing.

Map of the Town of Concord

1852

Monument at the "Old North Bridge"

CARLISLE

PART OF CAR

VI

VII

V

ANNURSNACK HILL

ASSABET RIVER

LEE HILL

CONCORD VILLAGE

DAMONS MILLS

IV

FITCHBURG RAIL ROAD

Rail Road Station

I

WALDEN POND
64.04 A.

L N

CONCORD RIVER

SUDBURY

WHITE POND
40 A.

NINE ACRE CORNER

III

FAIR HAVEN BAY

FITCHBURG

REMARKS.

Concord was settled in 1635 & then included within limits, nearly
the whole of Carlisle, Bedford, Lincoln, Sudbury, & Acton.
The Total Length of Public Highways is   55 Mile
The Length of the Fitchburg R.R. in Concord is   4½ "
Total Area of the town   15175 Acres
Area Covered by water about   723 "
Area occupied by Roads & Rail Roads about   250 "
Population in 1850   2249

Distances from the Town Pump, opposite the Town Hall are marked on the Roads
The Town Lines are laid down principally from old Surveys. White Pond &
Walden Pond from Surveys by H.D.Thoreau, Civ. Engr.

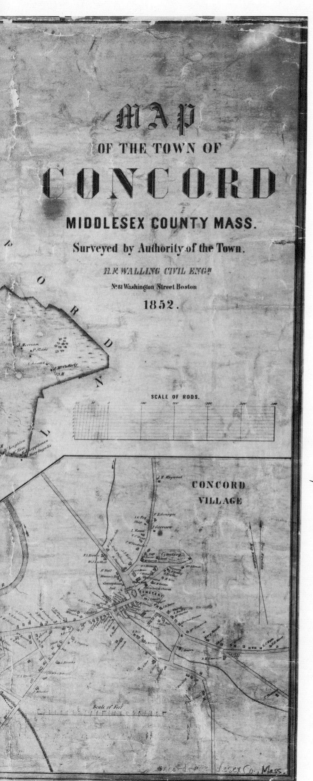

MAP
OF THE TOWN OF
CONCORD
MIDDLESEX COUNTY MASS.

Surveyed by Authority of the Town.

H.F. WALLING CIVIL ENG.ᴿ
N.º 81 Washington Street Boston
1852.

SCALE OF RODS.

CONCORD
VILLAGE

Scale of Feet

Concord Middlesex Co., Mass.

Henry D. Thoreau

Birds by a Lakeside Cabin

[*Walden*, one of the most influential books ever written in America, was first published in 1854. While it is often read merely as a delightful tale of camping in a snug cabin in the woods, it is far more than that. It is a literary treatment of a way of life.

Thoreau was always a man of independent character and a nonconformist, but his New England conscience demanded that he provide for his own needs. How was he to obtain without too great an expenditure of time and effort the necessities for a self-respecting life? At his Harvard graduation he was one of three speakers on the subject, "The Commercial Spirit of Modern Times, Considered in its Influence on the Political, Moral, and Literary Character of a Nation." Thoreau advanced the idea that the Biblical injunction that man should labor six days and rest on the seventh was not good. Instead, he believed one day only should be spent in earning the necessities of life. The other six should not be spent in idleness but in what he called "poetical living." Thoreau had great admiration for the Greeks and he noted the fact that they had enjoyed genuine leisure, not simply as time off from work, but as an opportunity to produce some of the world's finest literature and some of its greatest philosophical concepts. He wanted to fill his life with purposeful thought and activity, not waste it in conventional labor for money and things. Like the Greeks, he needed leisure to observe, to think, to read, and for walking in the woods and rowing on the waters, and for polishing his sentences until they were a distillation of truth and sparkled like sudden shafts of light.

Thoreau's problem, then, was to obtain sufficient leisure and use this leisure to produce the results which he deemed important. In order to devote most of his days to observation, writing, and thinking, he decided he must simplify his life. He must have no single possession unessential to his plan of life. He must eat simply for healthful reasons and to make his slender means cover his needs. He must dress simply. His was a universal problem faced by all poor people who wish to create. Thoreau never suggested that others solve their problem as he solved his, only that if their desire was great enough they could find some means both honorable and satisfactory for providing themselves with time to try to accomplish their dreams.

It has not been unusual in the history of the world for men to withdraw to solitary places in order to think or write. Knowledge that men had made use of time in solitary places to do some creative work must have had a strong influence on Thoreau, who lived in the social confusion of a boarding house. His good friend, William Ellery Channing, had lived alone for awhile on an Illinois prairie. But Thoreau did not want to leave Concord, for as far as he was concerned Concord held the best of the world. Instead of choosing some distant place for his period of seclusion, he wanted to remain in Concord and near his family and friends. This plan materialized when Emerson bought about fourteen acres of briar patch and pine woods beside Walden Pond and gave Thoreau permission to build a cabin on it. During his stay of two years, two months, and two days in the cabin which cost $28.12½ to build, Thoreau not only gathered much of the material used in *Walden* but he wrote some of the book. At Walden, wild creatures played by his doorstep and phoebes built in his woodshed while mice and squirrels moved inside with him.

To naturalists, Thoreau's poetic appreciation of the world about him makes *Walden* one of America's best nature books. To those who are poor and long to create, Thoreau's bean-patch economics give hope and courage. To those who long for freedom, his idea of resisting wrong or oppression by passive resistance brings resolute purpose. This idea rocked the British Empire when Gandhi put it into practice. In the southern United States many Negroes read Thoreau for ideas and encouragement in their struggle to gain their constitutional rights. In Asia and Africa the ideas in *Walden* and other writings by Thoreau are the chief bulwark against the ideas of Karl Marx.

Thoreau explained why he went to Walden.]

I went to the woods because I wished to live deliberately, to front only the essential facts of life, and see if I could not learn what it had to teach, and not, when I came to die, discover that I had not lived. I did not wish to live what was not life, living is so dear, nor did I wish to practise resignation, unless it was quite necessary. I wanted to live deep and suck out all the marrow of life, to live so sturdily and Spartan-like as to put to rout all that was not life, to cut a broad swath and shave close, to drive life into a corner, and reduce it to its lowest terms, and, if it proved to be mean, why then to get the whole and genuine meanness of it, and publish its meanness to the world; or if it were sublime, to know it by experience, and be able to give a true account of it in my next excursion. For most men, it appears to me, are in a strange uncertainty about it, whether it is of the devil or of God, and have *somewhat hastily* concluded that it is the chief end of man here to "glorify God and enjoy him forever."

[A few days before Thoreau died, his Aunt Louisa asked him if he had made his peace with God. He answered: "I did not know we had ever quarreled."

From this statement it is clear that Thoreau felt he had met life as he hoped to do when he went to Walden and had found it good.

Edith Emerson, shortly before her death, gave her father's woods to the state of Massachusetts for the "sole and exclusive purpose of aiding the Commonwealth in preserving the Walden of Emerson and Thoreau, its shores and woodlands, for the public who wish to enjoy the woods, the pond and Nature."

With the passing years, Walden Pond has grown in importance in the minds of those who read *Walden* and other works by Thoreau. But as the population of eastern Massachusetts swelled, the woods and pond were used more and more by those who merely wished to play or picnic and who gave little thought, or none at all, to the values that caused the area to be treasured by Thoreau and Emerson. The waters began to lose their purity. The woods were defaced by scattered trash. Boisterous shouts drowned the songs of birds. Quiet contemplation became impossible in the place where some of America's greatest thoughts developed.

Late in June, 1957, bulldozers and chainsaws were sent into the area to gouge out a new bathing beach, a swimming pool, a parking area, and roads. Worst of all was the plan to build a huge bathhouse which could be seen like a scowling fortification from all parts of Walden Pond.

A law suit was necessary before the desecration of this literary shrine could be halted. The Thoreau Society, singlehanded, raised more than $12,000 to pay the legal fees, and before the case was resolved, it had to be carried to the highest court in Massachusetts. Americans everywhere, and the people of the world, owe the Thoreau Society a great debt.

That children and adults need a place for play and recreation is granted by all. But the intent of the gift of Walden to Massachusetts was to preserve a place of historic and literary interest in which nature could be enjoyed as Thoreau and Emerson enjoyed it, a place where the waters would remain clean and the forest healthy, and where wildlife could live unharmed. While the courts temporarily stayed the destruction of the values which Thoreau enjoyed at Walden, only constant vigilance can continue to protect and preserve the most famous literary woodland and pond in all America.

There seems little doubt that the necessary vigilance will be maintained.

Walden has gone through more than one hundred and fifty editions. One of these, edited and illustrated with photographs by Edwin Way Teale, makes this more-than-a-century-old book seem as modern as tomorrow. *Walden* has been printed in at least fourteen languages beside English.

A bust of Thoreau by the distinguished sculptor, Malvina Hoffman, was placed in the Hall of Fame at New York University and dedicated on the centennial of his death on May 6, 1962. He is now officially placed among the greatest men of America.

The bird selections from *Walden* which follow are arranged in the order of their appearance in the book. It is not surprising that the first selection refers to the nests of birds. Thoreau, who enjoyed building his cabin, compared most men with species of birds which do not build their own nests: the cowbird and the European Cuckoo.

Two species of cowbird occur in the United States, but only the Brown-headed Cowbird is found in New England. Cowbirds do not build their own nests or care for their young. With great skill they locate the nests of such small birds as sparrows, vireos, and warblers in which the full clutch of eggs has not yet been laid. In such nests, the cowbird deposits one or more eggs. The cowbird egg hatches in about ten days, usually before the eggs of the species that incubated it. The young cowbird grows very rapidly and demands so much food that the young of the parasitized species either starve or are pushed from the nest. While this behavior of cowbirds is resented by many people, it must be remembered that over the centuries the cowbird has not had a damaging effect on the species it parasitizes.

European cuckoos never build their own nests but usually parasitize members of the crow family, especially magpies, often laying several eggs in the same nest. American cuckoos build their nests and care for their young. The Black-billed Cuckoo which is the common cuckoo in New England, builds a substantial nest a few feet above the ground in dense clumps of vegetation. From the two or three eggs come naked, coal-black young birds that bristle with pin feather tubes by the time they are six days old. When they are eight or nine days old, they are extremely strong and active, capable of climbing in the branches or of regaining the nest if they drop to the ground.]

. . . . There is some of the same fitness in a man's building his own house that there is in a bird's building its own nest. Who knows but if men constructed their dwellings with their own hands, and provided food for themselves and families simply and honestly enough, the poetic faculty would be universally developed, as birds universally sing when they are so engaged? But alas! we do like cowbirds and cuckoos, which lay their eggs in nests which other birds have built, and cheer no traveller with their chattering and unmusical notes.

[Since Thoreau wrote *Walden*, innumerable people across the American continent have discovered the pleasures of having birds in their gardens and close to their homes.

Feeding stations attract abnormal numbers of birds to an area. Except as a help during unusually severe weather, this artificial feeding of birds is largely selfish. Birds can find their own food if left to their own devices. Therefore a genuine responsibility for keeping a station stocked must be assumed, once feeding has started. Birds which normally might spend the winter in an area of abundant natural food, become dependents of the people who feed them.

The influence of *Walden* on Gandhi has already been mentioned. But the philosophy of India also influenced Thoreau. The Harivansa, an appendix to *Mahabharata*, concerned chiefly with Krishna, worshipped by many Hindus, was read by Thoreau while a member of the Emerson household. It played a part in the molding of his own philosophy.]

. . . . The Harivansa says, "An abode without birds is like a meat without seasoning." Such was not my abode, for I found myself suddenly neighbor to the birds; not by having imprisoned one, but having caged myself near them. I was not only nearer to some of those which commonly frequent the garden and the orchard, but to those wilder and more thrilling songsters of the forest which never, or rarely, serenade a villager—the wood thrush, the veery, the scarlet tanager, the field-sparrow, the whippoorwill, and many others. . . .

. . . . As I sit at my window this summer afternoon, hawks are circling about my clearing; the tantivy of wild pigeons, flying by twos and threes athwart my view, or perching restless on the white pine boughs behind my house, gives a voice to the air; a fish hawk dimples the glassy surface of the pond and brings up a fish; a mink steals out of the marsh before my door and seizes a frog by the shore; the sedge is bending under the weight of the reed-birds flitting hither and thither; and for the last half-hour I have heard the rattle of railroad cars, now dying away and then reviving like the beat of a partridge. . . .

[Thoreau was probably the first to record the regularity with which Whip-poor-wills begin their evening songs. Even in their winter habitat where they do not sing they continue their regular habits and can be depended upon to arrive at a favorite feeding perch each night at a stated time, giving then only a short *chuck*.]

Regularly at half-past seven, in one part of the summer, after the evening train had gone by, the whippoorwills chanted their vespers for half an hour, sitting on a stump by my door, or upon the ridge-pole of the house. They would begin to sing almost with as much precision as a clock, within five min-utes of a particular time, referred to the setting of the sun, every evening. I

had a rare opportunity to become acquainted with their habits. Sometimes I
heard four or five at once in different parts of the wood, by accident one a
bar behind another, and so near me that I distinguished not only the cluck
after each note, but often that singular buzzing sound like a fly in a spider's
web, only proportionally louder. Sometimes one would circle round and round
me in the woods a few feet distant as if tethered by a string, when probably
I was near its eggs. They sang at intervals throughout the night, and were
again as musical as ever just before and about dawn.

[Few bird watchers read as dark and dismal meanings in the wild and
wonderful calls of owls as did Thoreau. The call of the Screech Owl, soft and
tremulous and usually running down the scale, can easily be imitated. Such
imitations often attract this small owl to perches within a few feet of the bird
watcher. Barred Owls and occasionally Great Horned Owls may also be called
close to a good imitator of their songs. In past centuries the calls of owls were
heard with superstitous fear, and traces of this are found to-day in surprising
places. For instance, a teacher in New England refused to permit a pet owl
in the classroom, for it would, she said, bring bad luck.

If a large box is placed in a garden having several trees, Screech Owls often
move in and nest year after year. Barn Owls frequently nest in church belfreys,
attics of abandoned buildings, and empty water towers. This species has often
been called the "flying rat-trap" because it consumes so many of these rodents.
Great Horned Owls and Barred Owls occasionally move into city parks or
near garbage dumps where mice and rats are plentiful.

All species of owls are extremely interesting and play an important part in
maintaining a good balance between plants and small mammals. Unchecked
by predation, small mammals, particularly of the rodent tribe, would multiply
so fast they would outstrip their food supply and severely damage forests,
orchards, and fields by eating more than could be replaced by normal growth.]

When other birds are still, the screech owls take up the strain, like mourning women their ancient u-lu-lu. Their dismal scream is truly Ben Jonsonian.
Wise midnight hags! It is no honest and blunt tu-whit tu-who of the poets,
but, without jesting, a most solemn graveyard ditty, the mutual consolations
of suicide lovers remembering the pangs and the delights of supernal love in
the infernal groves. Yet I love to hear their wailing, their doleful responses,
trilled along the woodside; reminding me sometimes of music and singing
birds; as if it were the dark and tearful side of music, the regrets and sighs that
would fain be sung. They are the spirits, the low spirits and melancholy for-
bodings, of fallen souls that once in human shape night-walked the earth and
did the deeds of darkness, now expiating their sins with their wailing hymns
or threnodies in the scenery of their transgressions. They give me a new sense

of the variety and capacity of that nature which is our common dwelling. *Oh-o-o-o-o that I never had been bor-r-r-rn!* sighs one on this side of the pond, and circles with the restlessness of despair to some new perch on the gray oaks. Then—*That I never had been bor-r-r-r-n!* echoes another on the farther side with tremulous sincerity, and—*bor-r-r-r-n!* comes faintly from far in the Lincoln woods.

I was also serenaded by a hooting owl. Near at hand you could fancy it the most melancholy sound in Nature, as if she meant this to stereotype and make permanent in her choir the dying moans of a human being,—some poor weak relic of mortality who has left hope behind, and howls like an animal, yet with human sobs, on entering the dark valley, made more awful by a certain gurgling melodiousness,—I find myself beginning with the letters *gl* when I try to imitate it—expressive of a mind which has reached the gelatinous, mildewy stage in the mortification of all healthy and courageous thought. It reminded me of ghouls and idiots and insane howlings. But now one answers from far woods in a strain made really melodious by distance,—*Hoo hoo hoo, hoorer hoo*; and indeed for the most part it suggested only pleasing associations, whether heard by day or night, summer or winter.

I rejoice that there are owls. Let them do the idiotic and maniacal hooting for men. It is a sound admirably suited to swamps and twilight woods which no day illustrates, suggesting a vast and undeveloped nature which men have not recognized. They represent the stark twilight and unsatisfied thoughts which all have. All day the sun has shone on the surface of some savage swamp, where the single spruce stands hung with usnea lichens, and small hawks circulate above, and the chickadee lisps amid the evergreens, and the partridge and rabbit skulk beneath; but now a more dismal and fitting day dawns, and a different race of creatures awakes to express the meaning of Nature there.

[Seldom did Thoreau write a more magic description of a serene summer day shared with his neighbors, the birds, than the one which follows.

Brown Thrashers may eat the farmer's berries and small fruits but they are not likely to pull his corn and beans. It would be interesting to know if the words Thoreau applied to the Brown Thrasher's song originated with him. Forbush, more than three-quarters of a century later in *Birds of Massachusetts and Other New England States*, quotes these phrases as being generally applied to the song of this bird by country people.

All of Thoreau's remarks about the Passenger Pigeon are read with particular interest, for the last individual of this species died in 1914. Both Wilson and Audubon wrote of vast flocks that actually darkened the sun while taking hours to pass a given point. In 1805, Audubon wrote of seeing schooners on the Hudson River loaded with pigeons. Flocks of millions of these game birds were reported as late as the 1880s. A quarter of a century later not one remained alive.

The Eastern Nighthawk, close relative of the Whip-poor-will, and the hawk family had a particular appeal for Thoreau. He makes them come alive so the reader knows far more about them than if a scientific description is read. He watched these birds as he made a day of planting or tilling his field of beans.]

Near at hand, upon the topmost spray of a birch, sings the brown thrasher —or red mavis, as some love to call him—all the morning, glad of your society, that would find out another farmer's field if yours were not here. While you are planting the seed, he cries,—"Drop it, drop it,—cover it up, cover it up,—pull it up pull it up pull it up" But this was not corn and so it was safe from such enemies as he. You may wonder what his rigmarole, his amateur Paganini performances on one string or on twenty, have to do with your planting, and yet prefer it to leached ashes or plaster. It was a cheap sort of top dressing in which I had entire faith.

. . . . The nighthawk circled overhead in the sunny afternoons—for I sometimes made a day of it—like a mote in the eye, or in heaven's eye, falling from time to time with a swoop and a sound as if the heavens were rent, torn at last to very rags and tatters, and yet a seamless cope remained; small imps that fill the air and lay their eggs on the ground on bare sand or rocks on the tops of hills, where few have found them; graceful and slender like ripples caught up from the pond, as leaves are raised by the wind to float in the heavens; such kindredship is in Nature. The hawk is aerial brother of the wave which he sails over and surveys, those his perfect air-inflated wings answering to the elemental unfledged pinions of the sea. Or sometimes I watched a pair of hen-hawks circling high in the sky, alternately soaring and descending, approaching and leaving one another, as if they were the embodiment of my own thoughts. Or I was attracted by the passage of wild pigeons from this wood to that, with a slight quivering winnowing sound and carrier haste.

[Thoreau's advice to parents of young boys seems to be sound. It is most revealing to listen to a group of ornithologists and conservationists reminisce about the origin of their interest in birds. The majority seem to have been hunters, egg collectors, nest collectors, and so on, in their boyhood. As they matured, they developed an interest in the living birds. They realized also that each creature holds its life dear and deserves to live. They came to the realization that much greater pleasure can be found in studying the habits of wild creatures than was ever experienced in shooting or otherwise collecting them.]

. . . As for fowling, during the last years that I carried a gun my excuse was that I was studying ornithology, and sought only new or rare birds. But I confess that I am now inclined to think that there is a finer way of studying

ornithology than this. It requires so much closer attention to the habits of
the birds, that, if for that reason only, I have been willing to omit the gun.
Yet notwithstanding the objection on the score of humanity, I am compelled
to doubt if equally valuable sports are ever substituted for these; and when
some of my friends have asked me anxiously about their boys, whether they
should let them hunt, I have answered, yes,—remembering that it was one of
the best parts of my education,—*make* them hunters, though sportsmen only
at first, if possible, mighty hunters at last, so that they shall not find game
large enough for them in this or any vegetable wilderness,—hunters as well
as fishers of men. Thus far I am of the opinion of Chaucer's nun, who

> "yave not of the text a pulled hen
> That saith that hunters ben not holy men."

There is a period in the history of the individual, as of the race, when the
hunters are the "best men," as the Algonquins called them. We cannot but
pity the boy who has never fired a gun; he is no more humane, while his education has been sadly neglected. This was my answer with respect to those youths
who were bent on this pursuit, trusting that they would soon outgrow it. No
humane being, past the thoughtless age of boyhood, will wantonly murder
any creature which holds its life by the same tenure that he does. The hare in
its extremity cries like a child. I warn you, mothers, that my sympathies do
not always make the usual phil—*anthropic* distinctions.

[Phoebes and robins are common birds around most New England farms.
The Ruffed Grouse is not as well known. Throughout its entire range it is subject to great population fluctuations. Its numbers build up a peak over a
period of several years, then they decline quite abruptly. Usually no hunting
is permitted when its numbers are low in order to preserve breeding stock
which can rebuild the population. Nineteen Ruffed Grouse were counted in the
Concord area on the day of the 1961 Christmas Bird Count.

Ornithologists class the Woodcock with the shorebirds. As with most shorebirds, this species has four eggs in its clutch. The downy young look like bits
of fluff perched on toothpicks.

Mourning Doves (turtle doves) are common in the Concord area. Even in
winter, several dozen can be located there in a day devoted to earnest search
for them.]

A phoebe soon built in my shed, and a robin for protection in a pine which
grew against the house. In June the partridge (*Tetrao umbellus*), which is so
shy a bird, led her brood past my windows, from the woods in the rear to the
front of my house, clucking and calling to them like a hen, and in all her
behavior proving herself the hen of the woods. The young suddenly disperse
on your approach, at a signal from the mother, as if a whirlwind had swept

them away, and they so exactly resemble the dried leaves and twigs that many
a traveller has placed his foot in the midst of a brood, and heard the whir of
the old bird as she flew off, and her anxious calls and mewing, or seen her trail
her wings to attract his attention, without suspecting their neighborhood.
The parent will sometimes roll and spin round before you in such a dishabille,
that you cannot, for a few moments, detect what kind of creature it is. The
young squat still and flat, often running their heads under a leaf, and mind
only their mother's directions given from a distance, nor will your approach
make them run again and betray themselves. You may even tread on them, or
have your eyes on them for a minute, without discovering them. I have held
them in my open hand at such a time, and still their only care, obedient to
their mother and their instinct, was to squat there without fear or trembling.
So perfect is this instinct, that once, when I had laid them on the leaves again,
and one accidentally fell on its side, it was found with the rest in exactly the
same position ten minutes afterward. They are not callow like the young of
most birds, but more perfectly developed and precocious even than chickens.
The remarkably adult yet innocent expression of their open and serene eyes
is very memorable. All intelligence seems reflected in them. They suggest not
merely the purity of infancy, but a wisdom clarified by experience. Such an
eye was not born when the bird was, but is coeval with the sky it reflects.
The woods do not yield another such a gem. The traveller does not often look
into such a limpid well. The ignorant or reckless sportsman often shoots the
parent at such a time, and leaves these innocents to fall a prey to some
prowling beast or bird, or gradually mingle with the decaying leaves which
they so much resemble. It is said that when hatched by a hen they will directly
disperse on some alarm, and so are lost, for they never hear the mother's call
which gathers them again. These were my hens and chickens.

    . . . .Commonly I rested an hour or two in the shade at noon, after plant-
ing, and ate my lunch, and read a little by a spring which was the source of
a swamp and of a brook, oozing from under Brister's Hill, half a mile from
my field. The approach to this was through a succession of descending grassy
hollows, full of young pitch-pines, into a larger wood about the swamp. There,
in a very secluded and shaded spot, under a spreading white pine, there was
yet a clean, firm sward to sit on. I had dug out the spring and made a well of
clear gray water, where I could dip up a pailful without roiling it, and thither
I went for this purpose almost every day in midsummer, when the pond was
warmest. Thither too the woodcock led her brood, to probe the mud for
worms, flying but a foot above them down the bank, while they ran in a troop
beneath; but at last, spying me, she would leave her young and circle round
and round me, nearer and nearer till within four or five feet, pretending
broken wings and legs, to attract my attention, and get off her young, who
would already have taken up their march, with faint, wiry peep, single file

through the swamp, as she directed. Or I heard the peep of the young when I could not see the parent bird. There too the turtle doves sat over the spring, or fluttered from bough to bough of the soft white-pines over my head; . . . You only need sit still long enough in some attractive spot in the woods that all its inhabitants may exhibit themselves to you by turns.

[Loons are placed on the bottom rung of the evolutionary scale of American birds. Their wild, ringing calls, and devotion to remote, unspoiled northern lakes make them the spirit of the wilderness to many people.

The loon demands space for a breeding territory. Except when a lake is really large, only a single pair will be found nesting by it.

The legs of a loon are placed so far back on the body that they are useless for walking though they are in a superb position for fast swimming. On land, a loon can only push itself along clumsily with its breast on the ground. It cannot take wing from land. When a loon is confused by a storm or fog into mistaking a field for water, it is doomed unless it is rescued by some generous human and returned to water before a predator finds it.

Thoreau never heard a wolf, though he hoped to hear one when in the Maine woods. But whenever he heard a particularly wild sound, he thought of wolves, for their howl, he believed, must be one of the wildest of all sounds.]

In the fall the loon (*Colymbus glacialis*) came, as usual, to moult and bathe in the pond, making the woods ring with his wild laughter before I had risen. At rumor of his arrival all the Mill-dam sportsmen are on the alert, in gigs and on foot, two by two and three by three, with patent rifles and conical balls and spy-glasses. They come rustling through the woods like autumn leaves, at least ten men to one loon. Some station themselves on this side of the pond, some on that, for the poor bird cannot be omnipresent; if he dive here he must come up there. But now the kind October wind rises, rustling the leaves and rippling the surface of the water, so that no loon can be heard or seen, though his foes sweep the pond with spy-glasses, and make the woods resound with their discharges. The waves generously rise and dash angrily, taking sides with all waterfowl, and our sportsmen must beat a retreat to town and shop and unfinished jobs. But they were too often successful. When I went to get a pail of water early in the morning I frequently saw this stately bird sailing out of my cove within a few rods. If I endeavored to overtake him in a boat, in order to see how he would manoeuvre, he would dive and be completely lost, so that I did not discover him again, sometimes, till the latter part of the day. But I was more than a match for him on the surface. He commonly went off in a rain.

As I was paddling along the north shore one very calm October afternoon, for such days especially they settle on to the lakes, like the milkweed down, having looked in vain over the pond for a loon, suddenly one, sailing out from the shore toward the middle a few rods in front of me, set up his wild laugh and betrayed himself. I pursued with a paddle and he dived, but when he came up I was nearer than before. He dived again, but I miscalculated the direction he would take, and we were fifty rods apart when he came to the surface this time, for I had helped to widen the interval; and again he laughed long and loud, and with more reason than before. He manoeuvered so cunningly that I could not get within half a dozen rods of him. Each time, when he came to the surface, turning his head this way and that, he coolly surveyed the water and the land, and apparently chose his course so that he might come up where there was the widest expanse of water and at the greatest distance from the boat. It was surprising how quickly he made up his mind and put his resolve into execution. He led me at once to the widest part of the pond, and could not be driven from it. While he was thinking one thing in his brain, I was endeavoring to divine his thought in mine. It was a pretty game, played on the smooth surface of the pond, a man against the loon. Suddenly your adversary's checker disappears beneath the board, and the problem is to place yours nearest to where his will appear again. Sometimes he would come up unexpectedly on the opposite side of me, having apparently passed directly under the boat. So long-winded was he and so unweariable, that when he had swum farthest he would immediately plunge again, nevertheless; and then no wit could divine where in the deep pond, beneath the smooth surface, he might be speeding his way like a fish, for he had time and ability to visit the bottom of the pond in its deepest part. It is said that loons have been caught in the New York lakes eighty feet beneath the surface, with hooks set for trout,—though Walden is deeper than that. How surprised must the fishes be to see this ungainly visitor from another sphere speeding his way amid their schools! Yet he appeared to know his course as surely under water as on the surface, and swam much faster there. Once or twice I saw a ripple where he approached the surface, just put his head out to reconnoitre, and instantly dived again. I found that it was as well for me to rest on my oars and wait his reappearing as to endeavor to calculate where he would rise; for again and again, when I was straining my eyes over the surface one way, I would suddenly be startled by his unearthly laugh behind me. But why, after displaying so much cunning, did he invariably betray himself the moment he came up by that loud laugh? Did not his white breast enough betray him? He was indeed a silly loon, I thought. I could commonly hear the plash of the water when he came up, and so also detected him. But after an hour he seemed as fresh as ever, dived as willingly, and swam yet farther than at first. It was surprising to see how serenely he sailed off with unruffled breast when he came to the surface, doing all the work with his webbed feet beneath. His usual note was this demoniac laughter, yet somewhat like that of a water-fowl; but occasionally when he had balked me most successfully and come up a long

way off, he uttered a long-drawn unearthly howl, probably more like that of
a wolf than any bird; as when a beast puts his muzzle to the ground and
deliberately howls. This was his looning,—perhaps the wildest sound that is
ever heard here, making the woods ring far and wide. I concluded that he
laughed in derision of my efforts, confident of his own resources. Though the
sky was by this time overcast, the pond was so smooth that I could see where
he broke the surface when I did not hear him. His white breast, the stillness
of the air, and the smoothness of the water were all against him. At length,
having come up fifty rods off, he uttered one of those prolonged howls, as
if calling on the god of loons to aid him, and immediately there came a wind
from the east and rippled the surface, and filled the whole air with misty rain,
and I was impressed as if it were the prayer of the loon answered, and his
god was angry with me; and so I left him disappearing far away on the
tumultuous surface.

[To-day Louisiana is one of the foremost duck-hunting states in the country. Ducks need to be as wary there as they were on Walden Pond. However,
with the steadily increasing numbers of hunters making essential decreased
bag limits, more and more sportsmen are content to seek less than their legal
limits and spend more hours simply observing their game or trying to photo-
graph them, a sport far more demanding than shooting them.]

For hours, in fall days, I watched the ducks cunningly tack and veer and
hold the middle of the pond, far from the sportsman; tricks which they will
have less need to practise in Louisiana bayous. When compelled to rise they
would sometimes circle round and round and over the pond at a considerable
height, from which they could easily see to other ponds and the river, like
dark motes in the sky; and, when I thought they had gone off thither long
since, they would settle down by a slanting flight of a quarter of a mile on to
a distant part which was left free; but what beside safety they got by sailing
in the middle of Walden I do not know, unless they love its water for the
same reason that I do.

[Poets have sung of the passage of geese for ages. Sight or sound of migrating geese still means the coming of spring or autumn to many people in the
northeast. To those people, the geese are almost always Canada Geese though
several species occur in eastern North America.
Many Canada Geese now nest in hunting preserves, and in many state,
federal, and private sanctuaries in New England including the Great Meadows National Wildlife Refuge in Concord. This represents a marked change
since Thoreau's day when it is doubtful if any nested anywhere in New England. Geese usually feed early in the morning and again late in the afternoon.
As they move to and from their feeding grounds where they often graze like

cattle, they normally fly in formation, announcing their passage with a loud, wild clangor.]

At length the winter set in in good earnest, just as I had finished plastering, and the wind began to howl around the house as if it had not had permission to do so till then. Night after night the geese came lumbering in in the dark with a clangor and a whistling of wings, even after the ground was covered with snow, some to alight in Walden, and some flying low over the woods toward Fair Haven, bound for Mexico. Several times when returning from the village at ten or eleven o'clock at night, I heard the tread of a flock of geese, or else ducks, on the dry leaves in the woods by a pond-hole behind my dwelling, where they had come up to feed, and the faint honk or quack of their leader as they hurried off. . . .

[The Barred Owl is very common in New England. It prefers swampy woodlands and dense hemlock groves. Unlike the Great Horned Owl, it has no feather tufts on its head. It has dark eyes in a round face, while the Great Horned Owl has yellow eyes. Barred Owls have a baritone voice and their eight hoots are divided into groups of four. The Great Horned Owl has a bass voice and usually has five hoots given in a single group.

The two extracts from *Walden* which follow are the result of most careful observation on the part of Thoreau.]

. . . One afternoon I amused myself by watching a barred owl (*Strix nebulosa*) sitting on one of the lower dead limbs of a white-pine, close to the trunk, in broad daylight, I standing within a rod of him. He could hear me when I moved and cronched the snow with my feet, but could not plainly see me. When I made most noise he would stretch out his neck, and erect his neck feathers, and open his eyes wide; but their lids soon fell again, and he began to nod. I too felt a slumberous influence after watching him half an hour, as he sat thus with his eyes half open, like a cat, winged brother of the cat. There was only a narrow slit left between their lids, by which he preserved a peninsular relation to me; thus, with half-shut eyes, looking out from the land of dreams, and endeavoring to realize me, vague object or mote that interrupted his visions. At length, on some louder noise or my nearer approach, he would grow uneasy and sluggishly turn about on his perch, as if impatient at having his dreams disturbed; and when he launched himself off and flapped through the pines, spreading his wings to unexpected breadth, I could not hear the slightest sound from them. Thus, guided amid the pine boughs rather by a delicate sense of their neighborhood than by sight, feeling his twilight way, as it were, with his sensitive pinions, he found a new perch, where he might in peace await the dawning of his day.

For sounds in winter nights, and often in winter days, I heard the forlorn but melodious note of a hooting owl indefinitely far; such a sound as the frozen earth would yield if struck with a suitable plectrum, the very *lingua vernacula* of Walden Wood, and quite familiar to me at last, though I never saw the bird while it was making it. I seldom opened my door in a winter evening without hearing it; *Hoo hoo hoo, hoorer hoo*, sounded sonorously, and the first three syllables accented somewhat like *how der do*; or sometimes *hoo hoo* only. One night in the beginning of winter, before the pond froze over, about nine o'clock, I was startled by the loud honking of a goose, and, stepping to the door, heard the sound of their wings like a tempest in the woods as they flew low over my house. They passed over the pond toward Fair Haven, seemingly deterred from settling by my light, their commodore honking all the while with a regular beat. Suddenly an unmistakable cat-owl from very near me, with the most harsh and tremendous voice I ever heard from any inhabitant of the woods, responded at regular intervals to the goose, as if determined to expose and disgrace this intruder from Hudson's Bay by exhibiting a greater compass and volume of voice in a native, and *boo-hoo* him out of Concord horizon. What do you mean by alarming the citadel at this time of night consecrated to me? Do you think I am ever caught napping at such an hour, and that I have not got lungs and a larnyx as well as yourself? *Boo-hoo, boo-hoo, boo-hoo!* It was one of the most thrilling discords I ever heard. And yet, if you had a discriminating ear, there were in it the elements of a concord such as these plains never saw nor heard.

[Perhaps the most interesting feature of the following extract is the fact that Thoreau retained certain prejudices even as many people do to-day. He felt jays were thieves when they found food. Chickadees, on the other hand, were charming and intelligent when they found their food. He had not yet fully recognized the interrelationships of all forms of life, that all must feed to live, and that this food is obtained in a way dictated by forces outside each. The caterpillar must feed on the living leaf. The spider must catch insects. Vultures must eat carrion. The panther must catch mammals or birds.

When Thoreau read "The Succession of Forest Trees" to the Agricultural Society of Concord in 1860, his prejudices had been replaced by understanding. He had grasped the fact that no creature should be condemned because of its food habits, and that all animals had a right to live. Moreover, he recognized the vital part Blue Jays play in the continued health of the forest. (See Page 277.)]

At length the jays arrive, whose discordant screams were heard long before, as they were warily making their approach an eighth of a mile off, and in a stealthy and sneaking manner they flit from tree to tree, nearer and nearer, and pick up the kernels which the squirrels have dropped. Then, sitting on a pitch-pine bough, they attempt to swallow in their haste a kernel which is too big for their throats and chokes them; and after great labor they disgorge it, and spend an hour in the endeavor to crack it by repeated blows with their bills. They were manifestly thieves, and I had not much respect for them. . . .

Meanwhile also came the chickadees in flocks, which, picking up the crumbs the squirrels had dropped, flew to the nearest twig, and, placing them under their claws, hammered away at them with their little bills, as if it were an insect in the bark, till they were sufficiently reduced for their slender throats. A little flock of these titmice came daily to pick a dinner out of my wood-pile, or the crumbs at my door, with faint flitting lisping notes, like the tinkling of icicles in the grass, or else with sprightly *day day day*, or more rarely, in spring-like days, a wiry summery *phe-be* from the woodside. They were so familiar that at length one alighted on an armful of wood which I was carrying in, and pecked at the sticks without fear. I once had a sparrow alight upon my shoulder for a moment while I was hoeing in a village garden, and I felt that I was more distinguished by that circumstance than I should have been by any epaulet I could have worn. . . .

[When man introduces an exotic plant or animal into a new location, unexpected developments almost always follow. Ruffed Grouse were quick to discover that leaf and flower buds of apple trees, which were introduced in New England by the early settlers, provided them with a new and delicious food supply. Farmers, once so delighted by the "wild chickens," were angered at the damage done to their apple crop.]

When the ground was not yet quite covered, and again near the end of winter, when the snow was melted on my south hill-side and about my wood-pile, the partridges came out of the woods morning and evening to feed there. Whichever side you walk in the woods the partridge bursts away on whirring wings, jarring the snow from the dry leaves and twigs on high, which comes sifting down in the sunbeams like golden dust, for this brave bird is not to be scared by winter. It is frequently covered up by drifts, and, it is said, "sometimes plunges from on wing into the soft snow, where it remains concealed for a day or two." I used to start them in the open land also, where they had come out of the woods at sunset to "bud" the wild apple trees. They will come regularly every evening to particular trees, where the cunning sportsman lies in wait for them, and the distant orchards next to the woods suffer thus not a little. I am glad that the partridge gets fed, at any rate. It is Nature's own bird which lives on buds and diet-drink.

The first sparrow of spring! The year beginning with younger hope than ever! The faint silvery warblings heard over the partially bare and moist fields from the bluebird, the song sparrow, and the red-wing, as if the last flakes of winter tinkled as they fell! ... The marsh hawk, sailing low over the meadow is already seeking the first slimy life that awakes.

[The two selections which follow show the literary Thoreau at his best. Most of the first appeared in the *Journal* entry of March 26, 1846, very much as it is written in *Walden*. It is strong, vivid prose filled with poetic imagination. As Thoreau listened in early spring to the first full song of a Robin, he was carried beyond his Walden cabin and dimly glimpsed vast unknown arrangements of nature. In his *Journal* he wrote: "If I could ever find the twig he sits upon! Where does the minstrel really roost? We perceive it is not the bird of the ornithologist that is heard,—the *Turdus migratorius*." It is easy enough to locate the twig on which *Turdus migratorius* perchs to sing his song, but difficult indeed to hear the cosmic secrets that seem to lie behind it and are heard too faintly for the poet to quite grasp.

The small hawk (page 36) was probably a Marsh Hawk. By the end of April, Marsh Hawks which breed in Concord have arrived on territory. Their courtship flights are spectacular as they soar, plunge, and even turn somersaults in the air. They bound up and down in the air almost like rubber balls. These flights usually occur over marshes or meadows. Their rattling calls often are given during their aerial performances.]

The change from storm and winter to serene and mild weather, from dark and sluggish hours to bright and elastic ones, is a memorable crisis which all things proclaim. It is seemingly instantaneous at last. Suddenly an influx of light filled my house, though the evening was at hand, and the clouds of winter still overhung it, and the eaves were dripping with sleety rain. I looked out the window, and lo! where yesterday was cold gray ice there lay the transparent pond already calm and full of hope as in a summer evening, reflecting a summer evening sky in its bosom, though none was visible overhead, as if it had intelligence with some remote horizon. I heard a robin in the distance, the first I had heard for many a thousand years, methought, whose note I shall not forget for many a thousand more,—the same sweet and powerful song as of yore. O the evening robin, at the end of a New England summer day! If I could ever find the twig he sits upon! I mean *he*; I mean *the twig*. This at least is not the *Turdus migratorius*. The pitch-pines and shrub-oaks about my house, which had so long drooped, suddenly resumed their several characters, looked brighter, greener, and more erect and alive, as if effectually cleansed and restored by the rain. I knew that it would not rain any more. You may tell by looking at any twig of the forest, ay, at your very wood-pile, whether its winter is past or not. As it grew darker, I was startled by the honking of geese flying low over the woods, like weary travellers getting in late from southern lakes, and indulging at last in unrestrained complaint and

mutual consolation. Standing at my door, I could hear the rush of their wings;
when, driving toward my house, they suddenly spied my light, and with
hushed clamor wheeled and settled in the pond. So I came in, and shut the
door, and passed my first spring night in the woods.

In the morning I watched the geese from the door through the mist, sailing in the middle of the pond, fifty rods off, so large and tumultuous that
Walden appeared like an artificial pond for their amusement. But when I
stood on the shore they at once rose up with a great flapping of wings at
the signal of their commander, and when they had got into rank circled about
over my head, twenty-nine of them, and then steered straight to Canada, with
a regular *honk* from the leader at intervals, trusting to break their fast in
muddier pools. A "plump" of ducks rose at the same time, and took the route
to the north in the wake of their noisier cousins.

For a week I heard the circling, groping clangor of some solitary goose in
the foggy mornings, seeking its companion, and still peopling the woods with
the sound of a larger life than they could sustain. In April the pigeons were
seen again flying express in small flocks, and in due time I heard the martins
twittering over my clearing, though it had not seemed that the township contained so many that it could afford me any, and I fancied that they were
peculiarly of the ancient race that dwelt in hollow trees ere white men came.
In almost all climes the tortoise and the frog are among the precursors and
heralds of this season, and birds fly with song and glancing plumage, and
plants spring and bloom. . . .

On the 29th of April, as I was fishing from the bank of the river near the
Nine-Acre-Corner bridge, standing on the quaking grass and willow roots,
where the muskrats lurk, I heard a singular rattling sound, somewhat like
that of the sticks which boys play with their fingers, when, looking up, I
observed a very slight and graceful hawk, like a nighthawk, alternately soaring like a ripple and tumbling a rod or two over and over, showing the
under side of its wings, which gleamed like a satin ribbon in the sun, or like
the pearly inside of a shell. This sight reminded me of falconry and what
nobleness and poetry are associated with that sport. The Merlin it seemed to
me it might be called; but I care not for its name. It was the most ethereal
flight I had ever witnessed. It did not simply flutter like a butterfly, nor soar
like the larger hawks, but it sported with proud reliance in the fields of air;
mounting again and again with its strange chuckle, it repeated its free and
beautiful fall, turning over and over like a kite, and then recovering from its
lofty tumbling, as if it had never set its foot on *terra firma*. It appeared to
have no companion in the universe,—sporting there alone,—and to need none
but the morning and the ether with which it played. It was not lonely, but
made all the earth lonely beneath it. Where was the parent which hatched it,
its kindred, and its father in the heavens? The tenant of the air, it seemed

related to the earth but by an egg hatched sometime in the crevice of a crag,—
or was its native nest made in the angle of a cloud, woven of the rainbow's
trimmings and the sunset sky, and lined with some soft midsummer haze
caught up from earth? Its eyry now some cliffy cloud.

[The following selection contains a most eloquent plea for the preservation of wilderness areas. It is one that the leaders of small communities should
ponder as they plan for future growth.

Though the Wood Thrush has been recorded in Concord as early as mid-
April, it does not arrive in numbers until May. Probably Thoreau heard the
Hermit Thrush, the first thrush to arrive in Concord in spring and the last to
leave in autumn.]

Our village life would stagnate if it were not for the unexplored forests
and meadows which surround it. We need the tonic of wilderness,—to wade
sometimes in marshes where the bittern and the meadow-hen lurk, and hear
the booming of the snipe; to smell the whispering sedge where only some
wilder and more solitary fowl builds her nest, and the mink crawls with its
belly close to the ground. . . .

Early in May, the oaks, hickories, maples, and other trees, just putting out
amidst the pine woods around the pond, imparted a brightness like sunshine
to the landscape, especially in cloudy days, as if the sun were breaking
through mists and shining faintly on the hillsides here and there. On the
third or fourth of May I saw a loon in the pond, and during the first week of
the month I heard the whippoorwill, the brown-thrasher, the veery, the
wood-pewee, the chewink, and other birds. I had heard the wood-thrush long
before. The phoebe had already come once more and looked in at my door
and window, to see if my house was cavern-like enough for her, sustaining
herself on humming wings with clinched talons, as if she held by the air, while
she surveyed the premises.

Some Species of Birds
from Thoreau's Journal

THOREAU'S BIRDS OF CONCORD

[Students of Thoreau's writing are unanimous in recognizing the *Journal* as his greatest work, though it is granted that his finest writing is found in *Walden*. At his death Thoreau left forty notebooks, most of them packed in a wooden box which he had made himself.

In the notebooks Thoreau wrote nearly three million words about himself, his philosophy, his thoughts and convictions, about Concord and its people as well as the Indians who lived before them, and about the natural history of that area including the soil, rocks, waters, forests, and fields, and the many forms of life in those varied habitats.

In so varied a production there is necessarily variation in quality. There is also repetition as Thoreau reworked ideas to achieve greater clarity and truth, or when renewed observations revealed new facts. It must be kept in mind always that he wished to see beyond mere facts to the meaning behind what he observed.

In 1906, the *Journal*, edited by Bradford Torrey and Francis H. Allen, was published by Houghton Mifflin as fourteen volumes in the twenty-volume Walden edition which contains the major part of Thoreau's writings. This rare set is in such demand that second-hand dealers have waiting lists of those who wish to buy it, should one become available. It is well worth waiting for.

Edwin Way Teale stated a simple truth when he said, "There is a lifetime of good reading in Thoreau's *Journal*."

The *Journal* alone was republished in 1949, but that whole printing was quickly sold out. The *Journal* was then unavailable until 1962 when Dover Publications published it in two volumes, which are necessarily large but not at all unwieldy. It is hoped that the *Journal* will remain in print for a long time to come.

Here we are concerned with a single aspect of Thoreau's Concord studies: the birds. For a dozen years he watched birds without any optical aid. His references books, already discussed, were of limited help in identification and gave almost no clues to behavior. He did not want to collect birds, for it was his hope to name all the Concord species without resorting to the gun.

Three of his mystery birds were the Seringo, the Evergreen-forest Bird, and the Night Warbler. Several species of birds found in Concord have ecstatic flight songs and songs which are given at dusk or in the night. It is clear from Thoreau's own words in the *Journal* that his Night Warbler was not a single species but two or more. The Seringo was usually a sparrow, but again, several species were called by this name. At least once the Evergreen-forest Bird was the Black-throated Green Warbler, but the song, which Thoreau heard in the conifer woods, was probably almost any song he heard in that habitat and did not know.

Bird watchers to-day cannot help being surprised at some gaps in Thoreau's knowledge about birds, for we know what species to expect in an area, when to expect them, and in what habitat to look for them. It must be kept in mind that our knowledge rests on a solid foundation of compiled information—to which Thoreau contributed—which was gathered over more than a century.

Bradford Torrey, in the Introduction to the *Journal*, suggested that the means and methods of the ornithological amateur of the 1850s may be of particular interest to his readers. Moreover, he noted a desirable store of ornithological nuts to crack on winter evenings. But Francis H. Allen, the co-editor of the *Journal*, was an excellent bird student and probably solved all the "nuts" in bird identification for which there is sufficient data to permit more than a guess.

More than a century after Thoreau's death, Concord village still has a population under four thousand. Around the village many of Thoreau's special places can still be found, for the rural lands, hardwood swamps, pine woodlots, lakes, streams, and wet meadows are still there. Thoreau named many of the areas which he visited regularly. To-day the visitor to Concord, as well as the armchair explorer with the Concord map for reference, finds particular pleasure in locating such places as Owl Swamp where the Great Horned Owls hooted and Linnaea Hill, famous for Scarlet Tanagers. The Great Meadow is

permanently flooded and preserved as the Great Meadows National Wildlife
Refuge. Many more Wood Ducks can be found there to-day than when
Thoreau watched the species with such eloquent pleasure.

In the 1850s no area in all the United States was so thoroughly explored
for birds as was Concord by Thoreau. Its bird population is well documented
to-day. A bird list, periodically brought up to date, of species and their relative abundance is available from the U.S. Fish and Wildlife Service in Washington, D.C. Each winter a group of excellent bird students join in the conti-
nent-wide Christmas Bird Count, an activity sponsored by the National Audubon Society, which publishes the results of the hundreds of counts made during the Count period, the dates being set annually. Each count is made within
a circle having a diameter of fifteen miles. At least eight hours in the field
are required. The circle covered by the Concord Count includes the chief
areas explored by Thoreau. In addition to the Refuge list and the Concord
Christmas Bird Count, the records of visitors to Concord often find their way
into ornithological publications. Concord, then, since the middle of the last
century, has an unusually accurate picture of its bird life.

But it is not for facts, nor for identification of Concord species that Thoreau
is read to-day. To go through the year with him is to awaken a new appreciation of the turn of the earth through its seasons. The entries about birds open
the eyes of the reader to aspects of bird life he has never before considered.
Thoreau's wonder at the legs of the loon, so perfectly constructed for its life
in the water, arouses a similar wonder in his readers to-day. His account of
the death of a young hawk on November 9, 1858, brings to mind the emotion
felt when, reading the Iliad, we see the body of the brave son of Priam
dragged in the dust of Troy. Always he presents new ideas and a fresh approach to the enjoyment of the out of doors and birds.

Thoreau's birds are but a single part of his great literature. No more than
half of the bird material in the *Journal* is included here. Most of the material
is arranged according to species. When an entry sparkled with life but was
not limited to a single species, it was arbitrarily placed in a species group
which seemed suitable.

Perhaps the most remarkable contribution of Thoreau's writing is the way
it seems to sharpen the senses of the reader. For instance, when reading about
the Ruffed Grouse, one can feel the bitter cold of winter which that hardy
species must endure. One can see the bedraggled body of a grouse dangling
from a cunningly placed snare. The sound of a "drumming" grouse beats on
the ear. The anger of the farmers when the grouse comes out of the woods
to eat the buds of his apple trees is understood, while all sympathy goes to
the hungry bird. Admiration is awakened by the hen grouse trying to protect
her young. Thoreau's accounts of his observations arouse in the reader a con-

viction that he can go afield and really see, hear, and live as the Concord naturalist suggested in *A Week on the Concord and Merrimack Rivers*:]

> I hearing get, who had but ears,
>   And sight, who had but eyes before,
> I moments live, who lived but years,
>   And truth discern, who knew but learning's lore.

RED-THROATED LOON *(Gavia stellata)*

[Thoreau did not distinguish between this species and the Common Loon which anually settled on Walden Pond during migration. The Red-throated Loon is found in northern and arctic areas around the world. Its sharp, thin, uptilted bill, unlike the straight, rather heavy bill of the Common Loon, is the chief feature used in identifying the species in the winter. In breeding plumage the Red-throated Loon is far less brightly patterned than the Common Loon, but its gray head and rufous throat patch offer a pleasing contrast to the generally pale gray of its body.

The Red-throated Loon often nests on small bodies of water that have just space enough to permit takeoff and landing. Unlike the larger, heavier species, this loon can with effort walk upright. It is a strong flier and frequently takes to the air rather than dive. It is noisy on its breeding grounds but its voice, vaguely gooselike, is far less thrilling than that of the Common Loon.

No entries about the Common Loon are included here. However, Thoreau wrote a colorful undated account of this species between 1845 and 1846, and another on October 8, 1852. Drawing from these two entries, Thoreau wrote the dramatic episode of his contest with the loon in *Walden*. (See pages 29–31.)]

Nov. 11. [1858]   Goodwin brings me this afternoon a this year's loon, which he just killed on the river,—great northern diver, but a smaller specimen than Wilson describes and somewhat differently marked. . . . You are struck by its broad, flat, sharp-edged legs, made to cut through the water rather than to walk with, set far back and naturally stretched out backward, its long and powerful bill, conspicuous white throat and breast. Dislodged by winter in the north, it is slowly travelling toward a warmer clime, diving in the cool river this morning, which is now full of light, the trees and bushes on the brink having long since lost their leaves, and the neighboring fields are white with frost. Yet this hardy bird is comfortable and contented there if the sportsman would let it alone.

HORNED GREBE *(Podiceps auritus)*

[Thoreau's boat—which he kept in good repair—occasionally needed attention, but as he worked he observed what went on about him. He was quick
to see the agitation among the tame ducks when the Horned Grebe approached
them, for it was silly behavior on their part. However, wild birds also become
senselessly disturbed sometimes and a placid group of mixed herons and ducks
has been known to become highly agitated when a cormorant plunged among
them. Perhaps it results from a group resenting the intrusion of an outsider,
as has been known to happen among the human species.

In spring and early summer an adult Horned Grebe has conspicuous golden
ear tufts, and a rich rufous color runs down the throat and along the sides of
the white breast. Thoreau's little dipper was either an immature bird or an
adult in winter plumage. These compact little birds occur over much of the
northern part of the Northern Hemisphere. Their nests resemble small floating islands anchored to water vegetation. As they move southward after nesting is ended, they are much more common along the Massachusetts coast than
on inland waters near Concord. They can sink beneath the surface without
diving and they often swim under water for considerable distances—which
has earned them the name of Hell-diver, for many a person who has watched
one dive or sink from sight has never caught another glimpse of it.

The Horned Grebe is a rare vagrant on the waters of the Concord area.
Thoreau observed it once on the Concord River and once, on December 26,
1853, on Walden Pond.]

SEPT. 27. [1860]   Monroe's tame ducks sail along and feed close to me as I am
working there. Looking up, I see a little dipper, about one-half their size, in
the middle of the river, evidently attracted by these tame ducks, as to a place
of security. I sit down and watch it. The tame ducks have paddled four or
five rods down stream along the shore. They soon detect the dipper three or
four rods off, and betray alarm by a twittering note, especially when it dives,
as it does continually. At last, when it is two or three rods off and approaching them by diving, they all rush to the shore and come out on it in their
fear, but the dipper shows itself close to the shore, and when they enter the
water again joins them within two feet, still diving from time to time and
threatening to come up in their midst. They return upstream, more or less
alarmed and pursued in this wise by the dipper, who does not know what
to make of their fears, and soon the dipper is thus tolled along to within
twenty feet of where I sit, and I can watch it at my leisure. It has a dark bill
and considerable white on the sides of the head or neck, with black between
it, no tufts, and no observable white on back or tail. When at last disturbed

by me, it suddenly sinks low (all its body) in the water without diving. Thus it can float at various heights. (So on the 30th I saw one suddenly dash along the surface from the meadow ten rods before me to the middle of the river, and then dive, and though I watched fifteen minutes and examined the tufts of grass, I could see no more of it.)

Pied-billed Grebe *(Podilymbus podiceps)*

[This species of grebe is more common on the waters about Concord than the Horned Grebe. The fact that this dipper was all black and brownish indicates its species. To-day a bird watcher would have noted the chickenlike, light-colored bill and if the individual observed was an adult, this bill would have a distinctive black band around it.

Like the Horned Grebe, this species builds a floating island nest which is anchored to vegetation. The eggs, which may number as many as seven, are covered with wet trash when the grebe leaves them to feed.

Newly hatched young are brilliantly striped black and white. Often they climb on the back of the parent bird and nestle among her feathers as she swims about.]

SEPT. 9. [1858]   Watched a little dipper some ten rods off with my glass, but I could see no white on the breast. It was all black and brownish, and head not enlarged. Who knows how many little dippers are sailing and sedulously diving now along the edge of the pickerel-weed and the button-bushes on our river, unsuspected by most? This hot September afternoon all may be quiet amid the weeds, but the dipper, and the bittern, and the yellow-legs and the blue heron, and the rail are silently feeding there. At length the walker who sits meditating on a distant bank sees the little dipper sail out from amid the weeds and busily dive for its food along their edge. Yet ordinary eyes might range up and down the river all day and never detect its small black head above the water.

Great Blue Heron *(Ardea herodias)*

[This tallest bird of New England stands about four feet high and has a wing spread of about six feet. In sustained flight, it folds its neck so the head rests between the shoulders. The long legs trail straight behind.

Thoreau never saw a nesting colony of these large birds. One wonders what his reaction would have been to a group of a hundred or more Great

Blue Herons nesting within a small area. Such colonies may occasionally be found on islands off the coast of Maine. Nowhere in New England, however, are there such tremendous nesting colonies of these birds as are found in the South from Florida to Texas.]

APRIL 19. [1852]   Scared up three blue herons in the little pond close by, quite near us. It was a grand sight to see them rise, so slow and stately, so long and limber, with an undulating motion from head to foot, undulating also their large wings, undulating in two directions, and looking warily about them. With this graceful, limber, undulating motion they arose, as if so they got under way, their two legs trailing parallel far behind like an earthy residuum to be left behind. They are large, like birds of Syrian lands, and seemed to oppress the earth, and hush the hillside to silence, as they winged their way over it, looking back toward us. It would affect our thoughts, deepen and perhaps darken our reflections, if such huge birds flew in numbers in our sky. Have the effect of magnetic passes. They are few and rare.

MAY 14. [1853]   Suddenly there start up from the riverside at the entrance of Fair Haven Pond, scared by our sail, two great blue herons,—slate-color rather,—slowly flapping and undulating, their projecting breast-bones very visible,—or is it possibly their necks bent back?—their legs stuck out straight behind. Getting higher by their flight, they straight come back to reconnoitre us.

Land at Lee's Cliff, where the herons have preceded us and are perched on the oaks, conspicuous from afar, and again we have a fair view of their flight. . . .

Again we scare up the herons, who, methinks, will build hereabouts. They were standing by the waterside. And again they alight farther below, and we see their light-colored heads erect, and their bodies at various angles as they stoop to drink. And again they flap away with their great slate-blue wings, necks curled up (?) and legs straight out behind, and having attained a great elevation, they circle back over our heads, now seemingly black as crows against the sky,—crows with long wings they might be taken for,—but higher and higher they mount by stages in the sky, till heads and tails are lost and they are mere black wavelets amid the blue, one always following close behind the other. They are evidently mated. It would be worth the while if we could see them oftener in our sky.

AUG. 22. [1854]   Saw a blue heron—apparently a young bird, of a brownish blue—fly up from one of these pools, and a stake-driver from another, and also saw their great tracks on the mud, and the feathers they had shed,—some of the long, narrow white neck-feathers of the heron. The tracks of the heron were about six inches long. Here was a rare chance for the herons to transfix the imprisoned fish. It is a wonder that any escaped. I was surprised that any dead were left on the mud, but I judge from what the book says that they do not touch dead fish. To these remote shallow and muddy pools, usually surrounded by reeds and sedge, far amid the wet meadows,—to these, then, the blue heron resorts for its food. Here, too, is an abundance of the yellow lily on whose seeds they are said to feed. . . .

Thus the drought serves the herons, etc., confining their prey within narrower limits, and doubtless they are well acquainted with suitable retired pools far in the marshes to go a-fishing in.

Nov. 1. [1855]   As I pushed up the river past Hildreth's, I saw the blue heron (probably of last Monday) arise from the shore and disappear with heavily-flapping wings around a bend in front; the greatest of the bitterns (Ardea), with heavily-undulating wings, low over the water, seen against the woods just disappearing round a bend in front; with a great slate-colored expanse of wing, suited to the shadows of the stream, a tempered blue as of the sky and dark water commingled. This is the aspect under which the Musketaquid might be represented at this season; a long, smooth lake, reflecting the bare willows and button-bushes, the stubble, and the wool-grass on its tussock, a muskrat-cabin or two conspicuous on its margin amid the unsightly tops of pontederia, and a bittern disappearing on undulating wing around the bend.

Aug. 19. [1858]   Blue herons which have bred or been bred not far from us (plainly), are now at leisure, or are impelled to revisit our slow stream. I have not seen the last since spring.

When I see the first heron, like a dusky blue wave undulating over our meadows again, I think, since I saw them going northward the other day, how many of these forms have been added to the landscape, complete from bill to toe while, perhaps, I have idled! I see two herons. A small bird is pursuing the heron as it does a hawk. Perhaps it is a blackbird and the herons gobble up their young!

Aug. 14. [1859]   p.m.   To Barrett's Bar. When I reached the upper end of this weedy bar, at about 3 p.m., this warm day, I noticed some light-colored object in mid-river, near the other end of the bar. At first I thought of some large stake or board standing amid the weeds there, then of a fisherman in a brown holland sack, referring him to the shore beyond. Supposing it the last, I floated nearer and nearer till I saw plainly enough the motions of the person, whoever it was, and that it was no stake. Looking through my glass thirty or forty rods off, I thought certainly that I saw C., who had just bathed, making signals to me with his towel, for I referred the object to the shore twenty rods further. I saw his motions as he wiped himself,—the movements of his elbows and his towel. Then I saw that the person was nearer and therefore smaller, that it stood on the sand-bar in mid-stream in shallow water and must be some maiden [in] a bathing dress,—for it was the color of brown holland web,—and a very peculiar kind of dress it seemed. But about this time I discovered with my naked eye that it was a blue heron standing in very shallow water amid the weeds of the bar and pluming itself. I had not noticed its legs at all, and its head, neck, and wings being constantly moving, I had mistaken for arms, elbows, and towel of a bather, and when it stood stiller its shapely body looked like a peculiar bathing-dress. I floated to within twenty-five rods and watched it at my leisure. Standing on the shallowest part of the bar at that end it was busily dressing its feathers, passing its bill like a comb down its feathers from base to tip. From its form and color, as well as size, it was singularly distinct. Its great spear-shaped head and bill was very conspicuous, though least so when it turned toward me (whom it was eying from time to time). It coils its neck away from its back or breast as a sailor might a rope, but occasionally stretches itself to its full height, as tall as a man, and looks around at me. Growing shy, it begins to wade off, until its body is partly immersed amid the weeds,—potamogetons,—and then it looks more like a goose. The neck is continually varying in length, as it is doubled up or stretched out, and the legs also, as it wades in deeper or shallower water.

Suddenly comes a second, flying low, and alights on the bar yet nearer to me, almost high and dry. Then I hear a note from them, perhaps of warning, —a short, coarse, frog-like purring or eructating sound. You might easily mistake it for a frog. I heard it half a dozen times. It was not very loud. Anything but musical. The last proceeds to plume himself, looking warily at me from time to time, while the other continues to edge off through the weeds. Now and then the latter holds its neck as if it were ready to strike its prey,— stretched forward over the water,—but I saw no stroke. The arch may be lengthened or shortened, single or double, but the great spear-shaped bill and head are ever the same. A great hammer or pick, prepared to transfix fish, frog, or bird. At last, the water becoming too deep for wading, this one takes easily to wing,—though up to his body in water—and flies a few rods to the shore. It rather flies, then, than swims. It was evidently scared. These were probably birds of this season. I saw some distinct ferruginous on the angle of the wing. There they stood in the midst of the open river, on this shallow and weedy bar in the sun, the leisurely sentries, lazily pluming themselves, as if the day were too long for them. They gave a new character to the stream. Adjutant they were to my idea of the river, these two winged men . . .

How long may we have gazed on a particular scenery and think that we have seen and known it, when, at length, some bird or quadruped comes and takes possession of it before our eyes, and imparts to it a wholly new character. The heron uses these shallows as I cannot. I give them up to him.

GREEN HERON *(Butorides virescens)*

[This small heron looks rather crowlike when flying at a distance, but close views reveal its many bright colors. It is one of the most widely distributed of American herons, and large ponds, swamps, and marshes are seldom without one.

Usually the Green Heron is a solitary bird when nesting, but colonies of thirty or more pairs are occasionally found. The frail nest has no lining, the four or five greenish eggs resting on a small platform of loose sticks.]

Aug. 2. [1856]   To Hill. A green bittern comes, noiselessly flapping, with stealthy and inquisitive looking to this side the stream and then that, thirty feet above the water. This antediluvian bird, creature of the night, is a fit emblem of a dead stream like this Musketicook. This especially is the bird of the river. There is a sympathy between its sluggish flight and the sluggish flow of the stream—its slowly lapsing flight, even like the rills of Musketicook and my own pulse sometimes.

AMERICAN BITTERN *(Botaurus lentiginosus)*

[This species, at home in either fresh or salt bogs and marshes, has plumage which closly matches it surroundings. Many a person has looked directly at one without seeing it. Because of the strange, sometimes humanlike sounds which the American Bittern makes with its syrinx, the vocal organ of birds, many odd popular names have been applied to it. Among these are "thunder-pumper," "dunk-a-doo," and "stake driver." Thoreau most frequently used the latter name.

The eyes of a bittern are slung so low that even when it points its bill straight at the sky, it can see its toes. In company with other herons, the bittern has feathers known as powder downs. With their bills, they break up these yellowish powder-down feathers and rub them through their plumage when dressing it. Of course they also use oil pressed from their oil glands, which are located near the tail.

Bitterns are heard far oftener than they are seen. Their nest, a mere platform of grasses built a few inches above the water, is well hidden from inquisitive eyes.

Of course the bittern does not drive stakes or sticks into the ground, nor does it pump water. Nevertheless, the folk tales surrounding it, as well as its secretive habits, add to our interest in the species as they did to Thoreau's.]

Oct. 7. [1851]   Saw the *Ardea minor* walking along the shore, like a hen with long green legs. Its pencilled throat is so like the reeds and shore, amid which it holds its head erect to watch the passer, that it is difficult to discern it. You can get very near it, for it is unwilling to fly, preferring to hide amid the weeds.

June 20. [1852]   To Hubbard's Bathing-Place. The stake-driver is at it in his favorite meadow. I followed the sound. At last I got within two rods, it seeming always to recede and drawing you like a will-o'-the-wisp further away into the meadows. When thus near, I heard some lower sounds at the beginning, much more like striking on a stump or a stake, a dry, hard sound; and then followed the gurgling, pumping notes, fit to come from a meadow. This was just within the blueberry and *Pyrus arbutifolia* (choke-berry) bushes, and when the bird flew up alarmed, I went to the place, but could see no water, which makes me doubt if water is necessary to it in making the sound. Perhaps it thrusts its bill so deep as to reach the water where it is dry on the surface. It sounds the more like wood-chopping or pumping, because you seem to hear the echo of the stroke or the reverse motion of the pump-handle. I hear them morning and evening. After the warm weather has come, both morning and evening you hear the bittern pumping in the fens. It does not sound loud near at hand, and it is remarkable that it should be heard so far. Perhaps it is pitched on a favorable key. Is it not a call to its mate? Methinks that in the resemblance of this note to rural sounds, to sounds made by farmers, the protection, the security, of the bird is designed. Minott says: "I call them belcher-squelchers. They go *slug-toot, slug-toot, slug-toot.*"

Nov. 17. [1858]   I am surprised to see a stake-driver fly up from the weeds within a stone's throw of my boat's place. It drops its excrement from thirty feet in the air, and this falling, one part being heavier than another, takes the form of a snake, and suggests that this may be the origin of some of the stories of this bird swallowing a snake or eel which passed through it.

April 17. [1860]   Looking off on to the river meadow, I noticed, as I thought, a stout stick aslant in the meadow, three or more rods off, sharp at the top and rather light-colored on one side, as is often the case; yet at the same time, it occurred to me that a stake-driver often resembled a stake very much, but I thought, nevertheless, that there was no doubt about this being a stake. I took out my glass to look for ducks, and my companion, seeing what I had, and asking if it was not a stake-driver, I suffered my glass at last to rest on it, and I was much surprised to find that it was a stake-driver after all. The bird stood in shallow water near a tussock, perfectly still, with its long bill pointed upwards in the same direction with its body and neck, so as perfectly to resemble a stake aslant. If the bill had made an angle with the neck it would have been betrayed at once. Its resource evidently was to rely on its form and color and immobility solely for its concealment. This was its instinct, whether it implies any conscious artifice or not. I watched it for fifteen minutes, and at length it relaxed its muscles and changed its attitude, and I observed a slight motion; and soon after, when I moved toward it, it flew. It resembled more a piece of a rail than anything else,—more than anything that would have been seen there before the white man came. It is a question whether the bird consciously cooperates in each instance with its Maker, who contrived this concealment. I can never believe that this resemblance is a mere coincidence, not designed to answer this very end—which it does answer so perfectly and usefully.

CANADA GOOSE *(Branta canadensis)*

[Few species of birds appealed more deeply to Thoreau's imagination than did Canada Geese. There are many entries about geese in his *Journal* and all make delightful reading. He reworked two of them, written on March 26-27, 1846, and used them in one of the most beautiful passages of *Walden*.

At the time Thoreau watched the passage of geese, they were truly Canada Geese in eastern North America as far as their breeding range was concerned. Now, as a result of releasing partly tamed birds, there are scattered nesting groups throughout New England, including Concord itself.

During the winter the geese must move southward ahead of the ice, for they need open water as a resting place. Most stop north of or close to the Gulf Coast of the United States, but some continue as far south as Veracruz, Mexico.

Banding records indicate that geese customarily follow the same routes year after year and use the same resting places. No doubt Thoreau was quite right in believing that the large numbers of geese which passed over Concord at approximately the same hour each spring had spent the night in a favorite resting place where their ancestors had also stopped to rest.

Concord, with its network of rivers, its ponds, and flooded meadows, offered an ideal resting place for these large game birds. But the high population of hunters which preyed on the geese not only in autumn but in spring, reduced their numbers.

Place names used by Thoreau can be perplexing. In Concord, he bestowed his own names on places he often visited. The unwary may suspect that an obscure geographical term may also have originated with him. One of these is the long-forgotten King of Holland's Line. In the following selection, Thoreau referred to the northern boundary of lands claimed in America by the Dutch in 1614 by right of discovery. This boundary followed the 45 degree of latitude which lies across northeastern Massachusetts and southern New Hampshire; thus it was not far from Concord. The southern boundary of the Dutch-claimed lands lay along the 40th degree and was, therefore, slightly north of the Mason and Dixon Line.]

MARCH 21. [1840] . . . The wild goose is more a cosmopolite than we; he breaks his fast in Canada, takes a luncheon in the Susquehanna, and plumes himself for the night in a Lousiana bayou. The pigeon carries an acorn in his crop from the King of Holland's to the Mason and Dixon's line. Yet we think if rail fences are pulled down and stone walls set up on our farms, bounds are henceforth set to our lives and our fates decided. If you are chosen town clerk, forsooth, you can't go to Tierra del Fuego this summer.

MARCH 28. [1852] 10:15 P.M. The geese have just gone over, making a great cackling and awaking people in their beds. They will probably settle in the river. Who knows but they expected to find the pond open?

APRIL 15. [1852] How indispensable our one or two flocks of geese in spring and autumn! What would be a spring in which that sound was not heard: Coming to unlock the fetters of northern rivers. Those annual steamers of the air.

APRIL 18. [1852] Going through Dennis's field with C. [William Ellery Channing], saw a flock of geese on east side of river near willows. Twelve great birds on the troubled surface of the meadow, delayed by the storm. We lay on the ground behind an oak and our umbrella, eighty rods off, and watched them. Soon we heard a gun go off, but could see no smoke in the mist and rain. And the whole flock rose, spreading their great wings and flew with clangor a few rods and lit in the water again, then swam swiftly toward our shore with outstretched necks. I knew them first from ducks by their long necks. Soon appeared the man, running toward the shore in vain, in his great-coat; but he soon retired in vain. We remained close under our umbrella by the tree, ever and anon looking through a peep-hole between the umbrella and the tree at the birds. On they came, sometimes in two, sometimes in three, squads, warily, till we could see the steel-blue and green reflections from their necks. We held the dog close the while,—C., lying on his back in the rain, had him in his arms,—and thus we gradually edged round on the ground in this cold, wet, windy storm, keeping our feet to the tree, and the great wet calf of a dog with his eyes shut so meekly in our arms. We laughed well at our adventure. They swam fast and warily, seeing our umbrella. Occasionally one expanded a gray wing. They showed white on breasts. And not till after half an hour, sitting cramped and cold and wet on the ground, did we leave them.

APRIL 19. [1852] That last flock of geese yesterday is still in my eye. After hearing their clangor, looking southwest, we saw them just appearing over a dark pine wood, in an irregular waved line, one abreast of the other, as it were breasting the air, and pushing it before them. It made you think of the streams of Cayster. . . . They carry weight, such a weight of metal in the air. Their dark waved outline as they disappear. The grenadiers of the air. Man pigmifies himself at sight of these inhabitants of the air. These stormy days they do not love to fly; they alight in some retired marsh or river. From their lofty pathway they can easily spy out the most extensive and retired swamp. How many there must be, that one or more flocks are seen to go over almost every farm in New England in the spring! . . .

To see the larger and wilder birds, you must go forth in great storms like this. At such times they frequent our neighborhood and trust themselves in our midst. A life of fair-weather walks *might* never show you the goose sailing on our waters, or the great heron feeding here. When the storm increases, then these great birds that carry the mail of the seasons lay to. To see wild life you must go forth at a wild season. When it rains and blows, keeping men indoors, then the lover of Nature must forth. Then returns Nature to her wild estate. In pleasant sunny weather you may catch butterflies, but only when the storm rages that lays prostrate the forest and wrecks the mariner, do you come upon the feeding grounds of wildest fowl,—of herons and geese.

MARCH 26. [1853] Saw about 10 A.M. a gaggle of geese, forty-three in number, in a very perfect harrow flying northeasterly. One side [of] the harrow was a little longer than the other. They appeared to be four or five feet apart. At first I heard faintly, as I stood by Minott's gate, borne to me from the southwest through the confused sounds of the village, the indistinct honking of geese. I was somewhat surprised to find that Mr. Loring at his house should have heard and seen the same flock. I should think that the same flock was commonly seen and heard from the distance of a mile east and west. It is remarkable that we commonly see geese go over in the spring about 10 o'clock in the morning, as if they were accustomed to stop for the night at some place southward whence they reached us at that time.

DEC. 13. [1855] Sanborn tells me that he was waked up a few nights ago in Boston, about midnight, by the sound of a flock of geese passing over the city, probably about the same night I heard them here. They go honking over cities where the arts flourish, waking the inhabitants; over State-houses and capitols, where legislatures sit; over harbors where fleets lie at anchor; mistaking the city, perhaps, for a swamp or the edge of a lake, about settling in it, not suspecting that greater geese than they have settled there.

Nov. 8. [1857]   A warm cloudy, rain-threatening morning. About 10 A.M. a long flock of geese are going over from northeast to southeast, or parallel with the general direction of the coast and great mountain-ranges. The sonorous, quavering sounds of the geese are the voice of this cloudy air,—a sound that comes from directly between us and the sky; an aerial sound, and yet so distinct, heavy, and sonorous, a clanking chain drawn through the heavy air. I saw through my window some children looking up and pointing their tiny bows into the heavens, and I knew at once that the geese were in the air. It is always an exciting event. The children, instinctively aware of its importance, rushed into the house to tell their parents. These travellers are revealed to you by the upward-turned gaze of men. And though these undulating lines are melting into the southwestern sky, the sound comes clear and distinct to you as the clank of a chain in a neighboring stithy. So they migrate, not flitting from hedge to hedge, but from latitude to latitude, from State to State, steering boldly out into the ocean of the air. It is remarkable how these large objects, so plain when your vision is rightly directed, may be lost in the sky if you look away for a moment,—as hard to hit as a star with a telescope.

It is a sort of encouraging or soothing sound to assuage their painful fears when they go over a town, as a man moans to deaden physical pain. The direction of their flight each spring and autumn reminds us inlanders how the coast trends. In the afternoon I met Flood, who had just endeavored to draw my attention to a flock of geese in the mizzling air, but encountering me he lost sight of them, while I, at length, looking that way, discerned them though he could not. This was the third flock to-day. Now if ever, then, we may expect a change in the weather.

Nov. 30. [1857]   The air is full of geese. I saw five flocks within an hour, about 10 A.M., containing from thirty to fifty each, and afterward two more flocks, making in all from two hundred and fifty to three hundred at least, all flying southeast over Goose and Walden Ponds. The former was apparently well named Goose Pond. You first hear a faint honking from one or two in the northeast and think there are but a few wandering there, but, looking up, see forty or fifty coming on in a more or less broken harrow, wedging their way southwest. I suspect they honk more, at any rate they are more broken and alarmed, when passing over a village, and are seen falling into their ranks again, assuming the perfect harrow form. Hearing only one or two honking, even for the seventh time, you think there are but few till you see them. According to my calculation a thousand or fifteen hundred may have gone over Concord to-day.

APRIL 1. [1858]   I observed night before last, as often before, when geese were passing over in the twilight quite near, though the whole heavens were still light and I knew which way to look by the honking, I could not distinguish them. It takes but a little obscurity to hide a bird in the air. How difficult, even in broadest daylight, to discover again a hawk at a distance in the sky when you have once turned your eyes away!

MARCH 28. [1859]   When walking about on the low east shore at the Bedford bound, I heard a faint honk, and looked around over the water with my glass, thinking it came from that side or perhaps from a farmyard in that direction. I soon heard it again, quite on the other side of us and pretty high up. From time to time one of the company uttered a short note, that peculiarly metallic, clangorous sound. These were in a single undulating line, and, as usual, one or two were from time to time crowded out of the line, apparently by the crowding of those in the rear and were flying on one side and trying to recover their places, but at length a second short line was formed, meeting the long one at the usual angle and making a figure somewhat like a hay-hook. I suspect it will be found that there is really some advantage in large birds of passage flying in the wedge form and cleaving their way through the air,—that they really do overcome its resistance best in this way,—and perchance the direction and strength of the wind determine the comparative length of the two sides. . . .

Undoubtedly the geese fly more numerously over rivers which, like ours, flow northeasterly,—are more at home with the water under them. Each flock runs the gantlet of a thousand gunners, and when you see them steer off from you and your boat you may remember how great their experience in such matters may be, how many such boats and gunners they have seen and avoided between here and Mexico, and even now, perchance (though you, low plodding, little dream it), they see one or two more lying in wait ahead. They have an experienced ranger of the air for their guide. The echo of one gun hardly dies away before they see another pointed at them. How many bullets or smaller shot have sped in vain toward their ranks! . . . The geese rest in fair weather by day only in the midst of our broadest meadow or pond. So they go, anxious and earnest to hide their nests under the pole.

WILD DUCKS

[Ducks have a tremendous economic value to man. Some species have been domesticated. The wild ducks have inspired what amounts almost to a cult

among sportsmen. Multitudes have shared the exhilarating thrill aroused by
their migrating flocks both in spring and autumn and have watched spell-
bound as groups of ducks pitched into a marsh or took flight from it.

Until he bought his spyglass, Thoreau was not able to observe ducks closely
enough to identify them except on rare occasions. Nevertheless, he awaited
their coming with keen anticipation as their time for migration approached.
During the summer he frequently encountered, while boating, an occasional
Wood Duck family. Whether Thoreau wrote of ducks in general, or about a
particular species, he enriches the bird watcher's appreciation of these varied
birds.

Scientists divide ducks into two large groups: surface-feeding ducks which
feed in shallow water by "tipping up" and rarely dive, and diving ducks which
habitually dive for their food and frequently feed in very deep water. Though
they are diving ducks, mergansers with saw-edged bills useful in holding the
slippery fish which they chase and catch, and a few other ducks, are placed
in separate categories. The keen-eyed Thoreau noted that the surface-feeding
ducks were able to spring from the surface of the water into the air, while
the diving ducks first pattered along the surface when getting under way.]

MARCH 16. [1840]   The ducks alight at this season on the windward side of
the river, in the smooth water, and swim about by twos and threes, pluming
themselves and diving to peck at the root of the lily and the cranberries which
the frost has not loosened. It is impossible to approach them within gunshot
when they are accompanied by the gull, which rises sooner and makes them
restless. They fly to windward first, in order to get under weigh, and are
more easily reached by the shot if approached on that side. When preparing
to fly, they swim about with their heads erect, and then, gliding along a few
feet with their bodies just touching the surface, rise heavily with much splash-
ing and fly low at first, if not suddenly aroused, but otherwise rise directly
to survey the danger. The cunning sportsman is not in haste to desert his
position, but waits to ascertain if, having got themselves into flying trim, they
will not return over the ground in their course to a new resting place.

OCT. 12. [1852]   Paddled on Walden. A rippled surface. Scared up ducks.
Saw them first far over the surface, just risen,—two smaller, white-bellied,
one large, black. They circled round as usual, and the first went off, but the
black one went round and round and over the pond five or six times at a
considerable height and distance, when I thought several times he had gone
to the river, and at length settled down by a slanting flight of a quarter of
a mile into a distant part of the pond which I had left free; but what beside
safety these ducks get by sailing in the middle of Walden I don't know. That
black rolling-pin with wings, circling round you half a mile off for a quarter

of an hour, at that height from which he sees the river and Fair Haven all the while, from which he sees so many things, while I see almost him alone. Their wings set so far back. They are not handsome, but wild.

MARCH 12. [1855]   To Great Meadows. Two ducks in river, good size, white beneath with black heads, as they go over. They first rise some distance down-stream, and fly by on high, reconnoitring me, and I first see them on wing; then settle a quarter of a mile above by a long slanting flight, at last opposite the swimming-elm below Flint's. I come on up the bank with the sun in my face; start them again. Again they fly down-stream by me on high, turn and come round back by me again with outstretched heads, and go up to the Battle-Ground before they alight. Thus the river is no sooner fairly open than they are back again,—before I have got my boat launched, and long before the river has worn through Fair Haven Pond. I think I heard a quack or two.

MARCH 27. [1855]   6 A.M.—To Island. The ducks sleep these nights in the shallowest water which does not freeze, and there may be found early in the morning. I think that they prefer that part of the shore which is permanently covered.

APRIL 22. [1856]   It began to rain hard. . . . From time to time, from under my umbrella, I could see the ducks spinning before me, like great bees. For when they are flying low directly from you, you see hardly anything but their vanishing dark bodies, while the rapidly moving wings or paddles, seen edge-wise, are almost invisible.

OCT. 22. [1857]   As I go through the woods now, so many oak and other leaves have fallen the rustling noise somewhat disturbs my musing. However, Nature in this may have intended some kindness to the ducks, which are now loitering hereabouts on their migration southward, mostly young and inexper-ienced birds, for, as they are feeding [in] Goose Pond, for instance, the rustling of the leaves betrays the approach of the sportsman and his dog, or other foe; so perhaps the leaves on the ground protect them more than when on the trees.

OCT. 28. [1857]   All at once a low-slanted glade of sunlight from one of heaven's west windows behind me fell on the bare gray maples, lighting them up with an incredibly intense and pure white light; then, going out there, it lit up some white birch stems south of the pond, then the gray rocks and the pale reddish young oaks of the lower cliffs, and then the very pale brown meadow-grass, and at last the brilliant white breasts of two ducks, tossing on the agitated surface far off on the pond, which I had not detected before.

July 27. [1860]   How easy for the young ducks to hide amid the pickerel-weed along our river, while a boat goes by! and this plant attains its height when these water-fowl are of a size to need its shelter. Thousands of them might be concealed by it along our river, not to speak of the luxuriant sedge and grass of the meadows, much of it so wet as to be inaccessible. These ducks are diving scarcely two feet within the edge of the pickerel-weed yet one who had not first seen them exposed from a distance would never suspect their neighborhood.

BLACK DUCK *(Anas rubripes)*

[Bird watchers who read the following selections feel with Thoreau the biting wind on a brilliant March day and hear the crunch of dry leaves underfoot. Many people regard the Black Duck as the wariest, most alert of all the American ducks.

Thoreau wrote several accounts of his observations of Black Ducks. On April 1, 1853, he noted the light lining of their wings when in flight, the chief identification point by which bird watchers to-day pick them out of a flock. He sometimes heard of young Black Ducks in Concord, and on June 23, 1857, the local harness-maker told him of finding a nest with about a dozen eggs in it on June 14. Thoreau searched for the nest but failed to find it.

This duck breeds in some of the most densely populated areas of this country, and is common in the salt marshes along the Atlantic coast. The nest is usually well hidden under grass or dense shrubs. The greenish eggs, averaging nine in a clutch, are given extra protection by a nesting lining of down plucked from the breast of the female. Since the species has adapted itself so well to human disturbance, it would appear that its future is secure, and that hunters could be assured of continued sport with the species.

Submerged water plants make up a large part of the food of these ducks when shallow waters are open. As a consequence, more and more of these birds die each year from lead poisoning. Shots fall into their marshy feeding places during the hunting season. The ducks pick them up with their food. It takes but a pellet or two to spell the end of one of these fine ducks.]

April 1. [1853]   Saw ten black ducks at Clamshell. Had already started two, who probably occupied an outpost. They all went off with a loud and disagreeable quacking like ducks in a poultry-yard, their wings appearing lighter beneath.

MARCH 21. [1854] At sunrise to Clamshell Hill. River skimmed over at Willow Bay last night. Thought I should find ducks cornered up by the ice; they get behind this hill for shelter. Saw what looked like clods of plowed meadow rising above the ice. Looked with glass and found it to be more than thirty black ducks asleep with their heads in [sic] their backs, motionless, and thin ice formed about them. Soon one or two were moving about slowly. There was an open space, eight or ten rods by one or two. At first all within a space of apparently less than a rod [in] diameter. It was 6:30 A.M., and the sun shining on them but bitter cold. How tough they are! I crawled far on my stomach and got a near view of them, thirty rods off. At length they detected me and quacked. Some got out upon the ice, and when I rose up all took to flight in a great straggling flock which at a distance looked like crows, in no order. Yet, when you see two or three, the parallelism produced by their necks and bodies steering the same way gives the idea of order.

MARCH 31. [1858] I see about a dozen black ducks on Flint's Pond, asleep with their heads in their backs and drifting across the pond before the wind. I suspect they are nocturnal in their habits and therefore require much rest by day. So do the seasons revolve and every chink is filled. While the waves toss this bright day, the ducks, asleep, are drifting before it across the ponds. Every now and then one or two lift their heads and look about, as if they watched by turns . . . The leaves are now so dry and loose that it is almost impossible to approach the shore of the pond without being heard by the ducks.

WOOD DUCK *(Aix sponsa)*

[Thoreau began writing about Wood Ducks in his *Journal* as early as October 29, 1837, and many notes follow through the years. This duck is considered by many people the most beautiful duck in the entire world, and Thoreau delighted in watching it.

On November 9, 1855, Thoreau and his friend from Worcester, Massachusetts, Harrison G. O. Blake, were paddling on the river when suddenly they came upon a male Wood Duck. Imagine, if you can, never having heard of this duck or seen its picture and suddenly coming upon it. Only then can you fully appreciate Mr. Blake's delight. Most people remember vividly their first close view of this duck which is far more lovely than any painting can portray.

Thoreau always regretted the cutting of Concord trees, which he considered among the most valuable assets of the town. Most people of the village bought their winter supply of wood in the wood market. Thoreau, floating on a dark backwater on November 18, 1855, saw with sadness the trunks of felled trees reflected there. His thoughts suddenly lightened when before him appeared a brilliant Wood Duck. As he watched it, he felt though it could give him no physical warmth, it was worth being chilled that cold November day to see such beauty.

His entry on August 16, 1858, after he learned the fate of the Wood Ducks he had watched for weeks, is a powerful plea for the preservation of beauty for its own sake. There is an extension of Wood Ducks in his plea that places of great beauty be preserved, not in private ownership (see pages 247—248) but as public property for all men to enjoy freely.

Natural nesting places for Wood Ducks in Concord are decidedly limited. Since the establishment of the Great Meadows National Wildlife Refuge, boxes have provided many artificial sites for breeding pairs. This has greatly increased the population of Wood Ducks in the area.]

Aug. 6 [1855] At Ball's Hill see five summer ducks, a brood now grown, feeding amid the pads on the opposite side of the river, with a whitish ring, perhaps nearly around neck. A rather shrill squeaking quack when they go off. It is remarkable how much more game you will see if you are in the habit of *sitting* in the fields and woods. As you pass along with a noise it hides itself, but presently comes forth again.

Nov. 9. [1855] A.M. Grass white and stiff with frost. . . . Saw in the pool at the Hemlocks what I at first thought was a brighter leaf moved by the zephyr on the surface of the smooth dark water, but it was a splendid male summer duck, which allowed us to approach within seven or eight rods, sailing up close to the shore, and then rose and flew up the curving stream. We soon overhauled it again, and got a fair and long view of it. It was a splendid bird, a perfect floating gem, and Blake, who had never seen the like, was greatly surprised not knowing that so splendid a bird was found in this part of the world. There it was, constantly moving back and forth by invisible means and wheeling on the smooth surface, showing now its breast, now its side, now its rear. It had a large, rich, flowing, green burnished crest—a most ample head-dress,—two crescents of dazzling white on the side of the head and the black neck, a pinkish (?)-red bill (with black tip) and similar irides, and a long white mark under and at wing point on sides; the side, as if the form of a wing at this distance, a light bronze or greenish brown; but, above all, its breast, when it turns into the right light, all aglow with splendid purple (?) or ruby (?) reflections, *like the throat of the hummingbird.* It might not appear so close at hand. This was the most surprising to me. What an ornament to a river to see that glowing gem floating in contact with its water! As if the hummingbird should recline its ruby throat and its breast on the water. Like dipping a glowing coal in water! It so affected me.

It became excited, fluttered or flapped its wings with a slight whistling noise, and arose and flew two or three rods and alighted. It sailed close up to the edge of a rock, by which it lay pretty still, and finally sailed fast up one side of the river by the willows, etc., off the duck swamp beyond the spring, now and then turning and sailing back a foot or two, while we paddled up the opposite side a rod in the rear, for twenty or thirty rods. At length we went by it, and it flew back low a few rods to where we roused it. It never offered to dive. We came equally near it again on our return. Unless you are thus near, and have a glass, the splendor and beauty of its colors will not be discovered.

Nov. 18. [1855]   Instead of walking in the wood-market amid sharp-visaged teamsters, I float over dark reflecting waters in which I see mirrored the stumps on the bank, and am dazzled by the beauty of a summer duck. Though I should get no wood, I should get beauty perhaps more valuable. The price of this my wood, however high, is the very thing which I delight to pay.

Aug. 3. [1856]   To Lee's Cliff by river. Two small ducks (probably wood ducks) flying south. Already grown, and at least looking south! It reminds me of the swift revolution of the seasons.

Aug. 16. [1858]   In my boating of late I have several times scared up a couple of summer ducks of this year, bred in our meadows. They allowed me to come quite near, and helped to people the river. I have not seen them for some days. Would you know the end of our intercourse? Goodwin shot them, and Mrs. ——, who never sailed on the river, ate them. Of course, she knows not what she did. What if I should eat her canary? Thus we share each other's sins as well as burdens. The lady who watches admiringly the matador shares his deed. They belonged to me, as much as to any one, when they were alive, but it is considered of more importance that Mrs. —— should taste the flavor of them dead than that I should enjoy the beauty of them alive.

BUFFLEHEAD *(Bucephala albeola)*

[Spirit duck, Butterball, Spirit Dipper, and Woolhead are among the colloquial names applied to this very small duck, only slightly larger than the little teals. It is a rather silent duck, and was once called "buffalo-headed" because of its enormous black head with a conspicuous white triangular patch on the top. Its flight is extremely swift and it dives as readily as a grebe. Though they never nest in New England, they will remain there in winter if waters stay open.

Most Buffleheads nest in Canada and Alaska, though a few breed in the Northwest and Minnesota. Usually they choose holes deserted by flickers or other woodpeckers, but in areas where trees are scarce they have been known to lay their eggs in holes like those of kingfishers in banks along ponds and streams.]

APRIL 19. [1855] From Heywood's Peak I thought I saw the head of a loon in the pond, thirty-five or forty rods distant. Bringing my glass to bear, it seemed sunk very low in the water,—all the neck concealed,—but I could not tell which end was the bill. At length I discovered that it was the whole body of a little duck, asleep with its head in its back, exactly in the middle of the pond. It had a moderate-sized black head and neck, a white breast, and *seemed* dark-brown above, with a white spot on the side of the head, not reaching to the outside, from base of mandibles, and another, perhaps, at the end of the wing, with some black there. It sat drifting round a little, but with ever its breast toward the wind, and from time to time it raised its head and looked round to see if it were safe. I think it was the smallest duck I ever saw. Floating buoyantly asleep on the middle of Walden Pond. Was it not a female of the buffle-headed or spirit duck? I believed the wings looked blacker when it flew, with some white beneath. It floated like a little casket, and at first I doubted a good while if it possessed life, until I saw it raise its head and look around. It had chosen a place for its nap exactly equidistant between the two shores there, and, with its breast to the wind, swung round only as much as a vessel held by its anchors in the stream. At length the cars scared it.

COMMON MERGANSER *(Mergus merganser)*

[This fresh-water duck is also called the goosander and sheldrake. It often searches for its prey by swimming rapidly with its head half submerged, then when a fish is sighted, it dives in a flash and is fast enough to overtake and capture the fish.

Until he bought his spyglass, Thoreau often found it impossible to identify many of the ducks which he saw on Concord waters. He saw four ducks which he believed were mergansers on March 29, 1853, and wrote in his *Journal:*]

Would it not be well to carry a spyglass in order to watch these shy birds such as ducks and hawks? In some respects, methinks, it would be better than a gun. The latter brings them nearer dead, but the former alive. You can identify the species better by killing the bird, because it was a dead specimen that was so minutely described, but you can study the habits and appearance best in the living specimen. These ducks first flew north, or somewhat against the wind (was it to get under weigh?), then wheeled, flew nearer me, and went south up-stream, where I saw them afterward.

[The selections which follow were all written after Thoreau purchased his spyglass. Though he sold his gun before he went to live in the Walden Pond cabin, he examined dead birds whenever he had an opportunity. With what rejoicing he carried home, on April 6, 1855, a freshly killed Common Merganser which he found!

The female Common Merganser has a white, not a red throat, as Thoreau wrote on March 23, 1859. Her entire head and neck, except for the sharply defined white of the upper throat, are red. Without doubt this in one of those inexplicable errors which authors sometimes make, for on April 7, 1855, Thoreau wrote of seeing distinctly the reddish brown or sorrel on the neck of a female merganser and again on April 16, 1855, he watched a flock of mergansers and wrote:]

With my glass I see by their reddish heads that all of one party—the main body—are females. You see little more than their heads at a distance and not much white but on their throats, perchance.

[Common Mergansers nest either on the ground or in holes in trees. Young hatched in tree nests stay there two or three days. Then the female, on the ground, calls to them and they drop, unassisted, to the ground. They are then led to the water where they swim and dive with speed and ease.

Thoreau's records of this species remained the earliest (February 27, 1860) and the latest (April 19, 1858) spring records in Concord at the time *Birds of Concord* was published in 1948. Abundant in Thoreau's time, it declined until the 1930s when it began an increase which continues to the present time.]

APRIL 6. [1855]   You can hear all day, from time to time, in any part of the village, the sound of a gun fired at ducks. Yesterday I was wishing that I could find a dead duck floating on the water, as I had found muskrats, and a hare, and now I see something bright and reflecting the light from the edge of the alders, five or six rods off. Can it be a duck? I can hardly believe my eyes. I am near enough to see its green head and neck. I am delighted to find a perfect specimen of the *Mergus merganser,* or goosander, undoubtedly shot yesterday by the Fast-Day sportsmen, and I take a small flattened shot from its wing,—flattened against the wing-bone apparently. The wing is broken, and it is shot through the head. It is a perfectly fresh and very beautiful bird, and as I raise it, I get sight of its long, slender vermillion bill (color of red sealing-wax) and its clean, bright-orange legs and feet, and then of its perfectly smooth and spotlessly pure white breast and belly tinged with a faint salmon (or tinged with a delicate buff inclining to salmon).

This, according to Wilson, is one of the mergansers, or fisher ducks, of which there are nine or ten species and we have four in America. It is the largest of these four; feeds almost entirely on fin and shell fish; called water pheasant, sheldrake, fisherman diver, dun diver, sparkling fowl, harle, etc., as well as goosander. Go in April, return in November. Jardine has found seven trout in one female. Nuttall says they breed in the Russian Empire and are seen in Mississippi and Missouri in winter. He found a young brood in Pennsylvania. Yarrell says they are called also saw-bill and jack-saw; are sometimes sold in London market. Nest, according to Selby, on ground; according to others, in a hollow tree also. Found on the continent of Europe, northern Asia, and even in Japan(?). Some breed in the Orkneys and thereabouts. My bird is 25⅞ inches long and 35 in alar extent; from point of wing to end of primaries, 11 inches.

It is a great diver and does not mind the cold. It appears admirably fitted for diving and swimming. Its body is flat, and its tail short, flat, compact, and wedge-shaped; its eyes peer out a slight slit or semi-circle in the skin of the head; and its legs are flat and thin in one direction, and the toes shut up compactly so as to create the least friction when drawing them forward, but their broad webs spread them three and a half inches when they take a stroke. The web is extended three eighths of an inch beyond the inner toe of each foot. There are very conspicuous black teeth-like serrations along the edges of its bill, and this also is roughened so that it may hold its prey securely.

The breast *appeared* quite dry when I raised it from the water.

The head and neck are, as Wilson says, black glossed with green, but the lower part of the neck pure white, and these colors bound on each other so abruptly that one appears to be sewed on to the other.

It is a perfect wedge from the middle of its body to the end of its tail, and it is only three and a quarter inches deep from back to breast at the thickest part, while the greatest breadth horizontally (at the root of the legs) is five and a half inches. In these respects it reminds me of an otter, which however I have never seen.

I suspect that I have seen near a hundred of these birds this spring, but I never got so near one before. In Yarrell's plate the depth of the male goosander is to its length (*i.e.* from tip of tail to most forward part of breast) as thirty-seven to one hundred and three, or the depth is more than one third. This length in Yarrell's bird, calling the distance from the point of the wing to the end of the primaries eleven inches, is about fourteen and a half inches of which my three and a quarter is not one fourth. In Nuttall's plate the proportion is thirty-two to ninety-one, also more than one third. I think they have not represented the bird flat enough.

Yarrell says it is the largest of the British mergansers; is a winter visitor, though a few breed in the north of Britain; are rare in the southern countries. But, according to Yarrell, a Mr. Low in his Natural History of Orkney says they breed there, and, after breeding, the sexes separate; and Y. quotes Selby as saying that their nest is near the edge of the water, of grass, roots, etc., lined with down, sometimes among stones, in long grass, under bushes, or in a stump or hollow tree. Y. continues, egg "a uniform buff white," two and a half inches long. Sometimes carry their young on their backs in the water. It is common in Sweden and, according to the traveller Acerbi, in Lapland they give it a hollow tree to build in and then steal its eggs. The mother, he adds, carries her young to the water in her bill. Y. says it is well known in Russia and is found in Germany, Holland, France, Switzerland, Provence, and Italy. Has been seen near the Caucasus (and is found in Japan, according to one authority). Also in North America, Hudson's Bay, Greenland, and Iceland.

APRIL 7. [1855]   In my walk in the afternoon of to-day, I saw from Conantum, say fifty rods distant, two sheldrakes, male and probably female, sailing on A. Wheeler's cranberry meadow. I saw only the white of the male at first, but my glass revealed the female. The male is easily seen a great distance on the water, being a large white mark. But they will let you come only within some sixty rods ordinarily. I observed that they were uneasy at sight of me and began to sail away in different directions. I could plainly see that vermillion bill of the male and his orange legs when he flew (but he *appeared* all white above), and the reddish brown or sorrel of the neck of the female, and, when she lifted herself in the water, as it were preparatory to flight, her white breast and belly. She had a grayish look on the sides. Soon they approached each other again and seemed to be conferring, and then they rose and went off, at first low, down-stream, soon up-stream a hundred feet over the pond, the female leading, the male following close behind, the black at the end of his curved wings very conspicuous. I suspect that about all the conspicuous white ducks I see are goosanders.

I skinned my duck yesterday and stuffed it to-day. It is wonderful that a man, having undertaken such an enterprise, ever persevered in it to the end, and equally wonderful that he succeeded. To skin a bird, drawing backward, wrong side out, over the legs and wings down to the base of the mandibles! Who would expect to see a smooth feather again? This skin was very tender on the breast. I should have done better had I stuffed it at once or turned it back before the skin became stiff. Look out not to cut the ear and eyelid.

But what a pot-bellied thing is a stuffed bird compared even with the fresh dead one I found! It looks no longer like an otter, like a swift diver, but a mere waddling duck. How perfectly the vent of a bird is covered! There is no mark externally.

MARCH 1. [1856]   It is remarkable that though I have not been able to find any open place in the river almost all winter, except under the further stone

bridge and at Loring's Brook,—this winter so remarkable for ice and snow,—
Coombs should (as he says) have killed two sheldrakes at the falls by the
factory, a place which I had forgotten, some four or six weeks ago. Singular
that this hardy bird should have found this small opening, which I had forgotten, while the ice everywhere else was from one to two feet thick, and the
snow sixteen inches on a level. If there is a crack amid the rocks of some
waterfall, this bright diver is sure to know it. Ask the sheldrake whether the
rivers are completely sealed up.

The sheldrake has a peculiar long clipper look, often moving rapidly
straight forward over the water. It sinks to very various depths in the water
sometimes, as when apparently alarmed, showing only its head and neck and
the upper part of its back, and at others, when at ease, floating buoyantly on
the surface as if it had taken in more air, showing all its white breast and the
white along its sides. Sometimes it lifts itself up on the surface and flaps its
wings revealing its whole rosaceous breast and its lower parts, and looking
in form like a penguin. When I first saw them fly up-stream I suspected that
they had gone to Fair Haven Pond and would alight under the lea of the Cliff.
So, creeping slowly down through the woods four or five rods, I was enabled
to get a fair sight of them, and finally we sat exposed on the rocks within
twenty-five rods. They appear not to observe a person so high above them.

It was a pretty sight to see a pair of them tacking about, always within a
foot or two of each other and heading the same way, now on this short tack,
now on that, the male taking the lead, sinking deep and looking every way.
When the whole twelve had come together they would soon break up again,
and were continually changing their ground, though not diving, now sailing
slowly this way a dozen rods, and now that, and now coming in near the
shore. Then they would all go to preening themselves, thrusting their bills
into their backs and keeping up such a brisk motion that you could not get a
fair sight of one's head. From time to time you heard a slight titter, not of
alarm, but perhaps a breeding-note, for they were evidently selecting their
mates. I saw one scratch its ear or head with its foot. Then it was surprising
to see how, briskly sailing off one side, they went to diving, as if they had
suddenly come across a school of minnows. A whole company would disappear at once, never rising high as before. Now for nearly a minute there is
not a feather to be seen, and the next minute you see a party of half a dozen
there, chasing one another and making the water fly far and wide.

When returning, we saw, near the outlet of the pond, seven or eight sheldrakes standing still in a line on the edge of the ice, and others swimming
close by. They evidently love to stand on the ice for a change.

MARCH 28. [1858]   From Wheeler's plowed field on the top of Fair Haven
Hill, I look toward Fair Haven Pond, now quite smooth. There is not a duck

nor a gull to be seen on it. I can hardly believe that it was so alive with them yesterday. Apparently they improve this warm and pleasant day, with little or no wind, to continue their journey northward. The strong and cold north-west wind of about a week past has probably detained them. Knowing that the meadows and ponds were swarming with ducks yesterday, you go forth this particularly pleasant and still day to see them at your leisure, but find that they are all gone. No doubt there are some left, and many more will soon come with the April rains. It is a wild life that is associated with stormy and blustering weather. When the invalid comes forth on his cane, and misses improve the pleasant air to look for signs of vegetation, that wild life has withdrawn itself.

MARCH 29. [1858]   I do not see a duck on the Great Meadows to-day, as I did not up-stream yesterday. It is remarkable how suddenly and completely those that were here two days ago have left us. It is true the water has gone down still more on the meadows. I infer that water-fowl travel in pleaseant weather.

MARCH 30. [1858]   To my boat at Cardinal Shore and thence to Lee's Cliff. Landing at Bittern Cliff, I went round through the woods to get sight of ducks on the pond. Creeping down through the woods, I reached the rocks, and saw fifteen or twenty sheldrakes scattered about. The full-plumaged males, conspicuously black and white and often swimming in pairs, appeared to be the most wary, keeping furthest out. Others, with much less white and duller black, were very busily fishing just north of the inlet of the pond, where there is about three feet of water, and others still playing and preening themselves. These ducks, whose tame representatives are so sluggish and deliberate in their motions, were full of activity. A party of these ducks fishing and playing is a very lively scene. On one side, for instance, you will see a party of eight or ten busily diving and most of the time under water, not rising high when they come up, and soon plunging again. The whole surface will be in commotion there, though no ducks may be seen. I saw one come up with a large fish, whereupon all the rest, as they successively came to the surface, gave chase to it, while it held its prey over the water in its bill, and they pursued with a great rush and clatter a dozen or more rods over the surface, making a great furrow in the water, but, there being some trees in the way, I could not see the issue. I saw seven or eight all dive together as with one consent, remaining under half a minute or more. On another side you see a party which seem to be playing and pluming themselves. They will run and dive and come up and dive again every three or four feet, occasionally one pursuing another; will flutter in the water, making it fly, or erect them-selves at full length on the surface like a penguin, and flap their wings. This party makes an incessant noise. Again you will see some steadily tacking this way or that in the middle of the pond, and often they rest there asleep with their heads in their backs. They readily cross the pond, swimming from this side to that.

MARCH 23. [1859]   As we sit there, we see coming, swift and straight, northeast along the river valley, not seeing us and therefore not changing his course, a male goosander, so near that the green reflections of his head and neck are plainly visible. He looks like a paddle-wheel steamer, so oddly painted up, black and white and green, and moves along swift and straight like one. Ere long the same returns with his mate, the red-throated, the male taking the lead.

MARCH 16. [1860]   Saw a flock of sheldrakes a hundred rods off, on the Great Meadows, mostly males with a few females, all intent on fishing. They were coasting along a spit of bare ground that showed itself in the middle of the meadow, sometimes the whole twelve apparently in a straight line at nearly equal distances apart, each with its head under water, rapidly coasting along back and forth, and ever and anon one, having caught something, would be pursued by the others. It is remarkable that they find their finny prey on the middle of the meadow now, and even on the very inmost side, as I afterward saw, though the water is quite low. Of course, as soon as they are seen on the meadows there are fishes there to be caught. I never see them fish thus in the channel. Perhaps the fishes lie up there for warmth already.

MARCH 24. [1860]   The sheldrakes appear to be the most native to the river, briskly moving along up and down the side of the stream or the meadow, three-fourths immersed and with heads under water, like cutters collecting the revenue of the river bays, or like pirate crafts peculiar to the stream. They come the earliest and seem to be most at home.

The water is so low that all these birds are collected near the Holt. The inhabitants of the village, poultry-fanciers, perchance, though they be, [know not] these active and vigorous wild fowl (the sheldrakes) pursuing their finny prey ceaselessly within a mile of them, in March and April. Probably from the hen-yard fence with a good glass you can see them at it. They are as much at home on the water as the pickerel is within it. Their serrated bill reminds me of a pickerel's snout. You see a long row of these schooners, black above with a white stripe beneath, rapidly gliding along, and occasionally one rises erect on the surface and flaps its wings, showing its white lower parts. They are the duck most common and most identified with the stream at this season. They appear to get their food wholly within the water.

HAWKS

[Hawks made a lively impression on Thoreau. They stirred his imagination, and in their cries he heard the wildness of wolves and all things primitive. Not until he acquired his spyglass did he begin to identify the various species he watched fly over Concord. Nevertheless, in the selections that follow, the reader is quite content not to know which species Thoreau observed. His soaring, darting, screaming hawks are memorable enough without names. Perhaps Thoreau, when he called them skyscrapers on December 20, 1851, was the first to use this term now applied to tall steel and concrete structures.

Undoubtedly the hawks Thoreau observed on September 16, 1852, were migrants. Hawks have been so persecuted that their numbers are sadly low in comparison to the population of a hundred years ago. But on days of good flights at Hawk Mountain Sanctuary, Pennsylvania, a thousand or more are still seen. Thoreau was almost alone in his admiration for hawks. To-day hundreds of interested people gather to watch the stirring passage of these birds as they migrate, following certain ridges as their ancestors did for countless centuries.

All hawks were branded as bird-killers in Thoreau's day, and the farmers of Concord believed all hawks wished to prey exclusively on their poultry. Therefore they shot those they saw near their farm buildings and even searched the woods for hawk nests so they might destroy eggs and young. Though it is true that most hawks probably do take a bird occasionally, only the Accipters (the bird hawks)—the Goshawk, Sharp-shinned, and Cooper's—habitually feed on birds.

A large part of the stories told by his neighbors to Thoreau related to their adventures when hunting. Others told of observations which they claimed to have made. The entry of January 13, 1860, belongs in this latter category. While the reader is not convinced that the event took place as it was told, it is not as incredible as the tale of American Bitterns sucking up water and then making their odd pumping sounds as they expelled it, or of squirrels leaping aboard chips which they launched from a river bank, and then, raising their tails to catch the wind, sailing to the opposite shore.

Thoreau seldom saw hawks during the winter months, but some remain there throughout that season. Red-tailed Hawks, Red-shouldered Hawks and Sparrow Hawks, though few in number, are usually located when the Christmas Bird Count is made in Concord.]

Sept. 25. [1851]   Hawks, too, I perceive, sailing about in the clear air, looking white against the green pines, like the seeds of the milkweed. There is almost always a pair of hawks. Their shrill scream, that of the owls, and wolves are all related.

Oct. 9. [1851]   The circling hawk steers himself through the air, like a skater, without visible motion.

Dec. 20. [1851]   To Fair Haven Hill and plain below. Saw a large hawk circling over a pine wood below me, and screaming, apparently that he might discover his prey by their flight. Travelling ever by wider circles. What a symbol of the thoughts, now soaring, now descending, taking larger and larger circles, or smaller and smaller! It flies not directly whither it is bound, but advances by circles, like a courtier of the skies. No such noble progress! How it comes round, as with a wider sweep of thought! But the majesty is in the imagination of the beholder, for the bird is intent on its prey. Circling and ever circling, you cannot divine which way it will incline, till perchance it dives down straight as an arrow to its mark. It rises higher above where I stand, and I see with beautiful distinctness its wings against the sky,—primaries and secondaries, and the rich tracery of the outline of the latter (?), its inner wings, or wing linings, within the outer,—like a great moth seen against the sky. A will-o'-the-wind. Following its path, as it were, through the vortices of the air. The poetry of motion. Not as preferring one place to another, but enjoying each as long as possible. Most gracefully so surveys new scenes and revisits the old. As if that hawk were made to be a symbol of my thought, how bravely he came round over those parts of the wood which he had not surveyed, taking in a new segment, annexing new territories! Without "heave-yo!" it trims its sail. It goes about without the creaking of a block. That American yacht of the air that never makes tack, though it rounds the globe itself, takes in and shakes out its reefs without a flutter,—its skyscrapers all under its control. Holds up one wing, as if to admire, and sweeps off this way, then holds up the other and sweeps that. If there are two concentrically circling, it is such a regatta as Southhampton waters never witnessed. . . .

What made the hawk mount? Did you perceive the manouver? Did he fill himself with air? Before you were aware of it, he had mounted by his spiral path into the heavens.

June 15. [1852]   I hear the scream of a great hawk, sailing with a ragged wing against the high wood-side, apparently to scare his prey and so detect it—shrill, harsh, fitted to excite terror in sparrows and to issue from his split and curved bill. I see his open bill the while against the sky. Spit with force from his mouth with an undulatory quaver imparted to it from his wings or motion as he flies. A hawk's ragged wing will grow whole again, but so will not a poet's.

Sept. 16. [1852]   8 a.m.—To Fair Haven Pond. . . . What makes this such a day for hawks? There are eight or ten in sight from the Cliffs, large and small, one or more with a white rump. I detected the transit of the first by his shadow on the rock, and I look toward the sun for him. Though he is made light beneath to conceal him, his shadow betrays him. A hawk must get out of the wood, must get above it, where he can sail. It is narrow dodging for him amid the boughs. He cannot be a hawk there, but only perch gloomily. Now I see a large one—perchance an eagle, I say to myself! —down in the valley, circling and circling, higher and wider. This way he comes. How beautiful does he repose on the air, in the moment when he is directly over you, and you see the form and texture of his wings! How light he must make himself, how much earthy heaviness expel, before he can thus soar and sail! He carries no useless clogs there with him. They are out by families; while one is circling this way, another circles that. Kites without strings. Where is the boy that flies them? Are not the hawks most observed at this season?

MARCH 30. [1853]   The motions of a hawk correcting the flaws in the wind by raising his shoulder from time to time, are much like those of a leaf yielding to them. For the little hawks are hunting now. You have not to sit long on the Cliffs before you see one.

MARCH 2. [1855]   To Great Meadows to see the ice. Heard two hawks scream. There was something truly March-like in it, like a prolonged blast or whistling of the wind through a crevice in the sky, which, like a cracked blue saucer, overlaps the woods. Such are the first rude notes which prelude the summer's quire, learned of the whistling March wind.

JAN. 13. [1860]   Farmer says that he remembers his father's saying that as he stood in a field once, he saw a hawk soaring above and eying something on the ground. Looking round, he saw a weasel there eying the hawk. Just then the hawk stooped, and the weasel at the same instant sprang upon him, and up went the hawk with the weasel; but by and by the hawk began to come down as fast as he went up, rolling over and over, till he struck the ground. His father, going up, raised him up, when out hopped the weasel from under his wing and ran off none the worse for his fall.

SHARP-SHINNED HAWK *(Accipiter striatus)*

[This small Accipiter disappears as forest areas shrink. An examination of the contents of many stomachs of this species indicates that nearly 96 per cent of its food is small birds such as sparrows and warblers. Once considered a "bad" bird, scientists now recognize its value in harvesting the surplus of birds. It is essential that such cropping take place, for each wildlife community can support only so many individuals of each kind.

In the first selection, Thoreau gives a perfect description of the flight of a Sharp-shinned Hawk. So distinctive is its flight that the species may be identified by this alone long before any pattern can be seen.

Once most young birds leave the nest they never return to it. But hawks frequently use the nest as a feeding place long after they have taken flight from it.

The hurricane of September 21, 1938, destroyed all known nesting localities of this species in the Concord area. It is now considered an uncommon breeding hawk there.]

MAY 4. [1855]   Sitting in Abel Brook's Hollow, see a small hawk go over high in the air, with a long tail and distinct from wings. It advanced by a sort of limping flight yet rapidly, not circling nor tacking, but flapping briskly at intervals and then gliding straight ahead with rapidity, controlling itself with its tail. It seemed to be going on a journey.

JULY 21. [1858]—To Walden, with E. Bartlett and E. Emerson. The former wished to show me what he thought an owl's nest he had found. Near it, in Abel Brook's wood-lot, heard a note and saw a small hawk fly over. It was the nest of this bird. Saw several of the young flitting about and occasionally an old bird. The nest was in a middling-sized white pine, some twenty feet from the ground, resting on two limbs close to the main stem, on the south side of it. It was quite solid, composed entirely of twigs about as big round as a pipe-stem and less; was some fifteen inches in diameter and one inch deep, or nearly flat, and perhaps five inches thick. It was very much dirtied on the sides by the droppings of the young. As we were standing about the tree, we heard again the note of a young one approaching. We dropped upon the ground, and it alighted on the edge of the nest; another alighted near by, and a third a little further off. The young were apparently as big as the old, but still lingered about the nest and returned to it. I could hear them coming some distance off. Their note was a kind of peeping squeal, which you might at first suspect to be made by a jay; not very loud, but as if to attract the old and reveal their whereabouts. The note of the old bird which occasionally dashed past, was somewhat like that of the marsh hawk or pigeon woodpecker, a cackling or clattering sound, chiding us. The old bird was anxious about her inexperienced young, and was trying to get them off. At length she dashed close past us, and appeared to fairly strike one of the young, knocking him off his perch, and he soon followed her off. I saw the remains of several birds lying about in that neighborhood, and saw and heard again the young and old thereabouts for several days thereafter. A young man killed one of the young hawks, and I saw it. It was the *Falco fuscus*, the American brown or slate-colored hawk. Its length was thirteen inches; alar extent, twenty-three. The tail reached two or more inches beyond the closed wings. Nuttall says the upper parts are "a deep slate-color" (these were very dark brown); also that the nest is yet unknown. But Wilson describes his *F. velox* (which is the same as Nuttall's *F. fuscus*) as "whole upper parts very dark brown," but legs, greenish-yellow (these were yellow). The toes had the peculiar pendulous lobes which W. refers to. As I saw it in the woods, I was struck by its dark color above, its tawny throat and breast, brown-spotted, its clean, slender, long-yellow legs, feathered but little below the knee, its white vent, its wings distinctly and rather finely dark-barred beneath, short, black, much curved bill, and slender black sharp claws. Its tail with a dark bar near edge beneath. In hand I found it had the white spots on scapulars of the *F. fuscus*, and had not the white bars on tail of the *F. Pennsylvanicus*. It also had the fine sharp shin.

RED-TAILED HAWK *(Buteo jamaicensis)*

[This is the largest of the three buteos which are common in New England. It, the Red-shouldered Hawk, and Broad-winged Hawk, all have broad wings and broad, rather short tails. All soar in wide circles and add beauty to the summer skies. They have extraordinary eyesight, and can locate their prey from a great distance. All are commonly called hen-hawks, but research proves they are an asset to farms and ranches, for they eat large numbers of rodents. Occasionally a Red-tailed Hawk discovers an easy food supply in a farmer's chicken yard, but if the farmer is wise, he will protect his poultry with netting rather than destroy the valuable hawks. Hawks should be protected for economic reasons as well as for the beauty they lend to any skies they grace.

Thoreau found the Red-tailed Hawk one of the most interesting citizens of Concord. Its wildness, its freedom in the skies, and its independence of man all charmed him. These qualities meant so much to him that when Pratt, one of the local sportsmen, wanted to destroy the birds in a nest Thoreau found, he persuaded him to leave the hawks alone.

In the entry on October 28, 1857, Thoreau calls this a small bird. It has a wingspread of about four feet and therefore can be truly called small only in relation to the immensity of the sky in which it circles.

It is possible that some of the following selections referred to the Red-shouldered, not the Red-tailed Hawk, for both were, as stated above, commonly called Hen-hawks. However, the Red-tailed Hawk was the common species in Thoreau's day while today the Red-shouldered Hawk is the more abundant buteo in Concord.]

Sept. 7. [1851]   There were two hen-hawks soared and circled for our entertainment, when we were in the woods on that Boon Plain the other day, crossing each other's orbits from time to time, alternating like the squirrels of the morning, till, alarmed by our imitation of a hawk's shrill cry, they gradually inflated themselves, made themselves more aerial, and rose higher and higher into the heavens, and were at length lost to sight; yet all the while earnestly looking, scanning the surface of the earth for a stray mouse or rabbit.

June 8. [1853]   p.m.—To Well Meadow. As I stood by this pond, I heard a hawk scream, and, looking up, saw a pretty large one circling not far off and incessantly screaming, as I at first supposed to scare and so discover its prey, but its screaming was so incessant and it circled from time to time so near me, as I moved southward, that I began to think it had a nest near by and was angry at my intrusion into its domains. As I moved, the bird still followed and screamed, coming sometimes quite near or within gun-shot, then circling far off or high into the sky. At length, as I was looking up at it, thinking it the only living creature within view, I was singularly startled to behold, as my eye by chance penetrated deeper into the blue,—the abyss of blue above, which I had taken for a solitude,—its mate silently soaring at an immense height and seemingly indifferent to me. We are sur-prised to discover that there can be an eye on us on that side, and so little suspected, that the heavens are full of eyes, though they look so blue and spotless. Then I knew it was the female that circled and screamed below. At last the latter rose gradually to meet her mate, and they circled together there, as if they could not possibly feel any anxiety on my account. When I drew nearer to the tall trees where I suspected the nest to be, the female descended again, swept by screaming still nearer to me just over the tree-tops and finally, while I was looking for the orchis in the swamp, alighted on a white pine twenty or thirty rods off. (The great fringed orchis just open.) At length I detected the nest about eighty feet from the ground, in a very large white pine by the edge of the swamp. It was about three feet in diameter, of dry sticks, and a young hawk, apparently as big as its mother, stood on the edge of the nest looking down at me, and only moving its head when I moved. In its imperfect plumage and by the slow motion of its head it reminded me strongly of a vulture, so large and gaunt. It appeared a tawny brown on its neck and breast, and dark brown or blackish on wings. The mother was light beneath, and apparently lighter still on rump.

June 9. [1853]   8 a.m.—To Orchis Swamp; Well Meadow. I have come with a spy-glass to look at the hawks. They have detected me and are already screaming over my head more than half a mile from the nest. I find no

difficulty in looking at the young hawk (there appears to be one only, standing on the edge of the nest), resting the glass in the crotch of a young oak.
I can see every wink and the color of its iris. It watches me more steadily
than I it, now looking straight down at me with both eyes and outstretched
neck, now turning its head and looking with one eye. How its eye and its
whole head expresses anger! Its anger is more in its eye than in its beak. It
is quite hoary over the eye and on the chin. The mother meanwhile is incessantly circling about and above its charge and me, farther or nearer, sometimes withdrawing a quarter of a mile, but occasionally coming to alight for
a moment almost within gunshot, on the top of a tall white pine; but I hardly
bring my glass fairly to bear on her, and get sight of her angry eye through
the pine-needles, before she circles away again. Thus for an hour that I lay
there, screaming every minute or oftener with open bill. Now and then
pursued by a kingbird or a blackbird, who appear merely to annoy it by
dashing down at its back. Meanwhile the male is soaring, apparently quite
undisturbed, at a great height above, evidently not hunting, but amusing or
recreating himself in the thinner and cooler air, as if pleased with his own
circles, like a geometer, and enjoying the sublime scene. I doubt if he has
his eye fixed on any prey, or the earth. He probably descends to hunt.

JUNE 12. [1853]   I visited my hawk's nest, and the young hawk was perched
now four or five feet above the nest, still in the shade. It will soon fly. Now,
then, in secluded pine woods, the young hawks sit high on the edges of their
nests or on the twigs near by in the shade, waiting for their pinions to grow,
while their parents bring them their prey. Their silence also is remarkable,
not to betray themselves, nor will the old bird go to the nest while you are
in sight. She pursues me half a mile when I withdraw.

JUNE 13. [1853]   9 A.M.—To Orchis Swamp. Find that there are two
young hawks; one has left the nest and is perched on a small maple seven
or eight rods distant. This one appears much smaller than the former one.
I am struck by the large, naked head, so vulture-like, and large eyes, as if
the vulture's were an inferior stage through which the hawk passed. Its feet,
too, are large, remarkably developed, by which it holds to its perch securely
like an old bird, before its wings can perform their office. It has a buff breast,
striped with dark brown. Pratt, when I told him of this nest, said he would
like to carry one of his rifles down there. But I told him that I should be
sorry to have them killed. I would rather save one of these hawks than have
a hundred hens and chickens. It was worth more to see them soar, especially
now, that they are so rare in the landscape. It is easy to buy eggs, but not
to buy hen-hawks. My neighbors would not hesitate to shoot the last pair
of hen-hawks in the town to save a few of their chickens! But such economy

is narrow and grovelling. It is necessarily to sacrifice the greater value to the less. I would rather never taste chicken's meat or hen's eggs than never to see a hawk sailing through the upper air again. This sight is worth incomparably more than a chicken soup or a boiled egg. So we exterminate the deer and substitute the hog.

Nov. 9. [1858]   Now the young hen-hawks, full-grown but inexperienced, still white-breasted and brown (not red)-tailed, swoop down after the farmer's hens, between the barn and the house, often carrying one off in their clutches, and all the rest of the pack half fly, half run, to the barn. Unwarrantably bold, one ventures to stoop before the farmer's eyes. He clutches in haste his trusty gun, which hangs, ready loaded, on its pegs; he pursues warily to where the marauder sits teetering on a lofty pine, and when he is sailing scornfully away he meets his fate and comes fluttering head forward to earth. The exulting farmer hastes to secure his trophy. He treats the proud bird's body with indignity. He carries it home to show to his wife and children, for the hens were his wife's special care. He thinks it one of his best shots, full thirteen rods. This gun is "an *all-fired* good piece"—nothing but robin-shot. The body of the victim is delivered up to the children and the dog and like the body of Hector, is dragged so many times round Troy.

But alas for the youthful hawk, the proud bird of prey, the tenant of the skies! We shall no more see his wave-like outline against a cloud, nor hear his scream from behind one. He saw but a pheasant in the field, the food which nature has provided for him, and stooped to seize it. This was his offense. He, the native of these skies, must make way for those bog-trotters from another land, which never soar. The eye that was conversant with sublimity, that looked down on earth from under its sharp projecting brow, is closed; the head that was never made dizzy by any height is brought low; the feet that were not made to walk on earth now lie useless along it. With those trailing claws for grapnels it dragged the lower skies. Those wings which swept the sky must now dust the chimney-corner, perchance. So weaponed, with strong beak and talons, and wings, like a war-steamer, to carry them about. In vain were the brown-spotted eggs laid, in vain were ye cradled in the loftiest pine of the swamp. Where are your father and mother? Will they hear of your early death? before ye had acquired your full plumage, they who nursed and defended ye so faithfully?

FEB. 16. [1859]   The hen-hawk and the pine are friends. The same thing which keeps the hen-hawk in the woods, away from the cities, keeps me here. That bird settles with confidence on a white pine top and not upon your weathercock. That bird will not be poultry of yours, lays no eggs for you, forever hides its nest. Though willed, or *wild*, it is not willful in its wildness.

The unsympathizing man regards the wildness of some animals, their strangeness to him, as a sin; as if all their virtue consisted in their tamableness. He has always a charge in his gun ready for their extermination. What we call wildness is a civilization other than our own. The hen-hawk shuns the farmer, but it seeks the friendly shelter and support of the pine. It will not consent to walk in the barn-yard, but it loves to soar above the clouds. It has its own way and is beautiful, when we would fain subject it to our will. So any surpassing work of art is strange and wild to the mass of men, as is genius itself. No hawk that soars and steals poultry is wilder than genius, and none is more persecuted or above persecution. It can never be poet laureate, to say "pretty Poll" and "Polly want a cracker."

MARCH 15. [1860]   A hen-hawk sails away from the wood southward. I get a very fair sight of it sailing overhead. What a perfectly regular and neat outline it presents! an easily recognized figure anywhere. Yet I never see it represented in any books. The exact correspondence of the marks on one side to those on the other, as the black or dark tip of one wing to the other, and the dark line midway the wing. I have no idea that one can get as correct an idea of the form and color of the under sides of a hen-hawk's wings by spreading those of a dead specimen in his study as by looking up at a free and living hawk soaring above him in the fields. The penalty for obtaining a petty knowledge thus dishonestly is that it is less interesting to men generally, as it is less significant. Some, seeing and admiring the neat figure of the hawk sailing two or three hundred feet above their heads, wish to get nearer and hold it in their hands, perchance, not realizing that they can see it best at this distance, better now, perhaps, than ever they will again. What is an eagle in captivity!—screaming in a courtyard! I am not the wiser respecting eagles for having seen one there. I do not wish to know the length of its entrails.

How neat and all compact this hawk! Its wings and body are all one piece, the wings apparently the greater part, while its body is a mere fullness or protuberance between its wings, an inconspicuous pouch hung there. It suggests no insatiable maw, no corpulence, but looks like a larger moth, with little body in proportion to its wings, its body naturally etherealized as it soars higher.

These hawks, as usual, began to be common about the first of March, showing that they were returning from their winter quarters.

RED-SHOULDERED HAWK *(Buteo lineatus)*

[Averaging a foot less in wingspread than the Red-tailed Hawk, this is a graceful species. The adults have pale reddish underparts. Their wild, two-

syllabled scream is one of the finest and wildest sounds in nature, and is far
superior to the renowned scream of the eagle. It has frequently been stated
that Thoreau could not distinguish between the hawks called Hen-hawks.
On October 17, 1852, he indicated that he could, on occasion, identify the
Red-shouldered Hawk. Conversely, he frequently mentioned the red tail of
the adult Red-tailed Hawk.]

APRIL 17. [1852]   Undoubtedly the soaring and sailing of the hen-hawk,
the red-shouldered buzzard(?), is the most ornamental, graceful, stately,
beautiful to contemplate, of all the birds that ordinarily frequent our skies.
The eagle is but a rare and casual visitor. The goose, the osprey, the great blue
heron, though interesting, are either transient visitors or rarely seen; they
either move through the air as passengers or too exclusively looking for
their prey, but the hen-hawk soars like a creature of the air. The flight of
martins is interesting in the same way. When I was young and compelled
to pass my Sunday in the house without the aid of interesting books, I used
to spend many an hour till the wished-for sundown, watching the martins
soar, from an attic window; and fortunate indeed did I deem myself when
a hawk appeared in the heavens, though far toward the horizon against a
downy cloud, and I searched for hours till I had found his mate. They, at
least, took my thoughts from earthly things.

ROUGH-LEGGED HAWK *(Buteo lagopus)*

[This large hawk has a circumpolar distribution and only comes south to
the United States in winter. It likes open country and is sometimes mistaken
for the smaller Marsh Hawk, for it, too, has white at the base of its tail. It
sometimes hovers like an Osprey or a Sparrow Hawk over one spot. Like all
the buteos it is master at soaring, especially when migrating. When hunting
mice, its chief food, the Rough-legged Hawk alternately flaps and glides
over marshes and meadows fifty feet or more above the ground. It is not
surprising that Thoreau mistook this large, broad-winged hawk for an
eagle.]

MARCH 29. [1858]   To Ball's Hill. As I sit two thirds the way up the sunny
side of the pine hill, looking over the meadows, which are now almost completely bare, the crows, by their swift flight and scolding, reveal to me some
large bird of prey hovering over the river. I perceive by its markings and
size that it cannot be a hen-hawk, and now it settles on the topmost branch
of a white maple, bending it down. Its great armed and feathered legs dangle
helplessly in the air for a moment, as if feeling for the perch, while its body
is tipping this way and that. It sits there facing me some forty or fifty rods

off, pluming itself but keeping a good lookout. At this distance and in this light, it appears to have a rusty-brown head and breast and is white beneath, with rusty leg-feathers and a tail black beneath. When it flies again it is principally black varied with white, regular light spots on its tail and wings beneath, but chiefly a conspicuous white space on the forward part of the back; also some of the upper side of the tail or tail-coverts is white. It has broad, ragged, buzzard-like wings, and from the white of its back, as well as the shape and shortness of its wings and its not having a gull-like body, I think it must be an eagle. It lets itself down with its legs somewhat help-lessly dangling, as if feeling for something on the bare meadow, and then gradually flies away, soaring and circling higher and higher until lost in the downy clouds. This lofty soaring is at least a grand recreation, as if it were nourishing sublime ideas. I should like to know why it soars higher and higher so, whether its thoughts are really turned to earth, for it seems to be more nobly as well as highly employed than the laborers ditching in the meadow beneath or any others of my fellow-townsmen.

BALD EAGLE *(Haliaeetus leucocephalus)*

[One senses that Thoreau was disappointed by his first identification of the Bald Eagle. It appeared to be nothing more than a large hawk. This is some-thing all imaginative people can understand, for who has not dreamed of seeing some rare creature only to feel a certain disappointment because it was not as big, or as fierce, or as brilliantly colored as was expected? But repeated observations deepened Thoreau's interest and restored his sense of proportion. The Bald Eagle was truly a worthy symbol of his country.

This majestic bird builds a large nest, sometimes on a cliff, but more often in a tall tree. These are used year after year if the eagles are not disturbed by man, or by Great Horned Owls which sometimes appropriate them for their own eggs. Each year new material is added to the nest until the tree dies and falls over, or the nest crashes to earth from its own weight. A nest once occupied for many years in Vermilion, Ohio, was twelve feet deep, eight and a half feet in diameter, and was estimated to weigh nearly two tons. In St. Petersburgh, Florida, an eagle nest in a pine tree was nine and a half feet in diameter and twenty feet deep. Usually two, but sometimes three, eggs are laid.

Though the total population of Bald Eagles is decreasing alarmingly, one is occasionally detected as it migrates over Concord.]

APRIL 8. [1854] Saw a large bird sail along over the edge of Wheeler's cranberry meadow just below Fair Haven, which I at first thought a gull, but with my glass found it was a hawk and had a perfectly white head and tail and broad or blackish wings. It sailed and circled along over the low cliff, and the crows dived at it in the field of my glass, and I saw it well, both above and beneath, as it turned, and then it passed off to hover over the Cliffs at a greater height. It was undoubtedly a white-headed eagle. It was to the eye but a large hawk.

APRIL 23. [1854]   Saw my white-headed eagle again, first at the same place, the outlet of Fair Haven Pond. It was a fine sight, he is mainly—*i.e.* his wings and body—so black against the sky, and they contrast so strongly with his white head and tail. He was first flying low over the water; then rose gradually and circled westward toward White Pond. Lying on the ground with my glass, I could watch him easily, and by turns he gave me all possible views of himself. When I observed him edgewise I noticed that the tips of his wings curved upward slightly the more, like a stereotyped undulation. He rose very high at last, till I almost lost him in the clouds, circling or rather *looping* along westward, high over the river and wood and farm, effectually concealed in the sky. We who live this plodding life here below never know how many eagles fly over us. They are concealed in the empyrean. I think I have got the worth of my glass now that it has revealed to me the white-headed eagle. Now I see him edgewise like a black ripple in the air, his white head still as ever turned to earth and now he turns his under side to me, and I behold the full breadth of his broad black wings, somewhat ragged at the edges.

AUG. 22. [1858]   At Baker Farm a large bird rose up near us, which at first I took for a hen-hawk, but it appeared larger. It screamed the same, and finally soared higher and higher till it was almost lost amid the clouds, or could scarcely be distinguished except when it was seen against some white and glowing cumulus. I think it was at least half a mile high, or three quarters, and yet I distinctly heard it scream up there each time it came round, and with my glass saw its head steadily turned toward the ground, looking for its prey. Its head, seen in proper light, was distinctly whitish, and I suspect it may have been a white-headed eagle. It did not once flap its wings up there, as it circled and sailed, though I watched it for nearly a mile. How fit that these soaring birds should be haughty and fierce, not like doves to our race!

MARSH HAWK *(Circus cyaneus)*

[These hawks with narrow, somewhat angled wings and long slim bodies are beautiful fliers, and Thoreau enjoyed their movements along the river edges when the snows began to melt in spring. He frequently called them frog hawks, a name commonly applied to them in New England, for surely as the frogs emerge from their winter quarters the Marsh Hawks appear to eat them.

Adult males are pale gray with black wing tips. The females and young are brown. The white spot on the rump is the best field mark, but the long tail and wings held above the horizontal confirm the identification. As an adult Marsh Hawk looks squarely at the observer, its face is surprisingly owl-like.

At a nest recently under observation, about half the food brought to it was snakes. All hawks habitually carry their food in their powerful claws, but the Marsh Hawk (other species of hawks have been observed doing likewise) apparently found it difficult to transport snakes in her claws and she brought them in her bill instead. Oddly enough the smallest hawk at this nest was the first one to fly away.

The nest varies from a thin mat of grasses and weeds to a high mound depending on the water conditions in the meadow or marsh where it is securely hidden. Thoreau had not yet learned that this species was a ground nester on May 20, 1856, when he climbed several pines hoping to locate a Marsh Hawk nest.]

APRIL 23. [1855]   See a frog hawk beating the bushes regularly. What a peculiarly formed wing! It should be called the kite. Its wings are very narrow and pointed, and its form in front is a remarkable curve, and its body is not heavy and buzzard-like. It occasionally hovers over some parts of the meadow or hedge and circles back over it, only rising enough from time to time to clear the trees and fences.

MAY 14. [1855]   P.M.—To Cliffs *via* Hubbard's Bath. See a male hen-harrier skimming low along the side of the river, often within a foot of the muddy shore, looking for frogs, with a very compact flock of small birds, probably swallows, in pursuit. Occasionally he alights and walks or hops flutteringly a foot or two over the ground.

Nov. 5. [1855]   At Hubbard's Crossing I see a large male hen-harrier skimming over the meadow, its deep slate somewhat sprinkled or mixed with black; perhaps young. It flaps a little and then sails straight forward, so low it must rise at every fence. But I perceive that it follows the windings of the meadow over many fences.

MARCH 11. [1856]   The sight of a marsh hawk in Concord is worth more to me than the entry of the allies into Paris. In this sense I am not ambitious. I do not wish my native soil to become exhausted and run out through neglect. Only that travelling is good which reveals to me the value of home and enables me to enjoy it better. That man is richest whose pleasures are the cheapest.

APRIL 8. [1856]   Saw two marsh hawks this afternoon, circling low over the meadows along the water's edge. This shows that frogs must be out. Goodwin and Puffer both fired at one from William Wheeler's shore. They say they made him duck and disturbed his feathers some . . .

The marsh hawks flew in their usual irregular low tacking, wheeling, and circling flight, leisurely flapping and beating, now rising, now falling, in conformity with the contour of the ground. The last I think I have seen on the same beat in former years. He and his race must be well acquainted with the Musketicook and its meadows. No sooner is the snow off than he is back to his old haunts, scouring that part of the meadows that is bare, while the rest is melting. If he returns from so far to these meadows, shall the sons of Concord be leaving them at this season for slight cause?

MAY 20. [1856]   See and hear a stake-driver in the swamp. It took one short pull at its pump and stopped. Two marsh hawks, male and female, flew about me a long time, screaming, the female largest with ragged wings, as I stood on the neck of the peninsula. This induced me to climb four pines but I tore my clothes, got pitched all over, and found only squirrel; yet they have, no doubt, a nest thereabouts.

APRIL 19. [1858]   Spent the day hunting for my boat, which was stolen. As I go up the riverside, I see a male marsh hawk hunting. He skims steadily along exactly over the edge of the water, on the meadowy side, not more than three or four feet from the ground and winding with the shore, looking for frogs, for in such a tortuous line do the frogs sit. They probably know about what time to expect his visits, being regularly decimated. Particular hawks farm particular meadows. It must be easy for him to get a breakfast. Far as I can see with a glass, he is still tilting this way and that over the water-line.

MAY 2. [1858]   If I were to be a frog hawk for a month I should soon know some things about the frogs. How patiently they skim the meadows, occasionally alighting, and fluttering as if it were difficult ever to stand still on the ground. I have seen more of them than usual since I too have been looking for frogs.

MAY 30. [1858]   To hen-harrier's nest and to Ledum Swamp. Edward Emerson shows me the nest which he and another discovered. It is in the midst of the low wood, sometimes inundated, just southwest of Hubbard's Bath, the island of wood in the meadow. The hawk rises when we approach and circles about over the wood, uttering a note singularly like the common one of the flicker. The nest is in a more bushy or open place in this low wood, and consists of a large mass of sedge and stubble, with a very few small twigs, as it were accidentally intermingled. It is about twenty inches in diameter and remarkably flat, the slight depression in the middle not exceeding three quarters of an inch. The whole opening amid the low bushes is not more than two feet in diameter. The thickness of it raises the surface about four inches above the ground. The inner and upper part is uniformly rather fine and pale-brown sedge. There are two dirty, or rather dirtied, white eggs left (of four that were), one of them one and seven tenths inches long, and not "spherical," as Brewer says, but broad in proportion to length.

OSPREY *(Pandion haliaetus)*

[This large fish-eating hawk is the only American hawk which dives into water for its food. It plunges feet-first after its prey and carries the fish, head forward, to a favorite eating perch in a tree or on a cliff.

Thoreau regretted the loss of each Osprey which was shot in Concord. To-day this great bird, almost world-wide in distribution, is declining in numbers. Egg collectors were chiefly responsible for almost exterminating it in Great Britain. In the United States it has, like the Bald Eagle, been a victim of thoughtless gunners. The poison from insecticides, stored in the tissues of fish which it catches, is an additional threat to the species. This land will be the poorer if it vanishes from American skies.

Ospreys nest either alone or in loose colonies near salt and fresh water. They make huge mounds of sticks in trees, on man-made structures, on the ground, on cliffs and pinnacles. A seldom-mentioned spectacle of Yellowstone National Park is the Ospreys that nest on great thin pinnacles of rock in the Grand Canyon of the Yellowstone where they may be seen dropping onto their lofty nests while their loud, high-pitched whistled calls reverberate between the great rocky walls.

The Osprey is a fairly common migrant over Concord as it moves northward in spring. At other seasons it is seen occasionally, except in winter when it is unknown.]

MARCH 27. [1842]   Cliffs. Two little hawks have just come out to play, like butterflies rising one above another in endless alternation far below me. They swoop from side to side in the broad basin of the tree-tops, with wider and wider surges, as if swung by an invisible pendulum. They stoop down on this side and scale up on that.

Suddenly I look up and see a new bird, probably an eagle, quite above me, laboring with the wind not more than forty rods off. It was the largest bird of the falcon kind I ever saw. I was never so impressed by any flight. She sailed the air, and fell back from time to time like a ship on her beam ends, holding her talons up as if ready for the arrows. I never allowed before for the grotesque attitudes of our national bird.

[In *Excursions*, p. 110 (Riv. 136), what appears to be the same bird is described, and called the fish hawk.]

MARCH 31. [1842]   I cannot forget the majesty of that bird at the Cliff. It was no sloop or smaller craft hove in sight, but a ship of the line, worthy to struggle with the elements. It was a great presence, as of the master of river and forest. His eye would not have quailed before the owner of the soil; none could challenge his rights. And then his retreat, sailing so steadily away, was a kind of advance. How is it that man always feels like an interloper in nature, as if he had intruded on the domains of bird and beast?

Nov. 17. [1854]   Paddled up river to Clamshell and sailed back. I think it must have been a fish hawk which I saw hovering over the meadow and my boat (a raw cloudy afternoon), now and then sustaining itself in one place a hundred feet or more above the water, intent on a fish, with a hovering or fluttering motion of the wings somewhat like a kingfisher. Its wings were very long, slender, and curved in outline of front edge. I think there was some white on rump. It alighted near the top of an oak within rifle-shot of me and my boat, afterward on the tip-top of a maple by waterside, looking very large.

MAY 12. [1855]   From beyond the orchard saw a large bird far over the Cliff Hill, which, with my glass, I soon made out to be a fish hawk advancing. Even at that distance, half a mile off, I distinguished its gull-like body,—pirate-like fishing body fit to dive,—and that its wings did not curve upward at the ends like a hen-hawk's (at least I could not see that they did), but rather hung down. It came on steadily, bent on fishing, with long and *heavy* undulating wings, with an easy sauntering flight, over the river to the pond, and hovered over Pleasant Meadow a long time on one spot, when more than a hundred feet high, then making a very short circle or two and hovering again, then sauntering off against the woodside. At length he reappeared, passed downward over the shrub oak plain and alighted on an oak (of course now bare), standing this time apparently lengthwise on the limb. Soon took wing again and went to fishing down the stream a hundred feet high. When just below Bittern Cliff, I observed by its motions that it observed something.

It made a broad circle of observation in its course, lowering itself somewhat; then, by one or two steep sidewise flights, it reached the water, and, as near as the intervening trees would let me see, skimmed over it and endeavored to clutch its prey in passing. It failed the first time, but probably succeeded the second. Then it leisurely winged its way to a tall bare tree on the east side of the cliffs, and there we left it apparently pluming itself. It had a very white belly, and indeed appeared all white beneath its body. I saw broad black lines between the white crown and throat. . . .

Returning over Conantum, I directed my glass toward the dead tree on Cliffs, and was surprised to see the fish hawk still sitting there, about an hour after he first alighted; and now I found that he was eating a fish, which he had under his feet on the limb and ate as I have already described. At this distance his whole head looked white with his breast.

Oct. 26. [1857] I see two great fish hawks (*possibly* blue herons) slowly beating northeast against the storm, by what a curious tie circling ever near each other and in the same direction, as if you might expect to find the very motes in the air to be paired; two long undulating wings conveying a feathered body through the misty atmosphere, and this inseparably associated with another planet of the same species. I can just glimpse their undulating lines. Damon and Pythias they must be. The waves beneath, which are of kindred form, are still more social, multitudinous. . . . Where is my mate, beating against the storm with me? They fly according to the valley of the river, northeast or southwest.

April 28. [1858] Blustering northwest wind and wintry aspect. A.M.— Down river to look at willows. . . . I see the fish hawk again. . . . As it flies low, directly over my head, I see that its body is white beneath, and the white on the forward side of the wings beneath, if extended across the breast, would form a regular crescent. Its wings do not form a regular curve in front, but an abrupt angle. They are loose and broad at tips. This bird goes fishing slowly down one side of the river and up again on the other, forty to sixty feet high, continually poising itself almost or quite stationary, with its head to the northwest wind and looking down, flapping its wings enough to keep its place, sometimes stationary for about a minute. It is not shy. This boisterous weather is the time to see it.

Pigeon Hawk (*Falco columbarius*)

[This hawk, sometimes called the merlin by Thoreau, prefers woodland openings, swamps where it can hunt, and the borders of lakes and streams. They sometimes use old nests made by crows, sometimes build slight platforms for themselves, nest on the ground, usually on a small hill, on ledges or cliffs and holes in banks, and in trees. Few species accept a greater variety of nesting sites.

While Pigeon Hawks are adept in catching small birds, they also eat great numbers of insects, dragonflies being a favorite food.

This small hawk is a rare transient in Concord today and probably always has been.]

OCT. 22. [1855]   Another cloudy day without rain. P.M.—To Fair Haven *via* Hubbard's Grove. I sat on a bank at the brook crossing, beyond the grove, to watch a flock of *seringos*, perhaps Savannah sparrows, which, with some *F. hyemalis* and other sparrows, were actively flitting about amid the alders and dogwood. . . . Suddenly a pigeon hawk dashed over the bank very low and within a rod of me, and, striking its wings against the twigs with a clatter close to a sparrow, which escaped, it alighted amid the alders in front within four rods of me. It was attracted by the same objects which attracted me. It stayed a few moments, balancing itself and spreading its tail and wings,—a chubby little fellow. Its back appeared a sort of deep chocolate-brown. Every sparrow at once concealed itself, apparently deep in the bushes next the ground. Once or twice he dashed down there amid the alders and tried to catch one. In a few minutes he skimmed along the hedge by the path and disappeared westward. But presently, hearing the sound of his wings amid the bushes, I looked up and saw him dashing along through the willows and then out and upward high over the meadow in pursuit of a sparrow (perhaps a seringo). The sparrow flew pretty high and kept doubling. When it flew direct, the hawk gained, and got within two or three feet of it; but when it doubled, it gained on the hawk; so the latter soon gave up the chase, and the little bird flew right over my head, with a panting breath and a rippling ricochet flight, toward the high pine grove. When I passed along the path ten minutes after, I found that all those sparrows were still hid under the bushes by the ditch-side, close to the ground, and I saw nothing of them till I scared them out by going within two or three feet. No doubt they warned each other by a peculiar note. What a corsair the hawk is to them!—a little fellow hardly bigger than a quail.

Birds certainly are afraid of man. They [allow] all other creatures,—cows and horses, etc.,—excepting only one or two kinds, birds or beasts of prey, to come near them, but not man. What does this fact signify? Does it not signify that man, too, is a beast of prey to them? Is he, then, a true lord of creation, whose subjects are afraid of him, and with reason? They know very well that he is not humane, as he pretends to be!

RUFFED GROUSE *(Bonasa umbellus)*

[Thoreau quite naturally found most interesting those birds which he could easily observe. Ruffed Grouse (partridge) were common in the varied habitat around Concord. Moreover, they could be approached close enough for good observation.

Not only do the young leave the nest as soon as they are dry, but by the time they are twelve days old they can fly from twenty to thirty feet.

Thoreau's experiences with this species are enjoyed by all readers. Moreover, they can be duplicated to-day by observant bird watchers in the very same places where Thoreau watched the grouse.

Not until slow-motion moving pictures were made of Ruffed Grouse drumming was it definitely proved that the sound was made by fanning the air with the wings, not by striking the body or perch. The pulsing throb is produced by gradually increased speed until the movements of the wings are too fast for the eye to count them, and thumps merge into a whir. The movements tilt the grouse backward until his tail is pressed tightly against the log on which he stands and when the drumming stops, he springs upward as if by recoil.

Many creatures, including man, sometimes take refuge from cold by digging a shelter in the snow. Grouse have learned to fly into loose snow, or push their way backward into firm snow, for protection against severe cold. On rare occasions the snug shelter of the snow has turned into a death trap when sleet or freezing rain have formed a strong crust which the grouse cannot break so that they are held captive by the snow.

The reader must have become aware of Thoreau's habit of naming the places which he frequently visited. Often the name given was for a bird or plant characteristic of an area. Some of these names were Tanager Woods, Owl Swamp, Orchis Swamp, Bittern Cliff, Nut Meadow, Pink Azalea Woods, Trillium Woods, and Andromeda Ponds. His S. tristis Path in the section which follows might have more general appeal had he called it Dwarf Gray Willow Path instead of using the scientific name for the small shrub which grew beside this trail and at times sheltered the Ruffed Grouse.]

JUNE 4. [1850]   [A day spent fighting a field and forest fire.] The fire stopped within a few inches of a partridge's nest to-day, June 4th, whom we took off in our hands and found thirteen creamy-colored eggs.

FEB. 18. [1852]   I find the partridges among the fallen pine-tops on Fair Haven these afternoons, an hour before sundown, ready to commence budding in the neighboring orchard.

June 27. [1852]   I meet the partridge with her brood in the woods, a perfect little hen. She spreads her tail into a fan and beats the ground with her wings fearlessly within a few feet of me, to attract my attention while her young disperse; but they keep up a faint, wiry kind of peep, which betrays them, while she mews and squeaks as if giving them directions.

May 11. [1853]   I hear the distant drumming of a partridge. Its beat, however distant and low, falls still with a remarkably forcible, almost painful, impulse on the ear, like veritable little drumsticks on our tympanum, as if it were a throbbing or fluttering in our veins or brows or the chambers of the ear, and belonging to ourselves—as if it were produced by some little insect which had made its way up into the passages of the ear, so penetrating is it. It is as palpable to the ear as the sharpest note of a fife. Of course, that bird can drum with its wings on a log which can go off with such a powerful whir, beating the air. I have seen a thoroughly frightened hen and cockerel fly almost as powerfully, but neither can sustain it long. Beginning slowly and deliberately, the partridge's beat sounds faster and faster from far away under the boughs and through the aisles of the wood until it becomes a regular roll, but is speedily concluded. How many things shall we not see and be and do, when we walk there where the partridge drums!

June 12. [1853]   p.m.—To Bear Hill. Going up Pine Hill, disturbed a partridge and her brood. She ran in dishabille directly to me, within four feet, while her young, not larger than a chicken just hatched, dispersed, flying along a foot or two from the ground, just over the bushes, for a rod or two. The mother kept close at hand to attract my attention, and mewed and clucked and made a noise as when a hawk is in sight. She stepped about and held her head above the bushes and clucked just like a hen. What a remarkable instinct that which keeps the young so silent, and prevents their peeping and betraying themselves! The wild bird will run almost any risk to save her young. The young, I believe, make a fine sound at first in dispersing, something like a cherry-bird.

Jan. 31. [1855]   A clear, cold, beautiful day. Fine skating. As I skated near the shore under Lee's Cliff, I saw what I took to be some scrags or knotty stubs of a dead limb lying on the bank beneath a white oak, close by me. Yet while I looked directly at them I could not but admire their close resemblance of partridges. I had come along with a rapid whir and suddenly halted right against them, only two rods distant, and, as my eyes watered a little from skating against the wind, I was not convinced that they were birds till I had pulled out my glass, and deliberately examined them. They sat and stood, three of them, perfectly still with their heads erect, some darker feathers like ears, methinks, increasing their resemblance to scrabs [sic], as where a small limb is broken off. I was much surprised at the remarkable stillness they preserved, instinctively relying on the resemblance to the ground for their protection, *i.e.* withered grass, dry oak leaves, dead scrags, and broken twigs. I thought at first that it was a dead oak limb with a few stub ends or scrabbs [sic] sticking up, and for some time after I had noted the resemblance to birds, standing only two rods off, I could not be sure of their character on account of their perfect motionlessness, and it was not till I brought my glass to bear on them and saw their eyes distinctly, steadily glaring on me, their necks and every muscle tense with anxiety, that I was convinced. At length, on some signal which I did not perceive, they went off with a whir, as if shot, over the bushes.

FEB. 13. [1855] 10 A.M.—To Walden Woods. Not cold; sky somewhat overcast. The tracks of partridges are more remarkable in this snow than usual, it is so light, being at the same time a foot deep. I see where one has waddled along several rods, making a chain-like track about three inches wide (or two and a half), and at the end has squatted in the snow, making a perfectly smooth and regular oval impression, like the bowl of a spoon, five inches wide. Then, six inches beyond this, are the marks of its wings where it struck the snow on each side when it took flight. It must have risen at once without running. In one place I see where one, after running a little way, has left four impressions of its wings on the snow on each side, extending eighteen or twenty inches and twelve or fifteen in width. In one case almost the entire wing was distinctly impressed, eight primaries and five or six secondaries. In one place, when alighting, the primary quills, five of them, have marked the snow for a foot. I see where many have dived into the snow, apparently last night, on the side of a shrub oak hollow. In four places they have passed quite underneath it for more than a foot; in one place, eighteen inches. They appear to have dived or burrowed into it, then passed along a foot or more underneath and squatted there, perhaps, with their heads out, and have invariably left much dung at the end of this hole. I scared one from its hole only half a rod in front of me now at 11 A.M. . . . It is evidently a hardy bird, and in the above respects, too, is like the rabbit, which squats under a brake or bush on the snow. . . .

Looking further in an open place or glade amid the shrub oaks and low pitch pines, I found as many as twenty or thirty places where partridges had lodged in the snow, apparently the last night or the night before. You could see commonly where their bodies had first struck the snow and furrowed it for a foot or two, and six inches wide, and then entered and gone underneath two feet and rested at the further end, where the manure is left. Is it not likely that they remain quite under the snow there, and do not put their

heads out till ready to start? In many places they walked along before they
went under the snow. They do not go under deep, and the gallery they make
is mostly filled up behind them, leaving only a thin crust above. Then invariably, just beyond this resting-place, you could see the marks made by their
wings when they took their departure. These distinct impressions made by
their wings, in the pure snow, so common on all hands, though the bird
that made it is gone and there is no trace beyond, affect me like some Orien-
tal symbol,—the winged globe or what-not,—as if made by a spirit. In some
places you would see a furrow and hollow in the snow where there was no
track for rods around, as if a large snowball or a cannon-ball had struck it,
where apparently the birds had not paused in their flight. It is evidently a
regular thing with them thus to lodge in the snow.

MAY 7. [1855] P.M.—To Lee's Cliff. A partridge flew up from within
three or four feet of me with a loud whir; and betrayed one cream-colored
egg in a little hollow amid the leaves.

MAY 12. [1855]   I find the partridge-nest of the 7th partially covered with
dry oak leaves, and two more eggs only, three in all, cold. Probably the
bird is killed.

MAY 26. [1855]   The partridge which on the 12th had left three cold eggs
covered up with oak leaves is now sitting on eight. She apparently deserted
her nest for a time and covered it.

FEB. 11. [1856]   Saw a partridge by the riverside, opposite Fair Haven
Hill, which at first I mistook for the top of a fence-post above the snow,
amid some alders. I shouted and waved my hand four rods off, to see if it
was one, but there was no motion, and I thought surely it must be a post.
Nevertheless I resolved to investigate. Within three rods, I saw it to be
indeed a partridge, to my surprise, standing perfectly still, with its head
erect and neck stretched upward. It was as complete a deception as if it had
designedly placed itself on the line of the fence and in the proper place for
a post. It finally stepped off daintily with a teetering gait and head up, took
to wing.

MAY 24. [1856]   Humphrey Buttrick says that he . . . has known a partridge to fly at once from one to two miles after being wounded (tracked
them by the blood) without alighting. Says that he has caught as many as
a dozen partridges in his hands. He lies right down on them, or where he
knows them to be, then passes his hands back and forth under his body
till he feels them. You must not lift your body at all or they will surely

squeeze out, and when you feel one must be sure you get hold of their legs or head, and not feathers only.

MARCH 8. [1857] P.M.—To Hill. Get a glimpse of a hawk, the first of the season. The tree sparrows sing a little on this still sheltered and sunny side of the hill, but not elsewhere. A partridge goes off from amid the pitch pines. It lifts each wing so high above its back and flaps so low, and withal so rapidly, that they present the appearance of a broad wheel, almost a revolving sphere, as it whirs off like a cannon-ball shot from a gun.

DEC. 24. [1859] I saw the tracks of a partridge more than half an inch deep in the ice, extending from this island to the shore, she having walked there in the slosh. They were quite perfect and reminded me of bird-tracks in stone. She may have gone there to bud on these blueberry trees. I saw where she spent the night at the bottom of that largest clump, in the snow.

BOBWHITE *(Colinus virginianus)*

[This chunky little red-brown bird is scarcely as large as a meadowlark. Its whistled call is a clear *Bob-white!* or *Bob-bob-white!*

It is said that the cultivation of corn led to the northward spread of this species to the land of heavy winter snows. Not only does it hide in corn shocks but it eats such unharvested grain as it can find.

Concord is very near the northern extremity of its range and the Bob-white's hold is precarious there. In the past, severe winters have almost wiped it out. In 1948, after a very severe winter, not a single report of this species was made. It is considered a rarity to-day.]

FEB. 8 [1856] E. Garfield says there were many quails here last fall, but that they are suffering now. One night as he was spearing on Conant's cranberry meadow, just north the pond, his dog caught a sheldrake in the water by the shore. Some days ago he saw what he thought a hawk, as white as snow, fly over the pond, but it *may* have been a white owl (which last he never saw). He sometimes sees a hen-hawk at this season. Speaks again of that large speckled hawk he killed once, which some called a "cape eagle." Had a hum-bird's nest behind their house last summer, and was amused to see the bird drive off other birds; would pursue a robin and alight on his back; let none come near. I. Garfield saw one's nest on a horizontal branch of a white pine near the Charles Miles house, about seven feet from ground. E. Garfield spoke of the wren's nest as not uncommon, hung in the grass of the meadows, and how swiftly and easily the bird would run through a winrow of hay.

FEB. 6. [1857] One who has seen them tells me that a covey of thirteen quails daily visits Hayden's yard and barn, where he feeds them and can almost put his hands on them.

FEB. 7. [1857] Hayden the elder tells me that the quails have come to his yard every day for almost a month and are just as tame as chickens. They come about his wood-shed, he supposes to pick up the worms that have dropped out of the wood, and when it storms hard gather together in the corner of the shed. He walked within, say, three or four feet of them without disturbing them. They come out of the woods by the graveyard, and sometimes they go down toward the river. They will be about his yard the greater part of the day; were there yesterday, though it was so warm, but now probably they can get food enough elsewhere. They go just the same to Poland's across the road. About ten years ago there was a bevy of fifteen that used to come from the same woods, and one day, they being in the barn and scared by the cat, four ran into the hay and died there. The former do not go to the houses further from the woods. Thus it seems in severe winters the quails venture out of the woods and join the poultry of the farmer's yard, if it be near the edge of the wood. It is remarkable that this bird, which thus half domesticates itself, should not be found wholly domesticated before this.

VIRGINIA RAIL *(Rallus limicola)*

[Rails are chickenlike birds which are often called mud hens or marsh hens. They spend most of their time skulking through dense vegetation in marshes. They swim easily, and their long, slender feet enable them to run swiftly over mud flats. The reddish-brown Virginia Rail is about the size of a Bobwhite and has a long, slender, decurved bill. The young, even when full-grown, are sooty black.

So secretive are these birds that only those who drift in a boat along muddy shores of ponds or marshy streams, or hike through marshes are likely to see them. In spite of his interest in places where the Virginia Rail surely nested, Thoreau seldom saw the bird.

Though the Virginia Rail fluctuates in numbers from year to year, it is considered a common bird in summer and autumn on the Great Meadows.]

JUNE 16. [1853] Coming down the river, heard opposite the new houses, where I stopped to pluck the tall grass, a sound as of young blackbirds amid the button-bushes. After a long while gazing, standing on the roots of the button bushes, I detected a couple of meadow or mud hens (*Rallus Virginianus*) gliding about under the button-bushes over the mud and through the shallow water, and uttering a squeaking or squawking note, as if they had a nest there or young. Bodies about the size of a robin; short tail; wings and tail white-edged; bill about one and a half inches long, orange beneath in one bird; brown, deepening into black spots above; turtle-dove color on breasts and beneath; ashy about eyes and cheeks. Seemed not willing to fly, and for a long time unwilling to pass me, because it must come near to keep under the button-bushes.

AMERICAN WOODCOCK *(Philohela minor)*

[Since woodcock begin returning to Massachusetts in early March, Thoreau's first sight of one on April 22, 1860, was not an early date. This bird seems to hug the earth which it resembles in color and where it is seldom noticed until approached too closely. Then it bursts away with a twittering whistle.

One of the keen pleasures of early spring birding is a visit to a singing place of the woodcock. At dusk the males may be heard giving a nasal *pezeent* note rather like that of a nighthawk. The aerial song, believed to be made—at least in part—as air rushes through the strangely narrowed outer wing primaries, begins with a chippering trill as the bird ascends higher and higher. This changes to a bubbling warble as the woodcock drops. If the spot from which the woodcock arose is noted, it is possible to run to that place and actually see the bird alight after its aerial song, for they return to the same area.

The chief food of these rich-brown, chubby birds is earthworms for which they probe in the soft earth, apparently using both their sense of hearing and feeling to locate them. Their long bill is an extraordinary tool that can reach worms as much as three inches deep in the ground. The upper mandible is flexible at its outer end and thus the tip can be moved to reach around a worm though the bill is closed at the base. The four eggs are most often found in Massachusetts during April, and the woodcock has sometimes been found surrounded by snow as she incubated them.]

MAY 24. [1856]   Humphrey Buttrick says that he hears the note of the woodcock from the village in April and early in May (too late now); that there were some this year breeding or singing by the riverside in front of Abel Heywood's. He says that when you see one spring right up straight into the air, you may go to the spot, and he will surely come down again after some minutes to within a few feet of the same spot and of you.

JULY 3. [1856]   To Assabet River. I scare up one or two woodcocks in different places by the shore, where they are feeding, and in a meadow. They go off with a whistling flight. Can see where their bills have probed the mud.

Nov. 21. [1857]   Just above the grape-hung birches, my attention was drawn to a singular-looking dry leaf or parcel of leaves on the shore about a rod off. Then I thought it might be the dry and yellowed skeleton of a bird with all its ribs; then the shell of a turtle, or possibly some large dry oak leaves peculiarly curved and cut; and then, all at once, I saw that it was a woodcock, perfectly still, with its head drawn in, standing on its great pink feet. I had, apparently, noticed only the yellowish-brown portions of the plumage, referring the dark-brown to the shore behind it. May it not be that the yellowish-brown markings of the bird correspond somewhat to its skeleton? At any rate with my eye steadily on it from a point within a rod, I did not for a considerable time suspect it to be a living creature. Examining the shore after it had flown with a whistling flight, I saw that there was a clear space of mud between the water and the edge of ice-crystals about two inches wide, melted so far by the lapse of the water, and all along the edge of the ice, for a rod or two at least, there was a hole where it had thrust its bill down, probing, every half-inch, frequently closer. Some animal life must be collected at that depth just in that narrow space, savory morsels for this bird.

I was paddling along slowly, on the lookout for what was to be seen, when my attention was caught by a strange-looking leaf or bunch of leaves on the shore, close to the water's edge, a rod distant. I thought to myself, I may as well investigate that, and so pushed slowly toward it, my eyes resting on it all the while. It then looked like a small shipwrecked hulk and, strange to say, like the bare skeleton of a fowl that has been picked and turned yellowish, resting on its breast-bone, the color of a withered black or red oak leaf. Again I thought it must be such a leaf or cluster of leaves peculiarly curved and cut or torn on the upper edges.

The chubby bird dashed away zigzag, carrying its long tongue-case carefully before it, over the witch-hazel bushes. This is its walk,—the portion of the shore, the narrow strip, still kept open and unfrozen between the water's edge and the ice. The sportsman might discover its neighborhood by these probings.

April 22. [1860]   Scare up woodcock on the shore by my boat's place,—the first I had seen. It was feeding within a couple of rods, but I had not seen or thought of it. When I made a loud and sharp sound driving in my rowlocks, it suddenly flew up. It is evident that we very often come quite near woodcocks and snipe thus concealed on the ground, without starting them and so without suspecting that they are near. These marsh-birds, like the bittern, have this habit of keeping still and trusting to their resemblance to the ground.

COMMON SNIPE *(Capella gallinago)*

[During migration, a whole flock of these tight-sitting marsh waders can be overlooked until flushed almost from underfoot. It bursts into flight with a loud rasping note.

Common Snipe have a most interesting courtship flight in which they circle over marshy meadows with a loud, measured *chipa-chipa* repeated over and over. In addition, a winnowing sound, high-pitched and pulsating, carries a long distance, and because it is difficult to locate produces an eerie effect. It is said that this winnowing or humming effect is produced by the oddly formed tail feathers.

On April 9, 1858, Thoreau wondered that few Concord men noted the annual return of snipe to Concord. These same men, deaf to the strange sounds coming from the April sky, still knew all about the Germans and other visitors from far off places who appeared but once on the platform of the Concord Lyceum.

Thoreau never found the nest of a snipe, but in 1879 Brewster found three pairs nesting on the Great Meadows. To-day they vary in numbers, becoming more numerous in wet years and declining in dry years. There appears to be no recent record of a nest in the area and the National Wildlife Refuge records them as uncommon during the spring, summer, and autumn, and missing in winter.]

APRIL 1. [1853]   Now, at early starlight, I hear the snipe's hovering note as he circles over Nawshawtuct Meadow. Only once did I seem to see him; occasionally his squeak. He is now heard near, now farther, but is sure to circle round again. It sounds very much like a winnowing-machine increasing rapidly in intensity for a few seconds.

APRIL 16. [1855]   5 A.M.—To Hill. Clear and cool. A frost whitens the ground; yet a mist hangs over the village. There is a thin ice, reaching a foot from the water's edge, which the earliest sun rays will melt. I scare up several snipes feeding on the meadow's edge. It is remarkable how they conceal themselves when they alight on a bare spit of the meadow. I look with my glass to where one alighted four rods off, and at length detect its head rising amid the cranberry vines and withered grass blades,—which last it closely resembles in color,—with its eye steadily fixed on me.

APRIL 15. [1856]   I hear a part of the hovering note of my first snipe, circling over some distant meadow, a mere waif, and all is still again. *A-lulling* the watery meadows, fanning the air like a spirit over some far meadow's bay.

APRIL 25. [1856]   I landed on Merrick's pasture near the rock, and when I stepped out of the boat and drew it up, a snipe flew up, and lit again seven or eight rods off. After trying in vain for several minutes to see it on the ground there, I advanced a step and, to my surprise, scared up two more, which had squatted on the bare meadow all the while within a rod, while I drew up my boat and made a good deal of noise. In short, I scared up twelve, one or two at a time, within a few rods, which were feeding on the edge of the meadow just laid bare, each rising with a sound like *squeak squeak*, hoarsely. That part of the meadow seemed all alive with them. It is almost impossible to see one on the meadow, they squat and run so low, and are so completely the color of the ground. They rise from within a rod, fly half a dozen rods, and then drop down on the bare open meadow before your eyes, where there seems not stubble enough to conceal [them], and are at once lost as completely as if they had sunk into the earth. I observed that some, when finally scared from this island, flew off rising quite high, one a few rods behind the other, in their peculiar zigzag manner, rambling about high over the meadow, making it uncertain where they would settle, till at length I lost sight of one and saw the other drop down almost perpendicularly into the meadow as it appeared.

MARCH 29. [1858]   At the first pool I also scared up a snipe. It rises with a single *cra-a-ck* and goes off with its zigzag flight, with its bill presented to the earth, ready to charge bayonnets against the inhabitants of the mud.

APRIL 9. [1858]   I hear the booming of snipe this evening, and Sophia says she heard them on the 6th. The meadows having been bare so long, they may have begun yet earlier. Persons walking up or down our village street in still evenings at this season hear this singular *winnowing* sound in the sky over the meadows and know not what it is. This "booming" of the snipe is our regular serenade. I heard it this evening for the first time, as I sat in the house, through the window. Yet common and annual and remarkable as it is, not one in a hundred of the villagers hears it, and hardly so many know what it is. Yet the majority know of the Germanians who have only been here once. Mr. Hoar was almost the only inhabitant of this street whom I had heard speak of this note, which he used annually to hear and listen for in his sundown or evening walks.

APRIL 2. [1859]   As I go down the street just after sunset, I hear many snipe to-night. This sound is annually heard by the villagers, but always at this hour, i.e. in the twilight,—a hovering sound high in the air,—and they do not know what to refer it to. It is easily imitated by the breath. A sort of shuddering with the breath. It reminds me of calmer nights. Hardly one in a hundred hears it, and perhaps not as many know what creature makes it. Perhaps no one dreamed of snipe an hour ago, but as soon as the dusk begins, so that a bird's flight is concealed, you hear this peculiar spirit-suggesting sound, now far, now near, heard through and above the evening din of the village. I did not hear one when I returned up the street half an hour later.

UPLAND PLOVER *(Bartramia longicauda)*

[This thin-billed bird, about the size of a Robin, is not a plover despite its name. Scientists place it between the curlews and the sandpipers. It is a bird of open country such as the western prairies and extensive farmlands in the northeast. It sometimes finds golf courses acceptable as nesting places.

Thoreau found Upland Plovers nesting near Highland Light on Cape Cod. The nest is a small hollow in the ground lined with grasses. He never found a nest near Concord, though he suspected they bred there. According to William Brewster, they were extirpated as breeding birds in that area after 1871.]

JUNE 15. [1860]   I paddle to Clamshell. As I stood there I heard that peculiar hawk-like (for rhythm) but more resonant or clanging kind of scream which I may have heard before this year, plover-like, indefinitely far,—over the Clamshell plain. After proceeding half a dozen rods toward the hill, I heard the familiar willet note of the upland plover and looking up, saw one standing erect—like a large tell-tale, or chicken with its head stretched up—on the rail fence. After a while it flew off southwest and low, then wheeled and went a little higher down the river. Of pigeon size, but quick quivering wings. Finally rose higher and flew more or less zigzag, as if uncertain where it would alight, and at last, when almost out of sight, it pitched down into a field near Cyrus Hubbard's. It was the same note I heard so well on Cape Cod in July, '55, and probably the same I heard in the Shawsheen valley, May 15, 1858. I suspect, then, that it breeds here.

SPOTTED SANDPIPER *(Actitis mascularia)*

[This is the most widely distributed nesting sandpiper in the United States. Except in the southern states, it breeds by ponds, lakes, streams, and near swamps throughout the country. During the breeding season its breast is heavily spotted with black dots. It is frequently called teeter-tail because a habit of teetering, which is characteristic of many shorebirds, is so exaggerated in this species that it seems almost too delicately balanced.

The poignant regret expressed by Thoreau when Emerson collected a peetweet and spent most of his vacation breaking bottles is echoed by all who love the wilderness places and regret their desecration by uselessly broken scattered glass, or other litter.

Thoreau's ornithology was not sound on July 22, 1859, when he spoke of the Spotted Sandpiper as the only shorebird around Concord. Included here are selections about three other members of the shorebird group: American Woodcock, Common Snipe, and Upland Plover. Thoreau also saw the Killdeer, Semipalmated Plover, Solitary Sandpiper, and both Yellowlegs near Concord.]

JULY 2. [1853]   The peetweets are quite noisy about the rocks in Merrick's pasture when I approach; have eggs or young there, which they are anxious about.

JUNE 14. [1855]   Looked at the peetweet's nest which C. [Channing] found yesterday. It was very difficult to find again in the broad open meadow; no nest but a mere hollow in the dead cranberry leaves, the grass and stubble ruins, under a little alder. The old bird went off at last from under us; low in the grass at first and with *wings up*, making a worried sound which attracted other birds. I frequently noticed others afterward flying low over the meadow and alighting and uttering this same note of alarm. There [were] only four eggs in this nest yesterday, and to-day, to C.'s surprise, there are the two eggs which he left and a young peetweet beside; a gray pinch of down with a black centre to its back, but already so old and precocious that it runs with its long legs swiftly off from squatting beside the two eggs, and hides in the grass. We have some trouble to catch it. How came it here with these eggs, which will not be hatched for some days? C. saw nothing of it yesterday. J. Farmer says that young peetweets run at once like partridges and quails, and that they are the only birds he knows that do. These eggs were not addled (I had opened one, C. another). Did this bird come from another nest, or did it belong to an earlier brood? Eggs white, with black spots here and there all over, dim at great end.

AUG. 23. [1858]   Emerson says that he and Agassiz and Company broke some dozens of ale bottles, one after another, with their bullets, in the Adirondack country, using them for marks! It sounds rather Cockneyish. He says that he shot a peetweet for Agassiz, and this, I think he said, was the first game he ever bagged. He carried a double-barrelled gun—rifle and shotgun—which he bought for the purpose, which he says received much commendation—all parties thought it a very pretty piece. Think of Emerson shooting a peetweet (with shot) for Agassiz, and cracking an ale bottle (after emptying it) with his rifle at six rods! They cut several pounds of lead out of the tree. It is just what Mike Saunders, the merchant's clerk, did when he was there.

MAY 2. [1859] A peetweet and its mate at Mantatuket Rock. The river seems really inhabited when the peetweet is back. . . . This bird does not return to our stream until the weather is decidedly pleasant and warm. He is perched on the accustomed rock. Its note peoples the river, like the prattle of children once more in the yard of a home that has stood empty.

HERRING GULL *(Larus argentatus)*

[The Herring Gull population throughout its Northern Hemisphere habitat is much greater than it was a century ago when it was preyed upon by eggers and plume hunters. For many decades garbage and sewage have vastly increased the food supply of this scavenger. Protection and the adequate food supply explain the increase of this gull.

Though Thoreau never saw a gull on Walden Pond, today he would find them there during migration periods, and in winter if there is open water.

Gulls swim buoyantly. Their long, narrow, pointed wings enable them to fly, soar, and glide with grace surpassed by few birds. They usually nest in colonies, preferring rocky or grassy islands where they nest on the ground. The young are able to run about soon after they hatch.]

APRIL 15. [1852] Thinking of the value of the gull to the scenery of our river in the spring, when for a few weeks they are seen circling about so deliberately and heavily yet gracefully, without apparent object, beating like a vessel in the air, Gilpin says something to the purpose, that water-fowl "discover in their flight some determined aim. They eagerly coast the river, or return to the sea; bent on some purpose, of which they never lose sight. But the evolutions of the gull appear capricious, and undirected, both when she flies alone, and, as she often does, in large companies,—The more however her character suffers as a loiterer, the more it is raised in picturesque value, by her continuing longer before the eye; displaying, in her elegant sweeps along the air, her sharp-pointed wings, and her bright silvery hue,— She is beautiful also, not only on the wing, but when she floats, in numerous assemblies on the water; or when she rests on the shore, dotting either one, or the other with white spots; which, minute as they are, are very picturesque: . . . giving life and spirit to a view."

He seems to be describing our very bird. I do not *remember* to have seen them over or in our river meadows when there was not ice there. They come annually a-fishing here like royal hunters, to remind us of the sea and that our town, after all, lies but further up a creek of the universal sea, above the head of the tide. So ready is a deluge to overwhelm our lands, as the gulls circle hither in the spring freshets. To see a gull beating high over our meadowy flood in chill and windy March is akin to seeing a mackerel schooner on the coast. It is the nearest approach to sailing vessels in our scenery. I never saw one at Walden. Oh, how it salts our fresh, our sweet watered Fair Haven all at once to see this sharp-beaked, greedy sea-bird beating over it! For a while the water is brackish to my eyes. It is merely some herring pond, and if I climb the eastern bank I expect to see the Atlantic there covered with countless sails. We are so far maritime, do not dwell beyond the range of the seagoing gull, the littoral birds. Does not the gull come up after those suckers which I see? He is never to me perfectly in harmony with the scenery, but, like the high water, something unusual.

MARCH 29. [1854]   A gull of pure white,—a wave of foam in the air. How simple and wave-like its outline, the outline of the wings presenting two curves, between which the tail is merely the point of junction,—all wing like a birch scale; tail remarkably absorbed.

APRIL 15. [1855]   Before we rounded Ball's Hill,—the water now beautifully smooth,—at 2:30 P.M., we saw three gulls sailing on the glassy meadow at least half a mile off, by the oak peninsula,— the plainer because they were against the reflection of the hills. They looked larger than afterward close at hand, as if their whiteness was reflected and doubled. As we advanced into the Great Meadows, making the only ripples in their broad expanse, there being still not a ray of sunshine, only in subdued light through the thinner crescent in the north, the reflections of the maples, of Ponkawtasset and the poplar hill, and the whole township in the southwest, were as perfect as I ever saw. A wall which ran down to the water on the hillside, without any remarkable curve in it, was exaggerated by the reflection into the half of an ellipse. The meadow was expanded to a large lake, the shore-line being referred to the sides of the hills reflected in it. It was a scene worth many such voyages to see. It was remarkable how much light those white gulls, and also a bleached post on a distant shore, absorbed and reflected through that sombre atmosphere,—conspicuous almost as candles in the night. When we got near to the gulls, they rose heavily and flapped away, answering a more distant one, with a remarkable, deliberate, melancholy squeaking scream, mewing, or piping, almost a squeal. It was a *little* like the loon. Is this sound the origin of the name sea-mew? Not withstanding the smoothness of the water, we could not easily see black ducks against the reflection of the woods, but heard them rise at a distance before we saw them. The

birds were still in the middle of the day, but began to sing again by 4:30
P.M., probably because of the clouds. Saw and heard a kingfisher—do they
not come with the smooth waters of April?—hurrying over the meadow as
if on urgent business.

APRIL 22. [1857] A dozen gulls are circling over Fair Haven Pond, some
very white beneath, with very long, narrow-pointed, black-tipped wings, almost regular semicircles like the new moon. As they circle beneath a white
scud in this bright air, they are almost invisible against it, they are so nearly
the same color. What glorious fliers! But few birds are seen; only a crow
or two teetering along the water's edge looking for its food, with its large,
clumsy head, and on unusually long legs, as if stretched, or its pants pulled
up to keep it from the wet, and now flapping off with some large morsel in
its bill; or robins in the same place; or perhaps the sweet song of the tree
sparrows from the alders by the shore, or of a song sparrow or blackbird.
The phoebe is scarcely heard. Not a duck do we see!

MOURNING DOVE *(Zenaidura macroura)*

[This dove is considerably smaller than the Passenger Pigeon was. It is listed
as a game bird in most states. Its head looks far too small for its slim brown
body. Its long pointed tail is bordered with white.

Thoreau wrote little about this species and never during the winter season.
Yet two hundred and eleven were counted in Concord on the day of the 1962
Christmas Bird Count in that area.

On April 16, 1855, Thoreau marveled at the force with which doves landed
on his roof. Landing shocks are easily absorbed by a bird. They have powerful leg flexor muscles. Moreover, the thigh is held permanently forward and
encased in the body skin, providing a great cushioning effect. It must be
remembered that what is frequently mistaken in birds for a knee bent the
wrong way is in reality the bird's heel.]

JULY 12. [1852] The turtle dove flutters before you in shady wood-paths,
or looks out with extended neck, losing its balance, slow to leave its perch.

APRIL 16. [1855] I am startled sometimes these mornings to hear the sound
of doves alighting on the roof just over my head; they come down so hard
upon it, as if one had thrown a heavy stick on to it, and I wonder it does
not injure their organizations. Their legs must be cushioned in their sockets
to save them from the shock?

PASSENGER PIGEON *(Ectopistes migratorius)*

[Every word that Thoreau wrote about the Passenger Pigeon is of great interest to-day. The last survivor of this species died in captivity in a Cincinnati zoo in 1914.

John James Audubon and Alexander Wilson both estimated that migratory flocks which they saw numbered between one and two *billion* birds. Perhaps this was the most abundant bird that ever lived.

One of the last great nestings of Passenger Pigeons on record was in 1878. From this nesting more than a million and a half pigeons were shipped by railroad alone. Certainly man played a considerable part in the extinction of the Passenger Pigeon. No species, however numerous, can be killed by the millions year after year and not have its numbers decrease. The destruction of the beech forests as settlers pushed westward is believed to be an added factor, for beech mast was an important food item of these birds. It is too late for scientists to make a judgement based on actual studies, but many believe that once the pigeon population was reduced to a certain point biological factors were upset and reproduction ceased.

This was not only the largest American pigeon, but many scientists throughout the world considered it the finest of all pigeons. It was an abundant migrant through Massachusetts and once nested commonly in the Concord area. On September 2, 1868, a flock of about fifty pigeons was seen in Cambridge and between September 2 and 10, 1871, a heavy flight passed through eastern Massachusetts. Thousands were reportedly killed and the pigeon-netters in Concord used their nets profitably as of old. Sometime between 1880 and 1890, Passenger Pigeons, which had been at home for centuries in Massachusetts between the months of March and October, vanished and were seen no more.

Many early observers described the havoc made among the pigeons both on their nesting grounds and their winter roosts. Men fell upon them with sticks and stones. They frightened them with flaming torches at night so that they fell to the ground in confusion and could be gathered up, caught by dogs, and eaten by pigs. Guns killed dozens at a single blast. Nets were baited and as many as 1,044 pigeons were taken by one man in a single day in 1878 at the Petosky, Michigan, nesting place. Audubon believed that Passenger Pigeons, which doubled and sometimes quadrupled their numbers in a nesting season, could endure all the destruction that man might offer and still survive. He believed that only the destruction of the forests could decrease the Passenger Pigeon. The Sandgrouse of Asia offer a rather parallel case in that they travel in great flocks and gather in concentrated masses around favorite water holes, where they are frequently shot in fantastic numbers. They no longer occur in as enormous numbers as they did at the turn of the century, but the maharajas of India, who entertain guests with shooting parties at the water holes where concentrations of these birds come, maintain the decrease is not due to overshooting.

Apparently Passenger Pigeons were still abundant in parts of the Middle West during the decade when they vanished from Massachusetts. Even there they were decreasing. By the end of the century they were practically gone and there is a reliable report of only fifty of them in 1900.

These birds formed a staple food on the frontier, for when they were present in an area they were taken easily. The Plymouth Colony found them a blessing in 1648, and Winthrop wrote, "it being incredible what multitudes of them were killed daily." During the first three-quarters of the nineteenth century such vast quantities were shipped to markets that they were one of the cheapest foods available.

The cause of their extinction is still debated. Whatever may have led to the final disappearance of this once incredibly abundant species, it should serve as a warning that research scientists should help determine the cropping of even the most abundant natural resources.

In Concord the last specimen of Passenger Pigeon, according to Brewster, was shot in August, 1886.]

AUG. ? [1845] I sit here at my window like a priest of Isis, and observe the phenomena of three thousand years ago, yet unimpaired. The tantivy of wild pigeons, an ancient race of birds, gives a voice to the air, flying by twos and threes athwart my view or perching restless on the white pine boughs occasionally.

JULY 21. [1851] Some pigeons here are resting in the thickest of the white pines during the heat of this day, migrating, no doubt. They are unwilling to move for me. Flies buzz and rain about my hat, and the dead twigs and leaves of the white pine, which the choppers have left here, exhale a dry and almost sickening scent. A cuckoo chuckles, half throttled, on a neighboring tree, and now, flying into the pine, scares out a pigeon, which flies with its handsome tail spread, dashes this side and that between the trees helplessly, like a ship carrying too much sail in the midst of a small creek, some great anima having no room to manoeuvre, —a fluttering flight.

SEPT. 12. [1851] Saw a pigeon-place on George Heywood's cleared lot,— the six dead trees set up for the pigeons to alight on, and the brush house close by to conceal the man. I was rather startled to find such a thing going now in Concord. The pigeons on the trees looked like fabulous birds with their long tails and their pointed breasts. I could hardly believe they were alive and not some wooden birds used for decoys, they sat so still; and, even when they moved their necks, I thought it was the effect of art. As they were not catching then, I approached and scared away a dozen birds who were perched on the trees, and found that they were freshly baited there, though the net was carried away, perchance to some other bed. The smooth sandy bed was covered with buckwheat, wheat or rye, and acorns. Sometimes they use corn, shaved off the ear in its present state with a knife. There were left the sticks with which they fastened the nets. As I stood there, I heard a rushing sound and, looking up, saw a flock of thirty or forty pigeons dashing toward the *trees,* who suddenly whirled on seeing me and circled round and made a new dash toward the bed, as if they would fain alight if I had not been there, then steered off. I crawled into the bough house and lay awhile looking through the leaves, hoping to see them come again and feed, but they did not while I stayed. This net and bed belong to one Harrington of Weston, as I hear. Several men still take pigeons in Concord every year; by a method, methinks, extremely old and which I seem to have seen pictured in some old books of fables or symbols, and yet few in Concord know exactly how it is done. And yet it is all done for money and because the birds fetch a good price, just as the farmers raise corn and potatoes. I am always expecting that those engaged in such a pursuit will be somewhat less grovelling and mercenary than the regular trader or farmer, but I fear it is not so.

MAY 9. [1852] Saw pigeons in the woods, with their inquisitive necks and long tails, but few representatives of the great flocks that once broke down our forests.

SEPT. 2. [1852] Small flocks of pigeons are seen these days. Distinguished from doves by their sharper wings and bodies.

SEPT. 2 [1853] Hear the sharp *quivet* of pigeons at the Thrush Alley clearing. Mistook it for a jay at first, but saw the narrow, swift flying bird soon.

DEC. 15. [1853] He [George Brooks of Concord] had ten live pigeons in a cage under his barn. He used them to attract others in the spring. The reflections from their necks were very beautiful. They made me think of shells cast up on a beach. He placed them in a cage on the bed and could hear them from the house.

JULY 18. [1854] Brooks has let out some of his pigeons, which stay about the stands or perches to bait the others. Wild ones nest in his woods quite often. He begins to catch them in middle of August.

SEPT. 5. [1854]   Saw two pigeons, which flew about his [Samuel Barrett, sawmill and gristmill owner] pond and then lit on the elms over his house. He said they had come to drink from Brooks' as they often did.

SEPT. 12. [1854]   I scare pigeons from Hubbard's oaks beyond. How like the creaking of trees the slight sounds they make! Thus they are concealed. Not only their *prating* or *quivet* is like a sharp creak, but I heard a sound from them like a dull grating or creaking of bough on bough. . . .

On a white oak beyond Everett's orchard by the road, I see quite a flock of pigeons, their blue-black droppings and their feathers spot the road. The bare limbs of the oak apparently attracted them, though its acorns are thick on the ground. These are found whole in their crops. They swallow them whole. I should think from the droppings that they had been eating berries. I hear that Weatherbee caught ninety-two dozen last week.

APRIL 16. [1855]   In the meanwhile heard the *quivet* through the wood, and, looking, saw through an opening a small compact flock of pigeons flying low about.

APRIL 27. [1855]   Heard a singular sort of screech, somewhat like a hawk, under the Cliff, and soon some pigeons flew out of a pine near me.

MAY 26. [1855]   Saw a beautiful blue-backed and long-tailed pigeon sitting daintily on a low white pine limb.

SEPT. 2 [1856]   P.M.—To Painted Cup Meadow....A few pigeons were seen a fortnight ago. I have noticed none in all walks, but G. Minott, whose mind runs to them so much, but whose age and infirmities confine him to his wood-shed on the hillside, saw a small flock a fortnight ago. I rarely pass at any season of the year but he asks if I have seen any pigeons. One man's mind running on pigeons, [he] will sit thus in the midst of a village, many of whose inhabitants never see nor dream of a pigeon except in the pot, and where even naturalists do not observe [them], and he, looking out with expectation and faith from morning till night, will surely see them.

SEPT. 16. [1856]   See a flock of pigeons dash by. From a stout breast they taper straightly and slenderly to the tail. They have been catching them a while.

MAY 14. [1857]   Abel Hosmer [Concord farmer] tells me that he has collected and sown white pine seed, and that he has found them in the crop of pigeons. (?)

Sept. 9. [1858]   R. [Israel Rice, Sudbury farmer] says that he has caught pigeons which had ripe grapes in their crops long before any were ripe here, and that they came from the southwest.

Sept. 13. [1858]   A small dense flock of wild pigeons dashes by over the side of the hill, from west to east,—perhaps from Wetherbee's to Brooks, for I see the latter's pigeon-place. They make a dark slate-gray impression.

Sept. 23. [1858]   Met a gunner from Lynn on the beach [of Rockport, Mass.] who had several pigeons which he had killed in the woods by the shore. Said they had been blown off the mainland.

May 7. [1859]   I frequently see pigeons dashing about in small flocks, or three or four at a time, over the woods here [in Acton]. Theirs is a peculiarly swift, dashing flight.

Sept. 9. [1859]   I start many pigeons now in a sprout-land.

Sept. 13. [1859]   It is a wonder how pigeons can swallow acorns whole, but they do.

Sept. 14. [1859]   They are catching pigeons nowadays. Coombs has a stand west of Nut Meadow, and he says that he has just shot fourteen hawks there, which were after the pigeons.

Sept. 15. [1859]   Dense flocks of pigeons hurry-skurry over the hill. Pass near Brooks' pigeon-stands. There was a flock perched on his poles, and they sat so still and in such regular order there, being also the color of the wood, that I thought they were wooden figures at first. They were perched not only in horizontal straight lines one above the other, which the cross-bars required, but at equal distances apart on these perches, which must be their own habit; and it struck me that they made just such a figure seen against the sky as pigeonholes cut in a dove's house do, *i.e.* a more or less triangular figure . . . and possibly the seeing them thus perched might have originally suggested this arrangement of the holes.

Pigeons dart by on every side,—a dry slate color, like weather-stained wood (the weather-stained birds), fit color for this aerial traveller, a more subdued and earthy blue than the sky, as its field (or path) is between the sky and the earth,—not black or brown, as is the earth, but a terrene or slaty-blue, suggesting their aerial resorts and habits.

Sept. 21 [1859]   I sat near Coombs' pigeon-place by White Pond. The pigeons sat motionless on his bare perches, from time to time dropping down into the bed and uttering a *quivet* or two. Some stood on the perch; others squatted flat. I could see their dove-colored breasts. Then all at once, being alarmed, would take flight, but ere long return in straggling parties. He tells me that he has fifteen dozen baited, but does not intend to catch any more at present, or for two or three weeks, hoping to attract others. Rice says that white oak acorns pounded up, shells and all, make the best bait for them.

Sept. 28. [1859]   The white pine seed is very abundant this year, and this must attract more pigeons. Coombs tells me that he finds the seed in their crops. Also that he found within a day or two a full-formed egg with shell in one.

Nov. 8. [1859]   Coombs says that quite a little flock of pigeons bred here last summer. He found one nest in a small white pine near his pigeon-stand (where he baited them in the summer), so low he could put his hand in it (!?).

Jan. 23. [1860]   Minott says that pigeons alight in great flocks on the tops of hemlocks in March, and he thinks they eat the seed. (But he also thought for the same reason that they ate the white pine seed at the same season, when it is not there! They might find a little of the last adhering to the pitch.)

Sept. 4. [1860]   Saw flocks of pigeons the 2d and 3d.

Black-billed Cuckoo *(Coccyzus erythropthalmus)*

[Since this is the common species in the Concord area, it is assumed that all of Thoreau's references are related to the Black-billed Cuckoo. He frequently called it the St. Domingo Cuckoo after Nuttall. It was generally believed in Massachusetts that other species were afraid of the cuckoo. That Thoreau did not doubt this is evident from his entry on July 21, 1851.

When, on June 27, 1853, a cuckoo nest which Thoreau had found was robbed he wondered if the bird had broken her eggs because he had found the nest. This is not likely unless she was so startled that she left the nest abruptly enough to knock out the eggs. Dr. Arthur Allen has estimated that less than 20 per cent of the nests he finds each year actually endure until the young leave the nest of their own accord. Nature's surplus is cropped in various ways and eggs and young birds feed other birds, snakes, and mammals. If all the eggs and young of a single fairly common species

of birds all survived to maturity, that species, in a short time, would become so abundant as to be an unendurable pest.]

JUNE 18. [1853] Found the nest of a cuckoo,—a long, slender, handsome bird, probably St. Domingo cuckoo,—at the edge of the meadow on
a bent sallow, not in a crotch, covered by the broad shining leaves of a
swamp white oak, whose boughs stretched over it, two feet or more from
the ground. The nest was made of dry twigs and was small for the size of
the bird and very shallow, but handsomely lined with an abundance of
what looked like the dry yellowish-brown (?) catkins of the hickory, which
made a pleasing contrast with the surrounding grayish twigs. There were
some worm-eaten green leaves inwoven. It contained a single greenish-white
elliptical egg, an inch or more long. The bird flew off a little way and
clow-clow-clowed.

JUNE 27. [1853] The cuckoo's nest is robbed, or perhaps she broke her
egg because I found it. Thus three out of half a dozen nests which I have
revisited have been broken up. It is a very shallow nest, six or eight inches
in diameter by two and a half or three deep, on a low bending willow,
hardly half an inch deep within; concealed by overhanging leaves of a
swamp white oak on the edge of the river meadow, two to three feet
from the ground, made of slender twigs which are prettily ornamented
with much ramalina lichen, lined with hickory catkins and pitch pine needles.

MAY 14. [1854] A St. Domingo cuckoo, black-billed with red round the
eye, a silent, long, slender, graceful bird, dark cinnamon (?) above, pure
white beneath. It is in a leisurely manner picking the young caterpillars
out of a nest (now about a third of an inch long) with its long, curved
bill. Not timid.

JULY 17. [1854] The cuckoo is a very neat, slender, and graceful bird. It
belongs to the nobility of birds. It is elegant.

AUG. 20. [1857] As I stand there, I hear a peculiar sound which I mistake
for a woodpecker's tapping, but I soon see a cuckoo hopping near suspici-
ously or inquisitively, at length within twelve feet, from time to time uttering a hard, dry note, very much like a woodpecker tapping a dead dry tree
rapidly, its *full* clear white throat and breast toward me, and slowly lifting
its tail from time to time. Though somewhat allied to that throttled note
it makes by night, it was quite different to take.

OWLS

[The large eyes of these birds are fixed in their sockets making it necessary for them to turn their round heads in the direction they wish to look. So amazingly flexible is an owl's neck that the head can be turned more than one half of a circle. So quickly can the owl reverse the turn of its head that many a person is sure it twists its head around and around. Of all the birds in the world, only owls can blink their upper lids. This gives them a human-like look.

Their plumage is soft and fluffy. Their flight is almost soundless. Their hooked bills and talons are efficient tools in catching and devouring their prey. Most owls are nocturnal but they can, contrary to popular belief, see well in the daytime.]

Nov. 25. [1851]   When surveying in the swamp on the 20th last, at sundown, I heard the owls. Hosmer said: "If you ever minded it, it is about the surest sign of rain that there is. Don't you know that last Friday night you heard them and spoke of them, and the next day it rained?" This time there were other signs of rain in abundance. "But night before last," said I, "when you were not here, they hooted louder than ever, and we have had no rain yet." At any rate, it rained hard the 21st, and by that rain the river was raised higher than it has been this fall.

JAN. 4. [1860]   What if you could witness with owls' eyes the revelry of the wood mice some night, frisking about the wood like so many little kangaroos?

SCREECH OWL *(Otis asio)*

[Seldom indeed did Thoreau write as much about a species of bird as he did about the Screech Owl. His wonder and enjoyment of this small owl is evident. It is the smallest of the "horned" owls. It readily accepts a bird box fastened to a garden tree, and is common in orchards which have hallows or cavities in the old trees, in open woodlands, on farms, and in suburbs. Its note is easily imitated and it will often answer such a call even in the daytime.

This fairly common Concord owl suffered badly when the hurricane of September, 1938, destroyed many of its nesting places. It has never fully recovered from that disaster.]

MAY 7. [1855]   I observed a middling-sized red oak standing a little aslant on the side-hill over the swamp, with a pretty large hole in one side about

fifteen feet from the ground, where apparently a limb on which a felled
tree lodged had been cut some years before and so broke out a cavity. I
thought that such a hole was too good a one not to be improved by some
inhabitant of the wood. Perhaps the gray squirrels I had just seen had their
nest there. Or was not the entrance big enough to admit a screech owl? So
I thought I would tap on it and put my ear to the trunk and see if I could
hear anything stirring within it, but I heard nothing. Then I concluded to
look into it. So I shinned up, and when I reached up one hand to the
hole to pull myself up by it, the thought passed through my mind perhaps
something would take hold my fingers, but nothing did. The first limb was
nearly opposite to the hole, and, resting on this, I looked in, and, to my
great surprise, there squatted, filling the hole, which was about six inches
deep and five to six inches wide, a salmon-brown bird not so big as a partridge, seemingly asleep within three inches of the top and close to my
face. It was a minute or two before I made it out to be an owl. . . . It lay
crowded in that small space, with its tail somewhat bent up and one side
of its head turned up with one egret, and its large dark eye open only by
a long slit about a sixteenth of an inch wide; visible breathing. After a
while I put in one hand and stroked it repeatedly, whereupon it inclined its
head a little lower and closed its eye entirely. Though curious to know
what was under it, I disturbed it no farther at that time. . . .

Returning by owl's nest, about one hour before sunset, I climbed up and
looked in again. The owl was gone, but there were four nearly round *dirty
brownish white* eggs quite warm, on nothing but the bits of rotten wood
which made the bottom of the nest. . . .

MAY 12. [1855]   As I approached the owl's nest, I saw her run past the
hole up into that part of the hollow above it, and probably she was there
when I thought she had flown on the 7th. I looked in, and at first did not
know what I saw. One of the three remaining eggs was hatched, and a little
downy *white* young one, two or three times as long as an egg, lay helpless,
between the two remaining eggs. Also a dead white-bellied mouse (*Mus
leucopus*) lay with them, its tail curled round one of the eggs. Wilson says
his red owl (*Strix asio*),—with which this apparently corresponds, and not
with the mottled, though my egg is not "pure white,"—that "the young are
at first covered with a whitish down." . . .

Just before sundown, took our seats before the owl's nest and sat perfectly still and awaited her appearance. We sat for half an hour, and it
was surprising what various distinct sounds we heard there deep in the
wood, as if the aisles of the wood were so many ear-trumpets,—the cawing
of crows, the peeping of hylas in the swamp and perhaps the croaking of
a tree-toad, the oven-bird, the *yorrick* of Wilson's thrush, a distant stake-

driver, the night-warbler and black and white creeper, the lowing of cows, the late supper horn, the voices of boys, the singing of girls,—not all together but separately, distinctly, and musically, from where the partridge and the red-tailed hawk and the screech owl sit on their nests.

MAY 26. [1855]   At the screech owl's nest I now find two young slumbering, almost uniformly gray above, about five inches long, with little dark-grayish tufts for incipient horns(?). Their heads were about as broad as their bodies. I handle them without their stirring or opening their eyes. There are the feathers of a small bird and the leg of the *Mus leucopus* in the nest.

OCT. 28. [1855]   P.M.—By boat to Leaning Hemlocks. As I paddle up the Hemlock bank this cloudy afternoon, about 3 o'clock, I see a screech owl sitting on the edge of a hollow hemlock stump about three feet high, at the base of a large hemlock. It sits with its head drawn in, eyeing me, with its eyes partly open, about twenty feet off. When it hears me move, it turns its head toward me, perhaps one eye only open, with its great glaring golden iris. You see two whitish triangular lines above the eyes meeting at the bill, with a sharp reddish-brown triangle between and a narrow curved line of black under each eye. At this distance and in this light, you see only a black spot where the eye is, and the question is whether the eyes are open or not. It sits on the lee side of the tree this raw and windy day. You would say that this is a bird without a neck. Its short bill, which rests upon its breast, scarcely projects at all, but in a state of rest the whole upper part of the bird from the wings is rounded off smoothly excepting the horns, which stand up conspicuously or are slanted back. After watching it ten minutes from the boat, I landed two rods above, and, stealing quietly up behind the hemlock, though from the windward, I looked carefully around it, and, to my surprise, saw the owl still sitting there. So I sprang round quickly, with my arm outstretched, and caught it in my hand. It was so surprised that it offered no resistance at first, only glared at me in mute astonishment with eyes as big as saucers. But ere long it began to snap its bill, making quite a noise, and, as I rolled it up in my handkerchief and put it in my pocket, it bit my finger slightly. I soon took it out of my pocket and, tying the handkerchief, left it on the bottom of the boat. So I carried it home and made a small cage in which to keep it for the night. When I took it up, it clung so tightly to my hand as to sink its claws into fingers and bring blood.

When alarmed or provoked most, it snaps its bill and hisses. It puffs up its feathers to nearly twice its usual size, stretches out its neck, and, with wide-open eye, stares this way and that, moving its head slowly and undulatingly from side to side with a curious motion. While I write this evening, I see that there is ground for much superstition in it. It looks out on me from a dusky corner of its box with its great solemn eyes, so perfectly still itself. I was surprised to find that I could imitate its note as I remember it, by a *gutteral* whinnering.

A remarkably squat figure, being very broad in proportion to its length, with a short tail, and very cat-like in the face with its horns and great eyes. Remarkably large feet and talons, legs thickly clothed with whitish down, down to the talons. It brought blood from my fingers by clinging to them. It would lower its head, stretch out its neck, and, bending it from side to side, peer at you with laughable circumspection; from side to side, as if to catch or absorb into its eyes every ray of light, strain at you with complacent yet with earnest scrutiny. Raising and lowering its head and moving it from side to side in a slow and regular manner, at the same time snapping its bill smartly perhaps, and faintly hissing, and puffing itself up more and more,—cat-like, turtle-like, both in hissing and swelling. The slowness and gravity, not to say solemnity, of this motion are striking. There plainly is no jesting in this case.

Oct. 29. [1855]   Carried my owl to the hill again. Had to shake him out of the box, for he did not go of his own accord. (He had learned to alight on his perch, and it was surprising how lightly and noiselessly he would hop upon it.) There he stood on the grass, at first bewildered, with his horns pricked up and looking toward me. In this strong light the pupils of his eyes suddenly contracted and the iris expanded till they were two great brazen orbs with a center spot merely. His attitude expressed astonishment more than anything. I was obliged to toss him up a little that he might feel his wings, and then he flapped away low and heavily to a hickory on the hillside twenty rods off. (I had let him out in the plain just east of the hill.) Thither I followed and tried to start him again. He was now on the *qui vive*, yet would not start. He erected his head, showing some neck, narrower than the round head above. His eyes were broad brazen rings around bullets of black. His horns stood quite an inch high, as not before. As I moved around him, he turned his head always toward me, till he looked *directly* behind himself as he sat crosswise on a bough. He behaved as if bewildered and dazzled, gathering all the light he could and ever straining his great eyes toward [you] to make out who you are, but not inclining to fly. I had to lift him again with a stick to make him fly, and then he only rose to a higher perch, where at last he seemed to seek the shelter of a thicker cluster of the sere leaves, partly crouching there. He never appeared so much alarmed as surprised and astonished.

When I first saw him yesterday, he sat on the edge of a hollow hemlock stump about three feet high, at the bottom of a large hemlock, amid the darkness of the evergreens that cloudy day. (It threatened to rain every moment.) At the bottom of the hollow, or eighteen inches beneath him, was a very soft bed of the fine green moss (hypnum) which grows on the bank close by, probably his own bed. It had recently been put there.

GREAT HORNED OWL *(Bubo virginianus)*

[Thoreau often called this species the cat owl. Both the Great Horned and the Barred Owls are commonly called hoot owls, but Thoreau's description of the calls makes it clear which owl he listened to.

These owls, associated in the minds of most people with deep, wild forests, sometimes move into city parks where rats offer an abundant food supply. They eat anything from beetles and snakes to rabbits and skunks that happen to be available in their habitat. These owls defend their nests bravely and will attack a human who attempts to disturb them. Their soft feathers make possible silent flight and they can strike the intruder before he is aware of them. A blow by their powerful claws can be dangerous.

Thoreau enjoyed music, and the flute which he often played in the woods or on the waters of Concord is preserved among his relics. He delighted in the wild sounds of nature and particularly the calls of owls, for they were the same sounds that had echoed through the woods in ancient times long before Europeans arrived in America. It seems likely that Thoreau was thinking of music rather than poetry on December 9, 1856, as he listened to the owl calls. Did he recall *Miserere*, the most famous composition of the great Italian composer, Allegri, as he listened to the strange harmony of the distant owls? It seems logical that his ears were hearing fragments of music rather than sentences from either prose or poetry.]

Nov. 18. [1851]   Now at sundown I hear the hooting of an owl,—*hoo hoo hoo, hoorer hoo*. It sounds like the hooting of an idiot or a maniac broke loose. This is faintly answered in a different strain, apparently from a greater distance, almost as if it were the echo, *i.e.* so far as the *succession* is concerned. This is my music each evening. I heard it last evening. The men who help me call it the "hooting owl" and think it is the cat owl. It is a sound admirably suited [to] the swamp and to the twilight woods, suggesting a vast undeveloped nature which men have not recognized nor satisfied. I rejoice that there are owls. They represent the stark, twilight, unsatisfied thoughts I have. Let owls do the idiotic and maniacal hooting for men. This sound faintly suggests the infinite roominess of nature, that there is a world in which owls live. Yet how few are seen, even by the hunters! The sun has shone this day over this savage swamp, where the single spruce stands covered with usnea moss, which a Concord merchant mortgaged once to the trustees of the ministerial fund and lost, but now for a different race of creatures a new day dawns over this wilderness, which one would have thought was sufficiently dismal before.

JAN. 7. [1854]   P.M.—To Ministerial Swamp. I went to these woods partly to hear an owl, but did not; but now that I have left them nearly a mile behind, I hear one distinctly, *hoorer hoo*. Strange that we should hear this sound so often, loud and far,—a voice which we call the owl,—and yet so rarely see the bird. Oftenest at twilight. It has a singular prominence as a sound; is louder than the voice of a dear friend. Yet we see the friend perhaps daily and the owl but a few times in our lives. It is a sound which the wood or the horizon makes.

DEC. 9. [1856]   The winter day in the woods or fields has commonly the stillness of twilight. The pond is perfectly smooth and full of light. I hear only the strokes of a lingering woodchopper at a distance, and the melodious hooting of an owl, which is as common and marked a sound as the axe or the locomotive whistle. Yet where does the ubiquitous hooter sit, and who sees him? In whose wood-lot is he to be found? Few eyes have rested on him hooting. Few on him silent on his perch even. Yet cut away the wood never so much year after year, though the chopper had not seen him and only a grove or two is left, still his aboriginal voice is heard indefinitely far and sweet, mingled oft, in strange harmony, with the newly invented din of trade, like a sentence of Allegri sounded in our streets,—hooting from invisible perch at his foes the woodchoppers, who are invading his domains. As the earth only a few inches beneath the surface is undisturbed and what it was anciently, so are heard still some primeval sounds in the air. Some of my townsmen I never see, and of a great proportion I do not hear the voices in a year, though they live within my horizon; but every week almost I hear the loud voice of the hooting owl, though I do not see the bird more than once in ten years.

DEC. 15. [1856]   3 P.M.—To Walden. The hooting of the owl! That is a sound which my red predecessors heard here more than a thousand years ago. It rings far and wide, occupying the spaces rightfully,—grand, primeval, aboriginal sound. There is no whisper in it of the Buckleys, the Flints, the Hosmers who recently squatted here, nor of the first parrish, nor of Concord Fight, nor of the last town meeting.

BARRED OWL *(Strix varia)*

[This streaked and barred brown owl is little more than eighteen inches in length. It has a large, round head without "horns." Its eyes are dark, whereas all other owls (except Barn Owls) have yellow eyes.

Probably no more than a single pair of these owls nest in the Concord area today.]

DEC. 14. [1858]   I see at Derby's shop a barred owl *(Strix nebulosa),* taken in the woods west of the factory on the 11th, found (with its wing broke [sic]) by a woodchopper. It measures about three and a half feet in alar extent by eighteen to twenty inches long, or *nearly* the same as the cat owl, but is small and without horns. It is very mild and quiet, bears handling perfectly well, and only snaps its bill with a loud sound at the sight of a cat or dog. It is apparently a female, since it is large and has white spots on the wings. The claws are quite dark rather than dark horn-color. It hopped into the basin of the scales, and I was surprised to find that it weighed only one pound and one ounce. It may be thin-fleshed on account of its broken wing, but how light-bodied these fliers are! It has no yellow iris like the cat owl, and has the bristles about its yellow bill which the other had not. It has a very smooth and handsome round head, a brownish gray. Solemnity is what they express,—fit representatives of the night.

LONG-EARED OWL *(Asio otus)*

[These slender, crow-sized owls are found in many parts of the temperate zone of the Northern Hemisphere. It is larger than a Screech Owl and smaller by far than the Great Horned Owl. Thoreau describes the typical location for the nest of this species. Its usual call is rather dovelike, but it also has several wild, catlike whines.

Though the Concord area contains the right kind of country for breeding Long-eared Owls, the nest is rarely found. Nevertheless, there are many summer records for the species and it may nest there regularly.]

JUNE 24. [1857]   P.M.—To Farmer's Owl-Nest Swamp. Went to Farmer's Swamp to look for the screech owl's nest Farmer had found. You go about forty-five rods on the first path to the left in the woods and then turn to the left a few rods. I found the nest at last near the top of a middling-sized white pine, about thirty feet from the ground. As I stood by the tree, the old bird dashed by within a couple rods, uttering a peculiar mewing sound, which she kept up amid the bushes, a blackbird in close pursuit of her. I found the nest empty, on one side of the main stem but close to it, resting on some limbs. It was made of twigs rather less than an eighth of an inch thick and was almost flat above, only an inch lower in the middle than at the edge, about sixteen inches in diameter and six or eight inches thick, with the twigs in the midst, and beneath was mixed with sphagnum and sedge from the swamp beneath, and the lining or flooring was coarse strips of grape-vine bark; the whole pretty firmly matted together. How common and important a material is grape-vine bark for birds' nests! Nature wastes nothing. There were white droppings of the young on the nest and one large pellet of fur and small bones two and a half inches long. In the meanwhile, the old bird was uttering that hoarse worried note from time to time, somewhat like a partridge's, flying past from side to side and alighting amid the trees or bushes. When I had descended, I detected one young bird two thirds grown perched on a branch of the next tree, about fifteen feet from the ground, which was all the while staring at me with its great yellow eyes. It was gray with gray horns and a dark beak. As I walked past near it, it turned its head steadily, always facing me, without moving its body, till it looked directly the opposite way over its back, but never offered to fly. Just then I thought surely that I heard a puppy faintly barking at me four or five rods distant amid the bushes, having tracked me into the swamp,—*what what, what what what.* It was exactly such a noise as the barking of a very small dog or perhaps a fox. But it was the old owl, for I presently saw her making it. She repeated [sic] perched quite near. She was generally reddish-brown or partridge-colored, the breast mottled with dark brown and fawn-color in downward strings [sic] and had plain fawn-colored thighs.

WHIP-POOR-WILL *(Caprimulgus vociferus)*

[The strong vigorous call repeated over and over and over again is better known than the bird itself. Many people hear the song of the Whip-poor-will, but few see it from one year to the next. Its two slightly speckled white eggs are usually laid on dead leaves.

It is extremely difficult to find the nest of a Whip-poor-will. The bird blends so well with her surroundings that she is almost invisible. The eggs, too, seem to vanish against the background when they are left unsheltered. The only nest this editor has ever seen was found by the ornithologist, Dr. Olin Sewall Pettingill, Jr., who gave the most precise directions to its location. But in spite of the careful pinpointing of the nest, it took considerable searching through binoculars to detect the bird sitting on her eggs in the very middle of an abandoned trail exactly halfway between a large spruce blocking the trail and a sawdust pile.

Once a common breeding bird, only scattered pairs are found in the remaining woodlots of the Concord region today.]

JUNE 20. [1840]   The note of the whip-poor-will, borne over the fields, is the voice with which the woods and moonlight woo me.

JUNE 13. [1851]   It is not nightfall till the whip-poor-wills begin to sing.

JUNE 14. [1851]   Now the sun is fairly gone, I hear the dreaming frog, and the whip-poor-will from some *darker* wood. . . .

From Conant's summit I hear as many as fifteen whip-poor-wills—or whip-I-wills—at once, the succeeding cluck sounding strangely foreign, like a hewer at work elsewhere.

SEPT. 9. [1851]   [To Conantum by moonlight.] The whip-poor-wills now begin to sing in earnest about half an hour before sunrise, as if making haste to improve the short time that is left them. As far as my observation goes, they sing for several hours in the early part of the night, are silent commonly at midnight,—though you may meet [them] then sitting on a rock or flitting silently about,—then sing again just before sunrise.

COMMON NIGHTHAWK *(Chordeiles minor)*

[The aerial courtship flights of this species are beautiful to watch. The male plunges toward the earth until it seems that he will crash; but in time he zooms upward sharply with a booming sound, which has caused him to be called the Booming Nighthawk.

Thoreau found something rather mysterious about these slim-winged birds. Their bills are tiny but their mouths open to prodigious width, for they feed by swooping through the air with their mouths open and scooping in insects. Had he found the young birds when they were half-grown he would have been sure they were mysterious. Then the young birds have not only huge mouths but inside they are a smoky gray-blue color. When approached, they open their huge mouths and jump toward the intruder. The intruder instinctively retreats quickly from these tiny, helpless creatures.

This once-abundant species is steadily decreasing, though it is regularly recorded on migration at Concord. The last nesting record in that area was made in 1887.]

JUNE 23. [1851]   It is a pleasant sound to me, the squeaking and the booming of nighthawks flying over high open fields in the woods. They fly like butterflies, not to avoid birds of prey, but apparently, to secure their own insect prey. There is a particular part of the railroad just below the shanty where they may be heard and seen in greatest numbers. But often you must look a long while before you can detect the mote in the sky from which the note proceeds.

JUNE 1. [1853]   Walking up this side-hill, I disturbed a nighthawk eight or ten feet from me, which went, half-fluttering, half hopping, the mottled creature, like a winged toad, as Nuttall says the French of Louisiana (?) call them, down the hill as far as I could see. Without moving, I looked about and saw its two eggs on the bare ground, on a slight shelf of the hill, on the dead pine-needles and sand, without any cavity or nest whatever, very obvious when once you had detected them, but not easily detected from their color, a coarse gray formed of white spotted with a bluish or slaty brown, or umber,—a stone—granite-color, like the places it selects. I advanced and put my hand on them, and while I stooped, seeing a shadow on the ground, looked up and saw the bird, which had fluttered down the hill so blind and helpless, circling low and swiftly past over my head, showing the white spot on each wing in true nighthawk fashion. When I had gone a dozen rods, it appeared again higher in the air, with its peculiar flitting, limping kind of flight, all the while noiseless, and suddenly descending, it dashed at me within ten feet of my head, like an imp of darkness, then swept away high over the pond, dashing now to this side, now to that, on different tacks, as if, in pursuit of its prey, it had already forgotten its eggs on the earth. I can see how it might easily come to be regarded with superstitious awe.

JUNE 7. [1853]   Visited my nighthawk on her nest. Could hardly believe my eyes when I stood within seven feet and beheld her sitting on her eggs, her head to me. She looked so Saturnian, so one with the earth, so sphinx-like, a relic of the reign of Saturn which Jupiter did not destroy, a riddle that might well cause a man to go dash his head against a stone. It was not an actual living creature, far less a winged creature of the air, but a figure in stone or bronze, a fanciful production of art, like the gryphon or phoenix. In fact, with its breast toward me, and owing to its color or size no bill perceptible, it looked like the end [of] a brand, such as are common in a clearing, its breast mottled or alternately waved with dark brown and gray, its flat, grayish, weather-beaten crown, its eyes nearly closed, purposely, lest those bright beads should betray it, with the stony cunning of the sphinx. A fanciful work in bronze to ornament a mantel. It was enough to fill one with awe. The sight of this creature sitting on its eggs impressed me with the venerableness of the globe. There was nothing novel about it. All the while, this seemingly sleeping bronze sphinx, as motionless as the earth, was watching me with intense anxiety through those narrow slits in its eyelids. Another step, and it fluttered down the hill close to the ground, with a wabbling motion, as if touching the ground now with the tip of one wing, now with the other, so ten rods to the water, which [it] skimmed close over a few rods, then rose and soared in the air above me. Wonderful creature, which sits motionless on its eggs on the barest, most exposed hills, through pelting storms of rain or hail, as if it were a rock or a part of the earth itself, the outside of the globe, with its eyes shut and its wings folded, and, after the two days' storm, when you think it has become a fit symbol of the rheumatism, it suddenly rises into the air as a bird, one of the most aerial, supple, and graceful of creatures, without stiffness, in its wings or joints! It was a fit prelude to meeting Prometheus bound to his rock on Caucasus.

JUNE 17. [1853]   One of the nighthawk's eggs is hatched. The young is unlike any that I have seen, exactly like a pinch of rabbit's fur or down of that color dropped on the ground, not two inches long, with a dimpling or geometrical or somewhat regular arrangement of minute feathers in the middle, destined to become the wings and tail. Yet even it half opened its eye, and peeped if I mistake not. Was ever bird more completely protected, both by the color of its eggs and of its own body, that sits on them, and of the young bird just hatched? Accordingly the eggs and young are rarely discovered. There was one egg still, and by the side of it this little pinch of down, flattened out and not observed at first, and a foot down the hill had rolled a half of the egg it came out of. There was no callowness, as in the young of most birds. It seemed a singular place for a bird to begin its life,—to come out of its egg,—this little pinch of down,—and lie still on the exact spot where the egg lay, on a flat exposed shelf on the side of a bare hill, with nothing but the whole heavens, the broad universe above, to brood it when its mother was away.

CHIMNEY SWIFT *(Chaetura pelagica)*

[Though frequently called swallows, swifts are related not to that graceful family, but to hummingbirds. Their long paddlelike wings enable them to fly faster than other birds, but they usually dash about erratically rather than flying in a straight line. The reason for this is that they scoop up insects as they fly through the air. They rarely perch except in their nest cavities. Though most swifts still nest in natural cavities, Chimney Swifts have made use of chimneys and other such structures made by man.

While the Chimney Swift is a common summer resident in Concord to-day, large groups are seldom seen. One of the largest known flocks of this species to pass over Concord was seen by William Brewster on September 13, 1877. This flock contained several hundred swifts.]

JUNE 8. [1855]   G. Brooks told me on June 1st that a few evenings before he saw as many as a thousand chimney swallows pour down into Goodnow's chimney.

JULY. 29. [1856]   Pratt gave me a chimney swallow's nest, which he says fell down Weston's chimney with young in it two or three days ago. As it comes to me, it is in the form of the segment of the circumference of a sphere whose diameter is three and a half inches, the segment being two plus wide, one side, of course, longer than the other. It bears a little soot on the inner side. It may have been placed against a slanting part of the chimney, or perhaps some of the outer edge is broken off. It is composed wholly of stout twigs, one to two inches long, one sixteenth to one eighth inch [in] diameter, held quasi cob-fashion, so as to form a sort of basketwork one third to one half inch thick, without any lining, at least in this, but very open to the air. These twigs, which are quite knubby, seem to be of the apple, elm, and the like, and are firmly fastened together by a very conspicuous whitish semi-transparent glue, which is laid on pretty copiously, sometimes extending continuously one inch. It reminds me of the edible nests of the Chinese swallow. Who knows but their edibleness is due to a similar glue secreted by the bird and used still more profusely in building its nest? The chimney swallow is said to break off the twigs as it flies.

RUBY-THROATED HUMMINGBIRD *(Archilochus colubris)*

[This bird, which weighs no more than a penny, is the smallest species which occurs in New England. The feathers on the throat of the male are black, but at certain angles the light is refracted and glows with a fiery red color.

The nest, so small that a bottle cap will cover it, is saddled on a branch. It is formed of bud scales and plant down, the latter often taken from the stems of cinnamon fern. Lichens cover the outside of the nest and are held in place with spider silk. The nest looks very much like a natural knot on the branch.

The two pea-sized eggs are white. The young are naked when hatched and it is an almost frightening sight to watch the female (the male does not come to the nest) feed them by regurgitation, for she thrusts her needle-sharp bill into the delicate throats of the young. Her repeated jabbing motions are so violent that it seems as if she will impale the feeble creatures she feeds.]

June 23. [1853] Again I saw and heard the hummingbird visit the blue flags. He announces himself by a sudden loud humming.

May 22. [1854] A hummingbird dashes by like a loud bumblebee.

May 17. [1856] I hear the loud hum and see a splendid male hummingbird coming zigzag in long tacks, like a bee, but far swifter, along the edge of the swamp, in hot haste. He turns aside to taste the honey of the *Andromeda calyculata* (already visited by bees) within a rod of me. This golden-green gem. Its burnished back looks as if covered with green scales dusted with gold. It hovers, as it were stationary in the air, with an intense humming before each little flower-bell of the humble *Andromeda calyculata*, and inserts its long tongue in each, turning toward me that splendid ruby on its breast, that glowing ruby. Even this is coal-black in some lights! Then, along with me in the deep, wild swamp above the andromeda, amid the spruce. Its hum was heard afar at first, like that of a large bee, bringing a larger summer. This sight and sound would make me think I was in the tropics,—in Demerara or Maracaibo.

May 29. [1857] Soon I hear the low all-pervading hum of an approaching hummingbird circling above the rock, which afterward I mistake several times for the gruff voices of men approaching, unlike as these sounds are in some respects, and I perceive the resemblance even when I know better. Now I am sure it is a hummingbird, and now that it is two farmers approaching. But presently the hum becomes more sharp and thrilling, and the little fellow suddenly perches on an ash twig within a rod of me, and plumes himself while the rain is fairly beginning. He is quite out of proportion to the size of his perch. It does not acknowledge his weight.

July 9. [1860] There is a smart shower at 5 p.m., and in the midst of it a hummingbird is busy about the flowers in the garden unmindful of it though you would think that each big drop that struck him would be a serious accident.

Belted Kingfisher *(Megaceryle alcyon)*

[This is truly a continent-spanning species, for it nests in suitable habitat from Alaska to Labrador and south to the Gulf of Mexico. Its nest is made at the end of a hole three or four feet long, dug in a bank, road-cut, or river bluff. It lays from five to eight white eggs in a clutch.

Their shaggy heads, crested, look disproportionately large. Their pinkish toes are very short and blunt, looking as if they had been cut off.]

MAY 10. [1854]   Above the railroad bridge I saw a kingfisher twice sustain himself in one place, about forty feet above the meadow, by a rapid motion of his wings, somewhat like a devil's-needle, not progressing an inch, apparently over a fish.

APRIL 11. [1855]   Saw a kingfisher on a tree over the water. Does not its arrival mark some new movement in its finny prey? He is the bright buoy that betrays it!

APRIL 22. [1855]   The bluish band on the breast of the kingfisher leaves the pure white beneath in the form of a heart.

WOODPECKERS

[This is a large family having world-wide distribution. About twenty-two of the two hundred and ten species in the world occur in the United States.

Their bills are strong and chisel-like, and their nostrils are concealed by stiff bristles. Their tongues extend to a surprising length, have rather horny tips, and the sticky saliva aids in collecting food.

The tapping of a woodpecker can be a means of communication; it may indicate a bird searching for food; or it may indicate a bird chiseling a nest hole. Acute ears can often distinguish the reason for the tapping without seeing the bird.]

MARCH 3. [1852]   Moore's larch trees beyond Sleepy Hollow cut this winter. They were much decayed. The woodpeckers had stripped many of bark in pursuit of grubs. When the woodpeckers visit your trees in great numbers, you may suspect that it is time to cut them.

MARCH 22. [1853]   To Cliffs. The tapping of the woodpecker, *rat-tat-tat*, knocking at the door of some sluggish grub to tell him that the spring has arrived, and his fate, this is one of the season sounds, calling the roll of birds and insects, the reveille.

YELLOW-SHAFTED FLICKER *(Colaptes auratus)*

[The big, noisy flicker or pigeon woodpecker was a favorite of Thoreau. He enjoyed its loud calls, its drumming, and its handsome plumage. It brought the year around for him and its spring calls enlivened the woods for him. Flickers are the most conspicuous woodpeckers of Concord and occasionally are found nesting in trees along the streets of the town.

The fact that at least one hundred and twenty-five names have been applied to this species indicates how well-known it is. It feeds on the ground far more than other woodpeckers, and it eats vast numbers of ants. At least five thousand have been found in the stomach of a single flicker.]

APRIL 3. [1842] I have just heard the flicker among the oaks on the hillside ushering in a new dynasty. It is the age and youth of time. Why did Nature set this lure for sickly mortals: Eternity could not begin with more security and momentousness than the spring. The summer's eternity is reestablished by this note. All sights and sounds are seen and heard both in time and eternity. And when the eternity of any sight or sound strikes the eye or ear, they are intoxicated with delight.

JUNE 21. [1853] To-day I see two well-grown young woodpeckers about as big as the old, looking out at the hole, showing their handsome spotted breasts and calling lustily for something to eat, or, it may be, suffering from the heat. Young birds in some situations must suffer greatly from heat these days, so closely packed in their nests and perhaps insufficiently shaded. It is a wonder they remain so long there patiently. I saw a yellow-bird's nest in the willows on the causeway this afternoon and three young birds nearly ready to fly, overflowing the nest, all holding up their open bills and keeping them steadily open for a minute or more, on noise of my approach.

APRIL 27. [1856] Up Assabet. The tapping of a woodpecker is made a more remarkable and emphatic sound by the hollowness of the trunk, the expanse of water which conducts the sound, and the morning hour at which I commonly hear it. I think that the pigeon woodpeckers must be building, they frequent the old aspen now so much.

JUNE 10. [1856] In a hollow apple tree, hole eighteen inches deep, young pigeon woodpeckers, large and well feathered. They utter their squeaking hiss whenever I cover the hole with my hand, apparently taking it for the approach of the mother. A strong, rank fetid smell issues from the hole.

MARCH 17. [1858] Ah! there is the note of the first flicker, a prolonged, monotonous *wick-wick-wick-quick-quick-quick*, etc., or, if you please, *quick-quick*, heard far over and through the dry leaves. But how that single sound peoples and enriches all the woods and fields! They are no longer the same woods and fields that they were. This note really *quickens* what was dead.

It seems to put life into withered grass and leaves and bare twigs, and henceforth the days shall not be as they have been. It is as when a family, your neighbors, return to an empty house after a long absence, and you hear the cheerful hum of voices and the laughter of children, and see the smoke from the kitchen fire. The doors are thrown open, and children go screaming through the hall. So the flicker dashes through the aisles of the grove, throws up a window here and cackles out it, and then there, airing the house. It makes its voice ring up-stairs and down-stairs, and so, as it were, fits it for its habitation and ours, and takes possession. It is as good as a housewarming to all nature.

HAIRY WOODPECKER *(Dendrocopos villosus)*

[This white-backed woodpecker is about the size of a robin. The males have a bright red spot on the nape. They prefer forests, but in the autumn and winter many move into more open country and even come to villages.

Thoreau's admiration for apple trees had a by-product other than the apples they gave him. Many species of birds nest in apple trees, and in both the following selections he describes encounters with Hairy Woodpeckers among those trees.

Once a common breeding bird in Concord, this species, with the destruction of the forests, has become uncommon. It is most abundant during the winter.]

JUNE 4. [1857]   P.M.—To Bare Hill. In that first apple tree at Wyman's an apparent hairy woodpecker's nest (from the size of the bird), about ten feet from ground. The bird darts away with a shrill, loud chirping of alarm, incessantly repeated, long before I get there, and keeps it up as long as I stay in the neighborhood. The young keep up an incessant fine, breathing peep which can be heard across the road and is much increased when they hear you approach the hole, they evidently expecting the old bird. I perceive no offensive odor. I saw the bird fly out of this hole, May 1st, and probably the eggs were laid about that time.

MAY 18. [1860]   P.M.—To Walden. A hairy woodpecker betrays its hole in an apple tree by its anxiety. The ground is strewn with the chips it has made, over a large space. The hole, so far as I can see, is exactly like that of the downy woodpecker,—the entrance (though not so round) and the conical form within above,—only larger.

The bird scolds at me from a dozen rods off.

Downy Woodpecker *(Dendrocopos pubescens)*

[This species, which looks so much like the Hairy Woodpecker and is not enough smaller for size to be a good field mark, also nested in apple trees about Concord.

It chisels its nest cavity, often choosing a dead branch on an otherwise living tree, and in this lays four or five white eggs.

As young woodpeckers approach the age when they will leave the nest, they often become quite noisy and many a nest is discovered by keen ears rather than sharp eyes.]

JAN. 8. [1854] P.M.—To the Spruce Swamp in front of J. Farmer's. Can go across both rivers now. New routes are more practicable. Stood within a rod of a downy woodpecker on an apple tree. How curious and exciting the blood-red spot on its hindhead! I ask why it is there, but no answer is rendered by these snow-clad fields. It is so close to the bark I do not see its feet. It looks behind as if it had on a black cassock open behind and showing a white undergarment between the shoulders and down the back. It is briskly and incessantly tapping all round the dead limbs, but rare twice in a place, as if to sound the tree and so see if it has any worm in it, or perchance to start them. How much he deals with the bark of trees, all his life long tapping and inspecting it! He it is that scatters those fragments of bark and lichens about on the snow at the base of trees. What a lichenist he must be! Or rather, perhaps it is fungi makes his favorite study, for he deals most with dead limbs. How briskly he glides up or drops himself down a limb, creeping round and round, and hopping from limb to limb, and now flitting with a rippling sound of his wings to another tree!

JUNE 20. [1856] To Baker Farm. Walking under an apple tree in the little Baker Farm peach orchard, heard an incessant shrill musical twitter or peeping, as from young birds, over my head, and, looking up, saw a hole in an upright dead bough, some fifteen feet from the ground. Climbed up and, finding that the shrill twitter came from it, guessed it to be the nest of a downy woodpecker, which proved to be the case,—for it reminded me of the hissing squeak or squeaking hiss of young pigeon woodpeckers, but this was more musical or bird-like. The bough was about four and a half inches in diameter, and the hole perfectly circular, about an inch and a quarter in diameter. Apparently nests had been in holes above, now broken out, higher up. When I put my fingers in it, the young breathed their shrill twitter louder than ever. Anon the old appeared, and came quite near, while I stood in the tree, keeping up an incessant loud and shrill scolding note, and also after I descended; not to be relieved.

BLACK-BACKED THREE-TOED WOODPECKER
(Picoides arcticus)

[All bird watchers have experienced the delight Thoreau felt when he discovered a species that was new to him. This woodpecker seldom appears in the Concord area, but these had been attracted by the burned tract. After fires they often come to flake off the bark to obtain bark-boring beetles. Trees killed when beaver dams flood an area, or when an infestation of spruce budworm or larch sawfly occurs over a large area, also pull these northern woodpeckers south of their usual range.

The Black-backed Three-toed Woodpecker has been found nesting in the Katahdin region of Maine which Thoreau visited several times. It prefers to nest in a tree close to an opening in a forest. Like most birds that nest in holes, this woodpecker has white eggs, usually four in a clutch. Until recently, it was called the Arctic Three-toed Woodpecker.]

OCT. 8. [1860]   Standing by a pigeon-place on the north edge [of] Damon's lot, I saw on the dead top of a white pine four or five rods off—which had been stripped for fifteen feet downward that it might die and afford with its branches a perch for the pigeons about the place, like the more artificial ones that were set up—two woodpeckers that were new to me. They uttered a peculiar sharp *kek kek* on alighting (not so sharp as that of the hairy or downy woodpecker) and appeared to be about the size of the hairy woodpecker, or between that and the golden-winged. I had a good view of them with my glass as long as I desired. With the back to me, they were clear black all above, as well as their feet and bills, and each had a yellow or orange (possibly orange-scarlet?) front (the anterior part of the head at the base of the upper mandible). A long white line along the side of head to the neck, with a black one below it. The breast, as near as I could see, was gray specked with white, and the under side of the wing expanded was also gray, with small white spots. The throat white and vent also white or whitish. Is this the arctic three-toed? Probably many trees dying on this large burnt tract will attract many woodpeckers to it.

EASTERN KINGBIRD *(Tyrannus tyrannus)*

[This is the most definitely patterned of the Concord flycatchers. Its tail is black with a white terminal band. It is slate above, with a large dark head. It flies with stiff, quivering wings. Though it has a red streak on its crown, this is not usually visible.

Poultry raisers like to have kingbirds nest with them, for they will not hesitate to attack and drive away the large hawks—incidently protecting the farmer's chickens. Bee keepers, on the other hand, object to their presence, for they take so many honey bees that they are sometimes called bee martins.

The Eastern Kingbird was a very common breeding bird in Thoreau's day. According to Griscom in *Birds of Concord,* a decline in numbers in that area set in about 1895. This decline has continued slowly to the present time.]

JULY 16. [1851]   I hear the kingbird twittering or chattering like a stout-chested swallow.

JULY 22. [1851]   The pewee and kingbird are killing bees, perched on a post or a dead twig.

MAY 29. [1853]   How still the hot noon ; people have retired behind blinds. Yet the kingbird—lively bird, with belly and tail edged with white, and with its lively twittering—stirs and keeps the air brisk.

JUNE 5. [1854]   I see at a distance a kingbird or blackbird pursuing a crow lower down the hill, like a satelite revolving about a black planet.

AUG. 5. [1858]   Up river to Pantry Brook. The kingbird, by his activity and lively note and his white breast, keeps the air sweet. He sits now on a dead willow twig, akin to the flecks of mackerel sky, or its reflection in the water, or the white clamshell, wrong side out, opened by a musquash, or the fine particles of white quartz that may be found in the muddy river's sand. He is here to give a voice to all these. The willow's dead twig is aerial perch enough for him. Even the swallows deign to perch on it.

AUG. 6. [1858]   P.M.—Walk to Boulder Field. If our sluggish river, choked with potamogeton, might seem to have the slow-flying bittern for its peculiar genius, it has also the sprightly and aerial kingbird to twitter over and lift our thoughts to clouds as white as its own breast.

EASTERN PHOEBE *(Sayornis phoebe)*

[Phoebes, the first flycatchers to arrive in Concord in spring, are often called pewees or bridge pewees. Since the Wood Pewee would not be expected before the first week in May, all earlier dates of "pewees" may safely be attributed to the phoebe.

It wags its tail so regularly and emphatically that this is an important clue to the identification of the bird. It builds it moss-decked nest on cliffs,

in shallow caves, under bridges, and on ledges outside, or inside on rafters
of farm buildings.

There has been a decrease of breeding Eastern Phoebes in Concord
throughout the century since Thoreau recorded their appearance there in
the spring. A number of factors have contributed to the decline ranging
from winter kills due to cold in the south to increased use of pesticides
both on their breeding and wintering grounds.]

APRIL 2. [1852]   What ails the pewee's tail? It is loosely hung, pulsating
with life. What mean these way-tail birds? Cats and dogs, too, express some
of their life through their tails.

APRIL 2. [1856]   Just beyond Wood's Bridge, I hear the pewee. With what
confidence after the lapse of many months, I come out to this waterside,
some warm and pleasant spring morning, and, listening, hear, from farther
or nearer, through the still concave of the air, the note of the first pewee!
If there is one within half a mile, it will be here, and I shall be sure to
hear its simple notes from those trees, borne over the water. It is remarkable how large a mansion of the air you can explore with your ears in the
still morning by the waterside.

MAY 5. [1860]   See at Lee's a pewee (phoebe) building. She has just woven
in or laid on the edge, a fresh sprig of saxifrage in flower. I notice that
phoebes will build in the same recess in a cliff year after year. It is a constant thing here, though they are often disturbed. Think how many pewees
must have built under the eaves of this cliff since pewees were created and
this cliff itself built! You can possibly find the crumbling relices of how
many, if you should look carefully enough! It takes us many years to find
out that Nature repeats herself annually. But how perfectly regular and
calculable all her phenomena must appear to the mind that has observed
for a thousand years!

EASTERN WOOD PEWEE *(Contopus virens)*

[This species, like other members of the flycatcher family, likes to sally
forth from a perch to catch a passing insect and then return to the same
twig. This habit must have given Thoreau considerable pleasure, for he was
able to watch their behavior for long periods at a time.

Thoreau regarded this species as a common breeding bird in Concord,
where it inhabited not only the wooded sections but moved into apple
orchards. It abandoned the latter when House Sparrows arrived there in
numbers. Since then, the deterioration of the Concord forests has further

reduced its numbers. It became rare after the hurricane of 1938 and is still an uncommon summer bird.]

MAY 23. [1854]   The wood pewee sings now in the woods behind the spring in the heat of the day (2 P.M.), sitting on a low limb near me, *pe-a-wee, pe-a-wee*, etc., five or six times at short and regular intervals, looking about all the while, and then, naively, *pee-a-oo*, emphasizing the first syllable, and begins again. The last is, in emphasis, like the scream of a hen-hawk. It flies off occasionally a few feet, and catches an insect and returns to its perch between the bars, not allowing this to interrupt their order.

AUG. 14. [1858]   To the one-arched bridge. I have not been out early nor late, nor attended particularly to the birds. The more characteristic notes would appear to be the wood pewee's and the goldfinch's, with the squeal of young hawks. These might be called the pewee-days.

OLIVE-SIDED FLYCATCHER *(Nuttallornis borealis)*

[This nearly robin-sized flycatcher has a large head and a short tail. It is usually seen on the tip of the tallest tree in the area. It likes small lakes and bogs set in coniferous forests.

During the breeding season its *hic three-beers* is whistled loudly. Later in the season it repeats over and over again *pep-pep-pep* and seems an integral part of northern evergreen forests.

Though Brewster believed the species to nest in Concord as late as 1876, he failed to give concrete evidence of a definite breeding pair. It is now rarely seen there even during migration periods.]

MAY 15. [1855]   I hear from the top of a pitch pine in the swamp that loud, clear, familiar whistle which I have sometimes wrongly referred to the wood pewee,—*whip-ter-phe-ee*. Is it the whip-tom-kelly note which Sloane and Wilson gave to the red-eye, but which Nuttall says he never heard from it? Sometimes *ter-phee-e*. This is repeated at considerable intervals, the bird sitting quite still a long time. I saw it dart out once, catch an insect, and return to its perch muscicapa-like. As near as I could see it had a white throat, was whitish, streaked with dark, beneath, darker tail and wings, and maybe olivaceous shoulders; bright-yellow within bill.

MAY 29. [1857]   [A violent thunder-storm at Lee's Cliff.] The crashing thunder sounds like the overhauling of lumber on heaven's loft. And now, at last, after an hour of steady confinement, the clouds grow thin again, and the birds begin to sing. They make haste to conclude the day with their regular evening songs (before the rain is fairly over) according to the program. The pepe on some pine tree was heard almost in the midst of the storm.

JUNE 6. [1857]   As I sit on Lee's Cliff, I see a pe-pe on the topmost dead branch of a hickory eight or ten rods off. Regularly, at short intervals, it utters its monotonous note like *till-till-till* or *pe-pe-pe*. Looking round for its prey and occasionally changing its perch, it every now and then darts off (phoebe-like), even five or six rods, toward the earth to catch an insect, and then returns to its favorite perch. If I lose it for a moment, I soon see it settling on the dead twigs again and hear its *till, till, till*. It appears through the glass mouse-colored above and head (which is perhaps darker), white throat, and narrow white beneath, with no white on tail.

HORNED LARK *(Eremophila alpestris)*

[This species has benefitted by man's misuse of the land by overgrazing, lumbering, plowing, and general soil improverishment. It demands bare, unattractive country and leaves when good cover develops. In Thoreau's day these birds, in New England, were usually confined more or less to the ocean shore and islands such as Nantucket. They are much more widespread in the northeast to-day.]

MARCH 24. [1858]   P.M.—To Fair Haven Pond, east side. Returning about 5 P.M. across the Depot Field, I scare up from the ground a flock of about twenty birds, which fly low, making a short circuit to another part of the field. At first they remind me of bay-wings, except that they are in a flock, show no white in tail, are, I see, a little larger, and utter a faint *sveet sveet* merely, a sort of sibilant *chip*. Starting them again, I see that they have black tails, very conspicuous when they pass near. They fly in a flock somewhat like snow buntings, occasionally one surging upward a few feet in pursuit of another, and they alight about where they were first. It [is] almost impossible to discover them on the ground, they squat so flat and so much resemble it, running amid the stubble. But at length I stand within two rods of one and get a good view of its markings with my glass. They are the *Alauda alpestris*, or shore lark, quite a handsome bird.

SWALLOWS

[Swallows have a world-wide distribution. There are seventy-five species and of the eleven found in North America, six occur in Concord, and Thoreau noted the presence of all but the Rough-winged Swallow.

Birds in the swallow family have a small, flattened bill with a wide gape. Their wings are long and pointed. Legs are short and the toes are small and weak. They all feed by pursuing insects through the air and catching them in their open mouths.]

JULY 23. [1851]   The swallow's twitter is the sound of the lapsing waves of the air, or when they break and burst, as his wings represent the ripple. He has more air in his bones than other birds; his feet are defective. The fish of the air. His note is the voice of the air. As fishes may hear the sound of waves lapsing on the surface and see the outlines of the ripples, so we hear the note and see the flight of the swallow.

AUG. 4. [1855]   Just after bathing at the rock near the island this afternoon, after sunset, I saw a flock of thousands of barn swallows, and some white-bellied, and perhaps others, for it was too dark to distinguish them. They came flying over the river in loose array, wheeled and flew round in a great circle over the bay there, about eighty feet high, with a loud twittering as if seeking a resting place, then flew up the stream. I was very much surprised at their numbers. Directly after, hearing a buzzing sound, we found them all alighted on the dense golden willow hedge at Shattuck's shore, parallel with the shore, quite densely leaved and eighteen feet high. They were generally perched five or six feet from the top, amid the thick leaves, filling it for eight or ten rods. They were very restless, fluttering from one perch to another and about on another, and kept up a loud and remarkable buzzing or squeaking, breathing or hum, with only occasionally a regular twitter, now and then flitting alongside from one end of the row to the other. It was so dark we had to draw close to see them. At intervals they were perfectly still for a moment, as if at a signal. At length, after twenty or thirty minutes of bustle and hum, they all settled quietly to rest on their perches, I supposed for the night. We had rowed up within a rod of one end of the row, looking up so as to bring the birds between us and the sky, but they paid not the slightest attention to us. What was remarkable was: first, their numbers; second, their perching on densely leaved willows; third, their buzzing or humming, like a hive of bees, even squeaking notes; and fourth, their disregarding our nearness. I supposed that they were preparing to migrate, being the early broods.

AUG. 5. [1855]   4 A.M.—On river to see swallows. They are all gone; yet Fay saw them there last night after we passed. Probably they started very early. I asked Minott if he ever saw swallows migrating, not telling him what I had seen, and he said that [he] used to get up and go out to mow very early in the morning on his meadow, as early as he could see to strike, and once at that hour, hearing a noise, he looked up and could just distinguish high overhead fifty thousand swallows. He thought it was in the latter part of August.

What I saw is like what White says of the swallows, in the autumn, roosting "every night in the osier beds of the aits" of the river Thames; and his editor, Jesse, says, "Swallows in countless numbers still assemble every autumn on the willows growing on the aits of the river Thames." And Jardine, in his notes to Wilson, says that a clergyman of Rotherham describes in an anonymous pamphlet their assembling (in the words of the pamphlet) "at the willow ground, on the banks of the canal, preparatory to their migration," early in September, 1815, daily increasing in numbers until there were tens of thousands. Divided into bands every morning and sought their food. They finally left R. the 7th of October.

MAY 20. [1858] P.M.—Up Assabet. A cloudy afternoon, with a cool east wind producing a mist. Hundreds of swallows are now skimming close over the river, at its broadest part, where it is shallow and runs the swiftest, just below the Island, for a distance of twenty rods. There are bank, barn, cliff, and chimney swallows, all mingled together and continually scaling back and forth,—a very lively sight. They keep descending or stooping to within inches of the water on a curving wing, without quite touching it, and I suppose are attracted by some small insects which hover close over it. They also stoop low about me as I stand on the flat island there, but I do not perceive the insects. They rarely rise more than five feet above the surface, and a general twittering adds to the impression of sociability. The principle note is the low grating sound of the bank swallow, and I hear the *vit vit* of the barn swallow. The cliff swallow, then is here. Are the insects in any measure confined to that part of the river? Or are they congregated for the sake of society? I have also in other years noticed them over another swift place, at Hubbard's Bath, and also, when they first come, in smaller numbers, over the still and smooth water under the lee of the Island wood. They are thick as the gnats which perhaps they catch. Swallows are more confident and fly nearer to man than most birds. It may be because they are more protected by the sentiment and superstitions of man.

TREE SWALLOW *(Iridoprocne bicolor)*

[Thoreau always referred to the Tree Swallow as the white-bellied swallow, certainly a descriptive name for it. This species and the Purple Martin both accept bird houses, but the latter prefers an apartment type of house while the Tree Swallow wants to nest by itself. It also nests in natural cavities in trees or uses abandoned woodpecker holes.

When nesting has ended, Tree Swallows gather into huge flocks and often remain together throughout the winter in the South. Bayberry and Wax Myrtle berries are an important winter food. Their spectacular aerial maneuvers when ready to migrate are sights to remember.]

JUNE 12. [1852]   Small white-bellied (?) swallows in a row (a dozen) on the telegraph-wire over the water by the bridge. This perch is little enough departure from unobstructed air to suit them. Pluming themselves. If you could furnish a perch aerial enough, even birds of paradise would alight. Swallows have forked tails, and wings and tails are about the same length. They do not alight on trees, methinks, unless on dead and bare boughs, but stretch a wire over water and they perch on it. This is among the phenomena that cluster about the telegraph.

JUNE 14. [1855]   Up river. I told C. [Channing] to look into an old mortise-hole in Wood's Bridge for a white-bellied swallow's nest, as we were paddling under; but he laughed, incredulous. I insisted, and when he climbed up he scared out the bird. Five eggs. "You see the feathers about, do you not?" "Yes," said he.

BANK SWALLOW *(Riparia riparia)*

[This small brown-backed swallow nests in colonies. Far from being confined to North America, it is a nesting bird in Europe, Siberia, northwest Africa, parts of the Near East, northwest Indian, and Japan. Since its nest requirements are so specialized, it is surprising that it has such an intercontinental distribution. Natural steep sandy banks have a way of sliding down, or being swept away by floods. Man makes many steep-sided cuts in the land and these are frequently used by Bank Swallows. But those man-made banks are frequently changed by fresh slicing of the land, and nests are thus destroyed.

Their food is entirely insectivorous and as they feed, the Bank Swallows usually fly rather near the ground with a fluttery, erratic, twisting flight.]

MAY 7. [1856]   In the first hollow in the bank this side of Clamshell, where sand has been dug for the meadow, are a hundred or more bank swallows at 2 P.M. (I suspect I have seen them for some time) engaged in prospecting and digging their holes and circling about. It is a snug place for them,—though the upright portion of the bank is only four or five feet high,—a semi-circular recess facing the southeast. Some are within scratching out the sand,—I see it cast out of the holes behind them,— others hanging on to the entrance of the holes, others on the flat sandy space beneath in front, and others circling about, a dozen rods off over the meadow. Theirs is a low, dry, grating twitter, or rather rattle, less metallic or musical than the *vite vite* and twittering notes of barn and white-bellied swallows. They are white-bellied, dark-winged and tailed, with a crescent of white [sic] nearly around the lower part of the neck, and mouse-colored heads and backs. The upper and greater part of this bank is a coarse sliding gravel, and they build only in the perpendicular and sandy part (I sit and watch them within three or four rods) and close to the upper part of it. While I am looking, they all suddenly with one consent take to wing, and circle over the hillside and meadow, as if they chose to work at making their holes a little while at a time only. I find the holes on an average about a foot deep only as yet, some but a few inches.

JAN. 24. [1858]   Nut Meadow Brook. Between winter and summer there is, to my mind, an immeasurable interval. As, when I pry into the old bank swallows' holes to-day,—see the marks of their bills and even whole eggs left at the bottom,—it affects me as the phenomena of a former geological period. Yet perchance the very swallow which laid those eggs will revisit this hole next spring. The upper side of his gallery is a low arch, quite firm and durable.

BARN SWALLOW *(Hirundo rustica)*

[Since this country was settled by Europeans, Barn Swallows have almost entirely abandoned the caves and overhanging cliffs they once used as nesting sites and have moved into barns, under porches, and similar places. They are such energetic birds they reduce appreciably the flying insects about farm buildings and deserve all the protection man can give them.

When the nesting season is over, most of the Barn Swallows of the United States go to Panama or farther south to spend the winter.]

AUG. 17. [1851]   It has promised rain all day; cloudy and still and rather cool; from time to time a few drops gently spitting but no shower. The landscape wears a sober autumnal look. I hear a drop or two on my hat. I wear a thick coat. The birds seem to know that it will not rain just yet. The swallows skim low over the pastures, twittering as they fly near me with forked tail, dashing near me as if I scared up insects for them.

MAY 20. [1852]   So many birds that I have not attended much to any of late. A barn swallow accompanied me across the Depot Field, methinks attracted by the insects which I started, though I saw them not, wheeling and tacking incessantly on all sides and repeatedly dashing within a rod of me. It is an agreeable sight to watch one. Nothing lives in the air but is in rapid motion.

CLIFF SWALLOW *(Petrochelidon pyrrhonota)*

[It is a surprise to have Thoreau refer to this species as the *new* swallow, for it is well known to most New Englanders. Reference to ornithological history shows that it was unknown to Wilson and all earlier ornithologists except for a note by Forster in 1772 in which he called it Hirundo 35. Thomas Say named and described it from a specimen taken on Long's Expedition to the Rocky Mountains in 1820.

The name "Republican Swallow" originated with Audubon, who first saw the species at Henderson on the Ohio River in 1815. He wrote (1831): "I drew up a description at the time, naming the species *Hirundo republicana*, the republican swallow, in allusion to the mode in which individuals associate, for the purpose of forming their nests and rearing their young."]

JUNE 3. [1850] I saw in Sudbury twenty-five nests of the new (cliff?) swallow under the eaves of a barn. They seemed particularly social and loquacious neighbors, though their voices are rather squeaking. Their nests, built side by side, looked somewhat like large hornets' nests, enough so to prove a sort of connection. Their activity, sociability, and chattiness make them fit pensioners and neighbors of man—summer companions—for the barn-yard.

BLUE JAY *(Cyanocitta cristata)*

[In his early years of bird watching, Thoreau did not care much for Blue Jays, which he considered greedy. As his understanding of wildlife matured, he realized that jays play an invaluable part in forest health by planting seeds which result in a constant growth of young trees.

Due to the declining of suitable woodlands, resident Blue Jays have moved into the Concord estates, and during the winter they are regular visitors to feeding shelves. Their numbers are fewer by far than when Thoreau watched them carry away acorns.]

Nov. 16. [1850] I hear deep amid the birches some row among the birds or the squirrels, where evidently some mystery is being developed to them. The jay is on the alert, mimicking every woodland note. What *has* happened? Who's dead? The twitter retreats before you, and you are never let into the secret. Some tragedy surely is being enacted, but murder will out. How many little dramas are enacted in the depth of the woods at which man is not present.

DEC. 31. [1850]   The blue jays evidently notify each other of the presence of an intruder, and will sometimes make a great chattering about it, and so communicate the alarm to other birds and to beasts.

FEB. 2. [1854]   Up river on ice to Clematis Brook. The scream of the jay is a true winter sound. It is wholly without sentiment, and in harmony with winter.

FEB. 12. [1854]   The earth must be resonant if bare, and you hear the lisping tinkle of chickadees from time to time and the unrelenting steel-cold scream of a jay, unmelted, that never flows into a song, a sort of wintry trumpet, screaming cold; hard, tense, frozen music, like the winter sky itself; in the blue livery of winter's band. It is like a flourish of trumpets in the winter sky. There is no hint of incubation in the jay's scream. Like the creak of a cart-wheel. There is no cushion for sounds now. They tear our ears.

NOV. 3. [1858]   The jay is the bird of October. I have seen it repeatedly flitting amid the bright leaves, of a different color from them all and equally bright, and taking its flight from grove to grove. It, too, with its bright color, stands for some ripeness in the bird harvest. And its scream! it is as if it blowed on the edge of an October leaf. It is never more in its element and at home than when flitting amid these brilliant colors. No doubt it delights in bright color, and so has begged for itself a brilliant coat. It is not gathering seeds from the sod, too busy to look around, while fleeing the country. It is wide awake to what is going on, on the *qui vive*. It flies to some bright tree and bruits its splendors abroad.

NOV. 13. [1858]   I see some feathers of a blue jay scattered along a wood-path, and at length come to the body of the bird. What a neat and delicately ornamental creature, finer than any work of art in a lady's boudoir, with its soft light purplish-blue crest and its dark blue or purplish secondaries (the narrow half) finely barred with dusky. It is the more glorious to live in Concord because the jay is so splendidly painted.

OCT. 27. [1860]   [The white pine wood southeast of E. Wood's.] As I am coming out of this, looking for seedling oaks, I see a jay, which was scream-ing at me, fly to a white oak eight or ten rods from the wood in the pasture and directly alight on the ground, pick up an acorn, and fly back into the woods with it. This was one, perhaps the most effectual, way in which this wood was stocked with the numerous little oaks which I saw under that dense white pine grove. Where will you look for a jay sooner than in a dense pine thicket? It is there they commonly live, and build.

COMMON CROW *(Corvus brachyrhynchos)*

[The big black crow has adjusted to civilization and those who study the species find it a fascinating bird, as Thoreau surely did. In 1855 alone, he wrote at some length about the crow at least nine times.

Though they are abundant in Concord during migration, crows, formerly numerous as breeding birds, have become uncommon as a nesting species.]

JAN. 3. [1852]   The snow is so deep and the cold so intense that the crows are compelled to be very bold in seeking their food, and come very near the houses in the village. One is now walking about and pecking the dung in the street in front of Frank Monroe's. They remind me, as they sail along over the street, of the turkey buzzards of the South, and perhaps many hard winters in succession would make them as tame.

JAN. 12. [1855]   Perhaps what moves us in winter is some reminiscence of far-off summer. How we leap by the side of the open brooks! What beauty in the running brooks! What life! What society! The cold is merely superficial; it is summer still at the core, far, far within. It is in the cawing of the crow, the crowing of the cock, the warmth of the sun on our backs. I hear faintly the cawing of a crow far, far away, echoing from some unseen woodside, as if deadened by the springlike vapor which the sun is drawing from the ground. It mingles with the slight murmur of the village, the sound of children at play, as one stream empties gently into another, and the wild and tame are one. What a delicious sound! It is not merely crow calling to crow, for it speaks to me too. I am part of one great creature with him; if he has voice, I have ears. I can hear what he calls, and have engaged not to shoot nor stone him if he will caw to me each spring. On the other hand, it may be, is the sound of children at school saying their a, b, ab's, on the other, far in the wood-fringed horizon, the cawing of crows from their blessed eternal vacation, out at their long recess, children who have got dismissed! While the vaporous incense goes up from all fields of the spring, —if it were spring. Ah, bless the Lord, O my soul! bless him for wildness, for crows that will not alight within gunshot! and bless him for hens, too, that croak and cackle in the yard!

MAY 5. [1855]   Looking over my book, I found I had done my errands, and said to myself I would find a crow's nest. (I had heard a crow scold at a passing hawk a quarter of an hour before.) I had hardly taken this resolution when, looking up, I saw a crow wending his way across an interval in the woods toward the highest pines in the swamp, on which he alighted. I directed my steps to them, and was soon greeted with an angry *caw*, and, within five minutes from my resolve, I detected a new nest close to the top of the tallest white pine in the swamp. A crow circled cawing about it within gunshot, then over me surveying, and, perching on an oak directly over my head within thirty-five feet, cawed angrily. But suddenly, as if having taken a new resolution, it flitted away, and was joined by its mate and two more, and they went off silently a quarter of a mile or more and lit in a pasture, as if they had nothing to concern them in the wood.

MAY 11. [1855]   You can hardly walk in a thick pine wood now, especially a swamp, but presently you will have a crow or two over your head, either silently flitting over, to spy what you would be at and if its nest is in danger, or angrily cawing. It is most impressive when, looking for their nests, you first detect the presence of the bird by its shadow.

DEC. 15. [1855]   How like a bird of ill omen the crow behaves! Still holding its ground in our midst like a powwow that is not to be exterminated! Sometimes when I am going through the Deep Cut, I look up and see half a dozen black crows flitting silently across in front and ominously eying down; passing from one wood to another, yet as if their passage had reference to me.

JAN. 22. [1856]   Somebody has been fishing in the pond this morning, and the water in the holes is beginning to freeze. I see the track of a crow, the toes as usual less spread and the middle one making a more curved furrow in the snow than the partridge, as if they moved more unstably, recovering their balance,—feeble on their feet. The inner toe a little the nearest to the middle one. This track goes to every hole but one or two out of a dozen,— directly from hole to hole, sometimes flying a little,—and also to an apple-core on the snow. I am pretty sure that this bird was after the bait which is usually dropped on the ice or in the hole. E. Garfield says they come regularly to his holes for bait as soon as he has left. So, if the pickerel are not fed, it is. It had even visited, on the wing, a hole, now frozen and snowed up, which I made far from this in the middle of the pond several days since, as I discovered by its droppings, the same kind that it had left about the first holes. . . .

I brought home and examined some of the droppings of the crow. . . .

They were brown and dry, though partly frozen. After a long study with
a microscope, I discovered that they consisted of the seeds and skins and
other indigestible parts of red cedar berries and some barberries (I detected
the imbricated scale-like leaves of a berry stem and then the seeds and now
black skins of the cedar berries, but easily the large seeds of the barberries)
and perhaps something more, and I knew whence it had probably come,
i.e. from the cedar woods and barberry bushes by Flint's Pond. These, then,
make part of the food of crows in severe weather when the snow is deep,
as at present.

JAN. 24. [1856]   While the commentators and translators are disputing
about the meaning of this word or that, I hear only the resounding of the
ancient sea and put into it all the meaning I am possessed of, the deepest
murmurs I can recall, for I do not the least care where I get my ideas, or
what suggests them.

   I knew that a crow had that day plucked the cedar berries and barberries
by Flint's Pond and then flapped silently through the trackless air to Walden,
where it dined on fisherman's bait, though there was no living creature to
tell me.

FEB. 6. [1856]   Goodwin says that he has caught two crows this winter
in his traps set *in water* for mink, and baited with fish. The crows, probably
put to it for food and looking along the very few open brooks, attracted
by this bait, got their feet into the traps.

JAN. 22. [1859]   [A sudden thaw reveals thousands of dead insects and
spiders.] Crows which fared hard ten days ago must fare sumptuously now.
This will account for their tracks which I saw the other day leading to
every little bare strip [?] or exposed tuft of grass,—those warm days. Perhaps the caterpillars, etc., crawl forth in sunny and warm days in mid-
winter when the earth is bare, and so supply the birds, and are ready to
be washed away by a flow of water! . . . A sudden thaw is, then, a great
relief to crows and other birds that may have been put to it for food.
Their larders are now overstocked.

MARCH 4. [1859]   We stood still a few moments . . . and listened to hear
a spring bird. We heard only the jay screaming in the distance and the
cawing of a crow. What a perfectly New England sound is this voice of
the crow! If you stand perfectly still anywhere in the outskirts of the town
and listen, stilling the almost incessant hum of your own personal factory,
this is perhaps the sound which you will be most sure to hear rising above
all sounds of human industry and leading your thoughts to some far bay

in the woods where the crow is venting his disgust. This bird sees the white man come and the Indian withdraw, but it withdraws not. Its untamed voice is still heard above the tinkling of the forge. It sees a race pass away, but it passes not away. It remains to remind us of aboriginal nature.

DEC. 31. [1859]   Crows yesterday flitted silently, if not ominously, over the street, just after the snow had fallen, as if men, being further within, were just as far off as usual. This is a phenomenon of both cold weather and snowy. You hear nothing; you merely see these black apparitions, though they come near enough to look down your chimney and scent the boiling pot, and pass between the house and the barn.

BLACK-CAPPED CHICKADEE *(Parus atricapillus)*

[In *Walden* Thoreau told of the French Canadian woodchopper, Therien, who shared his lunch with the chickadees. He wrote, "In the winter he had a fire by which at noon he warmed his coffee in a kettle; and as he sat on a log to eat his dinner the chickadees would sometimes come round and alight on his arm and peck at the potato in his fingers; and he said that he 'liked to have the little *fellers* about him.' "

To-day many people share Therien's liking for chickadees and coax them to come to their windowsills in winter by offering them chopped nuts and other tidbits such as sunflower seeds and raisins. They are confiding little birds which readily accept humans as friendly creatures.

Thoreau frequently called chickadees titmice. These birds belong to the titmouse family.]

MARCH 10. [1852]   Heard the phoebe note of the chickadee to-day for the first time. I had at first heard their *day-day-day* ungratefully,—ah! you but carry my thoughts back to winter,—but anon I found that they too had become spring birds; they had changed their note. Even they feel the influence of spring.

DEC. 1. [1853]   To Cliffs. Those trees and shrubs which retain their withered leaves through the winter—shrub oaks and young white, red, and black oaks, the lower branches of larger trees of the last-mentioned species, hornbeam, etc., and young hickories—seem to form an intermediate class between deciduous and evergreen trees. They may almost be called the ever-reds. Their leaves, which are falling all winter long, serve as a shelter to rabbits and partridges and other winter quadrupeds and birds. Even the little chickadees love to skulk amid them and peep out from behind them. I hear their faint, silvery, lisping notes, like tinkling glass, and occasionally a sprightly *day-day-day*, as they inquisitively hop nearer and nearer to me. They are our most honest and innocent little bird, drawing yet nearer to us as the winter advances, and deserve best of any of the walker.

JAN. 7. [1855]   Still birds are very rare. Here comes a little flock of titmice, plainly to keep me company, with their black caps and throats making them look top-heavy, restlessly hopping along the alders, with a sharp, clear, lisping note.

JUNE 3. [1856]   Surveying for John Hosmer beyond pail-factory. While running a line in the woods, close to the water, on the southwest side of Loring's Pond, I observed a chickadee sitting quietly within a few feet. Suspecting a nest, I looked and found it in a small hollow maple stump which was about five inches in diameter and two feet high. I looked down about a foot and could just discern the eggs. Breaking off a little, I managed to get my hand in and took out some eggs. There were seven, making by their number an unusual figure as they lay in the nest, a sort of egg rosette, a circle around with one (or more) in the middle. In the meanwhile the bird sat silent, though rather restless, within three feet. The nest was very thick and warm, of average depth, and made of bluish-slate rabbit's (?) fur. The eggs were a perfect oval, five eighths inch long, white with small reddish-brown or rusty spots, especially about larger end, partly developed. The bird sat on the remaining eggs next day. I called off the boy in another direction that he might not find it.

DEC. 3. [1856]   Six weeks ago I noticed the advent of chickadees and their winter habits. As you walk along a wood-side, a restless little flock of them, whose notes you hear at a distance, will seem to say, "Oh, there he goes! Let's pay our respects to him." And they will flit after and close to you, and naively peck at the nearest twig to you, as if they were minding their own business all the while without any reference to you.

JAN. 12. [1860]   As I stand by the hemlocks, I am greeted by the lively and unusually prolonged *tche de de de de de* of a little flock of chickadees. The snow has ceased falling, the sun comes out, and it is warm and still, and this flock of chickadees, little birds that perchance were born in their midst, feeling the influences of this genial season, have begun to flit amid the snow-covered fans of the hemlocks, jarring down the snow,—for there are hardly bare twigs enough for them to rest on,—or they plume themselves in some snug recess on the sunny side of the tree, only pausing to utter their *tche de de de de*.

WHITE-BREASTED NUTHATCH *(Sitta carolinensis)*

[These chunky little birds with square-cut tails, black caps, slaty backs, and white cheeks which emphasize their beady black eyes are permanent residents in Concord. They are often called upside-down birds because of their habit of walking headfirst down perpendicular tree trunks as easily as they walk upward. Because they explore for insects, insect eggs, and so on, on the trunks and branches of trees as earnestly as do woodpeckers, many people confuse them with that group of birds. However, woodpeckers *never* walk headfirst down tree trunks and when they climb, they move upward with a series of hitching steps, their tails being propped against the tree trunk for added support.

Though sometimes considerable numbers of Red-breasted Nuthatches appear in Concord in winter, Thoreau mentioned the species (he called it the red-bellied nuthatch) only once in his *Journal*.]

JAN. 5. [1859]   As I go down the causeway, near the railroad bridge, I hear a fine busy twitter, and, looking up, see a nuthatch hopping along and about a swamp white oak branch, inspecting every side of it, as readily hanging head-downwards as standing upright, and then it utters a distinct *gnah*, as if to attract a companion. Indeed, that other, finer twitter seemed designed to keep some companion in tow, or else it was like a very busy man talking to himself. The companion was a single chickadee, which lisped six or eight feet off. There were, perhaps, no other birds than these two within a quarter of a mile. And when the nuthatch flitted to another tree two rods off, the chickadee unfailingly followed.

MARCH 5. [1859]   Going down-town this forenoon, I heard a white-bellied nuthatch on an elm within twenty feet, uttering peculiar notes and more like a song than I remember to have heard from it. There was a chickadee close by, to which it may have been addressed. It was something like *to-what what what what what*, rapidly repeated, and not the usual *gnah gnah*; and this instant it occurs to me that this may be that earliest spring note which I hear, and have referred to a woodpecker! (This is before *I* have chanced to see a bluebird, blackbird, or robin in Concord this year.) It is the spring note of the nuthatch. It paused in its progress about the trunk or branch and uttered this lively but peculiarly inarticulate song, an awkward attempt to warble almost in the face of the chickadee, as if it were one of its kind. It was thus giving vent to the spring within it. If I am not mistaken, it is what I have heard in former springs or winters long ago, fabulously early in the season, when we men had but just begun to anticipate the spring,—for it would seem that we, in our anticipations and sympathies, include in succession the moods and expressions of all creatures. When only the snow had begun to melt and no rill of song had broken loose, a note so dry and fettered still, so inarticulate and half thawed out, that you might (and would commonly) mistake for the tapping of a woodpecker. As if the young nuthatch in its hole had listened only to the tapping of woodpeckers and learned that music, and now, when it would sing and give vent to its spring ecstásy, it can modulate only some note like that. That is its theme still. That is its ruling idea of song and music,— only a little clangor and liquidity added to the tapping of the woodpecker. It was the handle by which my thoughts took firmly hold on spring.

This herald of spring is commonly unseen, it sits so close to the bark.

BROWN CREEPER *(Certhia familiaris)*

[This slim bird, smaller than a sparrow, with a slender curved bill, deserves its name. It creeps like a mouse up a tree trunk, spiraling around and around as it goes up, with its long stiff tail used as a prop.

Like many species in the Concord area, this one, once considered a common transient and winter resident, has decreased considerably in the last century. Yet, in 1962, a high count of sixteen Brown Creepers was recorded on the Christmas Count.]

Nov. 26. [1859]   I see here to-day one brown creeper busily inspecting the pitch pines. It begins at the base, and creeps rapidly upward by starts, adhering close to the bark and shifting a little from side to side often till near the top, then suddenly darts off downward to the base of another tree, where it repeats the same course. This has no black cockade, like the nuthatch.

CATBIRD *(Dumetella carolinensis)*

[This uniformly gray bird has a black cap and chestnut brown under-tail coverts. Once fruit ripens, that is its chief food, but when it is not available, the catbird eats insects and rears its young on insects almost wholly.

The catlike scolding mew of this bird is widely known, but it is a fine singer with a wide variety of notes which often go unrecognized. It prefers vine tangles and dense shrubbery, the latter often enticing the bird into village gardens.]

MAY 13. [1853]   At Corner Spring, stood listening to a catbird, sounding a good way off. Was surprised to detect the singer within a rod and a half on a low twig, the ventriloquist. Should not have believed it was he, if I had not seen the movements of his throat, corresponding to each note,— looking at this near singer whose notes sounded so far away.

JUNE 2. [1860]   A catbird has her nest in our grove. We cast out strips of white cotton cloth all of which she picked up and used. I saw a bird flying across the street with so long a strip of cloth, or the like, the other day, and so slowly that at first I thought it was a little boy's kite with a long tail. The catbird sings less now, while its mate is sitting, or maybe taking care of her young, and probably this is the case with robins and birds generally.

BROWN THRASHER *(Toxostoma rufum)*

[This long slim bird, bright rufous above and heavily striped below, with a long bill, a long tail, and yellow eyes, was one of Thoreau's favorite singers. Commonly the thrasher sings each phrase twice. Its deliberate notes are loud and musical. It is not a thrush, but is closely related to the catbird and mockingbird.

Thoreau's observation of the young Brown Thrashers suffering from heat on a torrid day has been noted by many naturalists since. Until they are covered with feathers, young song birds must be protected from the hot sun either by the parents or by shade from plants or other sources—or they will die.

To Thoreau the Brown Thrasher was an extremely abundant nesting bird, but the population appears to have suffered an abrupt decrease sometime late in the nineteenth century. Though cutting of the woodlands around Concord has created favorable habitats, the species, while commonly nesting there, cannot be considered abundant. A single individual lingered long enough to be included on the 1963 Christmas Bird Count.]

MAY 16. [1852]   P.M.—To Conantum. The thrasher has a sort of laugh in his strain which the catbird has not.

MAY 18. [1852]   This afternoon the brown thrashers are very numerous and musical. They plunge downward when they leave their perch, in a peculiar way. It is a bird that appears to make a business of singing for its own amusement. There is great variety in its strains. It is not easy to detect any repetition.

APRIL 30. [1856]   [Surveying the Tommy Wheeler farm.] A fine morning. I hear the first brown thrasher singing within three or four rods of me on the shrubby hillside in front of the Hadley place. I think I had a glimpse of one darting down a sapling-top into the bushes as I rode by the same place on the morning of the 28th. This, I think, is the very place to hear them early, a dry hillside sloping to the south, covered with young wood and shrub oaks. I am the more attracted to that house as a dwelling-place. To live where you would hear the first brown thrasher! First, perchance, you have a glimpse of one's ferruginous long brown back, instantly lost amid the shrub oaks, and are uncertain if it was the thrasher, or one of the other thrushes; and your uncertainty lasts commonly a day or two, until its rich and varied strain is heard. Surveying seemed a noble employment which brought me within hearing of this bird. I was trying to get the exact course of a wall thickly beset with shrub oaks and birches, making an opening through them with axe and knife, while the hillside seemed to quiver or pulsate with the sudden melody. Again, it is with the side of the ear that you hear. The music or the beauty belong not to your work itself but some of its accompaniments. You would fain devote yourself to the melody, but you will hear more of it if you devote yourself to your work.

JUNE 19. [1860]   To Flint's Pond. Observe a nest crowded full with four young brown thrashers half fledged. You would think they would die of heat, so densely packed and overflowing. Three head one way, and the other lies across. How quickly a fox would gobble them up!

ROBIN *(Turdus mirgratorius)*

[The robin is so well known throughout the northeast that it is used to "measure" other medium-sized birds; an unknown bird is described as the size of, or bigger or smaller than a robin. When it sang around the homes of the first settlers, they promptly named it for a smaller English bird (a member of the blackbird, not the thrush, family) which they had known in their former gardens and hedgerows.]

APRIL 1. [1852]   I hear a robin singing in the woods south of Hosmer's just before sunset. It is a sound associated with New England village life. It brings to my thoughts summer evenings when the children are playing in the yards before the doors and their parents conversing at the open windows. It foretells all this now, before those summer hours are come.

APRIL 6. [1853]   6 A.M.—To Cliffs. The robin is the singer at present, such is its power and universality, being found both in garden and wood. Morning and evening it does not fail, perched on some elm or the like, and in rainy days it is one long morning or evening.

MAY 4. [1855]   A robin sings when I, in the house, cannot distinguish the earliest dawning from the full moonlight. His song first advertises me of the daybreak, when I thought it was night, as I lay looking out into the full moonlight. I heard a robin begin his strain, and yielded the point to him, believing he was better acquainted with the springs of the day than I,—with the signs of day. 5 A.M.—To Hill.

JUNE 20. [1855]   A robin's nest with young, which was lately, in the great wind, blown down and somehow lodged on the lower part of an evergreen by arbor,—without spilling the young!

JAN. 11. [1856]   Mother reminds me that when we lived at the Parkman house she lost a ruff a yard and a half long and with an edging three yards long to it, which she had laid on the grass to whiten, and, looking for it, she saw a robin tugging at the tape string of a stay on the line. He would repeatedly get it in his mouth, fly off and be brought up when he got to the end of his tether. Miss Ward thereupon tore a fine linen handkerchief into strips and threw them out, and the robin carried them all off. She had no doubt that he took the ruff.

APRIL 16. [1856]   The robins sing with a will now. What a burst of melody! It gurgles out of all conduits now; they are choked with it. There is such a tide and rush of song as when a river is straightened between two rocky walls. It seems as if the morning's throat were not large enough to emit all this sound. The robin sings most before 6 o'clock now. I note where some suddenly cease their song, making a quite remarkable vacuum.

WOOD THRUSH *(Hylocichla mustelina)*

[Much has been made of the fact that Thoreau did not distinguish between the song of the Wood Thrush and that of the Hermit Thrush. Both species have exquisite songs and preference of one over the other is largely a matter of opinion and perhaps familiarity. Since the Wood Thrush is commonly heard in and around suburban villages, it is the favorite of many people— though musicians claim the song of the Hermit Thrush has greater melody and is delivered with great brilliance. F. Schuyler Mathews was reminded of Beethovan's *Fifth Symphony* when he listened to the Wood Thrush, and of his *Moonlight Sonata* when the Hermit Thrush sang.

On June 19, 1858, Thoreau was taken by some boys to see a nest fourteen feet up in a slender maple sapling. It had one blue egg in it at that time. It was surely a Wood Thrush's nest. Thoreau collected the empty nest on

July 31 and described it in some detail in his *Journal* entry of that day. This is the nest he referred to in the selection for August 9, included here.]

JULY 27. [1840]   By the last breath of the May air I inhale I am reminded that the ages never got so far down as this before. The wood thrush is a more modern philosopher than Plato and Aristotle. They are now a dogma, but he preaches the doctrine of this hour.

MAY 31. [1850]   There is a sweet wild world which lies along the strain of the wood thrush—the rich intervales which border the stream of its song —more thoroughly genial to my nature than any other.

JUNE 22. [1851]   I hear around me, but never in sight, the many wood thrushes whetting their steel-like notes. Such keen singers! It takes a fiery heat, many dry pine leaves added to the furnace of the sun, to temper their strains! Always they are either rising or falling to a new strain. After what a moderate pause they deliver themselves again! saying ever a new thing, avoiding repetition, methinks answering one another. While most other birds take their siesta, the wood thrush discharges his song. It is delivered like a bolas, or a piece of jingling steel.

JULY 21. [1851]   On Conantum. Never yet did I chance to sit in a house, except my own house in the woods, and hear a wood thrush sing. Would it not be well to sit in such a chamber within sound of the finest songster of the grove?

JUNE 23. [1852]   5 A.M.—To Laurel Glen. The wood thrush sings at all hours. I associate it with the cool morning, sultry noon, and serene evening. At this hour it suggests a cool vigor.

JULY 5. [1852]   Some birds are poets and sing all summer. They are the true singers. Any man can write verses during the love season. I am reminded of this while we rest in the shade on the Major Heywood road and listen to a wood thrush, now just before sunset. We are most interested in those birds who sing for the love of the music, and not of their mates; who meditate their strains, and *amuse* themselves with singing; the birds, the strains, of deeper sentiment; not bobolinks, that lose their plumage, their bright colors, and their song so early. . . .

The wood thrush's is no opera music; it is not so much the composition as the strain, the tone—cool bars of melody from the atmosphere of everlasting morning or evening. It is the quality of the song, not the sequence. In the peawai's note there is some sultriness, but in the thrush's, though heard at noon, there is the liquid coolness of things that are just drawn from the bottom of springs. The thrush alone declares the immortal wealth and vigor that is in the forest. Here is a bird in whose strain the story is told, though Nature waited for the science of aesthetics to discover it to man.⟦Whenever man hears it, he is young, and Nature is in her spring. Wherever he hears it, it is a new world and a free country, and the gates of heaven are not shut against him.⟧ Most other birds sing from the level of my ordinary cheerful hours—a carol; but this bird never fails to speak to me out of an ether purer than that I breathe, of immortal beauty and vigor. He deepens the significance of all things seen in the light of his strain. He sings to make men take higher and truer views of things. He sings to amend their institutions; to relieve the slave on the plantation and the prisoner in the dungeon, the slave in the house of luxury and the prisoner of his own low thoughts.

JULY 27. [1852]   How cool and assuaging the thrush's note after the fever of the day! I doubt if they have anything so richly wild in Europe. So long a civilization must have banished it. It will only be heard in America, per-chance, while our star is in the ascendant. I should be very much surprised if I were to hear in the strain of the nightingale such unexplored wildness and fertility, reaching to sundown, inciting to emigration. Such a bird must itself have emigrated long ago. Why, then, was I born in America? I might ask.

MAY 17. [1853]   The river reflects the golden light of the sun just before his setting. The sough of the wind in the pines is more noticeable, as if the air were otherwise more still and hollow. The wood thrush has sung for some time. He touches a depth in me which no other bird's song does. He has learned to sing, and no thrumming of the strings or tuning disturbs you. Other birds may whistle pretty well, but he is a master of a finer-toned instrument. His song is musical, not from association merely, not from variety, but the character of its tone. It is all divine,—a Shakespeare among birds, and a Homer too.

JUNE 14. [1853]   The wood thrush launches forth his evening strains from the midst of the pines. I admire the moderation of this master. There is nothing tumultuous in his song. He launches forth one strain with all his heart and life and soul, of pure and unmatchable melody, and then he pauses and gives the hearer and himself time to digest this, and then another, and another at suitable intervals. Men talk of the *rich* song of other birds—the thrasher, mocking-bird, nightingale. But I doubt, I doubt. They know not what they say! There is as great an interval between the thrasher and the wood thrush as between Thomson's *Seasons* and Homer. The sweetness of the day crystallizes in this morning coolness.

JUNE 22. [1853]   5:30 P.M.—To Walden and Fair Haven Hill. As I come over the hill, I hear the wood thrush singing his evening lay. This is the only bird whose note affects me like music, affects the flow and tenor of my thought, my fancy and imagination. It lifts and exhilarates me. It is inspiring. It is a medicative draught to my soul. It is an elixir to my eyes and a fountain of youth to all my senses. It changes all hours to an eternal morning. It banishes all trivialness. It reinstates me in my dominion, makes me the lord of creation, is the chief musician of my court. This minstrel sings in a time, a heroic age, with which no event in the village can be contemporary. How can they be contemporary when only the latter is *temporary* at all? How can the infinite and eternal be contemporary with the finite and temporal? So there is something in the music of the cow-bell, something sweeter and more nutritious, than in the milk which the farmers drink. This thrush's song is a *ranz des vaches* to me. I long for wildness, a nature which I cannot put my foot through, woods where the wood thrush forever sings, where the hours are early morning ones, and there is dew on the grass, and the day is forever unproved, where I might have a fertile unknown for a soil about me. I would go after the cows, I would watch the flocks of Admetus there forever, only for my board and clothes. A New Hampshire everlasting and unfallen. . . .

All that was ripest and fairest in the wilderness and the wild man is preserved and transmitted to us in the strain of the wood thrush. It is the mediator between barbarism and civilization. It is unrepentant as Greece.

DEC. 31. [1853]   There are a few sounds still which never fail to affect me. The notes of the wood thrush and the sound of a vibrating chord, these affect me as many sounds once did often, and as almost all should. The strains of the aeolian harp and of the wood thrush are the truest and loftiest preachers that I know now left on earth. I know of no missionaries to us heathen comparable to them. They, as it were, lift us up in spite of ourselves. They intoxicate, they charm us.

MAY 11. [1854]   The true poet will ever live aloof from society, wild to it, as the finest singer is the wood thrush, a forest bird.

MAY 28. [1855]   While we sit by the path in the depths of the woods three quarters of a mile beyond Hayden's, confessing the influence of almost the first summer warmth, the wood thrush sings steadily for half an hour, now at 2:30 P.M., amid the pines,—loud and clear and sweet. While other birds are warbling betweenwhiles and catching their prey, he alone appears to make a business of singing, like a true minstrel.

Aug. 30. [1856]   A cold white horizon sky in the north, forerunner of the fall of the year. I go to bed and dream of cranberry-pickers far in the cold north. With windows partly closed, with continent concentrated thoughts, I dream. I get my new experiences still, not at the opera listening to the Swedish Nightingale, but at Beck Stow's Swamp listening to the native wood thrush.

Hermit Thrush *(Hylocichla guttata)*

[The Hermit Thrush habitually nests on the ground while the Wood Thrush builds anywhere from five to twenty-five feet above it.

Thoreau recognized the Hermit Thrush when he was able to see it clearly. On April 26, 1854, he found a dead one and noted its fox-colored tail.

Though he recognized the Hermit Thrush, he used the inclusive term "wood thrush" for all the beautiful thrush songs he heard. This is not surprising, for his two most important references, Wilson and Audubon, both wrote that the Hermit Thrush was destitute of song. Some of the selections included under Wood Thrush may refer to the Hermit Thrush, but since there is not enough information to be sure, all are left under the preceeding heading except April selections and that of May 3, 1852. The Hermit Thrush arrives in Concord in late March or early April, but the Wood Thrush is not expected before May 5.]

June 15. [1851]   I sit in the shade of the pines to hear a wood thrush at noon. The ground smells of dry leaves; the heat is oppressive. The bird begins on a low strain, i.e. it first delivers a strain on a lower key, then a moment after another a little higher, then another still varied from the others,—no two successive strains alike, but either ascending or descending. He confines himself to his few notes, in which he is unrivalled, as if his kind had learned this and no more anciently.

April 30. [1852]   I hear a wood thrush here, with a fine metallic ring to his note. This sound most adequately expresses the immortal beauty and wildness of the woods. I go in search of him. He sounds no nearer. On a low bough of a small maple near the brook in the swamp, he sits with ruffled feathers, singing more low or with less power, as it were ventriloquizing; for though I am scarcely more than a rod off, he seems further off than ever.

MAY 3. [1852]   5 A.M.—To Cliffs. The wood thrush reminds me of cool mountain springs and morning walks.

APRIL 27. [1854]   7 A.M.—To Cliffs. The wood thrush from afar,—so superior a strain to that of other birds. I was doubting if it would affect me as of yore, but it did measurably. I did not believe there could be such differences. This is the gospel according to the wood thrush. He makes a sabbath out of a week-day. I could go to hear him, could buy a pew in his church. Did he ever practice pulpit eloquence? He is right about the slavery question.

VEERY *(Hylocichla fuscescens)*

[Of all the thrushes, this species has the most indistinctly, the least spotted, breast. Above it is uniformly cinnamon-brown.

Thoreau noted that the young men at Harvard called this species the *Yorrick*, and sometimes mentioned hearing this call in the Concord woods. Several times he found its nest and on July 2, 1852, he wrote: "It is starlight. Near woods the veery is a steady singer at this hour."]

MAY 17. [1853]   The west slope of Fair Haven orchard an hour before sunset. With the stillness of the air comes the stillness of the water. The sweetest singers among the birds are heard more distinctly now, as the reflections are seen more distinctly in the water,—the veery constantly now.

JUNE 19. [1853]   In the middle of the path to Wharf Rock at Flint's Pond, the nest of a Wilson's thrush, five or six inches high, between the green stems of three or four golden-rods, made of dried grass or fibres of bark, wide, to deceive the eye. Two blue eggs. Like an accidental heap. Who with dry oak leaves attached loosely, making the whole nine or ten inches taught it to do thus?

EASTERN BLUEBIRD *(Sialis sialis)*

[The sweet liquid warble of this early spring migrant was music Thoreau looked forward to with eagerness. While the bright blue back of the male pleased his eyes, even more pleasing to him was the song delivered in flight or on a perch. When finally the bluebird song reached his ears, spring seemed at last to have put the Concord winter to rout.]

MARCH 15. [1852]   A mild spring day. I must hie to the Great Meadows. The air is full of bluebirds. The ground almost entirely bare. The villagers are out in the sun, and every man is happy whose work takes him outdoors. I go by Sleepy Hollow toward the Great Fields. I lean over a rail to hear what is in the air, liquid with the bluebirds' warble.

APRIL 3. [1852]   The bluebird carries the sky on his back.

MARCH 18. [1853]   I no sooner step out of the house than I hear the blue-birds in the air, and far and near, everywhere except in the woods, through-out the town you may hear them,—the blue curls of their warblings,—harbingers of serene and warm weather, little azure rills of melody trickling here and there from out the air, their short warble trilled in the air remind-ing of so many corkscrews assaulting and thawing the torpid mass of winter, assisting the ice and snow to melt and the streams to flow.

APRIL 5. [1853]   The bluebird comes to us bright in his vernal dress as a bridegroom.

MARCH 7. [1854]   To Annursnack. Heard the first bluebird,—something like *pe-a-wor*,—and then other slight warblings, as if farther off. Was sur-prised to see the bird within seven or eight rods on the top of an oak on the orchard's edge under the hill. But he appeared silent, while I heard others faintly warbling and twittering far in the orchard. When he flew I heard no more, and then I suspected that he had been ventriloquizing; as if he hardly dared open his mouth yet, while there was so much winter left. It is an overcast and moist but rather warm afternoon. He revisits the apple trees, and appears to find some worms. Probably not till now was his food to be found abundantly.

MARCH 11. [1854]   Fair weather after three rainy days. . . . Bluebirds' warbling curls in elms.

FEB. 18. [1857]   I am excited by this wonderful air and go listening for the note of the bluebird or other comer. The very grain of the air seems to have undergone a change and is ready to split into the form of the bluebird's warble. Methinks if it were visible, or I could cast up some fine dust which would betray it, it would take a corresponding shape. The blue-bird does not come till the air consents and his wedge will enter easily. The air over these fields is a foundry full of molds for casting bluebirds' warbles. Any sound uttered now would take that form, not of the harsh, vibrating, rending scream of the jay, but a softer, flowing, curling warble, like a purling stream or the lobes of flowing sand and clay. Here is the soft air and moist expectant apple trees, but not yet the bluebird. They do not yet quite attain to song.

Feb. 24. [1857]   As I cross the causeway to the hill, thinking of the bluebird, I that instant hear one's note from deep in the softened air. . . . As
the day advances I hear more bluebirds and see their azure flakes settling
on the fence-posts. Their short, rich, crispy warble curls through the air.
Its grain now lies parallel to the curve of the bluebird's warble, like boards
of the same lot. It *seems* to be one of those early springs of which we have
heard but have never experienced.

March 17. [1858]   Hear the first bluebird. p.m.—To the Hill. A remarkably warm and pleasant day with a south or southwest wind, but still very
bad walking, the frost coming out and the snow that was left going off.
The air is full of bluebirds. I hear them far and near on all sides of the
hill, warbling in the tree-tops, though I do not distinctly see them. . . .
   How much more habitable a few birds make the field! At the end of
winter, when the fields are bare and there is nothing to relieve the monotony
of the withered vegetation, our life seems reduced to its lowest terms. But
let a bluebird come and warble over them, and what a change! The note
of the first bluebird in the air answers to the purling rill of melted snow
beneath. It is eminently soft and soothing, and, as surely as the thermometer,
indicates a higher temperature. It is modulated by the south wind. The
song sparrow is more sprightly, mingling its notes with the rustling of the
brash along the watersides, but it is at the same time more *terrene* than the
bluebird. The first woodpecker comes screaming into the empty house and
throws open doors and windows wide, calling out each of them to let the
neighbors know of its return. But heard further off it is very suggestive
of ineffable associations which cannot be distinctly recalled,—of long-drawn
summer hours,—and thus it, also, has the effect of music. I was not aware
that the capacity to hear the woodpecker had slumbered within me so long.
When the blackbird gets to a *conqueree* he seems to be dreaming of the
sprays that are to be and on which he is to perch. The robin does not come
singing, but utters a somewhat anxious or inquisitive peep at first. The
song sparrow is immediately most at home of any that I have named. I
see this afternoon as many as a dozen bluebirds on the warm side of a wood.

March 2. [1859]   The bluebird which some woodchopper or inspired
walker is said to have seen in that sunny interval between the snow-storms
is like a speck of clear blue sky seen near the end of a storm, reminding us
of an ethereal region and a heaven which we had forgotten. Princes and
magistrates are often styled serene, but what is their turbid serenity to that
ethereal serenity which the bluebird embodies? His Most Serene Birdship!
His soft warble melts in the ear,. as the snow is melting in the valleys
around. The bluebird comes and with his warble drills the ice and sets free

the rivers and ponds and frozen ground. As the sand flows down the slopes a little way, assuming the forms of foliage where the frost comes out of the ground, so this little rill of melody flows a short way down the concave of the sky. The sharp whistle of the blackbird, too, is heard like single sparks or a shower of them shot up from the swamps and seen against the dark winter in the rear.

MARCH 7. [1859]   It is a good plan to go to some old orchard on the south side of a hill, sit down, and listen, especially in the morning when all is still. You can thus often hear the distant warble of some bluebird lately arrived, which, if you had been walking, would not have been audible to you. As I walk, these first mild spring days, with my coat thrown open, stepping over tinkling rills of melting snow, excited by the sight of the bare gound, especially the reddish subsoil, where it is exposed by a cutting, and by the few green radical leaves, I stand still, shut my eyes, and listen from time to time, in order to hear the note of some bird of passage just arrived.

GOLDEN-CROWNED KINGLET *(Regulus satrapa)*

[The smallest individuals of this species are only three and one-fourth inches long. Yet they manage to raise as many as nine young in a single brood. As quick and restless as warblers, they are difficult to observe. The Ruby-crowned Kinglet has a ring around its eyes—making them look large. This species has a stripe over the eyes. The golden crown is often concealed by other feathers on the crown, which can be parted at will, to reveal the yellow on the female and the orange on the male.

For many years Thoreau was sure he saw only the Ruby-crowned Kinglet, but his *Journal* entry of December 25, 1859, is proof that he added a new bird to his Concord list on that Christmas Day.]

DEC. 25. [1859]   To Carlisle Bridge on river and meadow. Standing by the side of the river at Eleazer Davis's Hill,—prepared to pace across it,—I hear a sharp fine *screep* from some bird, which at length I detect amid the button-bushes and willows. The *screep* was a note of recognition meant for me. I saw that it was a novel bird to me. Watching it a long time, with my glass and without it, I at length made out these marks: It was slate-colored above and dirty-white beneath, with a broad and very conspicuous bright-orange crown, which in some lights was *red-orange*, along the middle of the head; this was bounded on each side by a black segment, beneath which was a yellow or whitish line. There was also some yellow and a black spot on the middle of the closed wings, and yellow within the tail-feathers. The ends of the wings and the tail above were dusky, and the tail forked.

It was so very active that I could not get a steady view of it. It kept drifting about behind the stems of the button-bushes, etc., half the time on the ice, and again on the lower twigs, busily looking for its prey, turning its body this way and that with great restlessness, appearing to hide from me behind the stems of the button-bush and the withered coarse grass. When I came nearest it would utter its peculiar *screep,* or *screep screep,* or even *screep screep screep.* Yet it was unwilling to leave the spot, and when I cornered it, it hopped back within ten feet of me. However, I could see its brilliant crown, even between the twigs of the button-bush and through the withered grass, when I could detect no other part.

It was evidently the golden-crested wren, which I have not made out before. This little creature was contentedly seeking its food here alone this cold winter day on the shore of our frozen river. If it does not visit us often it is strange that it should choose such a season.

RUBY-CROWNED KINGLET *(Regulus calendula)*

[The tiny Ruby-crowned Kinglet which nests high in evergreen forests of the north, or in scattered spruces in bogs, has an amazingly loud voice. Some of its call notes have a wrenlike quality which led early ornithologists to call it a wren. Of all the birds that nest in the northeast, only the Ruby-throated Hummingbird and Golden-crowned Kinglet are smaller. Yet this tiny bird usually lays a clutch of eggs numbering eight or nine.

In the entry for April 25, 1854, Thoreau originally wrote "golden-crested wren" in the first line, but this was crossed out by Thoreau or someone else and "ruby" written in with a pencil. The correction was used here since the song described by Thoreau was clearly that of a Ruby-crowned Kinglet— not the delicate, unmusical Golden-crowned Kinglet's song.]

APRIL 25. [1854]   Saw a ruby-crested wren in the woods near Goose Pond. . . . It sounded far off and like an imitation of a robin,—a long strain and often repeated. I was quite near it before I was aware of it, sounding like a faint imitation of a robin. Some chickadees and yellow redpoll were first apparent, then my wren on the pitch pines and young oaks. He appeared curious to observe me. A very interesting and active little fellow, darting about amid the tree-tops, and his song quite remarkable and rich and loud for his size. Begins with a very fine note, before its pipes are filled, not audible at a little distance, then *woriter weter,* etc., etc., winding up with *teter teter,* all clear and round. This was at 4 P.M., when most birds do not sing. I saw it yesterday, pluming itself and stretching its little wings. Our smallest bird, methinks, except the hummingbird.

CEDAR WAXWING *(Bombycilla cedrorum)*

[This sleek, crested brown bird has a wide yellow band on the end of its tail. On its secondary wing feathers are strange red waxlike spots, a characteristic shared by all three species of waxwings.

Thoreau was undoubtedly correct in thinking the waxwings were the only species except swallows he saw in flocks about Concord in early June. By that time, most species had established territories and were busy with nest activities.]

JULY 19. [1851]   The cherry-birds are making their *seringo* sound as they flit past. They soon find out the locality of the cherry trees.

JUNE 14. [1855]   A cherry-bird's nest and two eggs in an apple tree fourteen feet from ground. One egg, round black spots and a few oblong, about equally but thinly dispersed over the whole, and a dim, internal, purplish tinge about the large end. It is difficult to see anything of the bird, for she steals away early, and you may neither see nor hear anything of her while examining the nest, and so think it deserted. Approach very warily and look out for them a dozen or more rods off.

MARCH 1. [1856]   Goodwin says that somewhere where he lived they called cherry-birds "port-royals."

MARCH 20. [1858]   On that same tree by Conant's orchard, I see a flock of cherry-birds with that alert, chieftain-like look, and hear their *seringo* note, as if made by their swift flight through the air. They have been seen a week or two.

AUG. 26. [1859]   I see a cherry-bird peck from the middle of its upright (vertical) web on a bush one of those large (I think yellow-marked) spiders within a rod of me. It dropped to the ground, and then the bird picked it up. It left a hole or rent in the middle of the web. The spider cunningly spreads his net for feebler insects, and then takes up his post in the centre, but perchance a passing bird picks him from his conspicuous station.

SEPT. 1. [1859]   If you would study the birds now, go where their food is, *i.e.* the berries, especially to the wild black cherries, elder-berries, poke berries, mountain-ash berries, and ere long the barberries, and for pigeons the acorns. In the sprout-land behind Britton's Camp, I came to a small black cherry full of fruit, and then, for the first time for a long while, I see and hear cherry-birds—their shrill and fine seringo—and the note of robins, which of late are scarce. We sit near the tree and listen to the now unusual sounds of these birds, and from time to time one or two come dashing from out the sky toward this tree, till, seeing us, they whirl, disappointed, and perhaps alight on some neighboring twigs and wait till we are gone. The cherry-birds and robins seem to know the locality of every wild cherry in the town. You are as sure to find them on them now, as bees and butter-flies on the thistles. If we stay long, they go off with a fling, to some other cherry tree, which they know of but we do not. The neighborhood of a wild cherry full of fruit is now, for the notes of birds, a little spring come back again, and when, a mile or two from this, I was plucking a basketful of elder-berries (for which it was rather early yet), there too, to my surprise, I came on a flock of golden robins and of bluebirds, apparently feeding on them. Excepting the vacciniums, now past prime and drying up, the cherries and elder-berries are the two prevailing fruits now. We had remarked on the general scarcity and silence of the birds, but when we came to the localities of these fruits, there again we found the berry-eating birds assembled.

NORTHERN SHRIKE *(Lanius excubitor)*

[Shrikes are often called butcher-birds because of their habit of impaling their catch of insects, small birds, or mice on thorns or the barbs of barbed-wire fences. Even young shrikes have been included in such larders, and one wonders if those young shrikes happened to die in the nest of the shrikes that impaled them or if they robbed another shrike nest of its young.

The Northern Shrike does not nest as far south as the United States, but every fourth year when there is an upsurge in the mouse population they move far south of their breeding range to feast on those small rodents.

Thoreau was fortunate to hear not only the calls but the full song of the shrike. It is fairly silent in winter and comparatively few people hear either its calls, or its harsh but somewhat thrasherlike song.]

DEC. 24. [1850] Saw a shrike pecking to pieces a small bird, apparently a snowbird. At length he took him up in his bill, almost half as big as him-self, and flew slowly off with his prey dangling from his beak. I find that I had not associated such actions with my idea of birds. It was not birdlike.

DEC. 29. [1855] Down railroad to Andromeda Ponds. I occasionally see a small snowflake in the air against the woods. It is quite cold, and a serious storm seems to be beginning. Just before reaching the Cut I see a shrike flying low beneath the level of the railroad, which rises and alights on the topmost twig of an elm within four or five rods. All ash or bluish-slate above down to middle of wings; dirty-white breast, and a broad black mark through eyes on side of head; primaries(?) black, and some white appears when it flies. Most distinctive its small hooked bill (upper mandible). It makes no sound, but flies to the *top* of an oak further off. Probably a male.

MARCH 7. [1859]   To Hill. I come out to hear a spring bird, the ground generally covered with snow yet and the channel of the river only partly open. On the Hill I hear first the tapping of a small woodpecker. Then I see a bird alight on the dead top of the highest white oak on the hilltop, on the topmost branches. It is a shrike. While I am watching him eight or ten rods off, I hear robins down below, west of the hill. Then, to my surprise, the shrike begins to sing. It is at first a wholly ineffectual and inarticulate sound without any solid tone to it, a mere hoarse breathing, as if he were clearing his throat, unlike any bird that I know,—a shrill hissing. Then he uttered a kind of mew, a very decided mewing, clear and wiry, between that of a catbird and the note of the nuthatch, as if to lure a nuthatch within his reach; then rose into the sharpest, shrillest vibratory or tremulous whistling or chirruping on the very highest key. This high gurgling jingle was like some of the notes of a robin singing in summer. But they were very short spurts in all these directions, though there was all this variety. Unless you saw the shrike it would be hard to tell what bird it was. This variety of notes covered considerable time, but were sparingly uttered with intervals. It was a decided chinking sound—the clearest strain—suggesting much ice in the stream. I heard this bird sing once before, but that was also in early spring, or about this time. It is said that they imitate the notes of the birds in order to attract them within their reach. Why, then, have I never heard them sing in winter? (I have seen seven or eight of them the past winter quite near.) The birds which it imitated—if it imitated any this morning—were the catbird and the robin, neither of which probably would it catch,—and the first is not here to be caught. Hear—a peep, I looked up and saw three or four birds passing rather [sic], which suddenly descended and settled on this oak-top. They were robins, but the shrike instantly hid himself behind a bough and in half a minute flew off to a walnut and alighted, as usual, on its very topmost twig, apparently afraid of its visitors. The robins kept their ground, one alighting on the very point which the shrike vacated. Is not this, then, probably the spring note or pairing note or notes of the shrike?

RED-EYED VIREO *(Vireo olivaceus)*

[This is the most common and widely distributed vireo. Its red eye can be seen only under ideal conditions, making it of little value to identification.

Its gray cap and black-bordered white stripe over the eye are the best field
marks for this sparrow-sized bird.

Its song, which is heard throughout the hottest summer days, is a rather
monotonous series of short phrases rather robinlike in character and repeated over and over again as the bird feeds.

All vireos build beautiful little hanging baskets for their eggs. The vireo
nest Thoreau found on February 14, 1855, was not necessarily a Red-eyed
Vireo nest.

Though only selections about the Red-eyed Vireo and Warbling Vireo are
included here, Thoreau identified the White-eyed, Yellow-throated, and
Solitary Vireos also.]

MAY 21. [1852] [Billington Sea, not Concord, but the song is the same
wherever it is heard.] The red-eyed vireo is a steady singer, sitting near the
top of a tree a long time alone,—the robin of the woods,—as the robin
sings at morning and evening on an elm in the village.

AUG. 20. [1854] When the red-eye ceases generally, then I think is a
crisis,—the woodland quire is dissolved. That, if I remember, was about a
fortnight ago.

FEB. 14. [1856] I walk in the bare maple swamps and detect the minute
pensile nest of some vireo high over my head, in the fork of some unat-
tainable twig, where I never suspected them in the summer,—a little basket
cradle that rocked so high in the wind. And where is that young family
now, while their cradle is filled with ice?

WARBLING VIREO *(Vireo gilvus)*

[In New England villages this species is most often found feeding or nesting in tall graceful elms. Thoreau noted the preference this species had for
the elm tree.

There have been several known fluctuations in the population of this
species in the Concord area. Thoreau found it a common summer bird in
the tree-lined streets of Concord. There was a sharp decline during the second decade of this century throughout the whole northeast. During the
forties there was a substantial increase in numbers which was noted in
Concord. Bird watchers are likely to find the tendency to fluctuations in
this species will continue, but it is hoped they will be well documented.]

SEPT. 6. [1859] I hear occasionally a half-warbled strain from a warbling
vireo in the elm-tops, as I go down the street nowadays. There is about

as much life in their notes now as in the enfeebled and yellowing elm tree leaves at present.

MAY 29. [1860]   Hearing a warbling vireo, he [Jacob Farmer] asked me what it was, and said that a man who lived with him thought it said, "Now I have caught it, O how it is sweet!" I am sure only of the last words, or perhaps, "Quick as I catch him I eat him. O it is very sweet."

WARBLERS

[The Wood Warblers belong entirely to the New World, and in the Americas one hundred and nine species are found. The bill is usually slender and pointed. In most species there is a distinct difference in plumage between the male and female. They are not only small birds, but they are extremely active. This makes prolonged observations of warblers, away from the nest, quite difficult—even with the aid of fine binoculars.

On May 15, 1854, Thoreau wrote:]

Have just been looking at Nuttall's "North American Sylva." Much research, fine plates and print and paper, and no objectionable periods, but no turpentine, or balsam, or quercitron, or salicin, or birch wine, or the aroma of the balm-of-Gilead. . . . The plates are greener and higher-colored than the words, etc., etc. It is sapless, if not leafless.

[A reader who tried to identify warblers from any of Thoreau's chief references (Wilson, Audubon, and Nuttall) would become confused. For instance, Audubon names the Yellow Warbler (*Dendroica petechia*) Children's Warbler on Plate 35, Rathbone's Warbler on Plate 65, and Blue-eyed Yellow Warbler on Plate 95. Nuttall calls it the Summer Yellow-bird, giving it the same scientific name, *Sylvia aestiva*, that Audubon gives to his Blue-eyed Yellow Warbler, but Wilson calls it *Sylvia citrinella*. The Magnolia Warbler (*Dendroica magnolia*) is called the Black and Yellow or Spotted Warbler by Nuttall, while Audubon calls it Swainson's Warbler on his Plate 50 and Black and Yellow Warbler on Plate 123. Wilson, Audubon, and Nuttall all describe the Blue Mountain Warbler, but this species, known only from the plates of the two artists, has never been satisfactorily identified with any known species. The more Thoreau's reference books are examined, the more one wonders that he identified as many species of warblers as he did.]

APRIL 19. [1854]   [Paddling on the Assabet.] I had chosen to come to the river that afternoon, for there, the air being warm though the earth was covered with snow, there was least change. The few sparrows and warblers along the water's edge and on the twigs over the water seemed to forget the wintry prospect. . . . That is a good stream to explore any summer weather, because the woods border it immediately and you can observe a greater variety of small birds. I can approach them more nearly in my boat than on foot. . . .

I thought yesterday that the sparrows must rejoice to sit in the sun again and dry their feathers and feel its warmth. . . .

It is remarkable how scarce and silent the birds are even in a pleasant afternoon like this, compared with the morning. Within a few days the warblers have begun to come. They are of every hue. Nature made them to show her colors with. There are as many as there are colors and shades. In certain lights, as yesterday against the snow, nothing can be more splendid and celestial than the color of the bluebird.

MAY 18. [1856] The swamp is all alive with warblers about the hoary expanding buds of oaks, maples, etc., and amid the pine and spruce. They swarm like gnats now. They fill the air with their little *tshree tshree* sprayey notes.

MAY 23. [1857] P.M.—To Holden Swamp by boat. This is the time and place to hear the new-arriving warblers, the first fine days after the May storm. When the leaves generally are just fairly expanding, and the deciduous trees are hoary with them,—a silvery hoariness,—then about the edges of the swamps in the woods, these birds are flitting about in the tree-tops like gnats, catching the insects about the expanding leaf-buds.

JUNE 4. [1860] The black-poll warblers (*Sylvia striata*) appear to have left, and some other warblers, if not generally, with this first clear and bright and warm, peculiarly June weather, immediately after the May rain. About a month ago, after the strong and cold winds of March and April and in the (in common years) rain and high water, the ducks, etc., left us for the north. Now there is a similar departure of the warblers, on the expansion of the leaves and advent of yet warmer weather. Their season with us, *i.e.* those that go further, is when the buds are bursting, till the leaves are about expanded; and probably they follow these phenomena northward till they get to their breeding-places, flying from tree to tree.

BLACK AND-WHITE WARBLER *(Mniotilta varia)*

[The creeperlike habits of this warbler make Thoreau's name for it most descriptive.

This is a very widespread warbler, nesting as far north as central Canada, and many winter in the southern United States—though some continue to northern South America. It hides its nest in a depression by a tree or under a log, and its four or five eggs are spotted heavily with purples and brown.

On May 16, 1860, Thoreau watched a Black-and-white Warbler. Later he made some general observations about warbler-watching which are as pertinent to-day as when he wrote in his *Journal* on that day, more than a hundred years ago.]

MAY 30. [1857]   In the midst of the shower, though it was not raining very hard, a black and white creeper came and inspected the limbs of a tree before my rock, in his usual zigzag, prying way, head downward often, and when it thundered loudest, heeded it not. Birds appear to be but little incommoded by the rain. Yet they do not often sing in it.

MAY 16. [1860]   To Copan and Beck Stow's. Near Peter's I see a small creeper hopping along the branches of the oaks and pines, ever turning this way and that as it hops, making various angles with the bough; then it flies across to another bough, or to the base of another tree, and traces that up, zigzag and prying into the crevices. Think how thoroughly the trees are thus explored by various birds. You can hardly sit near one for five minutes now, but either a woodpecker or creeper comes and examines its bark rapidly, or a warbler—a summer yellowbird, for example—makes a pretty thorough exploration about all its expanding leaflets, even to the topmost twig. The whole North American forest is thus explored for insect food now by several hundred (?) species of birds. Each is visited by many kinds, and thus the equilibrium of the insect and vegetable kingdom is preserved. Perhaps I may say that each opening bud is thus visited before it had fully expanded.

The golden robin utters from time to time a hoarse or grating *cr-r-ack*. The creepers are very common now.

Now that the warblers are here in such numbers is the very time on another account to study them, for the leaf-buds are generally but just expanding, and if you look toward the light you can see every bird that flits through a small grove, but a few weeks hence the leaves will conceal them.

PARULA WARBLER *(Parula americana)*

[This tiny bluish warbler measures about four and one-fourth inches in length. Like all warblers it is extremely active and constantly moving about.
In the northeast this species makes its nest almost entirely of usnea

lichen, building it in the midst of a natural clump of this lichen so that it is almost invisible. Except on migration, where it may be seen in almost any wooded habitat, it should be looked for where usnea lichen grows abundantly.]

MAY 17. [1856] Kalmia Swamp. The *Sylvia Americana* (parti-colored warbler, etc.) is very numerous there, darting about amid the hoary buds of the maples and oaks, etc. It seems the most restless of all birds, blue more [or] less deep above, with yellow dust on the back, yellow breast, and white beneath (male with bright-orange throat, and some with a rufous crescent on breast); wings and tail dark, black, with two white bars or marks, dark bill and legs.

YELLOW WARBLER *(Dendroica petechia)*

[Yellow Warblers are by no means confined to willow thickets but how often Thoreau's experience of finding them in such a habitat is repeated by bird watchers not only in New England but all across the continent from thickets of willow by muddy South Carolina rivers to chilly heights in Utah mountains and by sluggish streams on the flats of Manitoba.

The nest of this species is usually placed from three to five feet from the ground. It stands upright in the fork of a small tree, shrub, or rank weed. Rather funnel-shaped, it is a surprisingly deep nest for so small a bird and is made of silky plant fibers felted tightly together and has a rather silvery look. Cowbirds often place their eggs in Yellow Warbler nests and the warbler usually covers the egg with a thick new flooring. Its own eggs, numbering four or five, are bluish-white heavily speckled with brown.]

MAY 14. [1852] P.M.—To Second Division Brook. Going over the Corner causeway, the willow blossoms fill the air with a sweet fragrance, and I am ready to sing. Ah! willow, willow! These willows have yellow bark, bear yellow flowers and yellowish-green leaves, and are now haunted by the summer yellowbird and Maryland yellow-throat. They see this now conspicuous mass of yellowish verdure at a distance and fly to it.

MAY 10. [1853] At this season the traveller passes through a golden gate on causeways where these willows are planted, as if he were approaching the entrance to Fairyland; and there will surely be found the yellowbird, and already from a distance is heard his note, a *tche tche tche tche tche tche,*—ah, willow, willow. Could not he truly arrange for us the difficult family of the willows better than Borrer, or Barrett of Middletown? And as he passes between the portals, a sweet fragrance is wafted to him, and he not only breathes but scents and tastes the air, and he hears the low humming or susurrus of a myriad insects which are feeding on its sweets. It is, apparently, these that attract the yellowbird. The golden gates of the year, the *May*-gate.

June 21. [1853] p.m.—To Conantum. I saw a yellowbird's nest in the willows on the causeway this afternoon and three young birds, nearly ready to fly, overflowing the nest, all holding up their open bills and keeping them steadily open for a minute or more, on noise of my approach.

June 24. [1853] A yellowbird's nest (*vide* 21st) in a fork of a willow on Hubbard's Causeway, resting chiefly on the leading branch; of fine grass, lined with hair, bottom outside puffing out with a fine, light, flax-like fibre, perhaps the bark of some weed, by which also it is fastened to the twigs. It is surprising that so many birds find hair enough to line their nests with. If I wish for a horsehair for my compass sights I must go to the stable, but the hair-bird, with her sharp eyes, goes to the road.

Jan. 19. [1856] Gathered some dry water milkweed stems to compare with the materials of the bird's nest of the 18th. (It *may* be a yellowbird's.) [H.D.T.] The bird used, I am almost certain, the fibres of the bark of the stem,—not the pods,—just beneath the epidermis; only the bird's is older and more fuzzy and finer, like worn twine or string. The fibres and bark have otherwise the same appearance under the microscope. I stripped off some bark about one sixteenth of an inch wide and six inches long and, separating ten or twelve fibres from the epidermis, rolled it in my fingers, making a thread about the ordinary size. This I could not break by direct pulling, and no man could. I doubt if a thread of flax or hemp of the same size could be made so strong. What an admirable material for the Indian's fish-line! I can easily get much longer fibres. I hold a piece of the dead weed in my hands, strip off a narrow shred of the bark before my neighbor's eyes and separate ten or twelve fibres as fine as hair, roll them in my fingers, and offer him the thread to try its strength. He is surprised and mortified to find that he cannot break it. Probably both the Indian and the bird discovered for themselves this same (so to call it) wild hemp. The corresponding fibres of the mikania seem not so divisible, become not so fine and fuzzy; though somewhat similar, are not nearly so strong. I have a hangbird's nest from the riverside, made almost entirely of this, in narrow shreds or strips with the epidermis on, wound round and round the twigs and woven into a basket. That is, this bird has used perhaps the strongest fibres which the fields afforded and which most civilized men have not detected.

Knocked down the bottom of that summer yellowbird's nest made on the oak at the Island last summer. It is chiefly of fern wool and also, *apparently,* some sheep's wool (?), with a fine green moss (apparently that which grows on button-bushes) inmixed, and some milkweed fibre, and all very firmly agglutinated together. Some shreds of grape-vine bark about it. Do not know what portion of the whole nest it is.

MYRTLE WARBLER *(Dendroica coronata)*

[This is one of the most abundant warblers. Its yellow rump is so distinctive that it was recognized easily in the field by early observers who depended on their eyes unaided by optical assistance.

Not only is this the most abundant warbler in the north, but it goes farther north than any other species. It generally nests in an evergreen anywhere from five to fifty feet above the ground, and the nest is usually placed rather far out on the leafy part of the branch.

The drama of migration attracts much more attention to-day than when Thoreau lived. The turning off of the flood lights on the Empire State Building each spring and autumn attests to this interest. Even in the day-time, many birds crash against large window spaces in which they see the reflection of garden scenes. The annual toll of birds which die while on migration is enormous.

The Myrtle Warbler has always been considered a common spring and an abundant autumn migrant in the Concord area. As many as a thousand have been recorded there in a single day of southward migration during the middle years of the twentieth century. A heavy winter kill of this species in the south in 1957–58 reduced the numbers of this species sharply, but once again their numbers are increasing.]

APRIL 26. [1854] The woods are full of myrtle-birds this afternoon, more common and commonly heard than any, especially along the edge of woods on oaks, etc.,—their note an oft-repeated fine jingle, *a che che che che, che che,* or *a tweedle tweedle tweedle tweedle-twe.* As I heard the *tull lull* from the same quarter from time to time, I think it came from it. Perhaps it may be written, *a tea le, tea le, tea le.* These small birds—and all small birds— seen against the sky at a little distance look black. There is not breadth enough to their colors to make any impression; they are mere motes, inter-cepting the light, the substance of a shadow.

APRIL 28. [1855] A second cold but fair day. Landed at Ball's Hill to look for birds under the shelter of the hill in the sun. There were a great many myrtle-birds there,—they have been quite common for a week,—also yellow redpolls, and some song sparrows, tree sparrows, field sparrows, and one

F. hyemalis. In a cold and windy day like this you can find more birds than in a serene one, because they are collected under the wooded hillsides in the sun. The myrtle-birds flitted before . . . in great numbers, yet quite tame, uttering commonly only a *chip*, but sometimes a short trill or *che che, che che, che che.* Do I hear the *tull-lull* in the afternoon? It is a bird of many colors,—slate, yellow, black and white,—singularly spotted.

Oct. 21. [1857] I see many myrtle-birds now about the house this forenoon, on the advent of cooler weather. They keep flying up against the house and the window and fluttering there, as if they would come in, or alight on the wood-pile or pump. They would commonly be mistaken for sparrows, but show more white when they fly, beside the yellow on the rump and sides of breast seen near to and two white bars on the wings. Chubby birds.

BLACKBURNIAN WARBLER *(Dendroica fusca)*

[The males of this species in the breeding season have a fiery orange throat while the females are less brilliantly colored. Mostly black and white above, with a lot of white in the tail and conspicuous white areas in the wings, the male Blackburnian Warbler is an arresting sight in spring dress.

It prefers mature forests of conifers or mixed woodlands. Thoreau seldom saw this warbler, but he believed he saw one when he was descending from the summit of Mount Monadnock on June 4, 1858. Through he mentions seeing the species but once in Concord, his Hemlock Warbler may have been this species, for Thoreau often consulted Audubon's paintings and on Plate 134, that great artist shows female or immature Blackburnian Warblers as Hemlock Warblers, *Sylvia parus.* Wilson and Nuttall both accepted the female Blackburnian Warbler as a distinct species known as the Hemlock Warbler. Wilson regarded it as a very rare species. He found it in the Great Pine Swamp in Pennsylvania where it kept to the hemlock trees. Peabody, however, regarded the Hemlock Warbler so like the Pine Warbler that only on the authority of Audubon did he accept it as one of the birds of Massachusetts.]

May 26. [1855] Hear another note, very *smart* and somewhat sprayey, rasping, *tshrip tshrip tshrip tshrip*, or five or six times with equal force each time. The bird hops near, directly over my head. It is black, with a large white mark forward on wings and a fiery orange throat, above and below eye, and line on crown, yellowish beneath, white vent, forked tail, dusky legs and bill; holds its wings (which are light beneath) loosely. It inclines to examine about the lower branches of the white pines or midway up. The Blackburnian warbler, very plainly; whose note Nuttall knows nothing about.

PINE WARBLER *(Dendroica pinus)*

[Thoreau's identification of this species, almost always associated with pine trees, must sometimes be questioned; but perhaps it was accurate in all the selections which follow. The song of this warbler resembles that of a Chipping Sparrow but is more musical and slower in tempo.

Pine Warblers—sometimes called pine creepers from their habit of clinging and creeping on trunks and branches—are well-named, for they are seldom seen away from pines. They nest from central Canada south to Florida and the Bahamas, wherever pines are found.

With the disappearance of the tall white pines in Concord, this species has become a rare and very local breeding bird there.]

APRIL 9. [1856]   A very warm day. While I am looking at the hazel, I hear from the old locality, the edge of the great pines and oaks in the swamp by the railroad, the note of the pine warbler. It sounds far off and faint, but, coming out and sitting on the iron rail, I am surprised to see it within three or four rods, on the upper part of a white oak, where it is busily catching insects, hopping along toward the extremities of the limbs, and looking off on all sides, twice darting off like a wood pewee, two rods, over the railroad, after an insect and returning to the oak, and from time to time uttering its simple, rapidly iterated, cool-sounding notes. When heard a little within the wood, as he hops to that side of the oak, they sound particularly cool and inspiring, like a part of the evergreen forest itself, the trickling of the sap. Its bright-yellow or golden throat, etc., are conspicuous at this season, a greenish yellow above, with two white bars on its bluish-brown wings. It sits often with loose-hung wings and forked tail.

APRIL 11. [1856]   Hear in the old place, the pitch pine grove on the bank by the river, the pleasant ringing note of the pine warbler. Its *a-che, vitter vitter, vitter vitter, vitter vitter, vitter vitter, vet* rings through the open pine grove very rapidly. I also heard it at the old place by the railroad, as I came along. It is remarkable that I have so often heard it first in these two localities, *i.e.* where the railroad skirts the north edge of a small swamp filled with tall old white pines and a few white oaks, and in a young grove composed wholly of pitch pines on the otherwise bare, very high and level bank of the Assabet. When the season is advanced enough, I am pretty sure to hear its ringing note in both those places.

APRIL 2. [1858] Approaching the side of a wood on which were some
pines, this afternoon, I heard the note of the pine warbler, calling the pines
to life, though I did not see it. It has probably been here as long as I said
before. Returning, I saw a sparrow-like bird flit by in an orchard, and
turning my glass upon it, was surprised by its burning yellow. This higher
color in birds surprises us like an increase of warmth in the day.

APRIL 15. [1859] The warm pine woods are all alive this afternoon with
the jingle of the pine warbler, for the most part invisible minstrel. . . .
This warbler impresses me as if it were calling the trees to life. I think of
springing twigs. Its jingle rings through the wood at short intervals, as
if, like an electric shock, it imparted a fresh spring life to them. You hear
the same bird, now here now there, as it incessantly flits about, commonly
invisible and uttering its simple jingle on very different keys, and from
time to time a companion is heard farther or nearer. This is a peculiarly
summer-like sound. Go to a warm pine wood-side on a pleasant day at this
season after a storm, and hear it ring with the jingle of the pine warbler.

PALM WARBLER *(Dendroica palmarum)*

[Thoreau's notes about Palm Warblers are interesting chiefly because they
indicate his repeated observations of a species that migrates, spring and
autumn, through Concord.

The wagging or jerking of the tail is of great help in identifying this
species which varies greatly in plumage color and pattern. The distinctive
red-brown crown appears only on fully mature birds, but this crown color
led early ornithologists to call the species the Yellow Red-poll Warbler.
Many individuals arriving in Concord in April do not yet possess this
bright crown. The amount of yellow also varies. A few nest as far south
as Maine, but most go on to the spruce and tamarack bogs of Canada to
nest.

This species' nest was unknown in Thoreau's day; though Audubon found
the bird abundant in Labrador, he searched in vain for a nest. The first
recorded nest was found by a Mr. Kennicott on June 18, 1889, at Fort
Resolution in Arctic America. It was on the ground in a hummock at the
foot of a small spruce and contained five young.]

APRIL 8. [1854] Saw several yellow redpolls *(Sylvia petechia)* on the willows by the Hubbard Bridge. Am not sure I heard their note. May have mistaken it formerly for the pine warbler. Its chestnut crown would distinguish
it.

APRIL 9. [1854]   Saw several more yellow redpolls with their rich, glowing yellow breasts by the causeway sides.

APRIL 16. [1854]   The male yellow redpoll's breast and under parts are of a peculiarly splendid and lively yellow, glowing. It is remarkable that they too are found about willows, etc., along the water.

APRIL 23. [1854]   P.M.—To Lee's Cliff on foot. The yellow redpolls are very common on the willows and alders and in the road near the bridge. They keep jerking their tails. I heard one male sing a jingle like *che ve ve ve ve ve*, very fast, and accenting the last syllable. They are quite tame. I sit awhile on the lee side of Conant's Wood, in the sun, amid the dry oak leaves.

OVENBIRD *(Seiurus aurocapillus)*

[This little warbler walks with a mincing step and looks rather like a miniature thrush. It prefers an area rather close to water, and teeters very much as a Spotted Sandpiper does.

The song is a series of short, ringing, emphatic notes that grow louder and louder as the tempo increases. It is often called the teacher-bird because the song sounds like *teacher* repeated over and over again. The Ovenbird also has a beautiful flight song, most often heard in May and June, late in the afternoon or on moonlight nights. Many people believe that Thoreau's Night Warbler song was most often this song of the Ovenbird.

JUNE [undated] [1850]   Who taught the oven-bird to conceal her nest? It is on the ground, yet out of sight. What cunning there is in nature! No man could have arranged it more artfully for the purpose of concealment. Only the escape of the bird betrays it.

JULY 3. [1853]   The oven-bird's nest in Laurel Glen is near the edge of an open pine wood, under a fallen pine twig and a heap of dry oak leaves. Within these, on the ground, is the nest, with a dome-like top and an arched entrance of the whole height and width on one side. Lined within with dry pine-needles.

THOREAU'S NIGHT WARBLER

[Thoreau was not at all averse to a little mystery in nature. He was apparently little disturbed by the fact that he never identified to his satisfaction his mysterious "night-warbler." Since the unknown songs were probably in most instances the aerial song of the Ovenbird, the "night-warbler" selections follow that species. However, we know that on August 5, 1858, it was probably a Yellowthroat giving its flight song. Emerson, on May 3, 1857, passed along to Thoreau an opinion held by Dr. Thomas M. Brewer, the ornithologist, that the "night warbler" was probably a Nashville Warbler.

The selection which follows, written on June 11, 1851, is the first mention of the night warbler.

In the introduction to the *Journal*, Mr. Bradford Torrey wrote; "Some . . . reader, by a careful collation of the data which the publication of the journal as a whole puts at his disposal, will perhaps succeed in settling the identity of the famous 'night warbler,' a bird which some, we believe, have suspected to be nothing rarer than the almost superabundant ovenbird, but which, so far as we ourselves know, may have been almost any one (or any two or three) of our smaller common birds that are given to occasional ecstatic song-flights. Whatever it was, it was of use to Thoreau for the quickening of his imagination, and for literary purposes; and Emerson was well advised in warning him to beware of booking it, lest life henceforth should have so much the less to show him."]

JUNE 11. [1851]   I hear the night-warbler breaking out as in his dreams, made so from the first for some mysterious reason.

MAY 10. [1853]   Mill Brook Ditch Path. Hear the night warbler now distinctly. It does not soon repeat its note, and disappears with the sound.

JUNE 19. [1853]   Heard my night-warbler on a solitary white pine in the Heywood Clearing by the Peak. Discovered it at last, looking like a small piece of black bark curving partly over the limb. No fork to its tail. It appeared black beneath; was very shy, not bigger than a yellowbird, and very slender.

MAY 28. [1854]   By boat to Lee's Cliff. The night-warbler, after his strain, drops down almost perpendicularly into a tree-top and is lost.

MAY 19. [1858]   Heard the night-warbler *begin* his strain just like an oven-bird! I have noticed that when it drops down into the woods it darts suddenly *one side* to a perch when low.

AUG. 5. [1858]   Fair Haven Pond. While passing there, I heard what I should call my night-warbler's note, and, looking up, saw the bird dropping to a bush on the hillside. Looking through the glass, I saw that it was the

Maryland yellow-throat! ! and it afterward flew to the button-bushes in the meadow.

MAY 18. [1860]   The night-warbler is a powerful singer for so small a bird. It launches into the air above the forest, or over some hollow or open space in the woods, and challenges the attention of the woods by its rapid and impetuous warble, and then drops down swiftly into the tree-tops like a performer withdrawing behind the scenes, and he is lucky who detects where it alights.

YELLOWTHROAT *(Geothlypis trichas)*

[This is one of the most widely distributed warblers and varies considerably in appearance in different parts of the continent. It is active, inquisitive, and found in a variety of places but is commonest in swamps, near water, and flooded thickets.

The male has a glossy black mask across its eyes. Both sexes have a yellow throat, while the immature birds are nondescript and often show little yellow.

It has a flight song quite unlike its usual *witchity, witchity*, but this note is sometimes included in the jumbled short notes of the aerial song.]

JUNE 8. [1853]   P.M.—To Well Meadow. Nest of a Maryland yellow-throat by Utricularia Pool in a tuft of sedge; made of dry sedge, grass, and a few dry leaves; about four small eggs, a delicate white with reddish-brown spots on larger end; the nest well concealed.

JUNE 22. [1853]   Now is the time for young birds. You cannot go near any thicket but the old will scold at you, and you see the kingbird and the blackbird and swallows pursuing crows and hawks, for several weeks. I looked for the nest of the Maryland yellow-throat, but could not find it. Some animal has carried it off from the tuft of sedge, but I found one little egg which had dropped out. How many tragedies of this kind in the fields!

AMERICAN REDSTART *(Setophaga ruticilla)*

[Though the last of the Old Day Elections held on the last Wednesday of May occurred in 1831, the day was celebrated as a holiday for some years to come. Shooting matches were held on that day and birds of all kinds were shot. Thoreau referred to birds shot on Election Day as Election Day Birds. He recalled such birds when he observed the Redstart on May 10, 1853.

While some Redstarts return to Concord in late April, they do not arrive
in numbers until the first week in May. Thoreau probably had been hearing
this species for a week before he saw the first individual of the spring.]

MAY 10. [1853]   I hear, and have for a week, in the woods, the note of one
or more small birds somewhat like a yellowbird's. What is it? Is it the redstart? I now see one of these. The first I have distinguished. And now I
feel pretty certain that my black and yellow warbler of May 1st was this.
As I sit, it inquisitively hops nearer and nearer. It is one of the election-
birds of rare colors which I can remember, mingled dark and reddish. This
reminds me that I supposed much more variety and fertility in nature before
I had learned the numbers and the names of each order. I find that I had
expected such fertility in our Concord woods alone as not even the completest museum of stuffed birds of all the forms and colors from all parts
of the world comes up to.

MAY 29. [1855]   P.M.—To Island Neck. What is that bird I hear much
like the first part of the yellowbird's strain, only two thirds as long and
varied at end, and not so loud,—*a-che che che, che-á,* or *tche tche tche,
tche-a,* or *ah tche tche tche, chit-i-vet?*

It is very small, not timid, but incessantly changing its position on the
pitch pines, etc. Some a pure dull white, some tawny-white, beneath; some
cinereous, others more dusky still, above; with a flycatcher or muscicapa bill
and head (head rounded?), but—what is more remarkable—a very deeply
forked or divided tail with a broad black tip beneath, and toward its roots
a fire-brick color, this last color much brighter on the sides of the breast,
and some perhaps have not the last mark. Did I see some of the yellowish
on rump? Dark-ash above and some reddish-brown(?). One is very inquisitive; hops down toward me lower and lower on the pitch pine twigs, while
I hold out my hand till within five feet, but in such a light that I cannot
distinguish its colors. There are at least half a dozen of them about; continually flitting about, sometimes in a circle of a few rods' diameter, one
pursuing another, both male and female, back to near the same spot, but I
can hardly bring my glass to bear on them before they change their position.
It is undoubtedly young males and the females of the redstart, described
by Wilson,—very different from the full-plumaged black males.

BOBOLINK *(Dolichonyx orysivorus)*

[The song of the Bobolink has inspired many a poet. This may be delivered
from a perch but is best when sung in hovering flight, and the loud, bubbling

phrases rise higher and higher in pitch as it progresses, and tumble out faster and faster. Finally there is a quivering descent during which the rollicking song diminishes in ecstacy and ends when the bird alights.

Bobolinks nest on the ground in stands of heavy grass. The eggs vary considerably from bluish-gray to reddish-brown and are spotted with brown or purple. But one brood is raised each year. Since the breeding territory of this bird consists of large fields of grass or grain, the species has probably benefitted by man, who replaced an almost unbroken forest in the east by extensive fields. However, when grains and grass are harvested before mid-July, the nest or young are frequently destroyed by farm machinery.

Thoreau saw flocks of many hundreds in Concord, and it was then a common nesting species. Today it is found there only in a few scattered localities.]

JUNE 29. [1851]   At a distance in the meadow I hear still, at long intervals, the hurried commencement of the bobolink's strain, the bird just dashing into song, which is as suddenly checked, as it were, by the warder of the seasons, and the strain is left incomplete forever. Like human beings they are inspired to sing only for a short season.

JULY 22. [1852]   Flocks of yellow-breasted, russet-backed female bobolinks are seen flitting stragglingly across the meadows. The bobolink loses his song as he loses his colors.

[Some of the "female" Bobolinks were undoubtedly young birds and still others males already changed into winter dress.]

AUG. 15. [1852]   I see a dense, compact flock of bobolinks going off in the air over a field. They cover the rails and alders, and go rustling off with a brassy, tinkling note like a ripe crop as I approach, revealing their yellow breasts and bellies. This is an autumnal sight, that small flock of grown birds in the afternoon sky.

MAY 10. [1853]   All at once a strain which sounded like old times and recalled a hundred associations. Not at once did I remember that a year had elapsed since I heard it, and then the idea of the bobolink was formed in my mind, yet afterward doubted if it was not the imitation of a catbird. . . .

When I heard the first bobolink strain this morning I could not at first collect myself enough to tell what it was I heard,—a reminiscence of last May in all its prime occurring in the midst of the experience of this in its unripe state. Suddenly the season being sufficiently advanced, the atmosphere in the right condition, these flashing, scintillating notes are struck out from it where that dark mote disappears through it, as sparks by a flint, with a tinkling sound. This flashing, tinkling meteor bursts through the expectant meadow air, leaving a train of tinkling notes behind. Successive regiments of birds arrive and are disbanded in our fields, like soldiers still wearing their regimentals.

MAY 12. [1856]   We hear the first bobolink. How suddenly the birds arrive after the storm,—even yesterday before it was fairly over,—as if they had foreseen its end! How much life the note of the bobolink imparts to the meadow!

JUNE 1. [1857]   I hear the note of a bobolink concealed in the top of an apple tree behind me. Though this bird's full strain is ordinarily somewhat trivial, this one appears to be meditating a strain as yet unheard in meadow or orchard. *Paulo majora canamus.* He is just touching the strings of his theorbo, his glassichord, his water organ, and one or two notes globe themselves and fall in liquid bubbles from his teeming throat. It is as if he touched his harp within a vase of liquid melody, and when he lifted it out, the notes fell like bubbles from the trembling strings. Methinks they are the most *liquidly* sweet and melodious sounds I ever heard. They are refreshing to my ear as the first distant tinkling and gurgling of a rill to a thirsty man. Oh, never advance farther in your art, never let us hear your full strain, sir. But away he launches, and the meadow is all bespattered with melody. His notes fall with the apple blossoms, in the orchard. The very divinest part of his strain dropping from his overflowing breast *singultim,* in globes of melody. It is a foretaste of such strains as never fell on mortal ears, to hear which we should rush to our doors and contribute all we possess and are. Or it seemed as if in that vase full of melody some notes sphered themselves, and from time to time bubbled up to the surface and were with difficulty repressed.

JUNE 2. [1857]   That bobolink's song affected me as if one were endeavoring to keep down globes of melody within a vase full of liquid, but some bubbled up irrepressible,—kept thrusting them down with a stick, but they slipped and came up one side.
    A young sparrow already flies.

AUG. 16. [1858]   To Cardinal Ditch. Channing tells me that he saw a white bobolink in a large flock of them to-day. Almost all flowers and animals may be found white. As in a large number of cardinal flowers you may find a white one, so in a large flock of bobolinks, also, it seems, you may find a white one.

EASTERN MEADOWLARK *(Sturnella magna)*

[This bird of open country adds a welcome whistle, sweet and plaintive, best heard from a distance, to fields just unlocked from winter snows.

Seen from the back, a Meadowlark is a brown bird marked with buff and white. Its white outer tail feathers, which are conspicuous because of the constant jerking of the tail, form its only distinctive mark. But let the Meadowlark face the observer and he sees a brilliant yellow breast with a shiny black breast-band lying across it.

Near the end of the last century this species declined sharply because of winter kills. It is now uncommon and local in Concord, for many former agricultural fields which offered good nesting sites are gone.]

JULY 16. [1851]   The lark sings in the meadow; the very essence of the afternoon is in his strain. This is a New England sound, but the cricket is heard under all sounds.

APRIL 14. [1852]   Going down the railroad at 9 A.M., I hear the lark singing from over the snow. This for steady singing comes next to the robin now. It will come up very sweet from the meadows ere long.

Nov. 8. [1853]   Three larks rise from the sere grass on Minott's Hill before me, the white of their outer tail-feathers very conspicuous, reminding me of arctic snowbirds by their size and form also. The snow begins to whiten the plowed ground now, but it has not overcome the russet of the grass ground. Birds generally wear the russet dress of nature at this season. They have their fall no less than the plants; the bright tints depart from their foliage or feathers, and they flit past like withered leaves in rustling flocks.

MARCH 12. [1854]   Now I see and hear the lark sitting with head erect, neck outstretched, in the middle of a pasture, and I hear another far off singing. Sing when they first come. All these birds do their warbling especially in the still, sunny hour after sunrise, as rivers twinkle at their sources. Now is the time to be abroad and hear them, as you detect the slightest ripple in smooth water. As with tinkling sounds the sources of streams burst their icy fetters, so the rills of music begin to flow and swell the general quire of spring. Memorable is the warm light of the spring sun on russet fields in the morning.

RED-WINGED BLACKBIRD *(Agelaius phoeniceus)*

[It was an exciting moment for Thoreau, as it is for all who watch for early spring movements of birds, when the first lively flock of Redwinged

Blackbirds arrived in Concord and began to sing loudly in a group, each singing lustily and independently of the others.

Long before the plain brown females arrived, the males began to display their shoulder epaulets of glowing red. Using their voices and the display of their red shoulder patches, they attempted to claim and protect territories on which they would nest later. While their nesting places are usually in or near marshes, they may find their food in grain fields, orchards, and pastures a mile away, and as they feed, their brilliant red shoulder patches may be hidden or almost hidden behind their black feathers.

APRIL 22. [1852]   The strain of the red-wing on the willow spray over the water to-night is liquid, bubbling, watery, almost like a tinkling fountain, in perfect harmony with the meadow. It oozes, trickles, tinkles, bubbles from his throat,—*bob-y-lee-e-e,* and then its shrill, fine whistle.

MAY 14. [1853]   The still dead-looking willows and button-bushes are alive with red-wings, now perched on a yielding twig, now pursuing a female swiftly over the meadow, now darting across the stream. No two have epaulets equally brilliant. Some are small and almost white, and others a brilliant vermilion. They are handsomer than the golden robin, methinks. The yellowbird, kingbird, and pewee, beside many swallows, are also seen. But the rich colors and the rich and varied notes of the blackbirds surpass them all.

MAY 16. [1854]   Looked into several red-wing blackbirds' nests which are now being built, but no eggs yet. They are generally hung between two twigs, say of button-bush. I noticed at one nest what looked like a tow string securely tied about a twig at each end about six inches apart, left loose in the middle. It was not a string, but I think a strip of milkweed pod, etc.,—water asclepias probably,—maybe a foot long and very strong. How remarkable that this bird should have found out the strength of this, which I was so slow to find out!

JUNE 1. [1857]   P.M.—To Hill. A red-wing's nest, four eggs, low in a tuft of sedge in an open meadow. What Champollion can translate the hieroglyphics on these eggs? It is always writing of the same character, though much diversified. While the bird picks up the material and lays the egg, who determines the style of the marking? When you approach, away dashes the dark mother, betraying her nest, and then chatters her anxiety from a neighboring bush, where she is soon joined by the red-shouldered male, who comes scolding over your head, chattering and uttering a sharp *phe phee-e.*

MARCH 13. [1859] I see a small flock of blackbirds flying over, some rising, others falling, yet all advancing together, one flock but many birds,
some silent, others tchucking,—incessant alternation. This harmonious movement as in a dance, this agreeing to differ, makes the charm of the spectacle
to me. One bird looks fractional, naked, like a single thread or raveling
from the web to which it belongs. Alternation! Alternation! Heaven and
hell! Here again in the flight of a bird, its ricochet motion, is that undulation observed in so many materials, as in the mackerel sky.

MARCH 28. [1859] As we were paddling over the Great Meadows, I saw
at a distance, high in the air above the middle of the meadow, a very compact flock of blackbirds, advancing against the sun. Though there were more
than a hundred, they did not appear to occupy more than six feet in breadth,
but the whole flock was dashing first to the right and then to the left. When
advancing straight toward me and the sun, they made but little impression
on the eye—so many fine dark points merely, seen against the sky—but as
often as they wheeled to the right or left, displaying their wings flatwise
and the whole length of their bodies, they were a very conspicuous black
mass. This fluctuation in the amount of dark surface was a very pleasing
phenomenon. It reminded me [of] those blinds whose sashes [sic] are made
to move all together by a stick, now admitted nearly all the light and now
entirely excluding it; so the flock of blackbirds opened and shut. But at
length they suddenly spread out and dispersed, some flying off this way
and others that, as, when a wave strikes against a cliff, it is dashed upward
and lost in fine spray. So they lost their compactness and impetus and broke
up suddenly in mid-air.

APRIL 25. [1860] I hear the greatest concert of blackbirds,—red-wings and
crow blackbirds nowadays, especially of the former. . . . The maples and
willows along the river, and the button-bushes, are all alive with them. They
look like black fruit on the trees, distributed over the top at pretty equal
distances. It is worth while to see how slyly they hide at the base of the
thick and shaggy button-bushes at this stage of the water. They will suddenly cease their strains and flit away and secrete themselves low amid these
bushes till you are past; or you scare up an unexpectedly large flock from
such a place, where you had seen none.

I pass a large quire in full blast on the oaks, etc., on the island in the
meadow northeast of Peter's. Suddenly they are hushed, and I hear the loud
rippling rush made by their wings as they dash away, and, looking up, I
see what I take to be a sharp-shinned hawk just alighting on the trees
where they were, having failed to catch one. They retreat some forty rods
off, to another tree, and renew their concert there. The hawk plumes himself,

and then flies off, rising gradually and beginning to circle, and soon it joins its mate, and soars with it high in the sky and out of sight, as if the thought of so terrestrial a thing as a blackbird had never entered its head.

APRIL 29. [1860]   I listen to a concert of red-wings,—their rich sprayey notes, amid which a few more liquid and deep in a lower tone or under-tone, as if it bubbled up from the very water beneath the button-bushes; as if those singers sat lower. Some old and skillful performer touches these deep and liquid notes, and the rest seem to get up a concert just to encourage him. Yet it is ever a prelude or essay with him, as are all good things, and the melody he is capable of and which he did not hear this time is what we remember. The future will draw him out. The different individuals sit singing and pluming themselves and not appearing to have any conversation with one another. They are only tuning all at once; they never seriously perform; the hour has not arrived.

BALTIMORE ORIOLE *(Icterus galbula)*

[The deep silvery bag of the Baltimore Oriole was frequently hung from the tips of branches on the elm trees of Concord streets.

Because the nest is placed so far toward the tip of slender branches which are generally too high to permit examination of the eggs, few see the four to six gray eggs which are scrawled and blotched with black and brown at the large end.

This brilliantly colored species is probably as numerous today as when Thoreau watched them in Concord.]

MAY 8. [1852]   Two gold robins; they chatter like blackbirds; the fire bursts forth on their backs when they lift their wings. A fresh scent blows off from the meadow, the river rapidly going down.

MAY 18. [1852]   These days the golden robin is the important bird in the streets, on the elms.

RUSTY BLACKBIRD *(Euphagus carolinus)*

[Thoreau described in his *Journal* the only song of the Rusty Blackbird. He always called this species the grackle—which could confuse some readers since there is a grackle in New England. However, Thoreau called that species the crow blackbird.

Rusty Blackbirds spend much of the year in flocks, often mingling with other blackbirds, but during the nesting season they are solitary. Then they seek wet woods and swamps filled with trees—alders and willows interspersed with shallow pools.

Their southward movement through Concord takes place chiefly during September and October. March and April witness the passage of the majority of Rusty Blackbirds on their return in spring as they travel toward their nesting grounds in the mountains of New England or farther north to Ontario, Quebec, and Labrador.]

APRIL 9. [1855]   Wilson says that the only note of the rusty grackle is a *chuck*, though he is told that at Hudson's Bay, at the breeding-time, they sing with a fine note. Here they utter not only a *chuck* but a *fine* shrill whistle. They cover the top of a tree now, and their concert is of this character: They all seem laboring together to get out a clear strain, as it were wetting their whistles against their arrival at Hudson's Bay. They begin as it were by disgorging or spitting it out, like so much tow, from a full throat, and conclude with a clear, fine, shrill, ear-piercing whistle. Then away they go, all chattering to-gether.

APRIL 11. [1856]   Going up the railroad, I see a male and female rusty grackle alight on an oak near me, the latter apparently a flaxen brown, with a black tail. She looks like a different species of bird. Wilson had heard only a *tchuck* from the grackle, but this male, who was courting his mate, broke into incipient warbles, like a bubble burst as soon as it came to the surface, it was so aerated. Its air would not be fixed long enough.

COMMON GRACKLE *(Quiscalus quiscula)*

[This foot-long blackbird has a long wedge-shaped tail. It has iridescent gleams of purple, blue, and bronze on its plumage and a pale yellow eye. The females are smaller and less iridescent than the males.

Grackles prefer to nest near water, but tall evergreens in open country are sometimes chosen. Occasionally they nest in colonies numbering as many as twenty-five pairs.]

MAY 11. [1854]   Over meadows in boat at sunset to Island. Now at last I see crow blackbirds without doubt. They have probably been here before, for they are put down under April in the bird book (for '37). They fly as if carrying or dragging their precious long tails, broad at the end, through the air. Their note is like a great rusty spring, and also a hoarse chuck.

JUNE 6. [1854]   Up Assabet. A crow blackbird's nest in a white maple this side the Leaning Hemlocks, in a crotch seven or eight feet from ground;

somewhat like a robin's but larger, made of coarse weed stems, mikania, and cranberry vines (without leaves), fish-lines, etc., without, and of mid lined with finer fibres or roots within; four large but blind young covered with dark brown.

BROWN-HEADED COWBIRD *(Molothrus ater)*

[These small members of the blackbird family, which Thoreau watched as they fed near a herd of cattle, attended the great bison herds before cows were brought to America.

Cowbirds do not build their own nests but place their eggs in the nests of such species as vireos, warblers, and sparrows. The foster parents incubate the eggs and rear the young which are ready to leave the nest in about ten days. The rightful young of the parasitized nest seldom survive.

The more one reads the reference material on which Thoreau had to rely, the more one appreciates the skill he developed in bird identification. It seems likely that the Ambiguous Sparrow of Audubon, Nuttall, and Peabody was a young cowbird. Nuttall describes it as a plain, mouse-colored sparrow that was shot near Cambridge and also said that he had seen an Ambiguous Sparrow in a Wilson's Thrush (Veery) nest. This must have misled many of his readers into believing that in Massachusetts there was a species of small land bird, other than the Cowbird, that parasitized small birds. Audubon called the Cowbird cow bunting and cow-pen bird, and Nuttall, even more generous with his names for the species, called it cow blackbird, cow troopial, and cow-bird. In spite of misleading information and many names, Thoreau became well acquainted with the voice and flight of the species.]

JULY 16. [1851]   The red-wings and crow blackbirds are heard chattering on the trees, and the cow troopials are accompanying the cows in the pastures for the sake of the insects they scare up. Oftentimes the thoughtless sportsman has lodged his charge of shot in the cow's legs in his eagerness to obtain the birds.

SEPT. 4. [1853]   In Potter's dry pasture I saw the ground black with blackbirds (troopials?). As I approach the front rank rises and flits a little further back into the midst of the flock,—it rolls up on the edges,—and, being then alarmed, they soon take flight, with a loud rippling rustle, but soon alight again. the rear wheeling swiftly into place like well-drilled soldiers. Instead of being an irregular and disorderly crowd, they appear to know and keep their places and wheel with the precision of drilled troops.

AUG. 25 [1855]   In Dennis's field this side of the river, I count about one hundred and fifty cowbirds about eight cows, running before their noses and in odd positions, awkwardly walking with a straddle, often their heads down and tails up a long time at once, occasionally flying to keep up with a cow, over the heads of the others, and following off after a single cow. They keep close to the cow's head and feet, and she does not mind them; but when all went off in a whirring (rippling?) flock at my approach, the cow (about whom they were all gathered) *looked off after them* for some time, as if she felt deserted.

SCARLET TANAGER *(Piranga olivacea)*

[The Latin name for Tanager means fire, a name most suitable for the male Scarlet Tanager. There is nothing soft or velvety about these birds, which gleam and shine like satin.

In the autumn, the males lose their brilliant red plumage which is replaced with bright green. Even the black wing feathers are tipped with green. Then the male looks much like the female, though even then she is rather duller than her mate.

The Scarlet Tanager as well as the Redstart was called election bird by Thoreau.]

MAY 18. [1851]   The scarlet tanagers are come. The oak leaves of all colors are just expanding, and are more beautiful than most flowers. The hickory buds are almost leaves. The landscape has a new life, and light infused into it. The deciduous trees are springing, to countenance the pines, which are evergreen. It seems to take but one summer day to fetch the summer in. The turning-point between winter and summer is reached. The birds are in full blast.

MAY 20. [1853]   Saw a tanager in Sleepy Hollow. It most takes the eye of any bird. You here have the red-wing reversed,—the deepest scarlet of the red-wing spread over the whole body, not on the wing-coverts merely, while the wings are black. It flies through the green foliage as if it would ignite the leaves.

MAY 23. [1853]   At Loring's Wood heard and saw a tanager. What a contrast of a *red* bird with the green pines and the blue sky! Even when I have heard his note and look for him and find the bloody fellow, sitting on a dead twig of a pine, I am always startled. (They seem to love the darkest and thickest pines.) That incredible red, with the green and blue, as if these were the trinity we wanted. Yet with his hoarse note he pays for his color. I am transported; these are not the woods I ordinarily walk in. He sunk

Concord in his thought. How he embraces the wildness and wealth of the woods! This and the emperor moth make the tropical phenomena of our zone. There is warmth in the pewee's strain, but this bird's colors and his notes tell of Brazil.

MAY 23. [1854]   We soon get through with Nature. She excites an expectation which she cannot satisfy. The merest child which has rambled into a copse-wood dreams of a wilderness so wild and strange and inexhaustible as Nature can never show him. The red-bird which I saw on my companion's string on election days, I thought but the outmost sentinel of the wild, immortal camp—of the wild and dazzling infantry of the wilderness—that the deeper woods abounded with redder birds still; but, now that I have threaded all our woods and waded the swamps, I have never yet met with his compeer, still less his wilder kindred. The red-bird which is the last of Nature is but the first of God. The White Mountains, likewise, were smooth mole-hills to my expectation. We *condescend* to climb the crags of earth. It is our weary legs alone that praise them. That forest on whose skirts the red-bird flits is not of earth. I expected a fauna more infinite and various, birds of more dazzling colors and more celestial song.

JUNE 24. [1857]   Looked over Farmer's eggs and list of names. He has several which I have not. . . . Among the rest I read, *"Fire never redder."* That must be the tanager. He laughed and said that this was the way he came to call it by that name: Many years ago, one election-day, when he and other boys, or young men, were out gunning to see how many birds they could kill, Jonathan Hildreth, who lived near by, saw one of these birds on the top of a tree before him in the woods, but he did not see a deep ditch that crossed his course between him and it. As he raised his gun, he exclaimed, "Fire never redder!" and, taking a step or two forward, with his eye fixed on the bird, fell headlong into the ditch, and so the name became a byword among his fellows.

MAY 24. [1860]   To Cliffs. As I sit just above the northwest end of the Cliff, I see a tanager perched on one of the topmost twigs of a hickory, holding by the tender leaflets, now five inches long, and evidently come to spy after me, peeping behind a leaflet. He is between me and the sun, and his plumage is incredibly brilliant, all aglow. It is our highest-colored bird,—a deep scarlet (with a yellower reflection when the sun strikes him), in the midst of which his pure-black wings look high-colored also. You can hardly believe that a living creature can wear such colors. A hickory, too, is the fittest perch for him.

THE FRINGILLIDAE

[This is a huge family of birds containing about four hundred and twenty-five species. It is world-wide in distribution, with the exception of Australia. It is frequently called the sparrow family in spite of the fact that it includes the grosbeaks, finches, and buntings as well as the sparrows. The characteristics of the various species are extremely varied, but typical bills are short and quite thick. One characteristic shared by all is nine primaries in the wing.

Thoreau had trouble in identifying the sparrows which he observed in Concord. This difficulty is shared by many to-day in spite of the excellent field guides and fine binoculars available to bird students. Many species are similar in many respects, and the immature birds are even more confusing. It is not surprising that frequently Thoreau simply called the small brownish birds, sparrows. Though it is not possible to identify them now, some of his observations about "sparrows" are too important to omit.]

SEPT. 11. [1850]   Autumnal mornings, when the feet of countless sparrows are heard like rain-drops on the roof by the boy who sleeps in the garret.

Nov. 9. [1850]   A rusty sparrow or two only remains to people the drear spaces. It goes to roost without neighbors.

OCT. 19. [1856]   To Conantum. The fall, now and for some weeks, is the time for flocks of sparrows of various kinds flitting from bush to bush and tree to tree—and both bushes and trees are thinly leaved or bare—and from one seared meadow to another. They are mingled together, and their notes, even, being faint, are, as well as their colors and motion, much alike. The sparrow youth are on the wing. They are still further concealed by their resemblance in color to the gray twigs and stems, which are now beginning to be bare. I have not noticed any kind of blackbird for a long time. . . .

I have often noticed the inquisitiveness of birds, as the other day of a sparrow, whose motions I should not have supposed to have any reference to me, if I had not watched it from first to last. I stood on the edge of a pine and birch wood. It flitted from seven or eight rods distant to a pine within a rod of me, where it hopped about stealthily and chirped awhile, then flew as many rods the other side and hopped about there a spell, then back to the pine again, as near me as it dared, and again to its first position, very restless all the while. Generally I should have supposed that there was more than one bird, or that it was altogether accidental,—that the chipping of this sparrow eight or ten rods [away] had no reference to

me,—for I could see nothing peculiar about it. But when I brought my glass
to bear on it, I found that it was almost steadily eying me and was all alive
with excitement.

Oct. 26. [1857] Those sparrows, too, are thoughts I have. They come and
go; they flit by quickly on their migrations, uttering only a faint *chip*, I
know not whither or why exactly. One will not rest upon its twig for me
to scrutinize it. The whole copse will be alive with my rambling thoughts,
bewildering me by their very multitude, but they will be all gone directly,
without leaving me a feather. My loftiest thought is somewhat like an eagle
that suddenly comes into the field of view, suggesting great things and
thrilling the beholder, as if it were bound hitherward with a message for
me; but it comes no nearer, but circles and soars away, growing dimmer,
disappointing me, till it is lost behind a cliff or a cloud.

Rose-breasted Grosbeak *(Pheucticus ludovicianus)*

[It is surprising that Thoreau did not discover this species until 1853, for it
is not shy and frequently nests in gardens and farmland thickets. The male
shares incubation duties and often sings as he covers the eggs and young.

The Rose-breasted Grosbeak is more common in New England now than
it was in the last century. Since it eats many insects which are considered
harmful by farmers and gardeners, its presence is desired by those people
who prefer natural controls for insect pests.]

June 13. [1853] What was that rare and beautiful bird in the dark woods
under the Cliffs, with black above and white spots and bars, a large triangular blood-red spot on breast, and sides of breast and beneath white? Note
a warble like the oriole, but softer and sweeter. It was quite tame. I cannot
find this bird described. I think it must be a grosbeak. At first I thought
I saw a chewink, [as] it sat within a rod sideways to me, and I was going
to call Sophia to look at it, but then it turned its breast full toward me
and I saw the blood-red breast, a *large* triangular painted spot occupying
the greater part of the breast. It was in the cool, shaded underwood by the
old path just under the Cliff. It is a memorable event to meet with so rare
a bird. Birds answer to flowers, both in their abundance and their rareness.
The meeting with some rare and beautiful flower, which you may never find
again, perchance, like the great purple fringed orchis, at least. How much
it enhances the wildness and the richness of the forest to see in it some
beautiful bird which you never detected before!

May 24. [1855] Hear a rose-breasted grosbeak. At first thought it a tanager, but soon I perceived its more *clear* and instrumental—should say whistle, if one could whistle like a flute; a noble singer, reminding me also of a robin; clear, loud and flute-like; on the oaks, hillside south of Great Fields. Black all above except white on wing, with a triangular red mark on breast but, as I saw, all white beneath this. Female quite different, yellowish olivaceous above, more like a muscicapa. Song not so sweet as clear and strong. Saw it fly off and catch an insect like a flycatcher.

MAY 21. [1856]   Saw two splendid rose-breasted grosbeaks with females in the young wood in Emerson's lot. What strong-colored fellows, black, white, and fiery rose-red breasts! Strong-natured, too, with their stout bills. A clear, sweet singer, like a tanager but hoarse somewhat, and not shy.

JUNE 14. [1859]   The rose-breasted Grosbeak is common now in the Flint's Pond woods. It is not at all shy, and our richest singer, perhaps, after the wood thrush. The rhythm is very like that of the tanager, but the strain is perfectly clear and sweet. One sits on the bare dead twig of a chestnut, high over the road, at Gourgas Wood, and over my head, and sings clear and loud at regular intervals,—the strain about ten or fifteen seconds long, rising and swelling to the end, with various modulations. Another, singing in emulation, regularly answers it, alternating with it, from a distance, at least a quarter of a mile off. It sings thus long at a time, and I leave it singing there, regardless of me.

INDIGO BUNTING *(Passerina cyanea)*

[In shadow or against the sky, the male Indigo Bunting looks dark, almost black, but in full sunlight he looks intensely blue. The female is nondescript in color and her uniform brown lacks definite field marks.

These birds prefer to nest in brushy thickets or old fields invaded by a sprinkling of small shrubs. Two broods are usually raised each season.]

JULY 21. [1851]   9 A.M. On Conantum.—A quarter of a mile is distance enough to make the atmosphere look blue now. This is never the case in spring or early summer. It was fit that I should see an indigo-bird here, concerned about its young, a perfect embodiment of the darkest blue that ever fills the valleys at this season.

JUNE 9. [1857]   To Violet Sorrel and Calla Swamp. In the sprout-land beyond the red huckleberry, an indigo-bird, which *chips* about me as if it had a nest there. This is a splendid and marked bird, high-colored as is the tanager, looking strange in this latitude. Glowing indigo. It flits from top of one bush to another, chirping as if anxious. Wilson says it sings, not like most other birds in the morning and evening chiefly, but also in the middle of the day. In this I notice it is like the tanager, the other fiery-plumaged bird. They seem to love the heat. It probably had its nest in one of those bushes.

PURPLE FINCH *(Carpodacus purpureus)*

[The Purple Finch is naturally a bird of the forest, preferring conifer woodlands, but it has adapted to villages where evergreens, particularly cedars whose berries it likes, are heavily planted in gardens and about the houses.

Purple Finches are permanent residents in Massachusetts, but they are most common during migration. In spring, these small, conical-billed birds are usually most abundant at Concord feeding stations at the time when red maples are in full bloom. The finches eat the buds of the maples and the male Purple Finches almost match them in color. Thoreau, who scattered crumbs by his Walden Pond cabin for the birds, would have enjoyed the intimacy of observation made possible to-day by well-stocked feeding shelves.

Thoreau never ceased to be astonished when the beautiful spring songs of birds were not heard by those who walked the streets of Concord. On April 3, 1858, he heard the rich strains of a Purple Finch coming from an elm, but he alone appeared to hear the music while everyone else in Concord had listened to, or at least heard about, the European singers who had given Lyceum concerts in the town.]

OCT. 7. [1842]   A little girl has just brought me a purple finch or American linnet. These birds are now moving south. It reminds me of the pine and spruce, and the juniper and cedar on whose berries it feeds. It has the crimson hues of the October evenings, and its plumage still shines as if it had caught and preserved some of their tint (beams?). We know it chiefly as a traveller. It reminds me of many things I had forgotten. Many a serene evening lies snugly packed under its wing.

APRIL 15. [1854]   The arrival of the purple finches appears to be coincident with the blossoming of the elm, on whose blossom it feeds.

APRIL 12. [1856]   There suddenly flits before me and alights on a small apple tree in Mackay's field, as I go to my boat, a splendid purple finch. Its glowing redness is revealed when it lifts its wings; as when the ashes is [*sic*] blown from a coal of fire. Just as the oriole displays its gold.

April 3. [1858]   Going down-town this morning, I am surprised by the
rich strain of the purple finch from the elms. Three or four have arrived
and lodged against the elms of our street, which runs east and west across
their course, and they are now mingling their loud and rich strains with
that of the tree sparrows, robins, bluebirds, etc. The hearing of this note
implies some improvement in the acoustics of the air. It reminds me of that
genial state of the air when the elms are in bloom. They sit still over the
street and make a business of warbling. They advertise me surely of some
additional warmth and serenity. How their note rings over the roofs of
the village! You wonder that even the sleepers are not awakened by it to
inquire who is there, and yet probably not another than myself in all the
town observes their coming, and not half a dozen ever distinguished them
in their lives. And yet the very mob of the town know the hard names of
Germanians or Swiss families which once sang here or elsewhere.

Pine Grosbeak *(Pinicola enucleator)*

[This is the largest of the grosbeaks and it breeds in boreal forests around
the whole Northern Hemisphere. The male is rose-red while the female is
greenish gray. The visits of this species to snow-covered Concord are always
events to remember. They seldom arrive there before November and their
numbers depend on available food supplies. If the cone crop in the north
is good, few may be seen in Massachusetts. But if the northern cone crops
fail, large flocks move southward where they quickly strip an area of food
and move on to another place that offers abundant food. During their excursions south of their breeding range they eat not only the seeds from conifer
cones, cedar berries, beechnuts, and ash seeds, but also the buds of deciduous
trees.]

Dec. 24. [1851]   Saw also some pine grosbeaks, magnificent winter birds,
among the weeds and on the apple trees; like large catbirds at a distance,
but, nearer at hand, some of them, when they flit by, are seen to have gorge-
ous heads, breasts, and rumps(?), with red or crimson reflections, more
beautiful than a steady bright red would be. The note I heard, a rather
faint and innocent whistle of two bars.

Dec. 11. [1855]   When some rare northern bird like the pine grosbeak
is seen thus far south in the winter, he does not suggest poverty, but dazzles
us with his beauty. There is in them a warmth akin to the warmth that melts
the icicle. Think of these brilliant, warm-colored, and richly warbling birds,
birds of paradise, dainty-footed, downy-clad, in the midst of a New England a Canadian winter. The woods and fields now somewhat solitary.

being deserted by their more tender summer residents, are now frequented
by these rich but delicately tinted and hardy northern immigrants of the
air. Here is no imperfection to be suggested. The winter, with its snow and
ice, is not an evil to be corrected. It is as it was designed and made to be,
for the artist has had leisure to add beauty to use. My acquaintances,
angels from the north. I had a vision thus prospectively of these birds as
I stood in the swamps. I saw this familiar—too *familiar*—fact at a different
angle, and I was charmed and haunted by it. But I could only attain to be
thrilled and enchanted, as by the sound of a strain of music dying away.
I had seen into paradisaic regions, with their air and sky, and I was no
longer wholly or merely a denizen of this vulgar earth. Yet had I hardly
a foothold there. I was only sure that I was charmed, and no mistake. It is
only necessary to behold thus the least fact or phenomenon, however familiar, from a point a hair's breadth aside from our habitual path or routine,
to be overcome, enchanted by its beauty and significance. Only what we
have touched and worn is trivial—our scurf, repetition, tradition, conformity. To perceive freshly, with fresh senses, is to be inspired. Great winter
itself looked like a precious gem, reflecting rainbow colors from one angle.

Common Redpoll *(Acanthis flammea)*

[This small bird, which breeds throughout the Northern Hemisphere from
the tundra southward, is found as a nesting bird of the United States only
in Alaska. During the winter they gather in flocks that wander about in
search of food which consists chiefly of seeds, those of the birch and alder
being preferred. But most weed seeds appearing above the snow are eaten
if necessary. Since food supplies may be poor in one area in a given season
but ample the next, this species, like the Pine Grosbeaks, Crossbills, and
other northern seed-eaters search for areas of abundance. Thus their movements from year to year are erratic, as they depend on supplies of their
preferred foods.

Thoreau found the Redpoll to be the most abundant bird in Concord
during the winter of 1851–52. Some winters not one was seen there, either
because there was ample food in the north, or plentiful supplies were found
elsewhere.

This species was once called *Fringilla linaria*, and Thoreau frequently
referred to them as linarias. He also called them passenger birds, ruby-
crowned wrens (apparently mistaking them occasionally for Ruby-crowned
Kinglets), and red-crowns.]

JAN. 3. [1853] The red-crowns here still. They appear to frequent one
clump of birches a long time, for here the snow beneath is covered with

the seeds they have loosened, while elsewhere there are none. They hang by the twigs while they peck the catkins, and others are busy on the snow beneath, picking up what drops. They are continually in motion, with a jingling twitter and occasional mew, and suddenly, when disturbed, go off with a loud jingle like the motion of a whole bag of nuts.

DEC. 19. [1854]   Off Clamshell I heard and saw a large flock of *Fringilla linaria* over the meadow. No doubt it was these I saw on the 15th. (But I saw then, and on the 10th, a larger and whiter bird also; may have been the bunting.) Suddenly they turn aside in their flight and dash across the river to a large white birch fifteen rods off, which plainly they had distinguished so far. I afterward saw many more in the Potter swamp up the river. They were commonly brown or dusky above, streaked with yellowish white or ash, and more or less white or ash beneath. Most had a crimson crown or frontlet, and a few crimson neck and breast, very handsome. Some with a bright-crimson crown and clear-white breasts. I suspect that these were young males. They keep up an incessant twittering, varied from time to time with some mewing notes, and occasionally, for some unknown reason, they will all suddenly dash away with that universal loud note (twitter) like a bag of nuts. They are busily clustered in the tops of the birches, picking the seeds out of the catkins, and sustain themselves in all kinds of attitudes, sometimes head downwards, while about this. Common as they are now, and were winter before last, I saw none last winter.

JAN. 19. [1855]   At noon it is still a driving snow-storm, and a little flock of redpolls is busily picking the seeds of the pig-weed, etc., in the garden. Almost all have more or less crimson; a few are very splendid, with their particularly bright crimson breasts. The white on the edge of their wing-coverts is very conspicuous. . . .

It may be that the linarias come into the gardens now not only because all nature is a wilderness to-day, but because the woods where the wind has not free play are so snowed up, the twigs are so deeply covered, that they cannot readily come at their food.

FEB. 12. [1855]   P.M.—To Walden. Under the birches, where the snow is covered with birch seeds and scales, I see the fine tracks, undoubtedly of linarias. The track of one of these birds in the light surface looks like a chain, or the ova of toads. Where a large flock has been feeding, the whole surface is scored over by them.

DEC. 11. [1855]   To Holden Swamp, Conantum . . . Standing there, though in this *bare* November landscape, I am reminded of the incredible phenomenon of small birds in winter,—that ere long, amid the cold powdery snow, as it were a fruit of the season, will come twittering a flock of delicate crimson-tinged birds, lesser redpolls, to sport and feed on the seeds and buds now just ripe for them on the sunny side of a wood, shaking down the powdery snow there in their cheerful social feeding, as if it were high midsummer to them. These crimson aerial creatures have wings which would bear them quickly to the regions of summer, but there is all the summer they want. What a rich contrast! tropical colors, crimson breasts, on cold white snow! Such etherealness, such delicacy in their forms, such ripeness in their colors, in this stern and barren season! It is as surprising as if you were to find a brilliant crimson flower which flourished amid the snows. They greet the chopper and the hunter in their furs. Their Maker gave them the last touch and launched them forth the day of the Great Snow. He made this bitter imprisoning cold before which man quails, but He made at the same time these warm and glowing creatures to twitter and be at home in it. He said not only, Let there be linnets in winter, but linnets of rich plumage and pleasing twitter, bearing summer in their natures. The snow will be three feet deep, the ice will be two feet thick, and last night, perchance, the mercury sank to thirty degrees below zero. All fountains of nature seem to be sealed up. The traveller is frozen on his way. But under the edge of yonder birch wood will be a little flock of crimson-breasted lesser redpolls, busily feeding on the seeds of birch and shaking down the powdery snow! As if a flower were created to be now in bloom, a peach to be now first fully ripe on its stem. I am struck by the perfect confidence and success of nature. There is no question about the existence of these delicate creatures, their adaptness to their circumstances. There is superadded superfluous paintings and adornments, a crystalline jewel-like health and soundness, like the colors reflected from ice-crystals.

AMERICAN GOLDFINCH *(Spinus tristis)*

[Usually by December when Thoreau watched the "burning" yellow goldfinches in the snow, the males have acquired their dull winter plumage and look quite like the females. Their winter flocks are not numerous in northern New England, but the occasional groups may be located by their chorus of sweet twittery high-pitched calls.

This is one of the last birds to nest in Massachusetts, for it delays until there is ample thistledown to line its nest. In fact, the association of this species with thistledown is so pronounced that Nuttall placed it in the subgenus *Carduelis* (from *carduus* for thistle), to which the European Goldfinch belongs. (See Aug. 14, 1858.) The nest is formed so compactly that it has been known to hold enough water to drown the young. The pale blue or white eggs number from four to six. Most young birds are fed some kind of animal food, and goldfinches might be expected to give their young soft insects or worms. Instead, they feed them partially digested seeds by regurgitation.

The undulatory flight of the goldfinch, accompanied by a cheerful *per-chic-o-ree*, is one of the familiar sights and sounds of New England summers.]

SEPT. 28. [1851] Piping goldfinches are flitting about like leaves and hopping up on to the bent grass stems in the garden, letting themselves down to the heavy heads, either shaking or picking out a seed or two, then alighting to pick it up. I am amused to see them hop up on to the slender, drooping grass stems, then slide down, or let themselves down, as it were foot over foot, with great fluttering, till they can pick at the head and release a few seeds; then alight to pick them up. They seem to prefer a coarse grass which grows like a weed in the garden between the potato-hills, also the amaranth.

AUG. 10. [1854] The tinkling notes of goldfinches and bobolinks which we hear nowadays are of one character and peculiar to the season. They are not voluminous flowers, but rather nuts, of sound,—ripened seed of sound. It is the tinkling of ripened grain in Nature's basket. It is like the sparkle on water,—a sound produced by friction on the crisped air.

AUG. 28. [1856] A goldfinch twitters away from every thistle now, and soon returns to it when I am past. I see the ground strewn with the thistle-down they have scattered on every side.

AUG. 14. [1858] The Canada thistle down is now begun to fly, and I see the goldfinch upon it. *Carduelis*. Often when I watch one go off, he flies at first one way, rising and falling, as if skimming close over unseen billows, but directly makes a great circuit as if he had changed his mind, and disappears in the opposite direction, or is seen to be joined there by his mate.

DEC. 22. [1858] To Walden. I see in the cut near the shanty-site quite a flock of *F. hyemalis* and goldfinches together, on the snow and weeds and ground. Hear the well-known mew and watery twitter of the last and the drier *chill chill* of the former. These burning yellow birds with a black cap and white on their coat-flaps look warm above the snow. There may be thirty goldfinches, very brisk and pretty tame. They hang head downwards on the weeds. I hear of their coming to pick sunflower seeds in Melvin's garden these days.

MARCH 24. [1859]   Returning, above the railroad causeway, I see a flock of goldfinches, first of *spring*, flitting along the causeway-bank. They have not yet the bright plumage they will have, but in some lights might be mistaken for sparrows. There is considerable difference in color between one and another, but the flaps of their coats are black, and their heads and shoulders more or less yellow. They are eating the seeds of the mullein and the large primrose, clinging to the plants sidewise in various positions and pecking at the seed-vessels.

RED CROSSBILL *(Loxia curvirostra)*

[This is one of the two species of birds in North America which have crossed bills. They are usually seen clinging to conifer cones, from which they dexterously extract the seeds with their bills, or in compact groups flying rapidly above the tree tops.

They are as erratic in their nesting habits as they are in their appearance in a given area. Their eggs have been found from January through August.

When Thoreau saw two Red Crossbills on April 13, 1860, he instantly recognized them as a species new to him, but being familiar with their description in his reference books, he was able to identify them.]

APRIL 13. [1860]   P.M.—I go up the Assabet to look at the sweet-gale . . . At first I had felt disinclined to make this excursion up the Assabet, but it distinctly occurred to me that, perhaps, if I came against my will, as it were, to look at the sweet-gale as a matter [of] business, I might discover something else interesting, as when I discovered the sheldrake. As I was paddling past the uppermost hemlocks, I saw two peculiar and plump birds near me on the bank there which reminded me of the cow blackbird and of the oriole at first. I saw at once that they were new to me, and guessed that they were crossbills, which was the case,—male and female. The former was dusky-greenish (through a glass), orange and red, the orange, etc., on head, breast, and rump, the vent white; dark, large bill; the female more of a dusky slate-color, and yellow instead of orange and red. They were very busily eating the seeds of the hemlock, whose cones were strewn on the ground, and they were very fearless, allowing me to approach quite near.

When I returned this way I looked for them again, and at the larger hemlocks heard a peculiar note, *cheep, cheep, cheep, cheep,* in the rhythm of a fish hawk but faster and rather loud, and looking up saw them fly to the north side and alight on the top of a swamp white oak, while I sat in my boat close under the south bank. But immediately they recrossed and went to feeding on the bank within a rod of me. They were very parrot-like both in color (especially the male, greenish and orange, etc.) and in their manner of feeding,—holding the hemlock cones in one claw and rapidly extracting the seeds with their bills, thus trying one cone after another very fast. But they kept their bills going [so] that, near as they were, I did not distinguish the cross. I should have looked at them in profile. At last the two hopped within six feet of me, and one within four feet, and they were coming still nearer, as if partly from curosity, though nibbling the cones all the while, when my chain fell down and rattled loudly,—for the wind shook the boat,—and they flew off a rod. In Bechstein I read that "it frequents fir and pine woods, but only when there are abundance of the cones." It may be that the abundance of white pine cones last fall had to do with their coming here. The hemlock cones were very abundant too, methinks.

RUFOUS SIDED TOWHEE *(Pipilo erythrophthalmus)*

[A few species of birds have a renewal of song after postbreeding moulting is completed. Usually such songs lack the exuberant qualities of spring songs and are often overlooked. Thoreau noted this lack of autumn vigor in the song of the towhee in September, 1858.

Towhees, called both chewink and ground-robin by Thoreau, demand a habitat having dense brushy cover under which they frequently scratch among the leaves. Usually they make their nest on the ground where their loosely built structure of coarse leaves, stems, and bark is lined with fine grasses and hair. They have two broods annually, and it is said that the second nest rather frequently is built off the ground up to a height of five feet.]

MAY 23. [1853] How different the . . . jingle of the chewink or any bird's note sounds now at 5 P.M. in the cooler, stiller air, when also the humming of insects is more distinctly heard, and perchance some impurity has begun to sink to earth strained by the air! Or is it, perchance, to be referred to the cooler, more clarified and pensive state of mind, when dews have begun to descend and clarify it? Chaste eve! A certain lateness in the sound, pleasing to hear, which releases me from the obligation to return in any particular season. I have passed the Rubicon of staying out. I have said to myself, that way is not homeward; I will wander further from what I have called my home—to the home which is forever inviting me. In such an hour the freedom of the woods is offered me, and the birds sing my despensation. In dreams the links of life are united; we forget that our friends are dead; we know them as of old.

Sept. 19. [1858]   Hear a chewink's *chewink*. But how ineffectual is the note of a bird now! We hear it as if we heard it not, and forgot it immediately. In spring it makes its due impression, and for a long time will not have done echoing, as it were, through our minds. It is even as if the atmosphere were in an unfavorable condition for this kind of music. Every musician knows how much depends on this.

SAVANNAH SPARROW *(Passerculus sandwichensis)*

[Thoreau made several references to the Savannah Sparrow in his *Journal*. But as late as June 26, 1856, when on a visit to his friend Daniel Ricketson in New Bedford, he expressed some uncertainty about the identification of the species. On June 12, 1857, he visited the natural-history room in Cambridge where he examined birds' eggs and noted that Savannah Sparrow eggs were about the size of Grasshopper Sparrow eggs but were dirty white with thick brown blotches.

Bradford Torrey appended a footnote in regard to Thoreau's entry concerning the Savannah Sparrow on May 1, 1852, as follows: "Though here, where the 'seringo-bird' makes it first appearance in the *Journal* its identity with the savanna sparrow seems to have been unquestioned by Thoreau, it proved afterwards . . . to be almost as puzzling to him as the ever elusive 'night warbler.' The probability is that the 'seringo' in this and most other cases was the Savannah sparrow, but it may sometimes have been the yellow-winged, or grasshopper sparrow, or even, as Thoreau once suspected, the grass finch, or vesper sparrow. It is quite likely that at times the bird he saw was not the bird he heard. . . ."

This open-country sparrow has a white stripe on the crown, a yellowish stripe over the eye, and a short tail. It looks rather like a short-tailed Song Sparrow. It nests in meadows of the Concord area.]

May 1. [1852]   I hear the note of the shy Savannah sparrow (*F. Savanna*), that plump bird with a dark-streaked breast that runs and hides in the grass, whose note sound so like a cricket's in the grass. (I used to hear it when I walked by moonlight last summer.) I hear it now from deep in the sod,— for there is hardly grass yet. The bird keeps so low you do not see it. You do not suspect how many there are till at length their heads appear. The word *seringo* reminds me of its note,—as if it were produced by some kind of fine metallic spring. It is an earth-sound.

VESPER SPARROW *(Pooecetes gramineus)*

[Thoreau called this species by any of several names including bay-wing, grass finch, grass-bird, and white-in-tail. The bird resembles a Song Sparrow but is much grayer, and its white outer tail feathers are conspicuous.

Vesper Sparrows are common in Massachusetts not only as migrants but as nesting birds. They do not become numerous until April though many arrive in March. By the end of November they have left the state for more southern areas.

With changing agricultural practices around Concord, Vesper Sparrows have decreased sharply in the past half-century until they are now uncommon and local in that area.]

Nov. 6. [1853]   To Lee's Cliff. It is remarkable how little we attend to what is passing before us constantly, unless our genius directs our attention that way. There are these little sparrows with white in tail, perhaps the prevailing bird of late, which have flitted before me so many falls and springs, and yet they have been as it were strangers to me, and I have not inquired whence they came or whither they were going, or what their habits were. It is surprising how little most of us are contented to know about the sparrows which drift about in the air before us just before the first snows. I hear the downy woodpecker's metallic *tchip* or peep. Now I see where many a bird builded last spring or summer. These are leaves which do not fall. How similar in the main the nests of birds and squirrels and mice! I am not absolutely certain that the mice do not make the whole nest in a bush sometimes, instead of building on a bird's nest. There is in the squirrel in this respect an approach to the bird.

JAN. 1. [1854]   The white-in-tails, or grass finches, linger pretty late, flitting in flocks before, but they come so near winter only as the white in their tails indicates. They let it come near enough to whiten their tails, perchance, and they are off. The snow buntings and the tree sparrows are the true spirits of the snow-storm; they are the animated beings that ride upon it and have their life in it.

MAY 12. [1857]   As the bay-wing sang many a thousand years ago, so sang he tonight. In the beginning God heard his song and pronounced it good, and hence it has endured. It reminded me of many a summer sunset, of many miles of gray rails, of many a rambling pasture, of the farmhouse far in the fields, its milk-pans and well-sweep, and the cows coming home from pasture.

I would thus from time to time take advice of the birds, correct my human views by listening to their volucral [*sic*]. He is a brother poet, this small gray bird (or bard), whose muse inspires mine. His lay is an idyl or pastoral, older and sweeter than any that is classic. He sits on some gray perch like himself, on a stake, perchance, in the midst of the field, and you can hardly see him against the plowed ground. You advance step by step as the twilight deepens, and lo! he is gone, and in vain you strain your eyes to see whither, but anon his tinkling strain is heard from some other quarter. One with the rocks and with us.

Methinks I hear these sounds, have these reminiscences, only when well employed, at any rate only when I have no reason to be ashamed of my employment. I am often aware of a certain compensation of this kind for doing something from a sense of duty, even unconsciously. Our past experience is a never-failing capital which can never be alienated, of which each kindred future event reminds us. If you would have the song of the sparrow inspire you a thousand years hence, let your life be in harmony with its strain to-day.

I ordinarily plod along a sort of whitewashed prison entry, subject to some indifferent or even grovelling mood. I do not distinctly realize my destiny. I have turned down my light to the merest glimmer and am doing some task which I have set myself. I take incredibly narrow views, live on the limits, and have no recollection of absolute truth. Mushroom institutions hedge me in. But suddenly, in some fortunate moment, the voice of eternal wisdom reaches me, even in the strain of the sparrow, and liberates me, whets and clarifies my senses, makes me a competent witness.

APRIL 15. [1859] The bay-wing now sings—the first I have been able to hear—both about the Texas house and the fields this side of Hayden's, both of them similar dry and open pastures. I heard it just before noon, when the sun began to come out, and at 3 P.M., singing loud and clear and incessantly. It sings with a pleasing deliberation, contrasting with the spring vivacity of the song sparrow, whose song many would confound with it. It comes to revive with its song the dry uplands and pastures and grassfields about the skirts of villages. Only think how finely our life is furnished in all its details,—sweet wild birds provided to fill its interstices with song! It is provided that while we are employed in our corporeal, or intellectual, or other exercises we shall be lulled and amused or cheered by the singing of birds. When the laborer rests on his spade to-day, the sun having just come out, he is not left wholly to the mercy of his thoughts, nature is not a mere void to him, but he can hardly fail to hear the pleasing and encouraging notes of some newly arrived bird. The strain of the grass finch is very likely to fall on his ear and convince him, whether he is conscious of it or not, that the world is beautiful and life a fair enterprise to engage in. It will make him calm and contented. If you yield for a moment to the impressions of sense, you hear some bird giving expression to its happiness in a pleasant strain. We are provided with singing birds and with ears to hear them. What an institution that! Nor are we obliged to catch and cage them, nor to be bird-fanciers in the common sense. Whether a man's work be hard or easy, whether he be happy or unhappy, a bird is appointed to sing to a man while he is at his work.

SLATE-COLORED JUNCO *(Junco hyemalis)*

[Few birds are mentioned more frequently in the *Journal* than Thoreau's *F. hyemalis*, the slate-colored snowbird, though he rarely wrote at any length about it. On June 2, 1858, Thoreau found the nest of this species on Mount Monadnock. He rejoiced about this discovery, for he noted in his *Journal* that Brewer said only one nest of the species was known to naturalists. It was on his mountain journeys and in the Maine wilderness that the Slate-colored Junco most impressed him.

Thoreau listened for the first songs of the junco in March, pleasant sound to hear on a cold day of early spring. He appreciated their company when he saw one of their flocks in late November and early December when the days were short and the hours of sunlight were limited.

The species is now a regular visitor to Concord feeding stations throughout the winter.]

MARCH 23. [1852] I heard, this forenoon, a pleasant jingling note from the slate-colored snowbird on the oaks in the sun on Minott's hillside. Apparently they sing with us in the pleasantest days before they go northward.

MARCH 28. [1853] The woods ring with the cheerful jingle of the *F. hyemalis*. This is a very trig and compact little bird, and appears to be in good condition. The straight edge of slate on their breasts contrasts remarkably with the white from beneath; the short, light-colored bill is also very conspicuous amid the dark slate; and when they fly from you, the two white feathers in their tails are very distinct at a good distance. They are very lively, pursuing each other from bush to bush.

APRIL 1. [1854] The birds sing this warm and showery day after a fortnight's cold (yesterday was wet too), with a universal burst and flood of melody. Great flocks of hyemalis, etc., pass overhead like schools of fishes in the water, many abreast. . . . The hyemalis is in the largest flocks of any at this season. You see them come drifting over a rising ground just like snowflakes before a northeast wind. . . . I hear the jingle of the hyemalis from within the house, sounding like a trill.

Dec. 1. [1865] p.m.—By path to Walden. Slate-colored snowbirds flit before me in the path, feeding on the seeds on the snow, the countless little brown seeds that begin to be scattered over the snow, so much more obvious to bird and beast. A hundred kinds of indigenous grain are harvested now, broadcast upon the surface of the snow. Thus at a critical season these seeds are shaken down on to a clean white napkin, unmixed with dirt and rubbish, and off this the little pensioners pick them. Their clean table is thus spread a few inches or feet above the ground. Will wonder become extinct in me? Shall I become insensible as a fungus?

Tree Sparrow *(Spizella arborea)*

[The Tree Sparrow breeds in the stunted trees and shrubs in the region just south of the arctic tundra. Those which winter in Concord find ample seeds held above the snow in weedy fields and brushy open country. As early as February their musical, sweet, variable warbles may be heard in sheltered tangles on sunny slopes.

Thoreau wrote many notes about Tree Sparrows, and the species added interest to his walks in the winter fields and woods. His descriptions of their songs and their feeding habits are exceptionally charming.]

Dec. 3. [1853] Up river by boat to Clamshell Hill. Saw two tree sparrows on Monroe's larch by the waterside. Larger than chip-birds, with more bay above and a distinct white bar on wings, not to mention bright-chestnut crown and obscure spot on breast; all beneath pale-ash. They were busily and very adroitly picking the seeds out of the larch cones. It would take man's clumsy fingers a good while to get at one, and then only by breaking off the scales, but they picked them out as rapidly as if they were insects on the outside of the cone, uttering from time to time a faint, tinkling chip.

Feb. 10. [1855] I hear the faint metallic chirp of a tree sparrow in the yard from time to time, or perchance the mew of a linaria. It is worth the while to let some pigweed grow in your garden, if only to attract these winter visitors. It would be a pity to have these weeds burned in the fall. Of the former I see in the winter but three or four commonly at a time; of the latter, large flocks. This in and after considerable snow-storms.

Dec. 4. [1856] Saw and heard cheep faintly one tree sparrow, the neat chestnut crowned and winged and white-barred bird, perched on a large and solitary white birch. So clean and tough, made to withstand the winter. This color reminds me of the upper side of the shrub oak leaf. I love the few homely colors of Nature at this season,—her strong wholesome browns, her sober and primeval grays, her celestial blue, her vivacious green, her pure, cold, snowy white.

Jan. 16. [1860]   I see a flock of tree sparrows busily picking something from the surface of the snow amid some bushes. I watch one attentively, and find that it is feeding on the very fine brown chaffy-looking seed of the panicled andromeda. It understands how to get its dinner, to make the place *give down*, perfectly. It flies up and alights on one of the dense brown panicles of the hard berries, and gives it a vigorous shaking and beating with its claws and bill, sending down a shower of the fine chaffy-looking seed on to the snow beneath. It lies very distinct, though fine almost as dust, on the spotless snow. It then hops down and briskly picks up from the snow what it wants. How very clean and agreeable to the imagination, and withal abundant, is this kind of food! How delicately they fare! These dry persistant seed-vessels hold their crusts of bread until shaken. The snow is the white table-cloth on which they fall. No anchorite with his water and his crust fares more simply. It shakes down a hundred times as much as it wants at each shrub, and shakes the same or another cluster after each successive snow. How bountifully Nature feeds them! No wonder they come to spend the winter with us, and are at ease in regard to their food. These shrubs ripen an abundant crop of seed to supply the wants of these immigrants from the far north which annually come to spend the winter with us. How neatly and simply it feeds!

This shrub grows unobserved by most, only known to botanists, and at length matures its hard, dry seed-vessels, which, if noticed, are hardly supposed to contain seed. But there is no shrub nor weed which is not known to some bird. Though you may have never noticed it, the tree sparrow comes from the north in the winter straight to this shrub, and confidently shakes its panicle, and then feasts on the fine shower of seeds that falls from it.

Chipping Sparrow (*Spizella passerina*)

[It is indeed wonderful that not only in Thoreau's day when horses were numerous in both town and on farms, but to-day when most horses are replaced by machines, the little dooryard Chipping Sparrow so frequently finds hair to add to its nest.

Though this has been a regular breeding bird in the Concord area since Thoreau's day, it is probably twice as numerous today as it was when he lived beside Walden Pond.]

[Undated. Between 1837 and 1847]   It is a marvel how the birds contrive to survive in this world. These tender sparrows that flit from bush to bush this evening, though it is so late, do not seem improvident, [but appear] to have found a roost for the night. They must succeed by weakness and reliance, for they are not bold and enterprising as their mode of life would seem to require, but very weak and tender creatures. I have seen a little chipping sparrow, come too early in the spring, shivering on an apple twig, drawing in its head and striving to warm it in its muffled feathers; and it had no voice to intercede with nature, but peeped as helpless as an infant, and was ready to yield up its spirit and die without any effort. And yet this was no new spring in the revolution of the seasons.

JUNE 2. [1853]   3:30 A.M. When I awake I hear the low universal chirping or twittering of the chip-birds, like the bursting bead on the surface of the uncorked day. First come, first served! You must taste the first glass of the day's nectar, if you would get all the spirit of it. Its fixed air begins to stir and escape. Also the robin's morning song is heard as in the spring, earlier than the notes of most other birds, thus bringing back the spring; now rarely heard or noticed in the course of the day.

JUNE 24. [1853]   It is surprising that so many birds find hair enough to line their nests with. If I wish for a horsehair for my compass sights I must go to the stable, but the hair-bird, with her sharp eyes, goes to the road.

FIELD SPARROW *(Spizella pusilla)*

[The Field Sparrow provided Thoreau with a focal point for some philosophical comments on literature and living, on July 18, 1852. On April 22, 1859, the same species caused him to think about the changes that take place in bird populations as the vegetation changes in character. His comments are good ecology, though that science had not yet been invented.

Field Sparrows have become uncommon nesting birds in the Concord area. Ludlow Griscom noted this decrease as long ago as 1948 and attributed it to some cause other than a loss of suitable habitat, for this is increasing in that area.]

JULY 18. [1852]   When I think of the London *Times* and the reviews here, the *Revue des Deux Mondes*, and the kind of life which it is possible to live here, I preceive that this, the natural side, has not got into literature. Think of an essay on human life, through all of which was heard the note of the huckleberry-bird still ringing, as here it rings ceaselessly. As if it were the muse invoked! The *Revue des Deux Mondes* does not embrace this view of things, nor imply it.

APRIL 22. [1859]   When setting the pines at Walden the last three days, I was sung to by the field sparrow. For music I heard their jingle from time to time. That the music the pines were set to, and I have no doubt they will build many a nest under their shelter. It would seem as if such a field as this—a dry open or half-open pasture in the woods, with small pines scattered in it—was well-nigh, if not quite, abandoned to this one alone among the sparrows. The surface of the earth is portioned out among them. By a beautiful law of distribution, one creature does not too much interfere with another. I do not hear the song sparrow here. As the pines gradually increase, and a wood-lot is formed, these birds will withdraw to new pastures, and the thrushes, etc., will take their place. Yes, as the walls of cities are fabled to have been built by music, so my pines were established by the song of the field sparrow. They commonly place their nests here under the shelter of a little pine in the field.

WHITE-THROATED SPARROW *(Zonotrichia albicollis)*

[Thoreau was long mistaken about the authorship of the plaintive, clear, high-pitched whistle of this bird. He first thought it was a song of the chickadee and later, of the Myrtle Warbler. As late as his 1857 excursion to the Maine Woods he still thought the Myrtle Warbler was the songster.

Thoreau knew this bird as a transient of variable numbers through Concord. It first appeared as a wintering species in Concord in 1937, but it is now a regular visitor at feeding stations throughout that season.]

APRIL 25. [1855]   P.M.—To Beck Stow's. Hear a faint cheep and at length detect the white-throated sparrow, the handsome and well-marked bird, the largest of the sparrows with a yellow spot on each side of the front, hopping along under the rubbish left by the woodchopper. I afterward hear a faint *cheep* very rapidly repeated, making a faint sharp jingle,—no doubt by the same. Many sparrows have a similar faint metallic *cheep*,—the tree sparrow and field sparrow, for instance. I first saw the white-throated sparrow at this date last year. Hear the peculiar *squeaking* notes of a pigeon woodpecker. Two black ducks circle around me three or four times, wishing to alight in the swamp, but finally go to the river meadows. I hear the whistling of their wings. Their bills point downward in flying.

FOX SPARROW *(Passerella iliaca)*

[This large sparrow with its heavily streaked breast and fox-colored tail nests in Canada as far south as the Gulf of St. Lawrence. Most of them winter south of Connecticut. Some linger in the Concord area through December. Their northward migration is fairly swift. It usually occurs in heavy waves, and bird watchers look forward in March to seeing some of the great flocks when a hundred or more may be found—perhaps all singing their delightful song. By the end of April, the Fox Sparrow becomes a rarity, and those who have been held indoors by cold or snow or rain may completely miss the concentrated and spectacular spring migration of this species.

Thoreau, who always wanted to watch the progression of spring, noted the Fox Sparrow each March from 1852 through 1860. In 1861, illness was causing him to restrict his walks, and his *Journal* entries became much more brief. But on April 6 he wrote: "The (are they cinnamon?) sparrows are the finest singers I have heard yet . . ."]

MARCH 31. [1852]   The song sparrow and the transient fox-colored sparrow,—have they brought me no message this year? Do they go to lead heroic lives in Rupert's Land? They are so small, I think their destinies must be large. Have I heard what this tiny passenger has to say, while it flits thus from tree to tree? Is not the coming of the fox-colored sparrow something more earnest and significant than I have dreamed of? Can I forgive myself if I let it go to Rupert's Land before I have appreciated it? God did not make this world in jest; no, nor in indifference. These migrating sparrows all bear messages that concern my life. I do not pluck the fruits in their season. I love the birds and beasts because they are mythologically in earnest. I see that the sparrow cheeps and flits and sings adequately to the great design of the universe; that man does not communicate with it, understand its language, because he is not at one with nature. I reproach myself because I have regarded with indifference the passage of the birds; I have thought them no better than I.

MARCH 14. [1854]   P.M.—To Great Meadows. Raw thickening mists, as if preceeding rain. A large company of fox-colored sparrows in Heywood's maple swamp close by. I heard their loud, sweet, canary-like whistle thirty or forty rods off, sounding richer than anything yet; some on the bushes singing, *twee twee twa twa ter tweer twa*,—This is the scheme of it only, there being no dental grit to it. They were shy, flitting before me, and I heard a slight susurrus where many were busily scratching amid the leaves of the swamp, without seeing them, and also saw many indistinctly. Wilson never heard but one sing, their common note there being a *cheep*.

APRIL 4. [1855]   P.M.—To Clematis Brook *via* Lee's. A pleasant day, growing warmer; a slight haze. Now the hedges and apple trees are alive with fox-colored sparrows, all over the town, and their imperfect strains are occasionally heard. Their clear, fox-colored backs are very handsome. I get quite near to them.

APRIL 6. [1856]   At Ivy Tree, hear the fine *tseep* of a sparrow, and detect the fox-colored sparrow on the lower twigs of the willows and from time to time scratching the ground beneath. It is quite tame,—a single one with its ashy head and mottled breast.

APRIL 9. [1856]   8 A.M.—By boat to V. palmata Swamp for *white birch sap*. A few rods off I hear some sparrows busily scratching the floor of the swamp, uttering a faint *tseep tseep* and from time to time a sweet strain. It is probably the fox-colored sparrow. These always feed thus, I think, in woody swamps, a flock of them rapidly advancing, flying before one another, through the swamp.

SONG SPARROW *(Melospiza melodia)*

[Song Sparrows are at home anywhere from the shrubs in gardens and parks to wild tangled swamps and young conifer plantings. No other American species of bird has been studied as exhaustively by a scientist as this species has been studied by Margaret Morse Nice. Its song has endeared it to people across the country, and, like Thoreau, they respond happily to its music which often rings through bleak cold days of March.

This bird is abundant in Concord during migration periods and is a common nesting bird in that area. Today, as in Thoreau's time, a rare wintering individual is discovered from time to time.

APRIL 1. [1852]   As I come over the Turnpike, the song sparrow's jingle comes up from every part of the meadow, as native as the tinkling rills or the blossoms of the spirea, the meadow-sweet, soon to spring. Its cheep is like the sound of opening buds. The sparrow is continually singing on the alders along the brook-side, while the sun is continually setting.

APRIL 2. [1852]   6 A.M.—To the riverside and Merrick's pasture. The sun is up. The water on the meadows is perfectly smooth and placid, reflecting the hills, and clouds and trees. The air is full of the notes of birds,—song sparrows, red-wings, robins (singing a strain), bluebirds,—and I hear also a lark,—as if all the earth had burst forth into song. The influence of this April morning has reached them, for they live out-of-doors all the night, and there is no danger that they will oversleep themselves such a morning. A few weeks ago, before the birds had come, there came to my mind in the night the twittering sound of birds in the early dawn of a spring morning, a semiprophecy of it, and last night I attended mentally as if I heard the spray-like dreaming sound of the midsummer frog and realized how glorious and full of revelations it was. Expectations may amount to prophecy.

APRIL 2. [1853]   The song sparrows, the three-spotted, away by the meadowsides, are very shy and cunning; instead of flying will frequently trot along the ground under the bushes, or dodge through a wall like a swallow; and I have observed that they generally bring some object, as a rail or branch, between themselves and the face of the walker,—often with outstretched necks will peep at him anxiously for five or ten minutes.

MAY 11. [1853]   P.M.—To Corner Spring *via* Hubbard's Bathing-Place. I nearly stepped upon a song sparrow and a striped snake at the same time. The bird fluttered away almost as if detained. I thought it was a case of charming, without doubt, and should think so still if I had not found her nest with five eggs there, which will account for her being so near the snake that was about to devour her.

SNOW BUNTING *(Plectrophenox nivalis)*

[These circumpolar birds nest on the tundra below the Arctic Ocean. Though Nuttall stated in his *Manual* that a few of their nests had been found in alpine declivities of the White Mountains in New Hampshire, actually they only come as far south as latitude 52 degrees north to breed.

The sun shines on Snow Buntings for almost twenty-four hours daily during their nesting season. They only leave the Arctic when deep snows bury their food. When they come to Concord, they seldom fail to discover the necessary seeds held by stiff stems above the snows. Even in mid-winter their musical twitter is frequently heard. As they were the real snow birds to Thoreau, so they are to bird watchers today.

In the selection which follows, the tracks Thoreau described may have been made by sparrows, redpolls, Pine Siskins, or other small, sparrowlike birds and not by Snow Buntings, for he applied the name, snowbird, promiscuously to any and all small winter birds.]

JAN. 20. [1853]   P.M.—To Walden. I see where snowbirds in troops have visited each withered chenopodium that rises above the snow in the yard— some are large and bushlike—for its seeds, their well-filled granary now. There are a few tracks reaching from weed to weed, where some have run, but under the larger plants the snow is entirely trodden and blackened, proving that a large flock has been there and flown.

DEC. 29. [1853]   The strong wind from the north blows the snow almost horizontally; and, beside freezing you, almost takes your breath away. The driving snow blinds you, and where you are protected, you can see but a little way, it is so thick. Yet in spite, or on account, of all, I see the first flock of arctic snowbirds (*Emberiza nivalis*) near the depot, white and black, with a sharp whistle-like note. An hour after I discovered half a pint of snow in each pocket of my greatcoat. . . .

These are the true winter birds for you, these winged snowballs. I could hardly see them, the air was so full of driving snow. What hardy creatures! Where do they spend the night.

JAN. 21. [1857]   [Twelve to fifteen inches of snow . . . drifts very large.] As I flounder along the Corner road against the root fence, a very large flock of snow buntings alight with a wheeling flight amid the weeds rising above the snow in Potter's heater-piece,—a hundred or two of them. They run restlessly amid the weeds, so that I can hardly get sight of them through my glass; then suddenly all arise and fly only two or three rods, alighting within three rods of me. (They keep up a constant twittering.) It was as if they were any instant ready for a longer flight, but their leader had not so ordered it. Suddenly away they sweep again, and I see them alight in a distant field where the weeds rise above the snow, but in a few minutes they have left that also and gone further north. Beside their *rippling* note, they have a vibratory twitter, and from the loiterers you hear quite a tender peep, as they fly after the vanishing flock.

What independent creatures! They go seeking their food from north to south. If New Hampshire and Maine are covered deeply with snow, they scale down to Massachusetts for their breakfasts. Not liking the grain in this field, away they dash to another distant one, attracted by the weeds rising above the snow. Who can guess in what field, by what river or mountain they breakfasted this morning. They did not seem to regard me so near, but as they went off, their wave actually broke over me as a rock. They have the pleasure of society at their feasts, a hundred dining at once, busily talking while eating, remembering what occurred at Grinnell Land. As they flew past me they presented a pretty appearance, somewhat like broad bars of white alternating with bars of black.

DEC. 12. [1858]   Crossing the fields west of our Texas house, I see an immense flock of snow buntings, I think the largest that I ever saw. There must be a thousand or two at least. There is but three inches, at most, of crusted and dry frozen snow, and they are running amid the weeds which rise above it. . . . The flock is at first about equally divided into two parts about twenty rods apart, but birds are incessantly flitting across the interval to join the pioneer flock until all are united. They are very restless, running amid the weeds and continually changing their ground. They will suddenly rise again a few seconds after they have alighted, as if alarmed, but after a short wheel settle close by. Flying from you, in some positions, you see only or chiefly the black part of their bodies, and then, as they wheel, the white comes into view, contrasted prettily with the former, and in all together at the same time. Seen flying higher against a cloudy sky they look like large snowflakes. When they rise all together their note is like the rattling of nuts in a bag, as if a whole binful were rolled from side to side. They also utter from time to time—*i.e.* individuals do—a clear rippling note, perhaps of alarm, or a call. It is remarkable that their notes above described should resemble the lesser redpolls! Away goes this great wheeling, rambling flock, rolling through the air, and you cannot easily tell where they will settle. Suddenly the pioneers (or a part not foremost) will change their course when in full career, and when at length they know it, the rushing flock on the other side will be fetched about as it were with an undulating jerk, as in a boy's game of snap-the-whip, and those that occupy the place of the snapper are gradually off after their leaders on the new track. As far as I observe, they confine themselves to upland, not alighting in the meadows. Like a snow-storm they come rushing down from the north. . . . I should like to know where all those snowbirds will roost to-night, for they will probably roost together. And what havoc an owl might make among them!

MARCH 3. [1859] Going by the solidago oak at Clamshell Hill bank, I heard a faint rippling note, and, looking up, saw about fifteen snow buntings sitting in the top of the oak, all with their white breasts toward me,— sitting so still and quite white, seen against the white cloudy sky, they did not look like birds but the ghosts of birds, and their boldness, allowing me to come quite near, enhanced this impression. These were almost as white as snowballs, and from time [to time] I heard a low, soft rippling note from them. I could see no features, but only the general outline of plump birds in white. It was a very spectral sight, and after I had watched them for several minutes, I can hardly say that I was prepared to see them fly away like ordinary buntings when I advanced further.

Thoreau's Ornithological Reference Books

Thoreau made use of as many reference books as were available to him in his attempt to identify the birds of Concord. For instance, after his discovery of a dead Common Merganser on April 6, 1855, he mentions information about the species, or others closely allied to it, gleaned from Wilson, Nuttall, Jardin, Yarrell, and Selby. But most often his information came from Nuttall, Wilson, and Audubon.

Today's uniformity in scientific and common names was lacking a century ago. A student, having located in one book a description which appeared to fit the bird he observed, might find no mention of the name in other reference books. This was most confusing when the bird under study had an indefinite or obscurely patterned plumage. Common, conspicuously colored species such as the Robin, Bluebird, and Baltimore Oriole presented little difficulty, nor did large birds such as geese, swans, gulls, and owls which were rather generally known. But many shorebirds and sparrows are very similar, and it may be necessary to see the color of the legs or a stripe on the head in order to determine the species. Warblers, though the males are often brilliantly colored, are tiny and move about rapidly—which makes it difficult to see them clearly. Moreover, those brilliant colors may be lost when the breeding season ends. To add confusion, the females often lack the colors of the males as do immature birds. Knowledge of plumage changes in many species was unknown in Thoreau's time.

Both Audubon and Wilson painted the adult Red-shouldered Hawk and also the same species in immature plumage—calling it "winter falcon."

Wilson's Winter Falcon [Plate I (1)] and Red-shouldered Hawk [Plate II (3)] are included here. The sketch of a Fish-hawk or Osprey in Nuttall [Plate III] and Wilson's Fish-hawk [Plate IV (1)] do not look like the same species. Wilson's is far more lifelike, but his sketches of the species in flight at left center of the plate would confuse a student. Instead of having pointed wings, the primaries as represented are widely spread at the end, giving a jagged, blunt look to the wings. However, the abrupt crook of the wings is well illustrated.

The Mourning Dove, Wilson's Turtle Dove [Plate V (1)] was easily identified by Thoreau. Only two wild pigeons occurred in Concord. The Passenger Pigeon, now extinct, was larger, had a longer tail, and a blue-gray head.

The heavy-headed, short-tailed Belted Kingfisher was well known to Thoreau, who encountered the species not only in Concord but in most areas where he traveled. Both Nuttall [Plate VI] and Wilson [Plate VII (1)] show the diagnostic features: large bill, shaggy crest, and banded breast that distinguish this species.

Perhaps because Thoreau most enjoyed the songs of thrushes when he was in the woods, he generally called them all "wood thrushes," though, if he saw them well, he was able to distinguish the Wood Thrush, Hermit Thrush, and Veery. Both Wilson [Plate V (2) and (3)] and Audubon [Plates VIII and IX] indicate the light speckling on the breast of the Hermit Thrush and the large, numerous spots on the breast and sides of the Wood Thrush. But how many readers both artists must have misled by dismissing the song of the Hermit Thrush as negligible in quality while enthusing about the song of the Wood Thrush! Today, most people, while granting the exquisite beauty of the Wood Thrush's song, consider that of the Hermit Thrush the most beautiful of any American bird.

Though Audubon, Nuttall, and Wilson described their birds from skins in the hand and often mentioned the color of the bill, they apparently failed to realize that there was a great similarity in the bills of warblers. Typically, they are slender and sharply pointed. Had Thoreau known this and examined the bill, he would not have believed the Black-throated Blue Warbler he saw in Concord was an Indigo Bunting. Wilson's Indigo Bird [Plate X (5)] clearly does not have a warbler-type bill.

Nuttall's American Redstart [Plate XI] and Wilson's [Plate X (6)] show the pattern of this species very well. Apparently Thoreau had no difficulty in identifying the male. He could easily identify a male Yellowthroat from Wilson [Plate X (1)]. Many people still use the old name, Maryland Yellowthroat, for this species. Other warblers painted by Wilson were not as useful for identification, though on Plate VII the Black and Yellow Warbler (2) (now called Magnolia Warbler), Blackburnian Warbler (3), and Water Thrush (5), show some of the outstanding characteristics of each species.

Even with today's excellent bird guides in hand, most experts are cautious about making quick identification of some sparrows, for the distinguishing characteristics are frequently subtle. The song is often much more useful than the fleeting glimpse which is all one sometimes has as a sparrow vanishes in tall grass.

Thoreau knew the common sparrows of the Concord area quite well and often wrote about their songs. He did surprisingly well when one considers that his references contained descriptions and pictures made from specimens only and that he was largely without guidance in the matter of distribution and habitat preference. He recognized the fact that Field Sparrows [Wilson, Plate XII (2)] move into an area when bushes and young trees reach a certain height, then abandon it when the growth becomes tall. It is interesting to compare Wilson [Plates XII and XIII] with Plates 57 and 58 of Peterson's *A Field Guide To The Birds* and to note the vast strides made in the past century and a half in the art of distinguishing between species of sparrows.

Thoreau must have been confused by the many names given a species by different authors. Nuttall [Plate XIV] called the Grasshopper Sparrow *(Ammodramus savannarum)* Savanna Finch or Yellow-shouldered Sparrow, while Wilson [Plate XV (5)] called it Yellow-winged Sparrow. Nuttall's [Plate XIV] description of the song of this species could scarcely be farther from reality, for it begins with a couple of low chucking notes followed by a rather faint locustlike buzz. Nuttall believed the Grasshopper Sparrow wintered in the West Indies, but we now know it winters from North Carolina to the Gulf.

Nuttall's Common Song Sparrow [Plate XVI] illustration fails to show the large central breast spot which every schoolchild recognizes as its best mark for field identification. The page reproduced here lists the scientific names given the species by Wilson and by Audubon. It also reveals some of the charm which a reader today can discover in the first American handbook of birds written when the science of ornithology was in its infancy.

1. *Winter Falcon*. 2. *Magpie*. 3. *Crow*.

35.

PLATE I

From Alexander Wilson: *American Ornithology,* Volume II, **1832**

Drawn from Nature by A. Wilson   Engraved by W.H. Lizars

1 Black Hawk. 2. Variety of d? 3. Red shouldered H? 4. Female Baltimore Oriole. 5. Female Towhee Bunting.
55.

PLATE II
From Alexander Wilson: *American Ornithology*, Volume II, 1832

FISH-HAWK, or OSPREY.

(*Falco haliætus*. LINN. AUDUBON, pl. 81, [excellent.] WILSON, **v.** p. 13, pl. 5. fig. 1. Philadelphia Museum, No. 144.)

SPEC. CHARACT. — Dark brown, beneath white ; cere and feet greyish-blue. — *Female* with the breast thinly spotted with pale brown. — *Young*, nearly all the feathers above terminated with yellowish-white tips.

THIS large and well known species, allied to the Eagles, is found near fresh and salt water in almost every country in the world. In summer it wanders into the arctic regions of Europe, Asia, and America ; it is also found equally prevalent in the milder parts of both continents, as in Greece and Egypt. In America it is found in the summer from Labrador, and the in-

PLATE III
From Thomas Nuttall: *A Manual of the Ornithology of the United States and Canada: The Land Birds,* 1832

210

Drawn from Nature by A. Wilson   Engraved by W.H.Lizars

1. Fish Hawk. 2. Fish Crow. 3. Ring Plover. 4. Least Snipe.
37.

PLATE IV
From Alexander Wilson: *American Ornithology*, Volume II, 1832

1. *Turtle Dove.* 2. *Hermit Thrush.* 3. *Tawney Thrush.* 4. *Pine swamp Warbler.*

Drawn from Nature by A Wilson.   Engraved by W H Lizars.

PLATE V
From Alexander Wilson: *American Ornithology,* Volume II, 1832

These are shy, solitary, and abstemious birds, feeding on insects, and diminutive aquatic animals, but principally on small fish, for which they assiduously watch while perched on some projecting stake or bough impending over the water; these they dexterously catch and swallow whole, at length casting up the scales, bones, and indigestible parts in the form of pellets. They fly for short distances with considerable celerity, skimming directly over the surface of the land or water. — Species are spread over the whole globe, but they abound most in warm climates. In the United States, as in Europe, there is but a solitary peculiar race in each country.

Bowen.

BELTED KING-FISHER.

(*Alcedo Alcyon*, L. Wilson, iii. p. 59. pl. 23. fig. 1.   Aud. pl. 77. Orn. Biog. i. p. 394.   Phil. Museum, No. 2145)

Sp. Charact. — Crested ; bluish slate-color ; breast with a bluish band ; a spot on either side of the eyes, with a large collar round the neck, as well as the vent, white. — *Female*, with the sides, and an additional belt on the breast, ferruginous.

PLATE VI
From Thomas Nuttall : *A Manual of the Ornithology of the United States and Canada : The Land Birds,* 1832

1.Belted Kingfisher. 2.Black and Yellow Warbler. 3.Blackburnian W. 4.Autumnal W. 5.Water Thrush.

23.

PLATE VII
From Alexander Wilson: *American Ornithology,* Volume I, 1832

Wood Thrush
Male 1. Female 2.
Common Dogwood.

Drawn from nature by J.J. Audubon F.R.S.F.L.S.   Lith & Printed by Endicott New York

PLATE VIII
From John James Audubon: *The Birds of America, from Drawings Made in
the United States and Their Territories,* Volume III, 1841

215

Hermit Thrush
Male 1. Female 2.
Plant Robin Wood.

Drawn from nature by J.J. Audubon F.R.S.ELS.   Lith & Printed by Endicott New York.

PLATE IX
From John James Audubon: *The Birds of America, from Drawings Made in
the United States and Their Territories*, Volume III, 1841

Engraved by W.H.Lizars

Drawn from Nature by A.Wilson

1.Maryland Yellow-throat. 2.Yellow-breasted Chat. 3.Summer Red Bird. 4.Female. 5.Indigo Bird. 6.American Redstart.

PLATE X
From Alexander **Wilson**: *American Ornithology,* Volume I, 1832

The moult of the male is double, and the voice musical like that of the Sylvias and Vireos, to which it is related, but sufficiently distinct. Nearly allied to the foreign *Malurus* of Vieillot, as well as to the Indian *Phœnicornis* of Swainson, in which the brilliant colors and their distribution are very similar, but in that the tail is long, and unequally graduated, and the bill more robust and strongly notched. The nest not pendulous, neat and somewhat artful, resembling that of the Sylvias. This section, including several species, holds probably the rank of a genus, but requires further comparison.

AMERICAN REDSTART.

(*Muscicapa ruticilla*, L. WILSON, i. p. 103. pl. 6. fig. 6. [adult male].
v. p. 119. pl. 45. fig. 2. [young]. AUDUBON, pl. 40. [in the act of
attacking a nest of hornets]. Philad. Museum, No. 6658.)

SP. CHARACT. — Black ; belly white ; sides of the breast, base of the
primaries and tail-feathers (the two middle ones excepted) reddish orange. — *Female, young*, and *autumnal male* greenish-olive ;
head cinereous ; beneath whitish ; sides of the breast and base of
the tail-feathers, yellow.

THIS beautiful and curious bird takes up its summer
residence in almost every part of the North-American

PLATE XI
From Thomas Nuttall: *A Manual of the Ornithology of the United States
and Canada: The Land Birds,* 1832

1.*American Sparrow Hawk.* 2.*Field Sparrow.* 3.*Tree Sp.* 4.*Song Sp.* 5.*Chipping Sp.* 6.*Snow Bird.*
16.

PLATE XII
From Alexander Wilson: *American Ornithology,* Volume I, 1832

1. Little Owl. 2. Sea-side Finch. 3. Sharp tailed F. 4. Savannah F.

34

PLATE XIII
From Alexander Wilson: *American Ornithology*, Volume II, 1832

SAVANNA FINCH, or YELLOW-SHOULDERED SPARROW.

(*Fringilla savanarum*, GMEL. LATHAM, i. p. 443. No. 31. and Synopsis, iii. p. 270. No. 27. *F. passerina*, WILSON, iii. p. 76. pl. 24. fig. 5. Phil. Museum, No. 6585.)

SP. CHARACT. — Breast pale brownish-yellow; line over the eye, shoulder, and lesser wing-coverts yellow; tail-feathers rather pointed, the outer partly whitish.

THIS small Sparrow is a summer resident in the United States, and is likewise, according to Sloane, a common species in the savannas or open glades of the island of Jamaica. From what little is known of it, as a bird of the United States, it appears to remain on the sheltered plains of the sea-coast of New York and New Jersey until the very commencement of winter. It is also observed in the lower parts of Pennsylvania, and about the middle of May or later, they are occasionally seen in the gardens of this vicinity, on their way apparently to some other breeding station. On these occasions they perch in sheltered trees in pairs, and sing in an agreeable voice somewhat like that of the Purple Finch, though less vigorously. In the West Indies, they live much on the ground, and run like Larks, flying low when flushed, and soon alighting. Their nest is likewise fixed on the ground, among the grass, where they collect their usual fare of seeds and insects. It is made of loose, dry stalks of dead grass, and lined with hair and root-fibres. The eggs, 5, are of a greyish-white, spotted with brown, and the female has been observed sitting as late as the 1st of August. They probably retire to the West Indies or Mexico to pass the winter, as they are not seen at this season in any of the Southern States.

The length of this species is from 4½ to 5 inches, alar extent about 8. Upper part of the head blackish, divided by a slight pale line;

hind-head and neck with touches of dusky-brown and white; cheeks brownish-white; back varied with blackish, brown, and pale ash; shoulders of the wings above and below, and lesser coverts of the same, olive-yellow; primaries and tail, drab, the feathers of the latter rather pointed; breast without spots, yellowish-white with a tinge of brown. Belly and vent white. Legs flesh-color. Bill dusky, pale bluish-white below.—The two sexes are nearly alike.

TREE SPARROW.

(*Fringilla canadensis*, LATH. *F. arborea*, WILSON, ii. p. 123. pl. 16. fig. 3. Phil. Museum, No. 6575.)

SP. CHARACT. — Crown bright bay; stripe over the eye, sides of the neck, chin, and breast, pale ash; wings with two white bars; bill black, the lower mandible yellow; legs and feet dusky; 1st primary shorter than the 5th and 2d.

THIS handsome winter Sparrow arrives from the northern regions in New England about the close of October, withdrawing from Hudson's Bay and the neighbouring countries some time in the month of September. The species, consequently, like many more of our *Fringillas*, only measures his speed by the resources of subsistence he is able to obtain, and thus straggling southward, as the winter advances, he enters Pennsylvania only about the beginning of November; there, as well as in the maritime parts of Massachusetts, and perhaps as far south as Virginia, the Tree Sparrow is often seen associated with the hardy Snow-Birds, gleaning a similar kind of subsistence; and when the severity of winter commences, leaving the woods, gardens, and uplands in which he is an occasional visitor, he seeks in company the shelter of some bushy swamp, thickly shaded brook, or spring. Near Fresh Pond, in this vicinity, they are at that season numerous, and roost together near the margin of the reeds, almost in the society of the Black-birds, who seek out a similar place of warmth and shelter as the chilling frosts begin to prevail.

PLATE XIV

From Thomas Nuttall: *A Manual of the Ornithology of the United States and Canada: The Land Birds*, 1832

1 Painted Bunting. 2 Female. 3 Prothonotary Warbler. 4 Wormeating W. 5 Yellow winged Sparrow. 6 Blue Grosbeak.

24

PLATE XV
From Alexander Wilson: *American Ornithology,* Volume I, 1832

COMMON SONG-SPARROW.

(*Fringilla melodia*, WILSON, ii. p. 125. pl. 16. fig. 4. AUDUBON, pl. 25. Orn. Biog. i. p. 126. *F. fasciata?* GMEL. Phil. Museum, No. 6573.)

SP. CHARACT. — Crown chesnut, divided by a greyish line; breast and flanks spotted with blackish-brown; tail cuneiform, unspotted; 1st primary shortest: body above varied with blackish, chesnut, and olive-grey.

THIS familiar and almost domestic bird is one of the most common and numerous Sparrows in the United States; it is, also, with the Blue-Bird, which it seems to accompany, one of the two earliest, sweetest, and most enduring warblers. Though many pass on to the Southern States at the commencement of winter, yet a few seem to brave the colds of New England, as long as the snowy waste does not conceal their last resource of nutriment. When the inundating storm, at length, arrives, they no longer, in the sheltering swamps, and borders of bushy streams, spend their time in gleaning an insufficient subsistence, but in the month of November, begin to retire to the warmer states; and here, on fine days,

PLATE XVI
From Thomas Nuttall: *A Manual of the Ornithology of the United States and Canada: The Land Birds*, 1832

General Bird Notes

[The following notes are arranged chronologically and not by subject. They are filled with thoughts and wisdom about bird watching which the reader will find challenging and thought-provoking.

The notes through the 1840s are almost exclusively philosophical. The one written on March 20, 1842, is particularly interesting in this day of shrinking wilderness. Thoughtful people believe that it is vital to our future to preserve for all time large blocks of genuine wilderness areas in order that we may learn many of her still unknown principles evolved through millions of years, from undamaged nature.]

MARCH 4. [1840] I learned to-day that my ornithology had done me no service. The birds I heard, which fortunately did not come within the scope of my science sung as freshly as if it had been the first morning of creation, and had for background to their song an untrodden wilderness, stretching through many a Carolina and Mexico of the soul.

APRIL 20. [1840] An early morning walk is a blessing for the whole day. To my neighbors who have risen in mist and rain I tell of a clear sunrise and the singing of birds as some traditionary mythus. I look back on those fresh but now remote hours as to the old dawn of time, when a solid and blooming health reigned and every deed was simple and heroic.

MARCH 20. [1842] Nature is very ample and roomy. She has left us plenty of space to move in. As far as I can see from this window, how little life in the landscape! The few birds that flit past do not crowd; they do not fill the valley. The traveller on the highway has no fellow-traveller for miles before or behind him. Nature was generous and not niggardly, certainly.

1 8 5 0 – 1 8 5 1

[Thoreau's philosophy still dominates his general notes during these years. On July 18, 1851, he points out how man's self-imposed rules of behavior have restricted his pleasure in each new day. In this period we not only have Thoreau marveling about the flying skill of swiftly-moving flocks of birds, which move as if controlled by a single brain. He also gives sound advice about locating nests in winter to make it easier to find active nests in spring and summer.]

[Undated] [1850]   Now about the first of September, you will see flocks of small birds forming compact and distinct masses, as if they were not only animated by one spirit but actually held together by some invisible fluid or film, and will hear the sound of their wings rippling or fanning the air, as they flow through it, flying, the whole mass, ricochet like a single bird,—or as they flow over the fence. Their mind must operate faster than man's, in proportion as their bodies do.

July 18. [1851]   Have you knowledge of the morning? Do you sympathize with that season of nature? Are you abroad early, brushing the dews aside? If the sun rises on you, slumbering, if you do not hear the morning cock-crow, if you do not witness the blushes of Aurora, if you are not acquainted with Venus as the morning star, what relation have you to wisdom and purity? You have then forgotten your Creator in the days of your youth! Your shutters were darkened till noon! You rose with a sick headache! In the morning sing, as do the birds. What of those birds which should slumber on their perches till the sun was an hour high? What kind of fowl would they be and new kind of bats and owls,—hedge sparrows or larks? then took a dish of tea or hot coffee before they began to sing?

Oct. 5 [1851]   I hear the red-wing blackbirds by the riverside again, as if it were a new spring. They appear to have come to bid farewell. The birds appear to depart with the coming of the frosts, which kill the vegetation and, directly, or indirectly, the insects on which they feed. The American bittern (*Ardea minor*) flew across the river, trailing his legs in the water, scared up by us. This, according to Peabody, is the boomer (stake-driver). In their sluggish flight they can hardly keep their legs up. Wonder if they can soar.

8 P.M.—To Cliffs. Moon three-quarters full. The nights now are very still, for there is hardly any noise of birds or of insects. The whip-poor-will is not heard, nor the mosquito; only the occasional lisping of some sparrow. . .

Standing on the Cliffs, no sound comes up from the woods. The earth has gradually turned more northward; the birds have fled south after the sun.

Nov. 9. [1851]   Now the leaves are gone the birds' nests are revealed, the brood being fledged and flown. There is a perfect adaptation in the material used in constructing a nest. There is one which I took from a maple on the causeway at Hubbard's Bridge. It is fastened to the twigs by white woolen strings (out of a shawl?), which it has picked up in the road, though it is more than half a mile from a house; and the sharp eyes of the bird have discovered plenty of horsehairs out of the tail or mane, with which to give it form by their spring; with fine meadow hay for a body, and the reddish woolly material which invests the ferns in the spring (apparently) for lining.

Nov. 8. [1851]   I, too, would fain set down something beside facts. Facts should only be as the frame to my pictures; they should be material to the mythology which I am writing; not facts to assist men to make money, farmers to farm profitably, in any common sense; facts to tell who I am, and where I have been or what I have thought.

1852

[There is a drastic change in the notes. Thoreau makes some generalizations about the food of birds, and the importance of food to their movements. We are made conscious of the rising tide of birds in spring, and the ebbing of song and activity as the young birds leave the nest and fend for themselves.

Thoreau often described the eggs of birds, but he seldom went beyond information which would help him to identify those he found. On July 30, 1852, he shares with his readers his appreciation of the beauty of eggs and their meaning.]

MARCH 12. [1852]   The little grain of wheat, *tritucum*, is the noblest food of man. The lesser grains of other grasses are the food of passerine birds at present. Their diet is like man's.

APRIL 4. [1852]   Going across Wheeler's large field beyond Potter's, saw a large flock of small birds go by. I am not sure what kind, the near ones continually overtaking the foremost, so that the whole flock appeared to roll over as it went forward. When they lit on a tree, they appeared at a distance to clothe it like dead leaves.

APRIL 24. [1852]   Vegetation starts when the earth's axis is sufficiently inclined; *i.e.* it follows the sun. Insects and all the smaller animals (as well as many larger) follow vegetation. The fishes, the small fry, start probably for this reason; worms come out of the trees; buffaloes finally seek new pastures; water-bugs appear on the water, etc., etc. Next, the large fish and fish hawks, etc., follow the small fry; flycatchers follow the insects, and worms. (The granivorous birds, who can depend on the supplies of the seasons, and can remain through the winter or come early in the spring, and they furnish food for a few birds of prey at that season.) Indians follow the buffaloes; trout, suckers, etc., follow the water-bugs, etc., reptiles follow vegetation, insects, and worms; birds of prey, the flycatchers, etc. Man follows all, and all follow the sun. The greater or less abundance of food determines migrations. If the buds are deceived and suffer from frost, then are the birds. The great necessary of life for the brute creation is food; next, perhaps, shelter, i.e. a suitable climate; thirdly, perhaps, security from foes.

MAY 1. [1852]   I hear the first towhee finch. He says *to-wee, to-wee*, and another, much farther off than I supposed when I went in search of him, says *whip your ch-r-r-r-r-r* with a metallic ring! I hear the first catbird also, mewing, and the wood thrush, which still thrills me,—a sound to be heard in a new country,—from one side of a clearing. I think I heard an oven-bird just now,—*wicher wicher whicher wich*. I am on the Cliff. It is about six. The flicker cackles. I hear a woodpecker tapping. The tinkle of the huckleberry-bird comes up from the shrub oak plain. He commonly lives away from the habitations of men, in retired bushy fields and sprout-lands. A partridge bursts away from under the rock below me on quivering wings, like some moths I have seen. We have, then, flowers, and the song of birds before the woods leave out,—like poetry. When leaving the woods I heard the hooting of an owl, which sounded very much like a clown calling to his team. Saw two large woodpeckers on an oak. I am tempted to say that they were other and larger than the flicker, but I have been deceived in him before.

MAY 7. [1852]   4:30 A.M.—To Cliffs. The sun now rises in a rosaceous amber. Methinks the birds sing more some mornings than others, when I cannot see the reason. I smell the damp path, and derive vigor from the earthy scent between Potter's and Haydens. Beginning, I may say, with robins, song sparrows, chip-birds, bluebirds, etc., I walked through larks, pewees, pigeon woodpeckers, chickadee *tull-a-lulls*, to towhees, huckleberry-birds, wood thrushes, brown thrasher, jay, catbird, etc., etc. Entered a cool stratum of air beyond Hayden's after the warmth of yesterday. . . . Hear the first partridge drum. The first oven-bird. A wood thrush which I thought a dozen rods off was only two or three, to my surprise, and betrayed himself by moving, like a large sparrow with ruffled feathers, and quirking his tail like a pewee, on a low branch. Blackbirds are seen going over the woods with a chattering bound to some meadow. . . .

Here [at Cliffs] at this hour the brown thrasher often drowns the other birds. The towhee has been a main bird for regular morning singing in the woods for a little while. The creeper is regularly heard, too. . . .

I think that birds vary their notes considerably with the seasons. When I hear a bird singing, I cannot think of any words that will imitate it. What word can stand in place of a bird's note? You would have to bury (?) it or surround it with a *chevaux de frise* of accents, and exhaust the art of the musical composer besides with your different bars, to represent it, and finally get a bird to sing it, to perform it. It has so little relation to words. The wood thrush says *ah-tully-tally* for one strain. There appear to be one or more little warblers in the woods this morning which are new to the season, about which I am in doubt, myrtle-birds among them. For now, before the leaves, they begin to people the trees in this warm weather. The first wave of summer from the south. The purple finch (sober-colored) is a rich singer. As I said the other day, something like the warbling vireo, only louder, clearer, mellower, and more various. . . .

P.M.—To Nawshawtuct. The vireo comes with warm weather, midwife to the leaves of the elm. . . . The first small pewee sings now *che-vet*, or rather chirrups *chevet, tche-vet*—a rather delicate bird with a large head and two white wing bars. The first summer yellowbirds on the willow causeway. The birds I have lately mentioned come not singly, as the earliest, but all at once, *i.e.* many yellowbirds all over town. Now I remember the yellowbird comes when the willows begin to leave out. (And the small pewee on the willows also.) So yellow. They bring summer with them and the sun, *tche-tche-tche-tcha-tcha-tchar*. Also they haunt the oaks, white and swamp white, where are not leaves. . . .

The first peetweet; myrtle birds numerous. The catbird does not make the corn-planting sounds. . . . The red-wing's shoulder, seen in a favorable light, throws all epaulets into the shade. It is General Abercrombie, methinks, when they wheel partly with the red to me. The crow blackbirds make a noise like crows, and also a singular and rarely heard scream or screech. They fly with lark-like wings.

MAY 8. [1852]   4.30.—The robin and the bluebird have sung for some time. The haziness is now like a sea-turn, through which the sun, shorn of beams, looks claret, and at length, when half an hour high, scarlet. You thought it might become rain. Many swallows flying in flocks *high* over the river,—the chimney swallow for one. What is the other? They sustain themselves sometimes on quivering wings, making little progress, as if to catch insects. . . . A singular noise from a jay this morning. Hear the yellowbird, the creeper, and the myrtle-bird this morning, all together; they are much alike. The creeper, a faint oven-bird note; the myrtle-bird, a little more of the s or t in it than the yellowbird and more various. I hear the *wit er che*, Maryland yellow-throat. Two gold robins; they chatter like blackbirds; the fire bursts forth on their backs when they lift their wings. . . .

The blackbirds have a rich *sprayey* warble now, sitting on the top [of] a willow or an elm. They possess the river now, flying back and forth across it. . . .

The blackbirds fly in flocks and sing in concert on the willows,—what a lively, chattering concert! a great deal of chattering with many liquid and rich warbling notes and clear whistles,—till now a hawk sails low, beating the bush; and they are silent or off, but soon begin again. Do any other birds sing in such deafening concert?

MAY 10. [1852]   I was reminded, this morning before I rose, of those undescribed ambrosial mornings of summer which I can remember, when a thousand birds were heard gently twittering and ushering in the light, like the argument to a new canto of an epic and heroic poem. The serenity, the infinite promise, of such a morning! The song or twitter of birds drips from the leaves like dew. Then there was something divine and immortal in our life. When I have waked up on my couch in the woods and seen the day dawning, and heard the twittering of the birds. . . .

P.M.—Through Deep Cut to Cliffs. I see flocks of a dozen bluebirds together. The warble of this bird is innocent and celestial, like its color. Saw a sparrow, perhaps a song sparrow, flitting amid the young oaks where the ground was covered with snow. I think that this is an indication that the ground is quite bare a little further south. Probably the spring birds never fly far over a snow-clad country.

JUNE 25. [1852]   I observe that young birds are usually of a duller color and more speckled than old ones, as if for their protection in their tender state. They have not yet the markings (and the beauty) which distinguish their species, and which betray it often, but by their colors are merged in the variety of colors of the season.

JULY 7. [1852]   4 A.M. The first really foggy morning. Yet before I rise I hear the song of birds from out of it, like the bursting of its bubbles with music, the bead on liquids just uncorked. Their song gilds thus the frost-work of the morning. As if the fog were a great sweet froth on the sur-face of land and water, whose fixed air escaped, whose bubbles burst with music. The sound of its evaporation, the fixed air of the morning just brought from the cellars of the night escaping. The morning twittering of birds in perfect harmony with it. I came near awaking this morning. I am older than last year; the mornings are further between; the days are fewer. Any excess—to have drunk too much water, even, the day before—is fatal to the morning's clarity, but in health the sound of a cow-bell is celestial music.

JULY 30. [1852]   What a gem is a bird's egg, especially a blue or a green one, when you see one broken or whole in the woods! I noticed a small blue egg this afternoon washed up by Flint's Pond and half buried by white sand, and as it lay there, alternately wet and dry, no color could be fairer, no gem could have a more advantageous or favorable setting. Probably it was shaken out of some nest which overhung the water. I frequently meet with broken egg-shells where a crow, perchance, or some other thief has been marauding. And is not that shell something very precious that houses that winged life?

1853

[Thoreau, who spent the previous year trying to identify as many species of birds as he was able, concentrated on the study of nests this year. Once more he took note of the arrival of spring birds and the departure of those that nest north of Concord.

On April 6, 1853, he brings out a point that many are unconsciously aware of, and the reason why the study of any phase of nature is inex-haustable. The most competent observer learns all he can to-day, but he finds that to-morrow and next year and on through decades to come, he constantly builds on his original true observation, but can never reach the end of knowledge about a single subject.]

MARCH 18. [1853]   How eagerly the birds of passage penetrate the northern ice, watching for a crack by which to enter! Forthwith the swift ducks will be seen winging their way along the rivers and up the coast. They watch the weather more sedulously than the teamster. All nature is thus forward to move with the revolution of the seasons. Now for some days the birds have been ready by myriads, a flight or two south, to invade our latitudes and, with this mild and serener weather, resume their flight. . . .

I stand still now and listen if I may hear the note of any new bird, for the sound of my steps hinders, and there are so few sounds at this season in a still afternoon like this that you are pretty sure to detect one within a considerable distance. Hark! Did I not hear the note of some bird then? Methinks it could not have been my own breathing through my nose. No, there it is again,—a robin; and we have put the winter so much further behind us. What mate does he call to in these deserted fields? It is, as it were, a scared note as he whisks by, followed by the familiar but still anxious *toot, toot, too*t. He does not sing as yet. There were one or two more fine bird-like tinkling sounds I could not trace home, not to be referred to my breathing. . . .

I came forth expecting to hear new birds, and I am not disappointed. We know well what to count upon. Their coming is more sure than the arrival of the sailing and steaming packets. Almost while I listen for this purpose, I hear the *chuck, chuck* of a blackbird in the sky, whom I cannot detect. So small an object is lost in the wide expanse of the heavens, though no obstacle intervenes. When your eye has detected it, you can follow it well enough, but it is difficult to bring your sight to bear on it, as to direct a telescope to a particular star. How many hawks may fly undetected, yet within sight, above our heads! And there's the great gull I came to see, already fishing in front of Bittern Cliff. Now he stoops to the water for his prey, but sluggishly, methinks. He requires a high and perhaps a head wind to make his motions graceful. I see no mate. He must have come up, methinks, before the storm was over, unless he started when I did. I believe it is only an easterly wind or storm brings him up.

Several times I hear and see blackbirds flying north singly, high overhead, chucking as if to find their mates, migrating; or are they even now getting near their own breeding-place? Perchance these are blackbirds that were hatched here—that know me! I saw a silent sparrow lurking amid the hazels and other shurbs by a wall and picking worms or what-not. . . . Soon after I heard a song sparrow distinctly. Could it have been this? I think not.

The bluebird and song sparrow sing immediately on their arrival, and hence deserve to enjoy some prominence. They give expression to the joy which the season inspires. But the robin and blackbird only peep and chuck at first, commonly, and the lark is silent and flitting. The bluebird at once fills the air with his sweet warbling, and the song sparrow from the top of a rail pours forth his most joyous strain. Both express their delight at the weather which permits them to return to their favorite haunts. They are the more welcome to man for it.

MARCH 22. [1853]   6 A.M.—To Cliffs. There is a white frost on the ground. One robin really sings on the elms. Even the cockerel crows with new lustiness. Already I hear from the railroad the plaintive strain of a lark or two. They sit now conspicuous on the bare russet ground. The tinkling bubbles of the song sparrow are wafted from distant fence-posts,—little rills of song that begin to flow and tinkle as soon as the frost is out of the ground. The blackbird tries to sing, as it were with a bone in his throat, or to whistle and sing at once. Whither so fast, the restless creature,—*chuck chuck*, at every rod, and now and then *whistle-ter-ee*? The *chill-lill* of the blue snow-birds is heard again. A partridge goes off on Fair Haven Hill-side with a sudden whir like the wad of a six-pounder, keeping just level with the tops of the sprouts. These birds and quails go off like a report. . . .

The tapping of the woodpecker, *rat-tat-tat*, knocking at the door of some sluggish grub to tell him that the spring has arrived, and his fate, this is one of the season sounds, calling the roll of birds and insects, the reveille. The Cliff woods are comparatively silent. Not yet the woodland birds, except, perhaps, the woodpecker, so far as it migrates; only the orchard and river birds have arrived.

APRIL 4. [1853]   After turning Lee's Cliff I heard, methinks, more birds singing even than in fair weather,—tree sparrows, whose song has the character of the canary's, *F. hyemalis's chill-lill*, the sweet strain of the fox-colored sparrow, song sparrows, a nuthatch, jays, crows, bluebirds, robins, and a large congregation of blackbirds. They suddenly alight with great din in a stubble-field just over the wall, not perceiving me and my umbrella behind the pitch pines, and there feed silently; then, getting uneasy or anxious, they fly up on to an apple tree, where being reassured, commences a rich but deafening concert, *o-gurgle-ee-e, o-gurgle-ee-e*, some of the most liquid notes ever heard, as if produced by some of the water of the Pierian spring, flowing through some kind of musical water-pipe and at the same time setting in motion a multitude of fine vibrating metallic springs. Like a shepherd merely meditating most enrapturing glees on such a water-pipe. A more liquid bagpipe or clarionet, immersed like bubbles in a thousand sprayey notes, the bubbles half lost in the spray. When I show myself, away they go with a loud harsh *charr-r, charr-r*. At first I had heard an inundation of blackbirds approaching, some beating time with a loud *chuck, chuck*, while the rest played a hurried, gurgling fugue.

APRIL 6. [1853]   If you make the least correct observation of nature this year, you will have occasion to repeat it with illustrations the next, and the season and life itself is prolonged.

MAY 4. [1853]   The woods and paths next them [the Cliffs] now ring with the silver jingle of the field sparrow, the medley of the brown thrasher, the honest *qui vive* of the chewink, or his jingle from the top of a low copse tree, while his mate scratches in the dry leaves beneath; the black and white creeper is hopping along the oak boughs, head downward, pausing from time to time to utter its note like a fine delicate saw-sharpening; and ever and anon rises clear over all the smooth, rich melody of the wood thrush.

MAY 10. [1853]   It is remarkable that I saw this morning for the first time the bobolink, gold robin, and kingbird,—and have since heard the first two in various parts of the town and am satisfied that they have just come,— and, in the woóds, the veery note. I hear the ringing sound of the toads borne on the rippling wind as I keep down the causeway.

He is richest who has most use for nature as raw material of tropes and symbols with which to describe his life. If these gates of golden willows affect me, they correspond to the beauty and promise of some experience on which I am entering. If I am overflowing with life, am rich in experience for which I lack expression, then nature will be my language full of poetry,— all nature will *fable,* and every natural phenomenon be a myth. The man of science, who is not seeking for expression but for a fact to be expressed merely, studies nature as a dead language. I pray for such inward experience as will make nature significant. . . .

There is now a multiplicity of sounds, in which the few faint spring ones are drowned. The birds are in full blast, singing, warbling, chirping, humming. Yet we do not receive more ideas through our ears than before. The storms and ducks of spring have swept by and left us in the repose of summer, the farmers to the ignoble pursuits of planting and hoeing corn and potatoes. The summer is not bracing, as when you hear the note of the jay in the cool air of October from the rustling chestnut woods. Hear the night warbler now distinctly. It does not repeat its note, and disappears with the sound.

AUG. 22. [1853]   I hear but a few notes of birds these days; no singing, but merely a few hurried notes or screams or twittering or peeping. I will enumerate such as I hear or see this still louring and showery afternoon. A hurried anxious note from a robin. Heard perhaps a dozen afterward. They flit now, accompanied by their young. A sharp, loud *che-wink* from a ground-robin. A goldfinch twitters over; several more heard afterward. A blue jay screams, and one or two fly over, showing to advantage their handsome forms, especially their regular tails, wedge-formed. Surprised to hear a very faint *bobolink* in the air; the link, link, once or twice later. A yellow-bird flew over the river. Swallows twittering, but flying high,—the chimney swallows and what I take to be the bank ditto. Scared up a green bittern from an oak by the riverside. Hear a peawai whose note is more like singing—as if it were still incubating—than any other. Some of the warble of the golden robin. A kingfisher, with his white collar, darted across the river and alighted on an oak. A peetweet flew along the shore and uttered its peculiar note. Their wings appear double as they fly by you, while their bill is cumbrously carried downward in front. The chipping of a song sparrow occasionally heard amid the bushes. A single duck scared up. And two nighthawks flying high over the river. At twilight many bats after the showers. These birds were heard or seen in the course of three or four hours on the river, but there were not sounds enough to disturb the general stillness.

Nov. 7. [1853]   The notes of one or two small birds, this cold morning, in the now comparatively leafless woods, sound like a nail dropped on an anvil, or a glass pendant tinkling against its neighbor.

1 8 5 4

[If, in his first years of noting birds, Thoreau largely confined himself to regarding them as vehicles for his thoughts, he had now reached a point where birds were extremely interesting fellow inhabitants of the world. He noted their association with certain flowers, and in winter their tracks on the snow led him to their granaries—seed pods he had thought were empty.

Thoreau bought his spyglass and from March onward he was able to observe birds, particularly ducks and hawks, better than ever before. In June he longed to know the birds better. His knowledge had reached the point where he understood how vast was the unknown world of birds in Concord.]

APRIL 15. [1854]   This cold, moist, snowy day it is easier to see the birds and get near them. They are driven to the first bare ground that shows itself in the road, and the weather, etc., makes them more indifferent to your approach. The tree sparrows look much stouter and more chubby than usual, their feathers being puffed up and darker also, perhaps with wet. Also the robins and bluebirds are puffed up. I see the white under sides of many purple finches, busily and silently feeding on the elm blossoms within a few feet of me, and now and then their bloody heads and breasts. They utter a faint, clear chip. Their feathers are much ruffled. The yellow redpoll hops along the limbs within four or five feet of me.

Martins the 13th first. The arrival of the purple finches appears to be coincident with the blossoming of the elm, on whose blossoms it feeds.

JUNE 9. [1854] I should like to know the birds of the woods better, what birds inhabit our woods? I hear their various notes ringing through them. What musicians compose our woodland quire? They must be forever strange and interesting to me.

1 8 5 5

[For the past three years, Thoreau named the birds as they arrived in Concord and spent much time describing their songs. Now he noted more behavior and spoke less of the songs, not because the songs affected him less, but because he understood more about the place of birds in nature.

In the last selection for this year, he again points out the value of locating nests in winter in order to know where to find nests in spring.]

MARCH 28. [1855] I run about these cold and blustering days, on the whole perhaps the worst to bear in the year,—partly because they disappoint expectation,—looking almost in vain for some animal or vegetable life stirring. The warmest springs hardly allow me the glimpse of a frog's heel as he settles himself in the mud, and I think I am lucky if I see one winter-defying hawk or a hardy duck or two at a distance on the water. As for the singing of birds,—the few that have come to us,—it is too cold for them to sing and for me to hear. The bluebird's warble comes feeble and frozen to my ear.

APRIL 17. [1855] P.M.—To Lee's Cliff. I leave off my greatcoat, though the wind rises rather fresh before I return. It is worth the while to walk so free and light, having got off both boots and greatcoat. Great flocks of grackles and red-wings about the Swamp Bridge Brook willows, perching restlessly on an apple tree all at once, and then, with a sweeping or curving flight, alighting on the ground. Many robins flit before me in flocks these days. I rarely find a nest (of the right species) near the river but it has a piece of a fish-line in it. . . .

I see by their droppings that many birds—perhaps robins—have lately roosted in that wine-glass apple scrub on Conantum, an excellent covert from the hawks, and there are three old nests in it, though it is only six or eight feet in diameter. I also see where birds have roosted in a thick white pine in Lee's Wood. It is easy to detect their roosting-places now, because they are in flocks. . . .

A sudden warm day, like yesterday and this, takes off some birds and adds others. It is a crisis in their career. The fox-colored sparrows seem to be gone, and I suspect that *most* of the tree sparrows and *F. hyemalis*, at least, went yesterday. So the pleasanter weather seems not an unmixed benefit.

MAY 3. [1855] P.M.—To Assabet Bath. Humphrey Buttrick, one of eight who alone returned from Texas out of twenty-four, says he can find woodcocks' eggs; now knows of several nests; has seen them setting with snow around them; and that Melvin has seen partridges' eggs some days ago. He has seen crows building this year. Found in a hen-hawk's nest once the legs of a cat. Has known of several goshawks' nests (or what he calls some kind of eagle; Garfield called it the Cape Eagle); one in a shrub oak, with eggs. Last year his dog caught seven black ducks so far grown that he got sixty cents a pair for them; takes a pretty active dog to catch such. He frequently finds or hears of them. Knew of a nest this year. Also finds wood ducks' nests. Has very often seen partridges drum close to him. Has watched one for an hour. They strike the body with their wings. He shot a white-headed eagle from Carlisle Bridge. It fell in the water, and his dog was glad to let it alone. He suggested that my fish hawks found pouts in holes made by ice.

JUNE 10. [1855] A remarkably strong wind from the southwest all day, racking the trees very much and filling the air with dust. I do not remember such violent and incessant gusts this season. Many eggs, if not young, must have been shaken out of birds' nests, for I hear of some fallen. It is almost impossible to hear birds—or keep your hat on.

DEC. 30. [1855] He who would study birds' nests must look for them in November and in winter as well as in midsummer, for then the trees are bare and he can see them, and the swamps and streams are frozen, and he can approach new kinds. He will often be surprised to find how many have haunted where he little suspected, and will receive many hints accordingly, which he can act upon in the summer. I am surprised to find many new ones (*i.e.* not new species) in groves which I had examined several times with particular care in the summer.

1 8 5 6

[Thoreau frequently took empty birds' nests home and pulled them apart to see what materials were used. This is reflected in the first note included here for 1856. In this year he speaks of birds as entomologists and as planters of trees.

His "pewee" of April 6 was a phoebe, of course, for the Wood Pewee is not expected in Concord until a month later. Thoreau used his ears to advantage to discover what new birds arrived from day to day. It was far easier to hear their song than to detect the early arrivals by sight.]

JAN. 13. [1856]   In Nature nothing is wasted. Every decayed leaf and twig and fibre is only the better fitted to serve in some other department, and all at last are gathered in her compost-heap. What a wonderful genius it is that leads the vireo to select the tough fibres of the inner bark, instead of the more brittle grasses, for its basket, the elastic pine-needles and the twigs, curved as they dried to give it form, and, as I suppose, the silk of cocoons, etc., etc., to bind it together with! I suspect that extensive use is made of these abandoned cocoons by the birds, and they, if anybody, know where to find them. There were at least seven materials used in constructing this [vireo] nest, and the bird visited as many distinct localities many times, always with the purpose or design to find some particular one of these materials, as much as if it had said to itself, "Now I will go and get some old hornets' nest from one of those that I saw last fall down in the maple swamp—perhaps thrust my bill into them—or some silk from those cocoons I saw this morning."

JAN. 18. [1856]   Observed some of those little hard galls on the high blueberry, pecked or eaten into by some bird (or *possibly* mouse), for the little white grubs which lie curled up in them. What entomologists the birds are! Most men do not suspect that there are grubs in them, and how secure the latter seem under these thick dry shells! Yet there is no secret but is confided to some one.

JAN. 24. [1856]   The snow is so deep along the sides of the river that I can now look into nests which I could hardly reach in the summer. I can hardly believe them the same. They have only an ice egg in them now. Thus we go about, raised, generally speaking, more than a foot above the summer level. So much higher do we carry our heads in winter. What a great odds such a little difference makes! When the snow raises us one foot higher than we have been accustomed to walk we are surprised at our elevation! So we soar.

FEB. 4. [1856]   To Walden. I have often wondered how red cedars could have sprung up in some pastures which I knew to be miles distant from the nearest fruit-bearing cedar, but it now occurs to me that these and barberries, etc., may be planted by the crows and probably other birds.

APRIL 6. [1856]   The meadow has frozen over, skimmed over in the night. The ducks must have had a cold night of it. I thought [I] heard white-bellied swallows over the house before I arose. The hedges resound with the song of the song sparrows. He sits high on a spray singing, while I stand near, but suddenly, becoming alarmed, drops down and skulks behind the bushes close to the ground, gradually removing far to one side. I am not certain but I have seen the grass-bird as well as song sparrow this year,—on the 2nd,—a sparrow with a light breast and less brown about the cheeks and head. The song sparrow I see now has a very warm breast. What a sly, skulking fellow! I have a glimpse of him skulking behind a stone or bush next to the ground, or perhaps he drops into a ditch just below me, and when I run forward he is not to be seen in it, having flitted down it four or five rods to where it intersected with another, and then up that, all beneath the level of the surface, till he is in the rear of me.

Just beyond Wood's Bridge, I hear the pewee. With what confidence after the lapse of many months, I come out to this waterside, some warm and pleasant spring morning, and listening, hear, from farther or nearer, through the still concave of the air, the note of the first pewee! If there is one within half a mile, it will be here, and I shall be sure to hear its simple notes from those trees, borne over the water. It is remarkable how large a mansion of the air you can explore with your ears in the still morning by the waterside.

APRIL 9. [1856]   7 A.M.—To Trillium Woods. The air is full of birds, and as I go down the causeway, I distinguish the seringo note. You have only to come forth each morning to be surely advertised of each newcomer into these broad meadows. Many a larger animal might be concealed, but a cunning ear detects the arrival of each new species of bird. These birds give evidence that they prefer the fields of New England to all other climes, deserting for them the warm and fertile south. Here is their paradise. It is here they express the most happiness by song and action. Though these spring mornings may often be frosty and rude, they are exactly tempered to their constitutions, and call forth the sweetest strains.

APRIL 15. [1856]   6:30 A.M.—To Hill. It is warmer and quite still; somewhat cloudy in the east. The water quite smooth,—April smooth waters. . . . The purple finch is singing on the elms about the house, together with the robin, whose strain it resembles, ending with a loud, shrill, ringing *chilt chilt chilt chilt*. I push across the meadow and ascend the hill. The white-bellied swallows are circling about and twittering above the apple trees and walnuts on the hillside. Not till I gain the hilltop do I hear the note of the *Fringilla juncorum* (huckleberry-bird) from the plains beyond. Returned again toward my boat, I hear the rich watery note of the martin, making haste over the edge of the flood. A warm morning, over smooth water, before the wind rises, is the time to hear it. Near the water are many recent skunk probings, as if a drove of pigs had passed along last night, death to many beetles and grubs. From amid the willows and alders along the wall there, I hear a bird sing, *a-chitter chitter chitter chitter chitter chitter, che che che che*, with increasing intensity and rapidity, and the yellow redpoll hops in sight. A grackle goes over (with two females), and I hear from him a sound like a watchman's rattle,—but a little more musical. . . .

Coming up from the riverside, I hear the harsh rasping *char-r char-r* of the crow blackbird, like a very coarsely vibrating metal, and, looking up, see three ·flying over.

1 8 5 7 – 1 8 5 8

[Though Thoreau's general notes grow fewer, a check of selections about species will show the reader that he continued to write much about birds, but with each passing year, what he wrote became more related to a particular species.

The first note is interesting because it indicates the vast amount of time Thoreau spent in the open. Not only did he spend about half of each day out of doors; he often walked at night when the moon was bright, and listened as he walked.

On June 6, 1858, Thoreau noted the predatory habits of crows, hawks, and owls. The part played by predatory creatures is better understood to-day. Nature is so fecund that if all her emerging life lived for just one year, the earth would be impossibly overcrowded. Predatory creatures help crop the overabundant life. It must be remembered that the dainty and beloved chickadee does its share of cropping also and even the exquisite flamingo eats living things. Man eats his share of living creatures. The fact that some birds eat things that man wants for himself, while other birds eat something he is glad to be rid of in no way indicates a faulty plan; nature's plan has evolved through millions of years while man's plans for the earth cover a short span of time and are very often both selfish and short-sighted.]

JAN. 7. [1857]   I go through the woods toward the Cliffs along the side of the Well Meadow Field.

There is nothing so sanative, so poetic, as a walk in the woods and fields even now, when I meet none abroad for pleasure. Nothing so inspires me and excites such serene and profitable thought. The objects are elevating. In the street and in society I am almost invariably cheap and dissipated, my life is unspeakably mean. No amount of gold or respectability would in the least redeem it,—dining with the Governor or a member of Congress!! But alone in distant woods or fields, in unpretending sprout-lands or pastures tracked by rabbits, even in a bleak and, to most, cheerless day, like this, when a villager would be thinking of his inn, I come to myself, I once more feel myself grandly related, and that cold and solitude are friends of mine. I suppose that this value, in my case, is equivalent to what others get by churchgoing and prayer. I come to my solitary woodland walk as the homesick go home. I thus dispose of the superfluous and see things as they are, grand and beautiful. I have told many that I walk every day about half the daylight, but I think they do not believe it.

FEB. 20 [1857]   What is the relation between a bird and the ear that appreciates its melody, to whom, perchance, it is more charming and significant than to any else? Certainly they are intimately related, and the one was made for the other. It is a natural fact. If I were to discover that a certain kind of stone by the pond-shore was affected, say partially disintegrated, by a particular natural sound, as of a bird or insect, I see that one could not be completely described without describing the other. I am that rock by the pond-side.

SEPT. 7. [1857]   To Dodge Brook Wood. Returning to my boat, at the white maple, I see a small round flock of birds, perhaps blackbirds, dart through the air, as thick as a charge of shot,—now comparatively thin, with regular intervals of sky between them, like the holes in the strainer of a watering-pot, now dense and dark, as if closing up their ranks when they roll over one another and stoop downward.

MARCH 18. [1858]   Each new year is a surprise to us. We find that we had virtually forgotten the note of each bird, and when we hear it again it is remembered like a dream, reminding us of a previous state of existence. How happens it that the associations it awakens are always pleasing, never saddening; reminiscences of our sanest hours? The voice of nature is always encouraging.

APRIL 15. [1858]   The naturalist accomplishes a great deal by patience, more perhaps than by activity. He must take his position, and then wait and watch. It is equally true of quadrupeds and reptiles. Sit still in the midst of their haunts.

JUNE 7. [1858]   It is evidence enough against crows and hawks and owls, proving their propensity to rob birds' nests of eggs and young, that smaller birds pursue them so often. You do not need the testimony of so many farmers' boys when you can see and hear the small birds daily crying "Thief and murder" after these spoilers. What does it signify, the kingbird, black-bird, swallow, etc., etc., pursuing a crow? They say plainly enough, "I know you of old, you villain, you want to devour my eggs or young, I have often caught you at it, and I'll publish you now." And probably the crow pursu-ing the fish hawk and eagle proves that the latter sometimes devour their young.

JUNE 16. [1858]   To Staple's Meadow Wood. It is pleasant to paddle over the meadows now, at this time of flood, and look down on the various meadow plants, for you can see more distinctly quite to the bottom than ever. . . . No doubt thousands of birds' nests have been destroyed by the flood,—blackbirds' boblinks', song sparrows', etc. I see a robin's nest high above the water with the young just dead and the old bird in the water, apparently killed by the abundance of rain and afterward I see a fresh song sparrow's nest which has been flooded and destroyed.

OCT. 2. [1858]   The garden is alive with migrating sparrows these morn-ings. The cat comes in from an early walk amid the weeds. She is full of sparrows and wants no more breakfast this morning, unless it be a saucer of milk, the dear creature. I saw her studying ornithology between the corn-rows.

1859–1860

[Though relatively few in number, the general notes included here from the years 1859–60 are important for the ideas they contain. We know now that soaring birds conform to air currents when they ride the rising thermals. We are familiar with the erratic movements of birds in winter. The note of April 4, 1860, reminds us of the massive waves of birds which sometimes sweep into New England in spring when weather conditions are right.

Some of Thoreau's most mature thoughts about nature are contained in the notes of December 17, 1859, and January 29, 1860. Not only did Thoreau find birds of intense interest, but he recognized their value to their habitat as no one had before him.]

NOV. 11. [1859]   October 24th, riding home from Acton, I saw the with-ered leaves blown from an oak by the roadside dashing off, gyrating, and surging upward into the air, so exactly like a flock of birds sporting with one another that, for a minute, at least, I could not be sure they were not birds; and it suggested how far the motions of birds, like those of these leaves, might be determined by currents of air, *i.e.*, how far the bird learns to conform to such currents.

Dec. 17. [1859]   By the side of the Pout's Nest, I see on the pure white snow what looks like dust for half a dozen inches under a twig. Looking closely, I find that the twig is hardhack and the dust its slender, light-brown, chaffy-looking seed, which falls still in copious showers, dusting the snow, when I jar it; and here are the tracks of a sparrow which has jarred the twig and picked the minute seeds a long time, making quite a hole in the snow. The seeds are so fine that it must have got more snow than seed at each peck. But they probably look large to its microscopic eyes. I see, when I jar it, that a meadow-sweet close by has quite similar, but larger, seeds. This the reason, then, that these plants rise so high above the snow and retain their seeds, dispersing it on the least jar over each successive layer of snow beneath them; or it is carried to a distance by the wind. What abundance and what variety in the diet of these small granivorous birds, while I find only a few nuts still! These stiff weeds which no snow can break down hold their provender. What the cereals are to men, these are to the sparrows. The only threshing they require is that the birds fly against their spikes or stalks. A little further I see the seed-box (?) (Ludweiga) full of still smaller, yellowish seeds. And on the ridge north is the track of a partridge amid the shrubs. It has hopped up to the low clusters of smooth sumach berries, sprinkled the snow with them, and eaten all but a few. Also, here only, or where it has evidently jarred them down—whether intentionally or not, I am not sure—are the large oval seeds of the stiff-stalked lespedeza, which I suspect it ate, with the sumach berries. There is much solid food in them. When the snow is deep the birds could easily pick the latter out of the heads as they stand on the snow.

I observe, then, eaten by birds to-day, the seed of hardhack and meadow-sweet, sumach, and probably lespedeza, and even seed-box.

Jan. 22. [1860]   Up river to Fair Haven Pond; return *via* Andromeda Ponds and railroad. Birds are commonly very rare in the winter. They are much more common at some times than at others. I see more tree sparrows in the beginning of the winter (especially when snow is falling) than in the course of it. I think that by observation I could tell in what kind of weather afterward these were most to be seen. Crows come about houses and streets in very cold weather and deep snows, and they are heard cawing in pleasant, thawing winter weather, and their note is then a pulse by which you feel the quality of the air, *i.e.*, when cocks crow. For the most part, lesser redpolls and pine grosbeaks do not appear at all. Snow buntings are very wandering. They were quite numerous a month ago, and now seem to have quit the town. They seem to ramble about the country at will.

Jan. 29. [1860]   Not only the Indian, but many wild birds and quadrupeds and insects, welcomed the apple tree to these shores. As it grew apace, the bluebird, robin, cherry-bird, kingbird, and many more came with a rush and built their nests in it, and so became orchard birds. The woodpecker found such a savory morsel under its bark that he perforated it in a ring quite round the tree, a thing he had never done before. It did not take the partridge long to find out how sweet its buds were, and every winter day she flew and still flies from the wood to pluck them, much to the farmer's sorrow. The rabbit too was not slow to learn the taste of its twigs and bark. The owl crept into the first one that became hollow, and fairly hooted with delight, finding it just the place for him. He settled into it, and has remained there ever since. The lackey caterpillar saddled her eggs on the very first twig that was formed, and it has since divided her affections with the wild cherry; and the canker-worm also in a measure abandoned the elm to feed on it. And when the fruit was ripe, the squirrel half carried, half rolled, it to his hole, and even the musquash crept up the bank and greedily devoured it; and when it was frozen and thawed, the crow and jay did not disdain to peck it. And the beautiful wood duck, having made up her mind to stay a while longer with us, has concluded that there is no better place for her too.

Feb. 16. [1860]   To Walden. All the birds' nests in the blueberry bushes are revealed, by the great snow-balls they hold.

April 4. [1860]   The birds sing quite numerously at sunrise about the villages,—robins, *tree sparrows*, and methinks I heard a purple finch. The birds are eager to sing, as the flowers to bloom, after raw weather has held them in check.

June 18. [1860]   The tumultuous singing of birds, a burst of melody, wakes me up (the window being open) these mornings at dawn. What a *matinade* to have poured into your slumber!

Sept. 1. [1860]   To Walden. See how artfully the seed of a cherry is placed in order that a bird may be compelled to transport it. It is placed in the very midst of a tempting pericarp, so that the creature that would devour a cherry must take a stone into its mouth. The bird is bribed with the pericarp to take the stone with it and do this little service for Nature. Cherries are especially birds' food, and many kinds are called birds' cherry, and unless we plant the seeds occasionally, I shall think the birds have the best right to them. Thus a bird's wing is added to the cherry-stone which is wingless, and it does not wait for winds to transport it. If you ever ate a cherry, and did not make two bites of it, you must have perceived it. There it is, right in the midst of the luscious morsel, an earthy residuum left on the tongue. And some wild men and children instinctively swallow it, like the birds, as the shortest way to get rid of it. And the consequence is that cherries not only grow here but there, and I know of some handsome young English cherries growing naturally in our woods, which I think of transplanting back again to my garden. If the seed had been placed in a leaf, or at the root, it would not have got transported thus. Consider how many seeds of plants we take into our mouths. Even stones as big as peas, a dozen at once.

IDENTIFICATION OF BIRDS

[Edmund Sewall arrived in Concord on March 23, 1840, to enter the Thoreau school. A few days later he wrote to his mother that he had gone for a walk to Walden Pond with Mr. Thoreau. On their return his teacher shot a slate-colored sparrow (Slate-colored Junco) which he wished to examine. But Thoreau was already forming an opinion that collected birds offered far less genuine information than could be learned from living ones. He sold his gun before he went to live for a while by Walden Pond.

In the *Journal* entry which follows, he considers the possible value of a spyglass in studying birds. In the next entry we learn what he did about it, and the third expresses satisfaction in the way he solved his problem. On April 23, 1854 (turn to "Bald Eagle" under "Birds of Concord" from the *Journal*), Thoreau felt he had already received a full return on his investment.]

MARCH 29. [1853]   Four ducks, two by two, are sailing conspicuously on the river. There appear to be two pairs. In each case one two-thirds white and another grayish-brown, and, I think, smaller. They are very shy and fly at fifty rods' distance. . . . Would it not be well to carry a spy-glass in order to watch these shy birds such as ducks and hawks? In some respects, methinks, it would be better than a gun. The latter brings them nearer dead, but the former alive. You can identify the species better by killing the bird, because it was a dead specimen that was so minutely described, but you can study the habits and appearance best in the living specimen.

MARCH 13. [1854]   To Boston. Bought a telescope to-day for eight dollars.

APRIL 10. [1854]   I bought me a spy-glass some weeks since. I buy but few things, and those not till long after I begin to want them, so that when I do get them I am prepared to make a perfect use of them and extract their whole sweet.

[Edwin Way Teale was once given the privilege of using this glass. He saw a robin sitting on an elm but before he could focus properly, the robin flew away. This glass with its narrow field was difficult to hold steady or focus quickly. It bears little resemblance to the spotting telescopes used to-day for watching birds. These instruments, mounted on tripods or gunstocks, have wide fields and admit much light, thus giving the viewer a brilliant image. Though Thoreau paid only $8.00 for his spyglass, his investment would be considered a waste today.

The reference books used by Thoreau in trying to identify birds have been discussed. He often spoke of the difference in appearance between a live bird and a dead one. Only the dead birds were described in his books. In his *Journal* entry of March 15, 1860 (turn to Red-tailed Hawk) he noted:]

What a perfectly regular and neat outline it presents! an easily recognized figure anywhere. Yet I never see it represented in any books.

[But such pictures as he longed for had not yet been made by any artist. Ernest Thompson Seton may have taken the idea for Jan's sketches of duck patterns in *Two Little Savages* from Thoreau. Dr. Roger Tory Peterson whose system of bird identification has gone round the world, attributes its origin in part to Seton. Whether or not Thoreau's desire for pictures of bird patterns led indirectly to the Peterson system cannot now be determined. Nevertheless, a foreshadowing of contemporary guidebook illustrations is found in Thoreau's *Journal*.

Even more impressive is his discussion which follows, of the need to revise the method of describing species. Here he drives home the need to emphasize the precise points which distinguish species and make each one unique. This, of course, is the heart of the Peterson system.]

MAY 25. [1853]   I quarrel with most botanists' description of different species, say of willows. It is a difference without a distinction. No stress is laid upon the peculiarity of the species in question, and it requires a very careful examination and comparison to detect any difference in the description. Having described you one species, he begins again at the beginning when he comes to the next and describes it *absolutely*, wasting time; in fact does not describe the species, but rather the genus or family; as if, in describing the particular races of men, you should say of each in its turn that it is but dust and to dust it shall return. The object should be to describe not those particulars in which a species resembles its genus, for they are many and that would be but a negative description, but those in which it is peculiar, for they are few and positive.

CONSERVATION

[Dr. Howard Zahniser, until his recent death executive secretary of the Wilderness Society and editor of *The Living Wilderness,* was one of many who rated Thoreau as the first and one of the very best American conservationists. To support this opinion, Dr. Zahniser quoted the entry in Thoreau's *Journal* for October 15, 1859.

The entry directly following this sums up in a single sentence the fact that preservation of habitat is essential to the preservation of species. His defense of hedgerows is supported by game management authorities aware of the value of these places as shelter, protection from enemies, and as a source of food for many species of birds and for small mammals as well.

Our state and national park systems were a thing of the future, but in 1861 Thoreau expresses a need to preserve beautiful natural features of towns and of wilderness areas as well.

In the very small section which follows, a very great amount of wisdom has been packed. It is well worth reading over and over again.]

MAY 17. [1853]   He who cuts down woods beyond a certain limit exterminates birds.

SEPT. 28. [1857]   I see that E. Wood has sent a couple of Irishmen, with axe and bush-whack, to cut off the natural hedges of sumach, Roxbury waxwork, grapes, etc., which have sprung up by the walls on this hill farm, in order that his cows may get a little more green. And they have cut down two or three of the very rare celtis trees, not found anywhere else in town. The Lord deliver us from these vandalic proprietors! The botanist and lover of nature has, perchance, discovered some rare tree which has sprung up by a farmer's wall-side to adorn and bless it, sole representative of its kind in these parts. Strangers send for a seed or a sprig from a distance, but, walking there again, he finds that the farmer has sent a raw Irishman, a hireling just arrived on these shores, who was never there before,—and, we trust, will never be let loose there again,—who knows not whether he is hacking at the upas tree or the Tree of Knowledge, with axe and stub-scythe to exterminate it, and he will know it no more forever. What is trespassing? This Hessian, the day after he was landed, was whirled twenty miles into the interior to do this deed of vandalism on our favorite hedge.

I would as soon admit a living mud turtle into my herbarium. If some are prosecuted for abusing children, others deserve to be prosecuted for mal-treating the face of nature committed to their care.

APR. 8. [1859]   When the question of the protection of birds comes up, the legislatures regard only a low use and never a high use; the best-disposed legislators employ one, perchance, only to examine their crops and see how many grubs or cherries they contain, and never to study their dispositions, or the beauty of their plumage, or listen and report on the sweetness of their song. The legislature will preserve a bird professedly not because it is a beautiful creature, but because it is a good scavenger or the like. This, at least, is the defense set up. It is as if the question were whether some cele-brated singer of the human race—some Jenny Lind or another—did more harm or good, should be destroyed, or not, and therefore a committee should be appointed, not to listen to her singing at all, but to examine the contents of her stomach and see if she devoured anything which was injurious to the farmers and gardeners, or which they cannot spare.

OCT. 15. [1859]   Each town should have a park, or rather primitive forest, of five hundred or a thousand acres, where a stick should never be cut for fuel, a common possession forever, for instruction and recreation. We hear of cow-commons and ministerial lots, but we want *men*-commons and lay lots, inalienable forever. Let us keep the New World *new*, preserve all the advantages of living in the country. There is a meadow and pasture and wood-lot for the town's poor. Why not a forest and huckleberry-field for the town's rich? All Walden Wood might have been preserved for our park forever, with Walden in its midst, and the Easterbrooks County, an unoc-cupied area of some four square miles, might have been our huckleberry-field. If any owners of these tracts are about to leave the world without natural heirs who need or deserve to be specially remembered, they will do wisely to abandon their possession to all, and not will them to some in-dividual who perhaps has enough already. As some give to Harvard College or another institution, why might not another give a forest or huckleberry-field to Concord? A town is an institution which deserves to be remembered. We boast of our system of education, but why stop at schoolmasters and schoolhouses? We are all schoolmasters, and our schoolhouse is the universe. To attend chiefly to the desk or schoolhouse while we neglect the scenery in which it is placed is absurd. If we do not look out we shall find our fine schoolhouse standing in a cow-yard one day.

JAN. 3. [1861]   The third considerable snowstorm. What are the natural features which make a township handsome? A river, with its waterfalls and meadows, a lake, a hill, a cliff or individual rocks, a forest, and ancient trees standing singly. Such things are beautiful; they have a high use which dollars and cents never represent. If the inhabitants of a town were wise, they would seek to preserve these things, though at a considerable expense; for such things educate far more than any hired teachers or preachers, or any at present recognized system of school education. I do not think him fit to be a founder of a state or even of a town who does not foresee the use of these things, but legislates chiefly for oxen, as it were. . . .

Think of a mountain-top in the township—even to the minds of the Indians a sacred place—only accessible through private grounds! a temple, as it were, which you cannot enter except by trespassing and at the risk of letting out or letting in somebody's cattle!—in fact the temple itself in this case private property and standing in a man's cow-yard,—for such is commonly the case!

New Hampshire courts have lately been deciding—as if it was for them to decide—whether the top of Mt. Washington belonged to A or B; and, it being decided in favor of B, as I hear it, he went up one winter with the proper officer and took formal possession of it. But I think that the top of Mt. Washington should not be private property; it should be left unappropriated for modesty and reverence's sake, or if only to suggest that earth has higher uses than we put her to. I know it is a mere figure of speech to talk about temples nowadays, when men recognize none, and indeed, associate the word with heathenism. . . .

But most men, it seems to me, do not care for Nature and would sell their share in all her beauty, as long as they may live, for a stated sum—many for a glass of rum. Thank God, men cannot as yet fly, and lay waste the sky as well as the earth! We are safe on that side for the present. It is for the very reason that some do not care for those things that we need to continue to protect all from the vandalism of a few.

SCIENCE

[Thoreau's remarks about science are biting, and as little heeded by the majority of scientists to-day as they were a century ago. He found most scientists working in stuffy laboratories as dull as their specimens, and their studies too limited to give any but the narrowest, most unimportant information about the subjects.

Nevertheless, after meeting Louis Agassiz, teaching at Harvard in the late 1840s, he collected quite a lot of fish, turtles, and mice for him. On August 18, 1854, he killed a cistudo (Box Turtle) and regretted it deeply. Throughout the following section he repeatedly expresses his belief that scientists approach their work from quite the wrong direction. Certainly his account on November 30, 1858, of the discovery in Walden Pond of a striped bream which was new to science, gives a vivid impression of the fish, and the reader would like to see it, as he would not care to do after reading the scientific description of the same small fish.

Though he did not care for scientific organizations, in 1850 he was elected a corresponding member of the Boston Society of Natural History for having given "a fine specimen of an American Goshawk" to its museum. But this was of too little importance to him to note the honor in his *Journal*. On March 5, 1853, he discusses his invitation to join the Association for the Advancement of Science. He did not join and to-day he would find the membership of that distinguished association even less to his liking, for there is now a far smaller proportion of natural scientists among its membership.

[Undated] [1837–47]   I hate museums; there is nothing so weighs upon my spirits. They are the catacombs of nature. One green bud of spring, one willow catkin, one faint trill from a migrating sparrow would set the world on its legs again. The life that is in a single green weed is of more worth than all this death. They are dead nature collected by dead men. I know not whether I muse most at the bodies stuffed with cotton and sawdust or those stuffed with bowels and fleshy fibre outside the cases.

DEC. 16. [1837]   How indispensable to a correct study of Nature is a perception of her true meaning. The fact will one day flower out into a truth. The season will mature and fructify what the understanding has cultivated. Mere accumulators of facts—collectors of materials for the master-workmen —are like those plants growing in dark forests, which "put forth only leaves instead of blossoms."

MARCH 5. [1853]   The secretary for the Association for the Advancement of Science requests me, as he probably has thousands of others, by a printed circular letter from Washington the other day, to fill the blank against certain questions, among which the most important one was what branch of science I was specially interested in, using the term science in the most comprehensive sense possible. Now, though I could state to a select few that department of human inquiry which engages me, and should be rejoiced at an opportunity to do so, I felt that it would be to make myself the laughing-stock of the scientific community to describe or attempt to describe to them that branch of science which specially interests me, inasmuch as they do not believe in a science which deals with the higher law. So I was obliged to speak to their condition and describe to them that poor part of me which alone they can understand. The fact is I am a mystic, a transcendentalist, and a natural philosopher to boot. Now I think of it, I should have told them at once that I was a transcendentalist. That would have been the shortest way of telling them that they would not understand my explanations.

How absurd that, though I probably stand as near to nature as any of them, and am by constitution as good an observer as most, yet a true account of my relation to nature should excite their ridicule only! If it had been the secretary of an association of which Plato or Aristotle was the president, I should not have hesitated to describe my studies at once and particularly.

MARCH 22. [1853]   A description of animals, too, from a dead specimen only, as if, in a work on man, you were to describe a dead man only, omitting his manners and customs, his institutions and divine faculties, from want of opportunity to observe them, suggesting, perchance, that the colors of the eye are said to be much more brilliant in the living specimen, and that some cannibal, your neighbor, who has tried him on the table, has found him to be sweet and nutritious, good on the gridiron. Having had no opportunity to observe his habits, because you do not live in the country. Only dindons and dandies. Nothing is known of his habits. Food: seeds of wheat, beef, pork, and potatoes.

MARCH 23. [1853]   Man cannot afford to be a naturalist, to look at Nature directly, but only with the side of his eye. He must look through and beyond her. To look at her is fatal as to look at the head of Medusa. It turns the man of science to stone.

MAY 10. [1854]   In Boston yesterday an ornithologist said significantly, "If you held the bird in your hand—;" but I would rather hold it in my affections.

MAY 17. [1854]   Who shall distinguish between the *law* by which a brook finds its river, the *instinct* [by which] a bird performs its migrations, and the *knowledge* by which a man steers his ship round the globe?

MAY 28. [1854]   The inhumanity of science concerns me, as when I am tempted to kill a rare snake that I may ascertain its species. I feel that this is not the means of acquiring true knowledge.

AUG. 18. [1854]   I have just been through the process of killing the cistudo for the sake of science; but I cannot excuse myself for this murder, and see that such actions are inconsistent with the poetic perception, however they may serve science, and will affect the quality of my observations. I pray that I may walk more innocently and serenely through nature. No reasoning whatever reconciles me to this act. It affects my day injuriously. I have lost some self-respect. I have a murderer's experience in a degree.

Nov. 30. [1858]   [Thoreau discovered a striped bream, in Walden Pond, which was new to science.] I cannot but see still in my mind's eye those little striped breams poised in Walden's glaucous water. They balance all the rest of the world in my estimation at present, for this is the bream that I have just found, and for the time I neglect all its brethren and am ready to kill the fatted calf on its account. For more than two centuries have men fished here and have not distinguished this permament settler of the township. It is not like a new bird, a transient visitor that may not be seen again for years, but there it dwells and has dwelt permanently, who can tell how long. When my eyes first rested on Walden the striped bream was poised in it, though I did not see it, and when Tahatawan paddled his canoe there. How wild it makes the pond and the township to find a new fish in it! America renews her youth here. But in my account of this bream I cannot go a hair's breadth beyond the mere statement that it exists—the miracle of its existence, my contemporary and neighbor, yet so different from me! I can only poise my thought there by its side and try to think like a bream for a moment. I can only think of precious jewels, of music, poetry, beauty, and the mystery of life. I only see the bream in its orbit, as I see a star, but I care not to measure its distance or weight. The bream, appreciated, floats in the pond as the centre of the system, another image of God. Its life no man can explain more than he can his own. I want you to perceive the mystery of the bream. I have a contemporary in Walden. It has fins where I have legs and arms. I have a friend among the fishes, at least a new acquaintance. Its character will interest me, I trust, not its clothes and anatomy. I do not want it to eat. Acquaintance with it is to make my life more rich and eventful. It is as if a poet or an anchorite had moved into the town, whom I can see from time to time and think of yet oftener. Perhaps there are a thousand of these striped bream which no one had thought of in that pond, —not their mere impressions in stone, but in the full tide of the bream life.

Though science may sometimes compare herself to a child picking up pebbles on the seashore, that is a rare mood with her; ordinarily her practical belief is that it is only a few pebbles which are *not* known, weighed and measured. A new species of fish signifies hardly more than a new name. See what is contributed in the scientific reports. One counts the fin-rays, another measures the intestines, a third daguerreotypes a scale, etc., etc.; otherwise there's nothing to be said. As if all but this were done, and these were very rich and generous contributions to science. Her votaries may be seen wandering along the shore of the ocean of truth, with their backs to that ocean, ready to seize the shells which are cast up. You would say that the scientific

bodies were terribly put to it for objects and subjects. A dead specimen of
an animal, if it is only well preserved in alcohol, is just as good for science
as a living one preserved in its native element.

What is the amount of my discovery to me? It is not that I have got one
in a bottle, that it has got a name in a book, but that I have a little fishy
friend in the pond. How was it when the youth first discovered fishes? Was
it the number of their fin-rays or their arrangement, or the place of the fish
in some system that made the boy dream of them? Is it these things that
interest mankind in the fish, the inhabitant of the water? No, but a faint
recognition of a living contemporary, a provoking mystery. One boy thinks
of fishes and goes a-fishing from the same motive that his brother searches
the poets for rare lines. It is the poetry of fishes which is their chief use;
their flesh is their lowest use. The beauty of the fish, that is what it is best
worth the while to measure. Its place in our systems is of comparatively little
importance. Generally the boy loses some of his perception and his interest
in the fish; he degenerates into a fisherman or an ichthyologist.

MARCH 5. [1860]   The old naturalists were so sensitive and sympathic to
nature that they could be surprised by the ordinary events of life. It was an
incessant miracle to them, and therefore gorgons and flying dragons were
not incredible to them. The greatest and saddest defect is not credulity, but
our habitual forgetfulness that our science is ignorance.

OCT. 9. [1860]   This haste to kill a bird or quadruped and make a skeleton
of it, which many young men and some old ones exhibit, reminds me of the
fable of the man who killed the hen that laid golden eggs, and so got no
more gold. It is a perfectly parallel case. Such is the knowledge which you
may get from the anatomy as compared with the knowledge you get from
the living creature. Every fowl lays golden eggs for him who can find them,
or can detect alloy and base metal.

THOREAU'S CONCORD BIRD LIST

[The birds Thoreau noted in his *Journal* are included in the following list.
Exceptions to this are such birds as his hemlock warbler and unspecificed
ducks and plovers which he mentioned and either did not describe at all or
too slightly for identification. The Connecticut Warbler, open to question,
has been included because he wrote a fairly accurate description of this
species in autumn plumage, and also Bonaparte's Gull, probably the black-
headed gull seen by Jacob Farmer (August 13, 1857), but perhaps never
seen by Thoreau.

To-day, visitors to Concord can locate many of the places which Thoreau visited regularly when making his Concord studies. Open to the public is the Great Meadows, now a National Wildlife Refuge and, though drastically changed since Thoreau watched birds there, is much better for waterfowl now than in the nineteenth century. The Great Meadows National Wildlife Refuge is one of the chain of waterfowl refuges extending from Canada to the Gulf of Mexico. It is small but a very important link in this chain. During spring floods Thoreau sailed over the Meadows. In summer he walked dryshod across them, and at that time the farmers harvested the wild grass by hand. With increased mechanized farming, the Great Meadows fell into disuse. In 1928 a distinguished lawyer, Mr. Samuel Hoar, diked part of the Meadows and found he had created a successful waterfowl area. In 1944 two hundred and fifty-three acres were made into the Great Meadows National Wildlife Refuge and since then the area has been constantly improved as a waterfowl habitat. Large numbers of nesting boxes have been erected there, leading to an exceptionally high density of Wood Ducks—a species Thoreau watched with particular pleasure. To-day two hundred and three acres of the Refuge are water and marsh. In the limited woodland along the borders, a surprisingly large number of land birds occur. Of all the areas in Concord that were well known to Thoreau, this one to-day is most frequently visited by bird watchers who have logged some one hundred and seventy-six species in or near the Refuge.

Thoreau saw none of the southern herons which to-day are regular summer and early autumn visitors to Concord, nor did he see either of the Night Herons. Of the twenty species of ducks listed for the Refuge, Thoreau definitely identified only nine.

He was keenly interested in hawks and thought they added more to a landscape than any other kind of bird. He identified all the common Concord species except the Broad-winged Hawk. He also identified some hawks which are considered rare in Concord to-day: Turkey Vulture, Goshawk, Rough-legged Hawk, and Bald Eagle.

Thoreau was less successful with the shorebirds and gulls. But he recorded the Common Tern, which is not on the present Concord bird list. He saw all the owls which regularly occur in Concord and may have seen the Snowy Owl which periodically moves southward when food is scare in the far north. He saw the Saw-whet Owl in the White Mountains, but never in Concord.

Oddly enough, he overlooked the Yellow-bellied Sapsucker which is a regular migrant through Concord. He saw the Pileated Woodpecker in Maine but never in Concord, though he once described squarish holes there which must have been made by that species.

He recorded all the swallows except the Rough-winged. He did poorly with the wrens, never seeing any species in the Great Meadows where the

House Wren, Winter Wren, Carolina Wren and both Marsh Wrens are recorded to-day, though it is true some species but rarely. However, due to the change in the entire habitat, the Long-billed Marsh Wren is common during the spring and summer.

Among the song birds, the thrushes gave Thoreau particular pleasure and he wrote at length about them. He also wrote often about the vireos, and his list is better than the present vireo list for the Refuge area. He had little to say about warblers though he described the majority of species which nest in or pass through Concord on migration. The Yellow Warbler, Pine Warbler, Redstart, and Ovenbird, together with his mysterious "night-warbler," were the subjects of some poetic prose; but the other species appear as little more than descriptions for the purpose of identification.

Thoreau identified all the Concord blackbirds. He did very well indeed with the huge fringillid family, though he frequently confused the songs of the sparrows.

Since his day the Passenger Pigeon, which he sometimes observed in great flocks, has become extinct. Pheasants, starlings, and house sparrows have been introduced and become common. Evening Grosbeaks from the northwest are regular winter visitors. Tufted Titmice have extended their range northward and while not common, are regularly seen there. Occasionally a Dickcissel, which Thoreau saw on Cape Cod but never in his town, is recorded in Concord in autumn or winter.

Though the changes in Concord are great, it has kept its beauty. The Concord of Thoreau can still be found in a limited and blurred way to-day. Allowing for the irregular and unpredictable appearance of many of the northern species, all the birds seen in Concord by Thoreau can be seen to-day with the exception of the extinct Passenger Pigeon. By using the map of Concord made by Herbert W. Gleason in 1906, a visitor to Concord can locate many of the places described by Thoreau in his *Journal* and in *Walden*. The bird watcher can record many of the birds in the very places where Thoreau saw them a century and more ago.]

LOON, COMMON (great northern diver)
    RED-THROATED (great northern diver)
GREBE, HORNED (little diver)
    PIED-BILLED (little diver)
HERON, GREAT BLUE (blue heron)
    GREEN (green bittern)
BITTERN, LEAST
    AMERICAN (stake-driver, great bittern)
GOOSE, CANADA (wild goose, Canadian goose)
BRANT (?)

DUCK, BLACK (dusky duck)
TEAL, GREEN-WINGED
     BLUE-WINGED
DUCK, WOOD (summer duck)
SCAUP (species ?)
GOLDENEYE, COMMON (whistler)
BUFFLEHEAD (buffle-headed duck, spirit duck)
MERGANSER, COMMON (goosander, sheldrake)
     RED-BREASTED
VULTURE, TURKEY
GOSHAWK (partridge hawk, Cape eagle)
HAWK, SHARP-SHINNED
    COOPER'S
    RED-TAILED (hen-hawk)
    RED-SHOULDERED (hen-hawk, red-shouldered buzzard)
    ROUGH-LEGGED
EAGLE, BALD (white-headed eagle)
HAWK, MARSH (frog hawk, hen-harrier)
OSPREY (fish hawk, fish eagle)
HAWK, PIGEON (merlin)
    SPARROW
GROUSE, RUFFED (partridge)
BOBWHITE (quail)
RAIL, VIRGINIA (meadow hen)
SORA (Carolina rail)
COOT, AMERICAN (cinereus coot)
KILLDEER
WOODCOCK, AMERICAN
SNIPE, COMMON
PLOVER, UPLAND
SANDPIPER, SPOTTED (peetweet)
    SOLITARY (solitary tattler)
WILLET
YELLOWLEGS, GREATER (telltale)
    LESSER (telltale)
SANDPIPER, PECTORAL
GULL, HERRING
    BONAPARTE'S (black-headed)
TERN, COMMON (mackerel gull)
DOVE, MOURNING (turtle dove)
PIGEON, PASSENGER (wild pigeon)

CUCKOO, BLACK-BILLED (St. Domingo)
OWL, SCREECH (red owl)
 GREAT HORNED (hoot owl, cat owl)
 BARRED (hoot owl)
 LONG-EARED
 SHORT-EARED
WHIP-POOR-WILL
NIGHTHAWK, COMMON
SWIFT, CHIMNEY (chimney swallow)
HUMMINGBIRD, RUBY-THROATED
KINGFISHER, BELTED
FLICKER, YELLOW-SHAFTED (pigeon woodpecker, golden-winged
 woodpecker)
KINGBIRD, EASTERN
PHOEBE, EASTERN (peewee, bridge pewee)
FLYCATCHER, LEAST (small pewee)
WOOD PEWEE, EASTERN (peawai)
FLYCATCHER, OLIVE-SIDED (pe-pe)
LARK, HORNED (shore lark)
SWALLOW, TREE (white-bellied swallow)
 BANK
 BARN
 CLIFF (republican swallow)
MARTIN, PURPLE
JAY, BLUE
CROW, COMMON
CHICADEE, BLACK-CAPPED (titmouse)
NUTHATCH, WHITE-BREASTED (white-bellied nuthatch)
 RED-BREASTED (red-bellied nuthatch)
CREEPER, BROWN
WREN, SHORT-BILLED MARSH
MOCKINGBIRD
CATBIRD
THRASHER, BROWN (red mavis)
ROBIN
THRUSH, WOOD
 HERMIT
VEERY (Wilson's thrush, yorrick)
BLUEBIRD, EASTERN
KINGLET, GOLDEN-CROWNED (golden-crested wren, golden-crowned
 wren)
 RUBY-CROWNED (ruby-crested wren, ruby-crowned wren)

PIPIT, WATER (titlark)
WAXWING, CEDAR (cherry-bird)
SHRIKE, NORTHERN (butcher-bird)
VIREO, WHITE-EYED
    YELLOW-THROATED
    SOLITARY
    RED-EYED (red-eye, robin of the woods)
    WARBLING
WARBLER, BLACK-AND-WHITE (black-and-white creeper)
    GOLDEN-WINGED
    NASHVILLE
    PARULA (tweezer-bird, parti-colored warbler, blue yellow-backed warbler)
    YELLOW (yellowbird, summer yellowbird)
    MAGNOLIA (black and yellow warbler)
    BLACK-THROATED BLUE (indigo-bird, May 4, 1853)
    MYRTLE (myrtle-bird, yellow-rump)
WARBLER, BLACK-THROATED GREEN (evergreen-forest bird)
    BLACKBURNIAN
    CHESTNUT-SIDED
    BLACKPOLL
    PINE
    PALM (yellow redpoll)
OVERBIRD (golden-crowned thrush, night-warbler)
WATERTHRUSH, NORTHERN
YELLOWTHROAT (Maryland yellowthroat, sometimes night-warbler)
WARBLER, CONNECTICUT (?)
    Canada
REDSTART, AMERICAN (election-bird)
BOBOLINK
MEADOWLARK, EASTERN (lark)
BLACKBIRD, REDWINGED (red-wing)
ORIOLE, BALTIMORE (hangbird, fiery hangbird, gold robin, golden robin)
BLACKBIRD, RUSTY (rusty grackle)
GRACKLE, COMMON (crow blackbird)
COWBIRD, BROWN-HEADED (cow troopial, cow blackbird)
TANAGER, SCARLET (election-bird, red-bird, fire-never-redder)
GROSBEAK, ROSE-BREASTED
BUNTING, INDIGO (indigo-bird)
FINCH, PURPLE
GROSBEAK, PINE

REDPOLL, COMMON (red-crown, linaria, lesser redpoll)
GOLDFINCH, AMERICAN
CROSSBILL, RED
TOWHEE, RUFOUS-SIDED (chewink, ground-robin, towhee finch)
SPARROW, SAVANNAH (sometimes seringo)
    GRASSHOPPER (yellow-winged)
    VESPER (bay-wing, grass finch, grass-bird, white-in-tail)
JUNCO, SLATE-COLORED (*Fringilla hyemalis*, slated-colored snowbird, blue snowbird)
SPARROW, TREE
    CHIPPING (chip-bird, hair-bird)
    FIELD (rush sparrow, huckleberry-bird)
    WHITE-THROATED
    FOX (fox-colored sparrow)
    SWAMP
    SONG
BUNTING, SNOW (snowbird, arctic snowbird)

Birds of Massachusetts

[Massachusetts is probably searched more thoroughly for birds than any other state in the Union. As a result, the number of species that have been identified within its boundaries has gone far beyond the two hundred and eight species known to occur there in Thoreau's day, and is moving close to the five hundred mark.

Thoreau's essay, "Natural History of Massachusetts," from which the bird section which follows was taken, contains much sound information. It ranges widely through the plant and animal life in the state and is salted throughout with Thoreau's philosophy and observations. In fact, it reflects his *Journal* far more than the report which it ostensibly reviews.

The opening paragraph of the essay sparks the imagination by taking the reader far from Thoreau's snow-bound state as he points out the cheer found in books of natural history.]

Books of natural history make the most cheerful winter reading. I read in Audubon with a thrill of delight, when the snow covers the ground, of the magnolia, and the Florida keys, and their warm sea breezes; of the fence-rail, and the cotton-tree, and the migrations of the rice-bird; of the breaking up of winter in Labrador, and the melting of the snow on the forks of the Missouri; and owe an accession of health to these reminiscenses of luxuriant nature. . . .

[Thoreau's pleasure in winter birds was shared by comparatively few of his contemporaries. To-day tens of thousands go to considerable thought, effort, and expense to attract birds to their gardens and windowsills by offering them food and water. More than ten thousand people took part in the most recent annual Christmas Bird Count, often braving extremely severe weather to do so.]

About two hundred and eighty birds either reside permanently in the State, or spend the summer only, or make us a passing visit. Those which spend the winter with us have obtained our warmest sympathy. The nuthatch and chickadee flitting in company through the dells of the wood, the one harshly scolding at the intruder, the other with a faint lisping note enticing him on; the jay screaming in the orchard; the crow cawing in unison with the storm; the partridge, like a russet link extended over from autumn to spring, preserving unbroken the chain of summers; the hawk with warrior-like firmness abiding the blasts of winter; the robin and the lark lurking by warm springs in the woods; the familiar snowbird culling a few seeds in the garden or a few crumbs in the yard; and occasionally the shrike, with heedless and unfrozen melody bringing back summer again:

> His steady sails he never furls
> At any time o' year,
> And perching now on Winter's curls,
> He whistles in his ear.

[In a footnote Thoreau added:]

A white robin and a white quail have occasionally been seen. It is mentioned in Audubon as remarkable that the nest of a robin should be found on the ground; but this bird seems to be less particular than most in the choice of a building-spot. I have seen its nest placed under the thatched roof of a deserted barn, and in one instance, where the adjacent country was nearly destitute of trees, together with two of the phoebe, upon the end of a board in the loft of a sawmill, but a few feet from the saw, which vibrated several inches with the motion of the machinery.

[Spring, when birds garbed in their brightest plumage sing their best songs, has always been the season when most attention is given to this large and varied group of creatures. Thoreau recalled the poetry of

Anacreon, the Greek poet of Teos, as he enjoyed the arrival of birds in New England.]

As spring advances, and the ice is melting in the river, our earliest and straggling visitors make their appearance. Again does the old Teian poet sing as well for New England as for Greece, in the

Return of Spring
Behold, how, Spring appearing,
The Graces send forth roses;
Behold, how the wave of the sea
Is smooth and calm;
Behold how the duck dives;
Behold, how the crane travells;
And Titan shines constantly bright.
The shadows of the clouds are moving;
The works of man shine;
The earth puts forth fruits;
The fruit of the olive puts forth.
The cup of Bacchus is crowned;
Along the leaves, along the branches,
The fruit, bending them down, flourishes.

The ducks alight at this season in the still water, in company with the gulls, which do not fail to improve an east wind to visit our meadows, and swim about by twos and threes, pluming themselves, and diving to peck at the root of the lily, and the cranberries which the frost has not loosened. The first flock of geese is seen beating to north, in long harrows and waving lines; the jingle of the song sparrow salutes us from the shrubs and fences; the plaintive note of the lark comes clear and sweet from the meadow; and the bluebird, like an azure ray, glances past us in our walk. The fish hawk, too, is occasionally seen at this season sailing majestically over the water, and he who has once observed it will not soon forget the majesty of its flight. It sails the air like a ship of the line, worthy to struggle with the elements, falling back from time to time like a ship on its beam ends, and holding its talons up as if ready for the arrows, in the attitude of the national bird. It is a great presence, as of the master of river and forest. Its eye would not quail before the owner of the soil, but make him feel like an intruder on its domain. And then its retreat, sailing so steadily away, is a kind of advance. I have by me one of a pair of ospreys, which have for some years fished in this vicinity, shot by a neighboring pond, meas-

uring more than two feet in length, and six in the stretch of its wings. Nuttall mentions that "the ancients, particularly Aristotle, pretended that the
ospreys taught their young to gaze at the sun, and those who were unable
to do so were destroyed. Linnaeus believed, on ancient authority, that one
of the feet of this bird had all toes divided, while the other was partly
webbed, so that it could swim with one foot, and grasp a fish with the
other." But that educated eye is now dim, and those talons are nerveless.
Its shrill scream seems still to linger in its throat, and the roar of the sea in
its wings. There is the tyranny of Jove in its claws, and his wrath in the
erectile feathers of the head and neck. It reminds me of the Argonautic
expedition, and would inspire the dullest to take flight over Parnassus.

The booming of the bittern, described by Goldsmith and Nuttall, is frequently heard in our fens, in the morning and evening, sounding like a
pump, or the chopping of wood in a frosty morning in some distant farmyard. The manner in which this sound is produced I have not seen anywhere described. On one occasion, the bird has been seen by one of my
neighbors to thrust its bill into the water, and suck up as much as it could
hold, then, raising its head, it pumped it out again with four or five heaves
of the neck, throwing it two or three feet, and making the sound each time.

[The description of an American Bittern making its strange sound, as
reported by Thoreau's neighbor, is pure fantasy. The bittern makes all of
its calls with the syrinx, the vocal organ of birds.]

At length the summer's eternity is ushered in by the cackle of the flicker
among the oaks on the hillside, and a new dynasty begins with calm
security.

In May and June the woodland quire is in full tune, and, given the immense spaces of hollow air, and this curious human ear, one does not see
how the void could be better filled.

> Each summer sound
> Is a summer round.

As the season advances, and those birds which make us but a passing
visit depart, the woods become silent again, and but few feathers ruffle the
drowsy air. But the solitary rambler may still find a response and expression
for every mood in the depths of the wood.

> Sometimes I hear the veery's clarion,
> Or brazen trump of the impatient jay,

And in secluded woods the chickadee
Doles out her scanty notes, which sing the praise
Of heroes, and set forth the loveliness
Of virtue evermore.

The phoebe still sings in harmony with the sultry weather by the brink of the pond, nor are the desultory hours of noon in the midst of the village without their minstrel.

Upon the lofty elm-tree sprays
The vireo rings the changes sweet,
During the trivial summer days,
Striving to lift our thoughts above the street.

With autumn begins in some measure a new spring. The plover is heard whistling high in the air over the dry pastures, the finches flit from tree to tree, the bobolinks and flickers fly in flocks, and the goldfinch rides on the earliest blast, like a winged hyla peeping amid the rustle of the leaves. The crows, too, begin now to congregate; you may stand and count them as they fly low and straggling over the landscape, singly or by twos and threes, at intervals of half a mile, until a hundred have passed.

[In few areas of traditional information have false beliefs been more consistently accepted than ancient "facts" about nature. Thoreau, who refused to accept generally believed "truths" in religion, social behavior, and economics without supporting evidence, extended this independence of thought to the natural world around him. Below, he demolishes the idea that the white man brought the crow to America.]

I have seen it suggested somewhere that the crow was brought to this country by the white man; but I shall as soon believe that the white man planted these pines and hemlocks. He is no spaniel to follow our steps; but rather flits about the clearings like the dusky spirit of the Indian, reminding me oftener of Philip and Powhatan than of Winthrop and Smith. He is a relic of the dark ages. By just so slight, by just so lasting a tenure does superstition hold the world ever; there is the rook in England, and the crow in New England.

Thou dusky spirit of the wood,
Bird of an ancient brood,

>   Flitting thy lonely way,
>   A meteor in the summer's day,
>   From wood to wood, from hill to hill,
>   Low over the forest, field, and rill,
>   What wouldst thou say?
>   Why shouldst thou haunt the day?
>   What makes thy melancholy float?
>   What bravery inspires thy throat,
>   And bears thee up above the clouds,
>   Over desponding human crowds,
>   Which far below
>   Lay thy haunts low.

The late walker or sailor, in the October evenings, may hear the murmurings of the snipe, circling over the meadows, the most spirit-like sound in nature; and still later in the autumn, when the frosts have tinged the leaves, a solitary loon pays a visit to our retired ponds, where he may lurk undisturbed till the season of moulting is passed, making the woods ring with his wild laughter. This bird, the Great Northern Diver, well deserves its name; for when pursued with a boat, it will dive, and swim like a fish under water, for sixty rods or more, as far as a boat can be paddled, and its pursuer, if he would discover his game again, must put his ear to the surface to hear where it comes up. When it comes to the surface, it throws the water off with one shake of its wings, and calmly swims about until again disturbed.

[Most bird watchers today, in spite of the wealth of aids at their disposal, have had the experience of hearing a new and strange bird note that defies identification. It may be an uncharacteristic note of a familiar species or a normal note heard in a situation that gives it an unreal quality. Often such notes remain a mystery and puzzle to remind the listener of the many unknowns that still lurk in the world about him. Thoreau next reminds the reader of those strange sights and sounds which sometime will surely puzzle the listener, the observer, and the thinker.]

These are the sights and sounds which reach our senses oftenest during the year. But sometimes one hears a quite new note, which has for background other Carolinas and Mexicos than the books describe, and learns that his ornithology has done him no service.

[This essay was written as a review of *Reports—on the Fishes, Reptiles, and Birds: the Herbaceous Plants and the Invertebrate Animals of Massachusetts*. Published agreeably to an order of the Legislature, by the Commissioners on the Zoological and Botanical Survey of the State. The essay is included in *Excursions*, and in writing it, Thoreau drew heavily on material in his *Journal*.]

By Boat as Far as the Mountains

A WEEK ON THE CONCORD AND MERRIMACK RIVERS

[This book, first published in 1849, is a delightful account of a trip made by Thoreau and his brother John. They left Concord on the last day of August, 1839, in a boat which they had made. While the brothers extended their journey beyond the highest point of navigation to the heart of the White Mountains, only the fluvial part of the adventure appears in the book. Most of the book was written at the Walden Pond cabin.

The great increase in population and expansion of cultivated lands have wrought great changes along the Concord and Merrimack since the Thoreau brothers rowed on them. But a traveler on these same waters to-day could hope to find the species of birds seen by Thoreau except for the Passenger Pigeon, now extinct.

The first selection from *A Week on the Concord and Merrimack Rivers* says very little about birds, yet it recreates the excitement of beginning a river adventure, and the birds are an inseparable part of it. As long as rivers are explored by youthful hearts, this book will remain a treasured tale of river exploration.

The Concord was called the Musketaquid or Grass-ground River by the Indians who inhabited the area before the English settled there. The beginning of the Thoreau adventure took the brothers by the wet fields now included in the Great Meadows National Wildlife Refuge where the present bird population is much greater than it was in 1839.

In the selection which follows, Thoreau brings alive the excitement of adventuring into new places with all senses alert. His magnificent prose must delight any reader, even those who never set off on a river trip. Not only does he portray the beauty and excitement of the day, but he awakens a desire in the reader for a similar adventure.]

[Saturday. The voyagers set out from Concord.] It is worth the while to make a voyage up this stream if you go no further than Sudbury, only to see how much country there is in the rear of us; great hills, and a hundred brooks, and farmhouses, and barns, and haystacks, you never saw before, and men everywhere; Sudbury, that is *Southborough* men, and Wayland, and Nine-Acre-Corner men, and Bound Rock, where four towns bound on a rock in the river, Lincoln, Wayland, Sudbury, Concord. Many waves are there agitated by the wind, keeping nature fresh, the spray blowing in your face, reeds and rushes waving; ducks by the hundred, all uneasy in the surf, in the raw wind, just ready to rise, and now going off with a clatter and whistling like riggers straight for Labrador, flying against the stiff gale with reefed wings, or else circling round first, with all their paddles briskly moving, just over the surf, to reconnoitre you before they leave these parts; gulls wheeling overhead, muskrats swimming for dear life, wet and cold, with no fires to warm them by that you know of, their labored homes rising here and there like haystacks; and countless mice and moles and winged titmice along the sunny, windy shore; cranberries tossed on the waves and heaving up on the beach, their little red skiffs beating about among the alders;— such healthy natural tumult as proves the last day is not yet at hand. And there stand all around the alders, and birches and oaks, and maples, full of glee and sap, holding their buds until the waters subside. You shall perhaps run aground on Cranberry Island, only some spires of last year's pipe-grass above water to show where the danger is, and get as good a freezing there as anywhere on the Northwest Coast. I never voyaged so far in all my life. You shall 'see men you never heard of before, whose names you don't know, going away down through the meadows with long ducking guns, with water-tight boots wading through the fowl-meadow grass, on bleak, wintry, distant shores, with guns at half-cock; and they shall see teal,—blue-winged green-winged,—sheldrakes, whistlers, black ducks, ospreys, and many other wild and noble sights before night, such as they who sit in parlors never dream of.

[Few people except those who arise with the sun have the good fortune to see such perfect reflections as Thoreau describes. For a short time after sunrise, broad expanses of water often reflect the surroundings perfectly, but as the earth warms unevenly a movement of the air shatters the image.]
[Sunday]   As we thus dipped our way along between fresh masses of foliage

overrun with the grape and smaller flowering vines, the surface was so calm, and both air and water so transparent, that the flight of a kingfisher or robin over the river was as distinctly seen reflected in the water below as in the air above. The birds seemed to flit through submerged groves, alighting on the yielding sprays, and their clear notes to come up from below.

[While it was old, the canal between the Concord and the Merrimack just above Billerica Falls plainly revealed its youthfulness in comparison to the untouched lands about it. Thoreau noted that birds that fed in, and creatures which swam in the waters were the first to be at home in the man-made waterway. Plants adjust themselves more slowly to areas disturbed by man. Though Thoreau at this time considered himself a student of the classics and a poet, the following passage indicates that he was beginning to see the landscape as a whole as an ecologist would view it.]

This canal, which is the oldest in the country, and has even an antique look beside the more modern railroads, is fed by the Concord, so that we were still floating on its familiar waters. It is so much water which the river *lets* for the advantage of commerce. There appeared some want of harmony in its scenery, since it was not of equal date with the woods and meadows through which it is led, and we missed the conciliatory influence of time on land and water; but in the lapse of ages, Nature will recover and indemnify herself, and gradually plant fit shrubs and flowers along its borders. Already the kingfisher sat upon a pine over the water, and the bream and pickerel swam below.

[On Monday afternoon the Thoreaus saw their first basswood, a tree new to them. This reminded them that they had reached a strange land quite unlike Concord. Thoreau speculated on the wonderful variety of nature's creations. The selection which follows cannot be called good science as far as the origin of species is concerned. If food chains are considered, a different light may be thrown on Thoreau's remarks. Leaves may be eaten by insects, which in turn are consumed by song birds, and the song birds may be devoured by a hawk. Thus the leaves may truly become a hawk.]

[Monday]   In all her products, Nature only develops her simplest germs. One would say that it was no great stretch of invention to create birds. The hawk which now takes his flight over the top of the wood was at first, perchance, only a leaf which fluttered in its aisles. From the rustling leaves she came in the course of ages to the loftier flight and clear carol of the bird.

[Near Litchfield, Thoreau saw an extensive desert area where sand had blown into dunes ten and twelve feet high. This recalled to his mind Plum

Island, which he had visited in the past, for he thought some of this desert sand might well be borne down the Merrimack to its mouth not far from Newburyport, and there form part of that island so well known to the birding clan. Of course, Thoreau did not come nearer to Plum Island on this river trip than the junction of the Concord and Merrimack, some thirty miles away.

But Thoreau's description of Plum Island is especially interesting to bird watchers. In his *Guide to Bird Finding*, Dr. Olin Sewall Pettingill, Jr., calls this one of the most famous ornithological areas of the eastern United States. Birds traveling north or south along the Atlantic coast funnel over this area, and multitudes drop down to rest and feed there. A trip to this island is particularly rewarding during the peak of shorebird migration in spring and fall.

The half-dozen houses of Thoreau's day have multiplied many times over. Nevertheless, ripe beach plums may still be picked there in September. Untracked sand, particularly in winter or after storms, may still be found.

The fact that Thoreau mentioned only a few beach birds running on the sand and some coots (scoters) riding the waves behind the surf reveals clearly that his interest in birds was dormant when he visited Plum Island. C. Russell Mason, then Executive Director of the Massachusetts Audubon Society, after an early September visit to Plum Island with Dr. Roger Tory Peterson, wrote, "Every shore-bird in the book can be found on Plum Island, and as for gulls, if rare species appear on the north-east coast, they will almost surely be spotted at Plum Island."

Plum Island is one of the most important areas covered by the Newburyport Christmas Bird Count. This Count is made at a time when weather is severe and one would expect bird life in that bleak area to be at a low ebb. Yet on the 1962 Count when winds blew off the ocean and the temperature scarcely rose into the thirties, when snow covered the ground and all the ponds were frozen, eighty-eight species and about twenty-eight thousand individual birds were seen.]

[Tuesday]   Plum Island, at the mouth of this river [The Merrimack] to whose formation, perhaps, these very banks have sent their contribution, is a similar desert of drifting sand, of various colors, blown into graceful curves by the wind. It is a mere sand-bar exposed, stretching nine miles parallel to the coast, and, exclusive of the marsh on the inside, rarely more than half a mile wide. There are but half a dozen houses on it, and it is almost without a tree, or a sod, or any green thing with which a countryman is familiar. The thin vegetation stands half buried in sand as in drifting snow. The only shrub, the beach plum, which gives the island its name, grows but a few feet high; but this is so abundant that parties of a hundred at once come from the mainland and down the Merrimack, in September, pitch their tents, and gather the plums, which are good to eat raw and to preserve. The graceful and delicate beach pea, too, grows abundantly amid the sand, and several strange moss-like and succulent plants. The island for its whole length is scalloped into low hills, not more than twenty feet high, by the wind, and, excepting a faint trail on the edge of the marsh, is as trackless as Sahara. There are dreary bluffs of sand and valleys plowed by the wind, where you might expect to discover the bones of a caravan. Schooners come from Boston to load with the sand for masons' uses, and in a few hours the wind obliterates all traces of their work. Yet you have only to dig a foot or two anywhere to come to fresh water; and you are surprised to learn that woodchucks abound here, and foxes are found, though you see not where they can burrow or hide themselves. I have walked down the whole length of its broad beach at low tide, at which time alone you can find a firm ground to walk on, and probably Massachusetts does not furnish a more grand and dreary walk. On the seaside there are only a distant sail and a few coots to break the grand monotony. A solitary stake stuck up, or a sharper sand-hill than usual, is remarkable as a landmark for miles; while for music you hear only the ceaseless sound of the surf, and the dreary peep of the beach-birds.

[Thoreau shot a Passenger Pigeon, one of a large flock near the mouth of the Souhegan River, and broiled it for supper. Scientists are not sure why these birds, once fantastically abundant, became extinct. Some attribute it to excessive slaughter on the breeding grounds and throughout the year. Some believe the destruction of the beech and oak forests was largely responsible. Some believe that the numbers having been severely reduced by overshooting, the species was no longer able to reproduce. Thoreau's concern about the dead pigeon was philosophical. Did he have a right to kill such a beautiful bird? Having killed it, he decided it should be eaten and not wasted. Many sensitive and thoughtful people wonder, as Thoreau did, why endless creatures must die to feed others.

Though Thoreau seldom saw a dead bird in the woods or fields, had he visited a nesting place of colonial birds, or walked along the drift of an ocean beach, he would have seen many dead birds. Probably the majority of song birds are finally caught and eaten by other creatures. Most of those that do die of disease or age, being quite small, are eaten by insects, mice, or even snakes, for the latter have been seen eating birds killed on highways. Certainly birds are never translated, as some of the Old Testament prophets were said to have been, being taken directly from earth to heaven without dying.]

[Tuesday. Passenger Pigeons near the mouth of the Souhegan River]   During the heat of the day, we rested on a large island a mile above the mouth of this river, pastured by a herd of cattle, with steep banks and scattered elms and oaks, and a sufficient channel for canal-boats on each side. When we made a fire to boil some rice for our dinner, the flames spreading amid the dry grass, and the smoke curling silently upward and casting grotesque shadows on the ground, seemed phenomena of the noon, and we fancied that we progressed up the stream without effort, and as naturally as the wind and tide went down, not outraging the calm days by unworthy bustle or impatience. The woods on the neighboring shore were alive with pigeons, which were moving south, looking for mast, but now, like ourselves, spending their noon in the shade. We could hear the slight, wiry, winnowing sound of their wings as they changed their roosts from time to time, and their gentle and tremulous cooing. They sojourned with us during the noon-tide, greater travellers far than we. You may frequently discover a single pair sitting upon the lower branches of the white pine in the depths of the woods, at this hour of the day, so silent and solitary, and with such a hermit-like appearance, as if they had never strayed beyond its skirts, while the acorn which was gathered in the forests of Maine is still undigested in their crops. We obtained one of these handsome birds, which lingered too long upon its perch, and plucked and broiled it here with some other game, to be carried along for our supper; for, beside provisions which we carried with us, we depended mainly on the river and forest for our supply. It is true, it did not seem to be putting this bird to its right use to pluck off its feathers, and extract its entrails, and broil its carcass on the coals; but we heroically persevered, nevertheless, waiting for further information. The same regard for Nature which excited our sympathy for her creatures nerved our hands to carry through what we had begun. For we would be honorable to the party we deserted; we would fulfill fate, and so at length, perhaps, detect the secret innocence of these incessant tragedies which Heaven allows. . . .

Nature herself has not provided the most graceful end for her creatures. What becomes of all these birds that people the air and forest for our solacement? The sparrows seem always *chipper*, never infirm. We do not see their bodies lie about. Yet there is a tragedy at the end of each one of their lives. They must perish miserably, not one of them is translated. True, "not a sparrow falleth to the ground without our Heavenly Father's knowledge," but they do fall, nevertheless.

[Thoreau's smaller bittern, the Green Heron, like all members of the heron family, catches its food with quick stabs of its bill. It does not probe the mud as do many species of shorebird. Since Green Herons often feed in still, shallow water, reflections may have caused Thoreau to think their bills were thrust into the mud. It must be remembered that Thoreau had no optical equipment at this time to aid his observations.]

[Wednesday. On the west bank of the Merrimack in the township of Bedford] As we shoved away from this rocky coast, before sunrise, the smaller bittern, the genius of the shore, was moping along its edge, or stood probing the mud for its food, with ever an eye on us, though so demurely at work, or else he ran along over the wet stones like a wrecker in his storm-coat, looking out for wrecks of snails and cockles. Now away he goes, with a limping flight, uncertain where he will alight, until a rod of clear sand amid the alders invites his feet; and now our steady approach compels him to seek a new retreat. It is a bird of the oldest Thalesian school, and no doubt believes in the priority of water to the other elements; the relic of a twilight ante-diluvian age which yet inhabits these bright American rivers with us Yankees. There is something venerable in this melancholy and contemplative race of birds, which may have trodden the earth while it was yet in a slimy and imperfect state. Perchance their tracks, too, are still visible on the stones. It still lingers into our glaring summers, bravely supporting its fate without sympathy from man, as if it looked forward to some second advent of which *he* has no assurance. One wonders if, by its patient study by rocks and sandy capes, it has wrested the whole of her secret from Nature yet. What a rich experience it must have gained, standing on one leg and looking out from its dull eye so long on sunshine and rain, moon and stars! What could it tell of stagnant pools and reeds and dank night fogs! It would be worth the while to look closely into the eye which has been open and seeing at such hours, and in such solitudes its dull, yellowish, greenish eye. Methinks my own soul must be a bright invisible green. I have seen these birds stand by the half dozen together in the shallower water along the shore, with their bills thrust into the mud at the bottom, probing for food, the whole head being concealed, while the neck and body formed an arch above the water.

On Thursday, Thoreau and his brother halted at a point east of Uncan-nunuc Mountain near Manchester, New Hampshire. They hung their tent and buffalo robes in a farmer's barn to dry and then continued on foot up the Merrimack until it became the Pemigewasset and then the Wild Amonoo-suck to its very fountainhead. This part of the adventure is not included in the book. However, Thursday morning as the brothers lay in their tent listening to the rain, they found such enjoyment in birds as those who never venture into a wet world can never know.]

[Thursday]   When we awoke this morning, we heard the faint, deliberate, and ominous sound of raindrops on our cotton roof. The rain had pattered all night, and now the whole country wept, the drops falling in the river, and on the alders, and in the pastures, and instead of any bow in the heavens, there was the trill of the hair-bird all the morning. The cheery faith of this little bird atoned for the silence of the whole woodland choir beside. . . .

The birds draw closer and are more familiar under the thick foilage, seemingly composing new strains upon their roots against the sunshine. What were the amusements of the drawing room and the library in comparison, if we had them here?

[Though *A Week on the Concord and Merrimack Rivers* began on the last day of August, Thoreau and his brother did not return to Concord until the middle of September because of the trip on foot into the heart of the White Mountains. Since the autumnal equinox does not always determine the arrival of the first autumnlike day, it is not surprising that Thoreau witnessed the passing of summer a few days ahead of the calendar.]

[Friday. Homeward bound.] We had gone to bed in summer, and we awoke in autumn; for summer passes into autumn in some unimaginable point of time, like the turning of a leaf. . . . As the mist gradually rolled away, and we were relieved from the trouble of watching for rocks, we saw by the flitting clouds, by the first russet tinge on the hills, by the rushing river, the cottages on shore, and the shore itself, so coolly fresh and shining with dew, and later in the day, by the hue of the grape-vine, the goldfinch on the willow, the flickers flying in flocks, and when we passed near enough to the shore, as we fancied, by the faces of men, that the fall had commenced. . . .

[Return to Concord, Friday evening.] The sun was just setting behind the edge of a wooded hill, so rich a sunset as would never have ended but for some reason unknown to men, and to be marked with brighter colors than ordinary in the scroll of time. Though the shadows of the hills were beginning to steal over the stream, the whole valley undulated with mild light, purer and more memorable than the noon. For so the day bids farewell even to solitary vales uninhabited by man. Two herons (*Ardea herodias*), with their long and slender limbs relieved against the sky, were seen traveling high over our heads,—their lofty and silent flight, as they were wending their way at evening, surely not to alight in any marsh on the earth's surface, but, perchance, on the other side of our atmosphere, a symbol for the ages to study, whether impressed upon the sky or sculptured amid the hieroglyphics of Egypt. Bound for some northern meadow, they held their stately, stationary flight, like the storks in the picture, and disappeared at length behind the clouds. Dense flocks of blackbirds were winging their way along the river's course, as if on a short evening pilgrimage to some shrine of theirs, or to celebrate so fair a sunset.

Navigation by the Stars

EXCURSIONS

[This book was first published by Ticknor and Fields in 1863 and included some of Thoreau's finest nature essays.

Though there is comparatively little about birds in *Excursions*, each essay is a delightful literary piece full of original ideas. Each opens new doors of interest to the out of doors. Whether Thoreau climbed a mountain, walked through the night when the moon was full, tasted wild apples and experimented with appropriate names for the varied flavors, observed the changing tints of autumn, or strode across fields, through the woods, and over the ice on a winter day, he had something both beautiful and original to say about each.]

A WALK TO WACHUSETT

[Though the climb to the summit of Wachusett Mountain is popular to-day, few would care to walk from Concord to the base of the mountain as Thoreau did. The unpaved road which made a pleasant footpath a century ago is now paved and congested with roaring cars. But once on the mountain trails, Red-eyed Vireos, Phoebes, Robins, and Cuckoos can be heard in spring and summer. From the summit, the surrounding country looks like a relief map and the climber sees many of the landmarks which birds must note as they travel above them.

Thoreau's suggestion that birds may possibly navigate by the stars is particularly interesting in view of contemporary research. Some of the world's great ornithologists have recently carried on exhaustive research with birds in planetariums. Their results convince many that birds actually do make use of the sun and stars as guides when on migration.]

We get a dim notion of the flight of birds, especially of such as fly high in the air, by having ascended a mountain. We can now see what landmarks mountains are to their migrations; how the Catskills and Highlands have hardly sunk to them, when Wachusett and Monadnock open a passage to the northeast; how they are guided too, in their course by the rivers and valleys; and who knows but by the stars, as well as the mountain ranges, and not by the petty landmarks which we use. The bird whose eye takes in the Green Mountains on the one side, and the ocean on the other, need not be at a loss to find its way.

A WINTER WALK

[In *A Winter Walk* Thoreau wrote: "though winter is represented in the almanac as an old man, facing the wind and sleet, and drawing his cloak about him, we rather think of him as a merry wood-chopper, and warm-blooded youth, as blithe as summer." Thoreau also described the fascinating "cabinet of curiosities" to be seen at that season and rejoiced that "the birds' nests are not hung on an artificial twig, but where they builded them."]

The chickadee and nuthatch are more inspiring society than statesmen and philosophers, and we shall return to these last as to more vulgar companions.

> And if perchance the chickadee
> Lisp a faint note anon,
> The snow is summer's canopy,
> Which she herself put on.

No domain of nature is quite closed to man at all times, and now we draw near to the empire of the fishes. Our feet glide swiftly over unfathomed depths, where in summer our line tempted the pout and perch, and where the stately pickerel lurked in the long corridors formed of bulrushes. The deep, impenetrable marsh, where the heron waded and bittern squatted, is made pervious to our swift shoes. . . . We skate near where the blackbird, the pewee, and the kingbird hung their nests over the water, and the hornets builded from the maple in the swamp. How many gay warblers, following the sun, have radiated from this nest of silver birch and thistle-down!

On the swamp's outer edge was hung the supermarine village where no foot penetrated. In this hollow tree the wood duck reared her brood, and slid away each day to forage in yonder fen.

THE SUCCESSION OF FOREST TREES

[This essay is regarded by many scientists as one of Thoreau's most important pieces of writing. It is an original contribution to the understanding of forests. It foreshadowed the science of ecology, the branch of biology which treats of the mutual relations between animal life and its environment. Only recently have scientists fully grasped the need for understanding this relationship if a healthy environment for man is to be maintained.

"The Succession of Forest Trees" was printed in the October 6, 1860, issue of the *New York Tribune*. Had Thoreau had time, he would undoubtedly have enlarged and enriched the essay by adding many of his observations included in his *Journal*, for his forest studies—pursued most earnestly during 1856–1857—were continued to the end of his life. During the time that remained to him after writing the essay as a lecture, he added considerably to his knowledge of forest succession, and many questions arose in his mind which he attempted to answer. But these remain scattered and unfinished in the *Journal*.

It was on December 3, 1860, that Thoreau went to Hill to measure a hickory, blown down by the wall. He found that it was sixteen inches in diameter, twelve feet from the ground, and "has 112 rings distinct, the first 50 within five and three quarters inches." At this time he was chilled and bronchitis developed. Against the doctor's orders, he kept a lecture engagement in Waterbury, Connecticut. There is little doubt that Thoreau had an attack of tuberculosis during his Harvard years. Now the old leisons in his lungs opened. This time the disease was terminal. Thoreau continued to observe and to write in his *Journal* through the following year. He died on May 6, 1862.]

Occasionally, when threading the woods in the fall, you will hear a sound as if some one had broken a twig, and, looking up, see a jay pecking at an acorn, or you will see a flock of them at once about it, in the top of an oak, and hear them break them off. They then fly to a suitable limb, and placing the acorn under one foot, hammer away at it busily, making a sound like a woodpecker's tapping, looking round from time to time to see if any foe is approaching, and soon reach the meat, and nibble at it, holding up their heads to swallow, while they hold the remainder very firmly with their claws. Nevertheless it often drops to the ground before the bird has done with it.

I can confirm what William Bartram wrote to Wilson, the ornithologist, that "the jay is one of the most useful agents in the economy of nature, for disseminating forest trees and other nuciferous and hard-seeded vegetables on which they feed. Their chief employment during the autumnal season is foraging to supply their winter stores. In performing this necessary duty they drop abundance of seed in their flight over fields, hedges, and by fences, where they alight to deposit them in the post-holes, etc. It is remarkable what numbers of young trees rise up in fields and pastures after a wet winter and spring. These birds alone are capable, in a few years' time, to replant all the cleared lands."

In the Great Northern Wilderness

[*The Maine Woods* by Henry David Thoreau, was published in 1864. Thoreau drew from material collected on three different trips in writing this book which was still unfinished at his death. The first two parts of the book had already been printed in magazines: "Ktaadin and the Maine Woods" in *The Union Magazine* in 1848, and "Chesuncook" in *The Atlantic Monthly* in 1858. Material for the third part, a trip to the Allegash and East Branch of the Penobscot, remained unpublished until the book appeared. Thoreau drew heavily from his *Journal* when preparing *The Maine Woods,* as he did when writing his other books.

A bird watcher on his way to the wilderness around Mount Katahdin (Thoreau always used the old spelling, Ktaadin) feels a rising excitement when he reaches Mattawamkeag, the town from which Thoreau first entered the wilderness. There the main highway is left behind. A paved road lies ahead of him for many miles. There will be small towns, trim farms, and smoky sawmills to pass. But occasional vistas reveal the wilderness ahead, and he lives again the happiness Thoreau felt as he entered that wilderness. If no strange northern species of bird has yet been seen, surely one is waiting just around the next curve. There is a sense of impending change, of adventure lurking over the brink of the next hill, as we approach Ktaadin, whose name is an Indian word signifying highest land. Before us is not only the highest land in Maine but the wildest land in that state.]

Early the next morning we had mounted our packs, and prepared for a tramp up the West Branch. . . . Leaping over a fence, we began to follow an obscure trail up the northern bank of the Penobscot. There was now no road further, the river being the only highway, and but half a dozen log huts, confined to its banks, to be met with for thirty miles. On either hand, and beyond, was a wholly uninhabited wilderness, stretching to Canada. Neither horse nor cow, nor vehicle of any kind, had ever passed over this ground; the cattle, and the few bulky articles which the loggers use, being got up in the winter on the ice, and down again before it breaks up. The evergreen woods had a decidedly sweet and bracing fragrance; the air was a sort of diet-drink, and we walked buoyantly in Indian file, stretching our legs. Occasionally there was a small opening on the bank, made for the purpose of log-rolling, where we got a sight of the river,—always a rocky and rippling stream. The roar of the rapids, the note of a whistler duck on the river, of the jay and chickadee around us, and of the pigeon woodpecker in the openings, were the sounds that we heard. That was what you might call a bran-new country; the only roads were of Nature's making, and the few houses were camps. Here, then, one could no longer accuse institutions and society, but must front the true source of evil.

[Of the remaining wilderness areas of eastern United States, the Mount Katahdin wilderness probably appeals most to the imagination of naturalists. This mile-high mountain towers grandly over a vast forest dotted with lakes and traced by a network of rivers and cold mountain streams, each supporting a complex variety of plants and animals.

The white pines which brought the lumbermen to the area were cut out a century ago. Since then spruce has replaced the pine in many areas. Where fires swept through the forest, gray birches, aspens, and maples now grow.

The spruce forest has a primeval appearance, for the trees are hoary with a thick encrustation of mosses and lichens. There is a dense ground cover of mosses, lichens, and ferns. Northern flowers such as dwarf cornel, twin flower, and lady slippers bloom in season. Northern birds are at home in this habitat.

In the deciduous woods, which are usually made up of young trees, deer are numerous. Sometimes one discovers a tiny fawn hidden in a bed of hay-scented fern. Vireos and Blue Jays are found here more often than in the conifers.

Numerous bogs have their own interesting plant and animal communities. Sphagnum moss, pitcher plants, and sundews grow in such wet places. Some of the bogs were formed by the filling in of ancient lake shores while others are of more recent origin, formed when beavers flooded an area with a dam. Moose often come to such places to feed. Olive-sided Flycatchers perch on the tips of the tallest dead tree above such a bog to await an insect.

Many ancient lumber camps, almost disintegrated to earth, are covered with dense tangles of wild raspberries. It is rather startling, when picking the ripe fruit, to see a bear on the opposite side of the berry patch rise on his haunches to see if the humans sharing the fruit are keeping their distance. Thoreau thought the huckleberries on Mount Katahdin also had a particularly wild flavor.

Above timberline lies the Tableland Plateau. There alpine plants hug the ground. Some that are but inches high may be a century old. The Katahdin butterfly, *Oensis polixenes katahdin*, a subspecies of a truly arctic species, is confined to this high Katahdin country. It is less than two inches long and yellowish-brown in color with a rather prominent submarginal band on the wings, which are dotted with a varying number of dark spots. Though only the Katahdin butterfly is unique to that small plateau, other arctic insect species occur there. The presence of these insects prove the truly arctic character of the high elevations of Katahdin. Nowhere else in eastern United States is the Water Pipit, which Thoreau called the titlark, known to nest.

Now the trails on Mount Katahdin are almost crowded on some fine summer days. Yet the wild aspect of the mountain remains. When the clouds settle over the rocky summit hiding climbers from one another, and the trail itself vanishes in the gray, cold mist, it seems as wild and desolate as it did to Thoreau, alone on that high peak. Even on sunny days when climbers continually pass one another, it is only necessary to step a few yards from the trail and look across the vast forest sprinkled with lakes to feel that here is a country that must look much as it did when Thoreau climbed to the summit.

Before venturing into the wilderness area of Mount Katahdin, it is wise to obtain not only a road map of the area, but a Katahdin region map issued by the Maine Appalachian Trail Club, Inc., and a Katahdin guide. Both may be obtained from the Appalachian Mountain Club, 5 Joy Street, Boston, Massachusetts.

According to *A Guide to Bird Finding East of the Mississippi*, by Olin Sewall Pettingill, Jr., June is the time to find the greatest number of birds in the Katahdin area. Thoreau climbed the mountain in early September when many birds had left the area, and those remaining were quiet. His second trip, which took him to Lake Chesuncook, began in mid-September. His Allegash trip began in late July. He never visited the Maine wilderness during the height of the bird season.

Those who wish to retrace Thoreau's trips may still do so, though dams which have been built since his day make extra carrys necessary. The Allegash with its frequent stretches of racing white water is regarded as a river to test the courage and skill of expert canoe men.

The lakes that Thoreau crossed are no longer as wild as when he saw them. But there are many secluded lakes in the area, where it is possible to camp for a week at a time without seeing another person.

Though paved roads now take one close to the wilderness, they end before it is reached. A fair dirt road leads to Roaring Brook. The tote road leading to Katahdin Stream is one which makes even reckless drivers keep within the twenty-mile speed limit.

More than a century has passed since Thoreau made his trips to the wilderness, but a genuine wilderness still remains. Except for the Bald Eagle which is now very rare, birders may duplicate Thoreau's bird list without too much difficulty. His was the first bird list to come from the Maine wilderness. It is therefore of considerable historical interest. But Thoreau's greatest contribution to present-day birding in the wilds of Maine is the fact that we may share with him the pleasure of seeing and hearing these same birds. Because of what he wrote, our senses are tuned to a higher, more sensitive key, and our enjoyment of the birds is deepened.

The Bald Eagle, our national symbol, is decreasing everywhere, and because of this a concerted effort by conservation organizations led by the National Audubon Society and directed by Alexander Sprunt IV, is trying to determine the number of Bald Eagles now living, and to save the species from extinction. As part of this effort, Charles Brookfield, during the summer of 1962, attempted to discover all the Bald Eagle nests now present in Maine. He found thirty-one nests and saw twenty-nine eagles. He counted eight fledglings at nests and saw three other immature eagles in areas where no nests were found. Two of the thirty-one nests were located in the Katahdin region. One of these, near Dobby Flowage on the Millinocket River, was in danger and no adults or young were observed there. The second nest on Shin Pond, some distance northeast of Katahdin, had one young in it on the last day of July.

Bald Eagles continued to nest regularly along the Maine coast long after they became very rare in the Katahdin area. Even a decade ago the sound of an aerial battle between an Osprey with a fish and a marauding eagle often drew the eyes of observers along the coast. Large birds such as the Bald Eagle and Osprey have a particular appeal to bird watchers to-day, just as they had for Thoreau. They bring a touch of wildness to any skies they grace.

Thoreau watched a battle between a Bald Eagle and an Osprey at Tom Fowler's homestead at the mouth of the Millinocket River not many miles from the endangered nest near Dobby Flowage.]

As we stood upon the pile of chips by the door, fish hawks were sailing overhead; and here, over Shad Pond, might daily be witnessed the tyranny of the bald eagle over that bird. Tom pointed away over the lake to a bald eagle's nest, which was plainly visible more than a mile off, on a pine, high above the surrounding forest, and was frequented from year to year by the same pair, and held sacred by him. There were these two houses only there, his low hut and the eagles' airy cartload of fagots.

[The legs of loons are placed so far back on the body that they cannot walk, but this position makes the legs superior aids to swimming. Loons, and grebes which also have their legs far back on the body, have a habit of raising one leg above the surface and waving it. This probably results from alarm or nervousness.

There are breaks in the forest around Quakish Lake to-day, but the ducks, a pair of loons, and some log booms may still be seen there.]

We were soon in the smooth water of Quakish Lake, and took our turns at rowing and paddling across it. It is a small, irregular, but handsome lake, shut in on all sides by the forest, and showing no traces of man but some low boom in a distant cove, reserved for spring use. The spruce and cedar on its shores, hung with gray lichens, looked at a distance like the ghosts of trees. Ducks were sailing here and there on its surface, and a solitary loon, like a more living wave,—a vital spot on the lake's surface,—laughed and frolicked, and showed its straight leg, for our amusement.

[The large Twin Lakes, like Quakish Lake, are really enlargements of the Penobscot River. It is easy for a canoeist, unfamiliar with the area, to spend long hours seeking the Penobscot inlet to the lakes. Thoreau and his party were fortunate to have an experienced guide, for they crossed the lake at night. The sound of a Great Horned Owl calling from the trees on the shore of North Twin Lake may be heard at night as it was a century ago.]

The shores seemed at an indefinite distance in the moonlight. Occasionally we paused in our singing and rested on our oars, while we listened to hear if the wolves howled, for this is a common serenade, and my companions affirmed that it was the most dismal and unearthly of sounds; but we heard none this time. If we did not *hear*, however, we did *listen*, not without a reasonable expectation; that at least I have to tell,—only some utterly uncivilized, big-throated owl hooted loud and dismally in the drear and boughy wilderness, plainly not nervous about his solitary life, nor afraid to hear the echoes of his voice there.

[Thoreau was probably the sixth man ever to reach the summit of Mount Katahdin. No doubt he drank some cold water from the spring which bears his name. One can only guess at the identity of the sparrows Thoreau saw. The White-throated Sparrow is the most abundant member of the sparrow family in this area. But he could have seen an American Water Pipit which would look rather sparrowlike as it hurtled past, driven by the wind and quickly lost in the clouds.]

Occasionally, as I came down, the wind would blow me a vista open, through which I could see the country, eastward, boundless forests, and lakes, and streams, gleaming in the sun, some of them emptying into the East Branch. There were also new mountains in sight in that direction. Now and then some small bird of the sparrow family would flit away before me, unable to command its course, like a fragment of the gray rock blown off by the wind.

[Thoreau left Boston on September 13, 1853, for his second trip to the Katahdin region of Maine. He sailed as far as Bangor where his cousin, George Thatcher, joined him, and took a stage coach to Greenville on the shore of Moosehead Lake. There he met his Indian guide, Joe Aitteon. They sailed to the head of the lake in a steamer. An ox cart carried their canoe and supplies to the Penobscot River. Supplies included a tent and food: hard-bread, pork, smoked beef, tea, and sugar.

When Thoreau reached the mouth of the Ragmuff, a small stream flowing into the Penobscot between Moosehead and Chesuncook, several birds attracted his attention. Purple Finches and Myrtle Warblers can be seen by campers at this place to-day. Canada Jays, now called Gray Jays, often visit camps and accept food or steal it. Both Ruffed Grouse and Spruce Grouse are often flushed by hikers. A male Spruce Grouse (Thoreau's pinnated or black grouse) has been known to become so immobile when approached that a photographer may take one-second or even five-second exposures of it without any trace of movement showing in the bird.

Animal psychologists might question Thoreau's remarks about the familiarity between lumbermen and wilderness birds. But the behavior of the birds on the Galapagos Islands, where man made a very recent appearance, lends a slight credence to his idea. On those islands, visitors can sometimes lift a hawk from its perch in a tree. Charles Darwin was astonished by the tameness of the birds. To collect such species as finches, wrens, flycatchers, doves, and carion buzzards, he did not need a gun but used a switch or even his hat.]

While we were trying for trout, Joe, Indian-like, wandered off up the Ragmuff on his own errands, and when we were ready to start was far beyond call. So we were compelled to make a fire and get our dinner here, not to lose time. Some dark reddish birds with grayer females (perhaps purple finches), and myrtle-birds in their summer dress, hopped within six or eight feet of us and our smoke. Perhaps they smelled the frying pork. The latter bird, or both, made the lisping notes which I had heard in the forest. They suggested that the few small birds found in the wilderness are on more familiar terms with the lumbermen and hunter than those of the orchard and clearing with the farmer. I have since found the Canada jay, and partridges, both the black and common, equally tame there, as if they had not yet learned to mistrust man entirely. The chickadee, which is at home alike in the primitive woods and in our wood-lots, still retains its confidence in the towns to a remarkable degree.

[Not until Thoreau and his party had passed the mouth of the Ragmuff on their return from Chesuncook Lake and were approaching Moosehead Lake did he again speak of birds. The same birds can be seen to-day on this stretch of the Penobscot River. Thoreau mentions that the deer is not found here, but a canoe party to-day is likely to see one feeding close to the bank or drinking from the river.]

We saw a few wood ducks, sheldrakes, and black ducks, but they were not so numerous there at that season as on our river at home. We scared the same family of wood ducks before us, going and returning. We also heard the note of one fish hawk, somewhat like that of a pigeon woodpecker, and soon after saw him perched near the top of a dead white pine against the island where we had first camped, while a company of peetweets were twittering and teetering about over the carcass of a moose on a low sandy spit just beneath. We drove the fish hawk from perch to perch, each time eliciting a scream or whistle, for many miles before us.

[In late July, 1857, Thoreau made his third and last trip to the Maine wilderness. This time he traveled on the Allegash, that almost legendary white-water river of Maine, and the East Branch of the Penobscot, once more crossing Moosehead Lake. Thus he finally completed a circuit around Mount Katahdin.

His other trips having been made in September, he now heard for the first time some songs of land birds in the Maine wilderness. As he paddled close to the eastern shore of Moosehead Lake, he saw mergansers which his Indian guide called *Shecorways,* Spotted Sandpipers which the Indian called *Naramekechus,* and loons called *Medawisla.* Thoreau noted the call of the Olive-sided Flycatcher, a sound which is heard throughout the entire region, and Wood Pewees and Kingfishers. He saw no bluebirds in 1857, nor would those who canoe on the same waters see them there to-day.

The black dippers of the following extract present a puzzle. Pied-billed Grebes are still called dippers by many New Englanders. But these dippers are clearly ducks, not grebes. The Hooded Merganser, a common nesting duck of the area, is a diving duck. The female is very dark and so are the young. Probably the black dippers were Hooded Mergansers.]

While we were getting breakfast, a brood of twelve black dippers, half grown, came paddling by within three or four rods, not at all alarmed; and they loitered about as long as we stayed, now huddled close together, within a circle of eighteen inches in diameter, now moving off in a long line, very cunningly. Yet they bore a certain proportion to the great Moosehead Lake on whose bosom they floated, and I felt as if they were under its protection.

The birds sang quite as in our woods,—the red-eye, redstart, veery, wood pewee, etc., but we saw no bluebirds in all our journey, and several told me in Bangor that they had not the bluebird there. Mount Kineo, which was generally visible, though occasionally concealed by islands or the mainland in front, had a level bar of cloud concealing its summit, and all the mountain-tops about the lake were cut off at the same height. Ducks of various kinds,— sheldrake, summer ducks, etc.,—were quite common, and ran over the water before us as fast as a horse trots. Thus they were soon out of sight.

[Sunday morning, July 26, 1857, while camped by the Penobscot River about fifteen miles southwest of Chesuncook Lake, Thoreau was wakened by White-throated Sparrows. In Massachusetts this sparrow is a common migrant, and some breed in the highland areas. Thoreau seldom mentioned them in his *Journal* and was slow in learning their song, which he first thought was sung by chickadees and later by Myrtle Warblers.]

The note of the white-throated sparrow, a very inspiriting but almost wiry sound, was the first heard in the morning, and with this all the woods rang. This was the prevailing bird in the northern part of Maine. The forest generally was all alive with them at this season, and they were proportionally numerous and musical about Bangor. They evidently breed in that State. Though commonly unseen, their simple *ah, te-te-te, te-te-te, te-te-te*, so sharp and piercing, was as distinct to the ear as the passage of a spark of fire shot into the darkest of the forest would be to the eye. I thought that they commonly uttered it as they flew. I hear this note for a few days only in the spring, as they go through Concord, and in the fall see them again going southward, but then they are mute. We were commonly aroused by their lively strain very early. What a glorious time they have in that wilderness, far from mankind and election day!

[Gray Jays are among the species bird watchers look for in the Maine wilderness. While they are numerous in that area, they are erratic in their movements. Sometimes they visit a camp several times in a single day, and then may not be seen again for a week or more. In addition to the names Thoreau mentions, Gray Jays are also called Whiskey Jack, Camp Robber, and Grease-bird.

The small hawk was probably a Pigeon Hawk.]

Three large slate-colored birds of the jay genus (*Garrulus Canadensis*), the Canada jay, moose-bird, meat-bird, or what not, came flitting silently and by degrees toward me, and hopped down the limbs inquisitively to within seven or eight feet. They were more clumsy and not nearly so handsome as the bluejay. Fish hawks, from the lake, uttered their sharp whistling notes low over the top of the forest near me, as if they were anxious about a nest there. . . .

At one place I heard a very clear and piercing note from a small hawk, like a single note from a white-throated sparrow, only very much louder, as he dashed through the tree-tops over my head. I wondered that he allowed himself to be disturbed by our presence, since it seemed as if he could not easily find his nest again himself in that wilderness.

[Bears are numerous in the wilderness around Mount Katahdin. Rumors grow that the panther is returning to the area, but the rumors are vague and unsatisfactory. It is hoped by naturalists that this big American cat will reestablish itself in the Maine wilderness. The predatory panther would help solve the problem of too many deer in the area.

Moose are there in good numbers. On a hot summer day it is not unusual to emerge from the forest to the shore of a lake where feeding conditions are good, and there see one or two of these great mammals feeding in water deep enough for them to completely submerge sometimes.

The wolves are gone. It is doubtful that they will ever return.

The wild cry of the loon is still a part of the wilderness. When it rings across the lake, the sound stirs the pulse of all who hear it. Loons must nest so close to the water that they can slide into it if danger threatens, for they cannot walk. Too many fishermen or hikers, too many outboard motors, and too many summer cottages have spelled the end of nesting loons on many lakes in Maine. Whether they can continue to find solitude before the rising tide of human population, will be answered in the future. If they vanish from the Katahdin wilderness, not only Chamberlain Lake, where Thoreau listened to their looning, but all America will be the poorer because they are gone.]

In the middle of the night, as indeed each time that we lay on the shore of a lake, we heard the voice of the loon, loud and distinct, from far over the lake. It is a very wild sound, quite in keeping with the place and the circumstances of the traveler, and very unlike the voice of a bird. I could lie awake for hours listening to it, it is so thrilling. When camping in such a wilderness as this, you are prepared to hear sounds from some of its inhabitants which will give voice to its wildness. Some idea of bears, wolves, or panthers runs in your head naturally, and when this note is first heard very far off at midnight, as you lie with your ear to the ground,—the forest being perfectly still about you, you take it for granted that it is the voice of a wolf or some other wild beast, for only the last part is heard when at a distance,—you conclude that it is a pack of wolves, baying the moon, or perchance, cantering after a moose. Strange as it may seem, the "mooing" of a cow on a mountain-side comes nearest to my idea of the voice of a bear; and this bird's note resembled that. It was the unfailing and characteristic sound of those lakes. We were not so lucky as to hear wolves though that is an occasional serenade. Soon friends of mine, who two years ago went up the Caucomgomoc River, were serenaded by wolves while moose-hunting by moonlight. It was a sudden burst, as if a hundred demons had broke loose,—a startling sound enough, which, if any, would make your hair stand on end, and all was still again. It lasted but a moment, and you'd have said there were twenty of them, when probably there were only two or three. They heard it twice only, and they said it gave expression to the wilderness, which it lacked before. I heard of some men, who, while skinning a moose lately in those woods, were driven off from the carcass by a pack of wolves which ate it up.

This of the loon,—I do not mean its laugh, but its looning,—is a long-drawn call, as it were, sometimes singularly human to my ear,—*hoo-hoo-ooooo*, like the hallooing of a man on a very high key, having thrown his voice into his head. I have heard a sound exactly like it when breathing heavily through my own nostrils, half awake at ten at night, suggesting my affinity to the loon; as if its language were but a dialect of my own, after all. Formerly, when lying awake at midnight in those woods, I had listened to hear some words or syllables of their language, but it chanced that I listened in vain until I heard the cry of the loon. I have heard it occasionally on the ponds of my native town, but there its wildness is not enhanced by the surrounding scenery.

I was awakened at midnight by some heavy, low-flying bird, probably a loon, flapping by close over my head, along the shore. So, turning the other side of my half-clad body to the fire, I sought slumber again.

[While still at the camp on Chamberlain Lake, Thoreau awakened very early on the morning of July 28, 1857. Once more he heard the morning serenade of the White-throated Sparrow.]

When we awoke, we found a heavy dew on our blankets. I lay awake very early, and listened to the clear, shrill, *ah, te, te, te, te, te* of the white-throated sparrow, repeated at short intervals, without the least variation, for half an hour, as if it could not enough express its happiness. Whether my companions heard it or not, I know not, but it was a kind of matins to me, and the event of that forenoon.

[Of the two episodes which follow, the first took place by the Webster Lake Dam, the second on Webster Stream.

Though travelers following Thoreau's route around Mount Katahdin seldom see as many mergansers, or sheldrakes, as he did, many ducks rise before a canoe. All three American species of merganser occur there: Hooded, Common, and Red-breasted. Both Common and Hooded Mergansers nest in holes in trees and are often seen on the waters of the area. The Red-breasted Merganser, which usually nests on the ground, is the rarest of the three species in this area.

Those who travel the wilderness streams and lakes by canoe, slipping along as quietly as a floating log, often surprise groups of ducklings, perhaps made up of several families. Then they see repeated the amusing actions of flightless young ducks which Thoreau witnessed. The ducks dash over the surface with their bodies almost perpendicular to it, their feet rapidly pattering the surface, and their wings flailing the air, leaving a long, straight wake behind them.]

We got our dinner on the shore, on the upper side of the dam. As we were sitting by our fire, concealed by the earth bank of the dam, a long line of the sheldrake, half-grown, came waddling over it from the water below, passing within about a rod of us, so that we could almost have caught them in our hands. They were very abundant on all the streams and lakes which we visited, and every two or three hours they would rush away in a long string over the water before us, twenty to fifty of them at once, rarely ever flying, but running with great rapidity up or down the stream, even in the midst of the most violent rapids, and apparently as fast up as down, or else crossing diagonally, the old, as it appeared, behind, and driving them, and flying to the front from time to time, as if to direct them. We also saw many small black dippers, which behaved in a similar manner, and, once or twice, a few black ducks.

Swiftly as the shallow and rocky river ran here, a continuous rapid with dancing waves, I saw, as I sat on the shore, a long string of sheldrakes, which something scared, run up the opposite side of the stream by me, with the same ease that they commonly did down it, just touching the surface of the waves, and getting an impulse from them as they flowed from under them; but they soon came back, driven by the Indian, who had fallen a little behind us on account of the windings.

[The Great Horned Owl (cat owl) is the largest owl which breeds in Maine and is seen by comparatively few people. The voice of the Great Horned Owl, a nocturnal hunter, is heard by many. Like most birds, it has a vocabulary of several calls, though its bass, impressive hooting is heard most often. One call is a strange and terrifying shriek. Whenever a camper in the Katahdin region has been awakened from a sound sleep by this powerful call, it sets his heart a-pounding lest a pack of wolves has returned and is on the prowl. Probably this wild cry of the Great Horned Owl has frightened more newcomers to the wilderness than have all the bears and other wild creatures that occur there.

As the Great Horned Owl was the largest owl which Thoreau saw, the Bald Eagle was the giant of the hawk family. Many ornithologists wish Thoreau's name, White-headed Eagle, had been retained for this species. Its head is white (an archaic meaning of white is bald) not bald, but there are several species of birds in America which do have bald heads. Among these are the vultures and the Wood Stork.

Mergansers were the largest ducks which Thoreau saw in the Maine wilderness. Having learned the Abenaki name, *shecorway*, for this species, Thoreau often used it in writing about them.

Thoreau's "red-headed" woodpecker was a Pileated Woodpecker, the largest woodpecker in the northeast.]

A red-headed woodpecker flew across the river, and the Indian remarked that it was good to eat. As we glided swiftly down the inclined plane of the river, a great cat owl launched itself across the stream, and the Indian, as usual, imitated its note. Soon the same bird flew back in front of us, and we afterwards passed it perched on a tree. Soon afterward a white-headed eagle sailed down the stream before us. We drove him several miles, while we were looking for a good place to camp, for we expected to be overtaken by a shower,—and still we could distinguish him by his white tail, sailing away from time to time from some tree by the shore still farther down the stream. Some shecorways being surprised by us, a part of them dived, and we passed directly over them, and could trace their course here and there by a bubble on the surface, but we did not see them come up.

FROM THE APPENDIX OF THE MAINE WOODS

List of Birds
Which I saw in Maine between July 24 and August 3, 1857

A very small hawk at Great Falls, on Webster Stream.

HALIAETUS LEUCOCEPHALUS (White-headed or Bald Eagle). At

Ragmuff, and above and below Hunt's, and on pond below Mattawamkeag.

PANDION HALIAETUS (Fish Hawk or Osprey), heard, also seen on East Branch.

BUBO VIRGINIANUS (Cat Owl), near Camp Island, also above mouth of Schoonis, from a stump back and forth, also near Hunt's on a tree.

ICTERUS PHOENICEUS (Red-winged Blackbird). Umbazookskus River.

CORVUS AMERICANUS (American Crow), a few, as at outlet of Grand Lake; a peculiar cawing.

FRINGILLA CANADENSIS (Tree Sparrow), think I saw one on Mount Kineo, July 24, which behaved as if it had a nest there.

GARRULUS CRISTATUS (Blue Jay).

PARUS ATRICAPILLUS (Chickadee), a few.

MUSCICAPA TYRANNUS (Kingbird).

MUSCICAPA COOPERII (Olive-sided Flycatcher), everywhere a prevailing bird

MUSCICAPA VIRENS (Wood Pewee), Moosehead, and I think beyond.

MUSCICAPA ACADICA (Small Pewee), common.

MUSCICAPA RUTICILLA (American Redstart), Moosehead.

VIREO OLIVACEUS (Red-eyed Vireo), everywhere common.

TURDUS MIGRATORIUS (Red-breasted Robin), some everywhere.

TURDUS MELODUS (Wood Thrush), common in all the woods.

TURDUS WILSONII (Wilson's Thrush), Moosehead and beyond.

TURDUS AUROCAPPILUS (Golden-crowned Thrush or Ovenbird), Moosehead.

FRINGILLA ALBICOLLIS (White-throated Sparrow), Kineo and after, apparently nesting; the prevailing bird early and late.

FRINGILLI MELODIA (Song Sparrow), at Moosehead or beyond.

SYLVIA PINUS (Pine Warbler), one part of voyage.

TRICHAS MARYLANDICA (Maryland Yellow-throat), everywhere.

COCCYZUS AMERICANUS (?) (Yellow-billed Cuckoo), common.

PICUS ERYTHROCEPHALUS (Red-headed Woodpecker), heard and saw, and good to eat.

SITTA CAROLINENSIS (?) (White-breasted Nuthatch), heard.

ALCEDO ALCYON (Belted Kingfisher), very common.

CAPRIMULGUS AMERICANUS (Nighthawk).

TETRAO UMBELLUS (Partridge). Moosehead Carry, etc.

TETRAO CUPIDO (?) (Pinnated Grouse), Webster Stream.

ARDEA CAERULEA (Blue Heron), lower part of Penobscot.

TOTANUS MACULARIUS (Spotted Sandpiper or Peetweet), everywhere.

LARUS ARGENTATUS (?) (Herring Gull), Heron Lake on rocks.

ANAS OBSCURA (Dusky or Black Duck), once in East Branch.

ANAS SPONSA (Summer or Wood Duck), everywhere.

FULIGULA ALBEOLA (Spirit Duck or Dipper), common.

COLYMBUS GLACIALIS (Great Northern Diver or Loon), in all the lakes.

MERGUS MERGANSER (Buff-breasted Merganser or Sheldrake), common on lakes and rivers.

A SWALLOW; the Night Warbler (?) once or twice.

THOREAU'S BIRD-LIST FROM
THE MAINE WOODS

[The Bald Eagle is rarely seen to-day in the Maine wilderness, or, for that matter, anywhere in the state. Only a few nests are still active in that state.

A very few pairs of Ospreys are still found nesting in the Katahdin region. Even along the coast, where it is now most abundant, it is steadily decreasing.

The Great Horned Owl is heard regularly. Probably each pair of these owls has a large territory, and the total number in the area is not great. The hooting is arresting and memorable and the sound carries for a long way.

Thoreau's crow with the peculiar caw was not a crow at all, but a Common Raven. Ravens occur regularly in this area. In addition to the call which is quite unlike that of a crow, the wedge-shaped tail helps in the identification of the species. The fact that it is decidedly larger than a crow is of little help, for size, without a means of comparison, is most unreliable in the identification of a bird.

Chipping Sparrows nest on Mount Kineo, and it was this species which Thoreau saw there. Tree Sparrows, which have a red-brown cap similar to that of the Chipping Sparrows, do not nest south of central Quebec. They nest north of the tree line.

Several species which Thoreau mentioned in his text were omitted on his list. One of these was the Gray Jay which is found in the area as well as the Blue Jay. Since the Gray Jay is rarely seen south of Maine, it is a species most bird watchers hope to see in the Katahdin region.

Both Black-capped and Boreal Chickadees are regular, and both species often hunt for crumbs around camp sites.

Several species of flycatchers are found in this region. Probably Thoreau's small pewee was an Alder Flycatcher. The Olive-sided Flycatcher is particularly conspicuous in August when nesting is finished. This species calls loudly and constantly from the tops of tall trees throughout this wilderness area. Thoreau mentions only four warblers: Pine Warbler, Ovenbird, Yellowthroat, and American Redstart. Many other species of warblers nest there or occur on migration, and will surely be discovered by bird watchers with good binoculars, particularly if they visit the area earlier in the summer than Thoreau ever did.

There is no record of the Wood Thrush in this region. The Hermit Thrush is common, and its song is perhaps the most beautiful of any American bird. Also present are the Veery, Swainson's Thrush and Gray-checked Thrush.

Though the Red-headed Woodpecker was once far more common in the northeast than it is to-day, it is doubtful if there is an authentic record for the species near Katahdin. Because most adult male woodpeckers have red on the head many people call any such woodpecker a Red-headed Woodpecker. The red on this species covers the entire head and neck like a helmet. Undoubtedly the woodpecker which Thoreau called a red-headed woodpecker was the crow-size Pileated Woodpecker, the largest member of the family in North America except for the almost extinct Ivory-billed Woodpecker. On Tuesday, September 20, 1854, Thoreau wrote in his *Journal*, "saw a large and new woodpecker, probably the red-headed, making a noise like the pigeon woodpecker." The call of the Pileated Woodpecker is very much like that of the Yellow-shafted Flicker (pigeon woodpecker) except it is more musical. Downy and Hairy Woodpeckers, Black-backed Three-toed Woodpeckers, and Yellow-bellied Sapsuckers also nest in the area.

Thoreau indicated with question marks that he was doubtful about some of the birds on his list. His cuckoo was undoubtedly a Black-billed Cuckoo. Both White-breasted and Red-breasted Nuthatches have been found nesting in Maine, but the latter species is the one to expect in conifer woods. Thoreau saw the Spruce Grouse, not the Pinnated Grouse. Both Ring-billed and Herring Gulls may be seen on the larger lakes in September.

No doubt Thoreau saw Spotted Sandpipers (peetweets), but other small shorebirds on migration at that time were present since he saw them "everywhere."

The Bufflehead (Spirit Duck) was known to Thoreau in Concord. He probably saw the duck but not in the numbers he indicated. The species has never been known definitely to nest in the area, though there are several summer and autumn records.

Bank, Barn, Tree, and Cliff Swallows have all been recorded in this area.

Here, as in Concord, Thoreau heard his mysterious bird singing in the night; his night warbler. While many ornithologists believe this was usually the night song of the Ovenbird, it must be remembered that this species prefers deciduous woods to conifer woods which then dominated the Maine wilderness. Perhaps in this instance Thoreau heard the aerial song of the Yellowthroat, which is a common nesting bird in the bogs and along the brush-bordered streams.]

Where Gulls Wheel Amid the Spray

[*Cape Cod,* edited by William Ellery Channing, was published first in 1865. Drawing from the *Journal* as was his habit, Thoreau continued to work on his Cape Cod material until his death.

Thoreau made four trips to Cape Cod. The first of these, a walking trip with Channing in October, 1849, provided the bulk of the material used in the book. Thoreau returned alone in June, 1850. In July, 1855, Channing again accompanied him to the Cape. The last trip was made in June, 1857.

Cape Cod has long been a famous birding place and many a bird watcher has retraced part or all of Thoreau's walking trip. He and his companion began their walk at Orleans and ended it at Provincetown, a distance of about twenty-six miles by road to-day. Their way was much longer, for they followed an erratic route from the bay to the ocean beach and back again.

Thoreau and Channing, riding in a stage coach, passed through many villages on the bay side of the Cape; Sandwich, Barnstable, Yarmouth, Dennis, and Brewster. Thus they did not approach Chatham with its tern island lying about a hundred yards off shore from the town wharf, and Monomoy Island now included in the Monomoy National Wildlife Refuge, which at times literally swarms with shorebirds and waterfowl. At Eastham they did walk along Nauset Beach, long regarded as an outstanding place for observing migrating shorebirds.

Much of the material used in *Cape Cod* was gathered the year that *A Week on the Concord and Merrimack Rivers* was published. Therefore it is particularly interesting to note the increase in bird observations. No longer do they serve chiefly as color for his prose or as philosophical springboards.

Thoreau had begun to watch birds as fellow creatures having interesting habits as well as beauty.

He quickly makes Cape Cod come alive to the reader and among those who know the Cape, he recreates many beloved scenes. He wrote:]

Every landscape which is dreary has a certain beauty to my eyes, and in this instance its permanent qualities were enhanced by the weather. Everything told of the sea, even when we did not see its wastes or hear its roar. For birds there were gulls, and for carts in the fields, boats turned bottom upward against the houses, and sometimes the rib of a whale was woven into the fence by the roadside.

[The windmills interested him. Of these he said:]

They looked loose and slightly locomotive, like huge wounded birds, trailing a wing or a leg.

[Thoreau's first material directly concerned with birds is largely historical, but when he returned to the Cape alone in 1850, he observed that blackbirds still flocked to the grain fields as they had in 1695. They are still there to-day.

Thoreau sees flocks of blackbirds and quotes from the early colonists.]

"In 1667 the town of [Eastham] voted that every housekeeper should kill twelve blackbirds, or three crows, which did great damage to the corn, and this vote was repeated for many years." In 1695 an additional order was passed, namely, that "every unmarried man in the township shall kill six blackbirds, or three crows, while he remains single; as a penalty for not doing it, shall not be married until he obey this order." The blackbirds, however, still molest the corn. I saw them at it the next summer, and there were many scarecrows, if not scare-blackbirds, in the fields, which I often mistook for men. From which I concluded, that their many men were not married, or many blackbirds were.

[Terns are quick to discover schools of small fish herded to the surface by feeding mackerel. Fishermen are often guided to big mackerel schools by the terns which they call Mackerel Gulls. Those which Thoreau saw off Cape Cod were probably chiefly Common Terns, though other species undoubtedly were in the flock. The "black" terns were young birds.

In the half-century following Thoreau's visits to Cape Cod, incredible numbers of shorebirds were killed. The demand for both tern and gull feathers for ladies' hats increased until finally not only Cape Cod but all our eastern seaboard was almost destitute of birds. An aroused public, led by the National Audubon Society, demanded that these birds be saved from extinction. To-day a visitor to Cape Cod will see gulls and terns in their former abundance. Most species of shorebirds have also made a good recovery from near extinction, but the once abundant Golden Plover is only now beginning to recover from the intensive market hunting of sixty years ago. The Eskimo Curlew remains so rare that comparatively few present-day bird watchers have ever seen one, though in the past few years the species on migration has been sighted many times and even photographed on Galveston Island, Texas.]

[The beach near Eastham]   Mackerel gulls were all the while flying over our heads and amid the breakers, sometimes two white ones pursuing a black one; quite at home in the storm, though they are as delicate organizations as sea-jellies and mosses; and we saw that they were adapted to their circumstances rather by their spirits than their bodies. Theirs must be an essentially wilder, that is, less human, nature, than that of larks and robins. Their note was like the sound of some vibrating metal, and harmonized well with the scenery and the roar of the surf, as if one had rudely touched the strings of the lyre, which ever lies on the shore; a ragged shred of ocean music tossed aloft by the spray. But if I were required to name a sound the remembrance of which most perfectly revives the impression which the beach has made, it would be the dreary peep of the piping plover (*Charadrius melodus*) which haunts there. Their voices, too, are heard as a fugacious part of the dirge which is ever played along the shore for those mariners who have been lost in the deep since first it was created. But through all this dreariness we seemed to have a pure and unqualified strain of eternal melody, for always the same strain which is a dirge to one household is a morning song of rejoicing to another.

A remarkable method of catching gulls, derived from the Indians, was practiced in Wellfleet in 1794. "The Gull House," it is said, "is built with crotches, fixed in the ground on the beach," poles being stretched across for the top, and the sides made close with stakes and seaweed. "The poles on the top [are] covered with lean whale. The man, being placed within, is not discovered by the fowls, and, while they are contending for and eating the flesh, he draws them in, one by one, between the poles, until he collected forty or fifty." Hence, perchance, a man is said to be *gulled*, when he is *taken in*. We read that one "sort of gull is called by the Dutch *mallemuche*, i.e., the foolish fly, because they fall upon a whale as eagerly as a fly, and, indeed, all gulls are foolishly bold and easy to be shot. The Norwegians call this bird *havhest*, sea-horse (and the English translator says, it is probably what we call boobies). If they have eaten too much, they throw it up, and eat it again till they are tired. It is this habit in the gulls of parting with their

property [disgorging the contents of their stomachs to the skuas], which
has given rise to the terms gull, guller, and gulling, among men." We also
read that they used to kill small birds which roosted on the beach at night,
by making a fire with hog's lard in a frying-pan. The Indians probably used
pine torches; the birds flocked to the light, and were knocked down with a
stick. We noticed holes dug near the edge of the bank, where gunners conceal themselves to shoot the large gulls which coast up and down a-fishing,
for these are considered good to eat.

[Many a bird has been trapped by some species of shellfish, until it starved
or was drowned by a rising tide. Allan Cruickshank once saw an adult Ring-
billed Gull struggling helplessly as the tide threatened to engulf it at St.
Petersburg, Florida. He waded in, discovered the gull had been caught by
an oyster, and he was able to pry the shell apart and release the gull.]

[Between Wellfleet and Truro] Our host [The Wellfleet Oysterman]
told us that the sea-clam, or hen, was not easily obtained; it was raked up,
but never on the Atlantic side, only cast ashore there in small quantities in
storms. The fisherman sometimes wades in water several feet deep, and
thrusts a pointed stick into the sand before him. When this enters between
the valves of a clam, he closes them on it, and is drawn out. It has been known
to catch and hold coot and teal which were preying on it. I chanced to be on
the bank of the Acushnet at New Bedford one day since this, watching some
ducks, when a man informed me that, having let out his young ducks to seek
their food amid the samphire (*Salicornia*) and other weeds along the riverside at low tide that morning, at length he noticed that one remained stationary, amid the weeds, something preventing it from following the others,
and going to it he found its foot tightly shut in a quahog's shell. He took up
both together, carried them to his home, and his wife opening the shell with
a knife released the duck and cooked the quahog.

[The Piping Plover (*Charadrius melodus*) nests regularly on the ocean
beaches of Cape Cod.
Phalaropes, called sea geese by fishermen, have caught popular fancy
because the female is more handsome than the male, is the aggressor in
courtship, lays four eggs in a nest built by the male, and then leaves him to
incubate the eggs and rear the young.
Thoreau's information about the feeding of the petrel was fallacious.
Petrels gather small fish, mollusks, and crustaceans from the surface of the
sea with their bills. They often follow ships and feed on wastes from it.
The editor has taken the liberty of inserting two short extracts from the
Journal at this point. Petrels are among the most interesting birds in the

world. They nest in burrows on oceanic islands. Seldom is one ever seen near the nesting island during the day. Exchange of nest duties is made at night. The Wilson's Petrel, which Thoreau saw, nests in the Southern Hemisphere during our winter. At times in summer, thousands of these birds congregate in Cape Cod Bay and the nearby waters.

The extract from June 18 is rather puzzling. Thoreau had a very keen sense of smell. Petrels have a distinctive scent, not unpleasant, which those who know petrels can detect if a single feather is held to the nose. This scent clings indefinitely. Even specimens long dusted with preservatives in museums retain that unique scent. It is odd that Thoreau did not notice this characteristic odor.]

[The birds of Truro Beach]   Sometimes we sat on the wet beach and watched the beach-birds, sandpipers, and others, trotting along close to each wave, and waiting for the sea to cast up their breakfast. The former (*Charadrius melodus*) ran with great rapidity, and then stood stock-still, remarkably erect, and hardly to be distinguished from the beach. The wet sand was covered with small skipping sea-fleas, which apparently made a part of their food. These last are the little scavengers of the beach, and are so numerous that they will devour large fishes which have been cast up, in a very short time. One little bird not larger than a sparrow—it may have been a phalarope —would alight on the turbulent surface where the breakers were five or six feet high, and float buoyantly there like a duck, cunningly taking to its wings and lifting itself a few feet through the air over the foaming crest of each breaker, but sometimes outriding safely a considerable billow which hid it some seconds, when its instinct told it that it would not break. It was a little creature this to sport with the ocean, but it was as perfect a success in its way as the breakers in theirs. There was also an almost uninterrupted line of coots rising and falling with the waves, a few rods from the shore, the whole length of the Cape. They made as constant a part of the ocean's border as the pads or pickerel-weed do of that of a pond. We read the following as to the storm petrel (*Thalassidroma Wilsonii*), which is seen in the Bay as well as on the outside. "The feathers on the breast of the Storm Petrel are, like those of all swimming birds, water-proof; but substances not susceptible of being wetted with water are, for that very reason, the best fitted for collecting oil from its surface. That function is performed by the feathers on the breast of the Storm Petrels as they touch the surface; and though that may not be the only way in which they procure their food, it is certainly that in which they obtain great part of it. They dash along till they have loaded their feathers and then they pause upon the waves and remove the oil with their bills."

JUNE 18. [1857] [Near Truro, Cape Cod]   I had shortly before picked up a Mother-Carey's-chicken, which was just washed up dead on the beach. This I carried tied to the tip of my umbrella, dangling outside. When the inhabitants saw me come up from the beach this stormy day, with this emblem dangling from my umbrella, and saw me set it up in a corner carefully to be out of the way of cats, they must have taken me for a crazy man. . . .

The Mother-Carey's-chicken was apparently about thirteen inches in alar extent, black-brown, with seven primaries, the second a little longer than the third; rump and vent white, making a sort of ring of white, breast ashy-brown, legs black with yellowish webs, bill black with a protuberance above.

JUNE 22. [1857]   [Thoreau leaves Cape Cod by ship] Took the steamer Acorn(?) about 9 A.M. for Boston in the fog. . . . . The monotony was only relieved by numerous petrels, those black sea-swallows, incessantly skimming over the undulating [surface], a few inches above and parallel with it, and occasionally picking some food from it. Now they dashed past our stern and now across our bows, as if we were stationary, though going at the rate of a dozen knots an hour.

[Bank Swallows are our smallest members of the swallow family. They dig their holes in steep sandy banks, often moving in after steam shovels have removed sand and left behind perpendicular walls suitable for Bank Swallow nests. Their colonies are not only destroyed at times by small boys, but those on river banks are sometimes washed away by floods. Sometimes a weasel or mink will destroy an entire colony. The nests which at first glance appear so safe are vulnerable to many dangers.

Common Grackles are still called crow blackbirds on Cape Cod.

Upland Plovers no longer nest near Highland Light. However, after several decades of decline, this species seems to be recovering and good numbers now nest in Massachusetts.

The Golden Plover makes one of the longest annual migration flights of any bird. It breeds around the Northern Hemisphere close to the Arctic Circle, many of those in eastern North America nesting on Baffin Island. After nesting they move southward and many are believed to make a nonstop flight from Nova Scotia to South America, where they may winter as far south as the plains of Bolivia and Argentina. On their return flight north to their nesting grounds, most move up the Mississippi Valley to the tundra, where they nest in the mosses and lichens.

Lighthouses in the path of migrating birds have cost the lives of incredible numbers of these winged creatures. Since lighthouses must continue to safeguard ships, the annual toll of birds goes on. But such lights as that on the tower of the Empire State Building are turned off during migration as a safety measure to keep birds from crashing into them.]

[Birds at Highland Light]   In this bank, above the clay, I counted in the summer two hundred holes of the bank swallow within a space six rods long, and there were at least one thousand old birds within three times that distance, twittering over the surf. I had never associated them in my thoughts with the beach before. One little boy who had been a-birds'-nesting had got eighty swallows' eggs for his share! Tell it not to the Humane Society! There were many young birds on the clay beneath, which had tumbled out and died. Also there were many crow blackbirds hopping about in the dry fields, and the upland plover was breeding close by the lighthouse. The keeper had once cut off one's wing while mowing, as she sat on her eggs there. This is also a favorite resort for gunners in the fall to shoot the golden plover. . . .

Our host said that the frost, too, on the windows caused him much trouble, and in sultry summer nights the moths covered them and dimmed his lights; sometimes even small birds flew against the thick plate glass, and were found on the ground beneath in the morning with their necks broken. In the spring of 1855 he found nineteen small yellow birds, perhaps goldfinches or myrtle-birds, thus lying dead around the lighthouse; and sometimes in the fall he had seen where a golden plover had struck the glass in the night, and left the down and the fatty part of its breast on it.

[Birds at Provincetown Harbor]   The Pilgrims say, "There was the greatest store of fowl that ever we saw."

We saw no fowl there, except gulls of various kinds; but the greatest store of them that ever we saw was on a flat but slightly covered with water on the east side of the harbor, and we observed a man who had landed there from a boat creeping along the shore in order to get a shot at them, but they all rose and flew away in a great scattering flock, too soon for him, having apparently got their dinners, though he did not get his.

Ceaseless Song in Tuckerman's Ravine

[The White Mountains, close to many great eastern cities, annually attract large numbers of bird watchers. Thoreau's account, in his *Journal*, of the birds he saw and heard there in 1858 is therefore of particular interest, though it contains little of his fine literary work.

The wild cry of the loon may still be heard on many lakes such as the Squam Lakes and Lake Winnepesaukee. Spotted Sandpipers, Thoreau's pee-tweets, teeter along the rocky shores. The sight of an eagle is rare enough to cause excitement when one is discovered. Thoreau's "screech owl" of July 9 was a Saw-whet Owl. This smallest of northern owls exhibits little fear of man. Its nest, in a tree cavity or old woodpecker hole, is found from time to time in these mountains.

It is not surprising that Thoreau, suffering from a sprained ankle, was unable to see one of the Winter Wrens whose song was so continuous in Tuckerman's Ravine on July 10. These wrens are very dark brown and so tiny they can vanish behind a leaf. Anyone who has climbed Tuckerman Ravine in late June or early July, particularly if it was raining, has been astonished by the loud incessant chorus of this species. The chorus of Winter Wrens is then so all-pervasive that it seems universal. Mingled with the songs of the Winter Wren are the plaintive whistled notes of White-throated Sparrows.

If it seems odd that Thoreau did not become acquainted during the Concord winters with the Red-breasted Nuthatch, it must be remembered that he possessed no good optical aid. Moreover, feeding shelves, which to-day attract this species and many others during the winter to windowsills where they may be observed easily, were unheard of in Thoreau's Concord. There is no doubt that Thoreau had a good look at a Red-breasted Nuthatch on July 15 for the first time in his life.

Bradford Torrey suggested in a footnote in the *Journal* that the wood thrush and veery which Thoreau mentioned on July 16 were instead the Olive-backed Thrush (now Swainson's Thrush) and Bicknell's Thrush (a subspecies of the Gray-cheeked Thrush). Thoreau probably heard these species, but surely he also heard the Hermit Thrush. Of all bird songs heard in the White Mountains, the song of the Hermit Thrush is doubtless considered the finest by most people. Many make a pilgrimage whenever possible to a favorite lake, valley, or mountain slope where good acoustics enhance the wonderful song of this bird as fine acoustics bring out the best of music.

Thoreau's evergreen-forest note may have been given by the Black-throated Green Warbler, for at least once in Concord he heard this warbler sing his evergreen-forest song. But of the many warblers that breed in the White Mountains, Thoreau mentioned only the Blackburnian Warbler and the Ovenbird. Of course it was too late in the season for the songs of these birds to be at their best. Nevertheless, an expert observer to-day who climbs one of the trails leading through the evergreen forest to the rocky summit of any of the peaks during the last week of June or the first two weeks in July would identify a dozen or more species of small, usually colorful warblers.

Now when the range of almost all species of North American birds has been established, it is difficult to realize that Thoreau's reference books, the best then available, gave no accurate indication of the breeding range for either the Rose-breasted Grosbeak or the Pine Grosbeak. Nevertheless, the discovery of something new is always a possibility of which bird watchers are aware. Bird watching offers as much excitement to-day as when Thoreau climbed the slopes of the White Mountains.

From his description of the behavior of the Pine Grosbeaks, it is clear that if they did not have a nest, they must have had young in the immediate vicinity. If young Pine Grosbeaks just out of the nest are discovered, it is possible to stand within a few feet of them while the adult birds bring food to the hungry fledglings.

Slate-colored Juncos (Thoreau's *F. hyemalis*) are common breeding birds in the evergreen forest of the White Mountains. Their little nests may be tucked in some such charming place as a bed of moss under an overhanging rock. Usually they are well concealed.

Thoreau believed that the top of Mount Washington should not be in private hands. His wish in this respect has come to pass, for it is now within the boundary of the White Mountain National Forest and is open for the enjoyment of all Americans.]

THOREAU'S BIRDS OF THE WHITE MOUNTAINS FROM THE *JOURNAL*

JULY 2. [1858]   Start for White Mountains in a private carriage with Edward Hoar. . . .

The wood thrush sings almost wherever I go, eternally reconsecrating the world, morning and evening, for us. And again it seems habitable and more than habitable to us.

JULY 4. [Overlooking Lake Winnepiseogee, now Winnepesaukee]   I hear song sparrows there among the rocks, with a totally new strain, ending *whit whit, whit whit, whit whit whit*. They had also the common strain. . . . The goldfinch was more common than at home, and the fragrant fern was perceived oftener. The evergreen-forest not frequently heard. . . . Camped within a mile of Senter Harbor, in a birch wood on the right near the lake. Heard in the night a loon, screech owl, and cuckoo.

JULY 5. [On the summit of Mount Ossippee]   Heard a chewink on the summit. Descended. . . . Here first, in Moultonboro, I hear the *tea-lee* of the white-throated sparrow.

JULY 6. Breakfast by shore of one of the Ossippe Lakes. . . . Hear and see loons and see a peetweet's egg washed up.

JULY 8. [On Mount Washington]   The only bird I had seen on the way up, above the limit of trees, was the *Fringilla hyemalis*. Willey says it flies over the summit and that a bear has been seen there. [Near Hermit Lake, Tuckerman's Ravine]   The wood thrush, which Wentforth called the nightingale, sang at evening and in the morning, and the same bird which I heard on Monadnock, I think, and then thought might be the Blackburnian warbler; also the veery.

JULY 9. [Tuckerman's Ravine]   We had the *Fringilla hyemalis* with its usual note about our camp, and Wentworth said it was common and bred about his house. I afterward saw it in the valleys about the mountains. I had seen the white-throated sparrow near his house. This also, he said, commonly bred there, on the ground. . . . Returning, I sprained my ankle in

jumping down the brook, so that I could not sleep that night, nor walk the
next day. . . . A small owl came in the evening and sat within twelve feet
of us, turning its head this way and that and peering at us inquisitively. It
was apparently a screech owl. [A Saw-whet Owl]

July 10. [Tuckerman's Ravine]   The *Fringilla hyemalis* was most common
in the upper part of the ravine, and I saw a large bird of prey, perhaps an
eagle, sailing over the head of the ravine. The wood thrush and veery sang
regularly, especially morning and evening. But, above all, the peculiar and
memorable songster was that Monadnock-like one, keeping up an exceed-
ingly brisk and lively strain. It was remarkable for its incessant twittering
flow. Yet we never got within sight of the bird, at least while singing, so that
I could not identify it, and my lameness prevented my pursuing it. I heard
it afterward, even in the Franconia Notch. It was surprising for its steady
and uninterrupted flow, for when one stopped, another appeared to take
up the strain. It reminded me of a fine corkscrew stream issuing with
incessant lisping tinkle from a cork, flowing rapidly, and I said that he had
pulled out the spile and left it running. That was the rhythm, but with a
sharper tinkle of course. It had no more variety than that, but it was more
remarkable for its continuance and monotonousness than any bird's note I
ever heard. It evidently belongs only to cool mountainsides, high up amid
the fir and spruce. I saw once flitting through the fir-tops restlessly a small
white and dark bird, sylvia-like, which may have been it. Sometimes they
appeared to be attracted by our smoke. The note was so incessant that at
length you only noticed when it ceased. [A Winter Wren]

July 15. [Ascent of Mount Lafayette]   At about a mile and a half up by path,
the spruce began to be small. Saw there a silent bird, dark slate and blackish
above, especially head, with a white line over the brows, then dark slate next
beneath, white throat and reddish belly, black bill. A little like a nuthatch.

[Red-breasted Nuthatch] Also saw an *F. hyemalis* on top of a dead tree. . . .
Heard one white-throated sparrow above the trees, and also saw a little bird
by the pond. Think I heard a song sparrow about latter place.
  About half-way down the mountain, amid the spruce, we saw two pine
grosbeaks, male and female, close by the path, and looked for a nest, but in
vain. They were remarkably tame, and the male a brilliant red orange,—
neck, head, breast beneath, and rump,—blackish wings and tail, with two
white bars on wings. (Female yellowish.) The male flew nearer inquisitively,
uttering a low twitter, and perched fearlessly within four feet of us,
eyeing us and pluming himself and plucking and eating the leaves of the
Amelanchier oligocarpa on which he sat for several minutes. They were

evidently breeding there. Yet neither Wilson nor Nuttall speak of their breeding in the United States.

At the base of the mountain, over the road, heard (and saw), at the same place where I heard him the evening before, a splendid rose-breasted grosbeak singing. I had mistaken him at first for a tanager, and then for a red-eye, but was not satisfied; but now, with my glass, I distinguished him sitting quite still, high above the road at the entrance of the mountain-path in the deep woods, and singing steadily for twenty-minutes. . . . It was much richer and sweeter and, I think, more powerful than the note of the tanager, and more sweetness and fullness than the red-eye. Wilson does not give their breeding-place. Nuttall quotes Pennant as saying that some breed in New York but most further north. They, too, appear to breed about the White Mountains.

Heard the evergreen-forest note on the sides of the mountains often. Heard no robins in the White Mountains.

July 16. [Thoreau continued on through Thornton and Campton] About the mountains were wilder and rarer birds, more or less arctic, like the vegetation. I did not even *hear* a robin on them, and when I had left them a few miles behind, it was a great change and surprise to hear the lark, the wood pewee, the robin, and the bobolink (for the last had not done singing). On the mountains, especially at Tuckerman's Ravine, the notes even of familiar birds sounded strange to me. I hardly knew the wood thrush and veery and ovenbird at first. They sing so differently there. In two instances,—going down the Mt. Jefferson road and along the road in the Franconia Notch,—I started an *F. hyemalis* within two feet, close to the roadside, but looked in vain for a nest. They alight and sit thus close. I doubt if the chipping sparrow is found about the mountain.

[It is not surprising that the songs of birds, familiar to Thoreau in Concord, sounded strange in Tuckerman's Ravine. The song of a Hermit Thrush sung from the tip of a tall, solitary tree has not the beauty of one sung on or near the ground on the shore of a lake. The song of a Canyon Wren heard within the great circular walls of a cave is far more beautiful than the same song sung in the open. So the great walls of Tuckerman Ravine would cause the songs to reverberate, to echo and re-echo and sound richer and louder than in the open Concord woods.]

To the Land of Wild Indians

[In 1905, four hundred and eighty-nine copies of *The First and Last Journeys of Thoreau*, edited by Franklin Benjamin Sanborn, were printed in two volumes for members only by the Bibliophile Society. For the first time, the scanty notes made on Thoreau's trip to Minnesota were published. This trip, not only the last but the longest, was made in a vain hope that his health, failing because of tuberculosis, would be restored. He hoped that either Channing or Harrison Blake would accompany him, but apparently he was well pleased when young Horace Mann, Jr., a quiet, highly intelligent son of the great educator and statesman, joined him. Already this young man was an excellent botanist. His career was cut short, for he died of tuberculosis at the age of twenty-four.

Thoreau left Concord on May 11, 1861. His train ticket permitted a stopover at Niagara Falls where he and young Mann arrived on May 16 and remained until May 20. At East Dubuque (then Dunleith) Thoreau and his companion boarded a boat bound up the Mississippi River. They arrived at St. Paul on May 26 and remained in that general area until June 17 when they joined a group traveling up the Minnesota River to an Indian Council at Redwood. At the time, a Minneapolis newspaper described the group as very choice, select, brilliant, and cultured. In fact, the newspaper continued, the group was composed mainly of the *crème de la crème*—the rich yellow skim from the mottled milk of frontier society. Thoreau, probably dressed in his oldest clothes as was his custom when traveling, was mentioned as "Henry D. Thoreau, Esq., the celebrated abolitionist, etc."

Near Redwood, Thoreau saw genuine wild Indians for the first time as the Sioux gathered to receive their annual payments from the United States. He wrote:]

In the afternoon the half-naked Indians performed a dance at the request of the Governor, for our amusement and their own benefit. Then we took leave of them, and of the officials who had come to treat with them. In the dance were thirty men dancing and twelve musicians with drums, while others struck their arrows against their bows. The dancers blew some flutes, and kept good time, moving their feet or their shoulders, sometimes one, sometimes both. They wear no shirts. Five bands of Indians came in, and were feasted on an ox cut into five parts, one for each band.

[That same afternoon Thoreau again boarded the *Frank Steele* to begin his return to Concord. On June 22, near Mankato, the captain ran his boat on a rock and Thoreau noted, "We see the same birds along the river as in Concord, except the grebe and the Turkey Buzzard." He arrived in Red Wing about two o'clock in the afternoon of June 23. He heard that as many as a hundred rattlesnakes had been killed there in a single day, but this did not deter him from using what time he had to explore the surrounding country for plants and animal life. He sailed from Red Wing on June 26 and arrived in Prairie du Chien on June 27. There he boarded a train for Milwaukee where he embarked on the steamer *Edith* for Mackinaw which he reached at 2:00 A.M. on June 30. He remained there until July 4, though the weather was miserably cold, studying the plants and observing and learning about the area. He sailed on the *Sun* for Goderich and arrived in that Canadian town in the late evening of July 5. The following day he continued his journey to Toronto where he stayed until July 8 when he sailed for Ogdensburg, New York. From that town he went by train across Vermont and New Hampshire, arriving in Concord on July 10, 1861. He returned fatigued after a shorter absence than he had planned.

This trip, which took Thoreau about four thousand miles, was not only his last but took him farther from Concord than he had even been before. It cost between $150 and $180. He packed in a carpetbag his best pants, three shirts, three pairs of socks, a flannel shirt, slippers, underclothing, five handkerchiefs, a waistcoat, one towel, soap, a half-thick coat (he also took a thin coat which he probably wore when traveling), and a supply of medicine and other little articles which he might need. He carried an umbrella.

For his studies, Thoreau took a compass and microscope, a plant book for specimens, insect boxes, a botany book (probably Gray's *Manual of Botany*), twine, cards, blotting paper, tape, and a dipper and bottle for foot journeys.

No doubt the coat he wore was one made to his particular specifications with pockets large enough for his notebook and his spyglass, a pencil, a foot rule or surveyer's tape, and other materials which he might need on a particular walk. He did not trust his memory for facts but made immediate notes about each observation. It was his custom to rework his notes, not just once but usually many times. But the notes made on this last trip were only fragmentary and he never reworked them to any extent. Thus they give us a better understanding of his field notes than does the *Journal*.

Thoreau had about ten months to live when he returned to Concord and whatever strength he could summon was directed toward revising his material about Cape Cod, the Maine woods, and some of his essays for publication. But time ran out too soon, and neither *Cape Cod* nor *The Maine Woods* was ready for publication when he died.

On May 3, 1861, Thoreau wrote to his friend, Harrison Blake of Worcester, that he expected to be away from Concord for three months, and he mentioned the stop planned for Niagara Falls. The two notes that follow were written during that stop. In the years since Thoreau watched the ducks below the Falls, many birds have been swept over the brink. This usually happens when mist or snow narrows the vision. A few years ago a large flock of migrating Whistling Swans settled above the Falls, shrouded by a heavy mist, and were swept over the precipice—a genuine loss, for these large, beautiful birds are not abundant.

The Oldsquaw, a common duck near Niagara Falls, is often called coween by duck hunters in western New York State.]

MAY 15. [1861]   To Niagara Falls. Afternoon to Goat Island. Sight of the Rapids from the Bridge like the sea off Cape Cod—most imposing sight as yet. The great apparent height of the waves tumbling over the immense ledges—at a distance; while the water view is broad and boundless in that direction, as if you were looking out to sea, you are so low. Yet the distances are very deceptive; the most distant billow was scarcely more than a quarter of a mile off, though it appeared two miles or more. Many ducks were constantly floating a little way down from the Rapids,—then flying back and alighting again.

MAY 17. [1861]   Go to the Suspension Bridge and walk up on the Canada side. The completest view of the Falls is from that side. . . . A man says he calls these ducks "coween," and that they and other ducks both wild and tame, alight in the mist and are often carried over the Falls.

[There is no question that on his trip to Minnesota Thoreau really saw a Red-headed Woodpecker. His description of this species is excellent. As has been noted, his "red-headed woodpecker" near Mount Katahdin was not that species but the Pileated Woodpecker.]

MAY 20. [1861]   Niagara Falls to Detroit . . . Wild fowl east of Lake St. Clair; of which a long and fine view on each side of the Thames. Crossing, saw about Thamesville a small plump bird,—red head and blackish or bluish back and wings, but with broad white on the rounded wing and tail. Probably the red-headed woodpecker.

[While Thoreau made fairly complete notes about the flowers and trees which he saw, his notes about birds were sketchy. He mentioned only very common species, with but few exceptions, which occurred in Concord, as well as along his route to Minnesota.]

MAY 24. [1861]   [From Dunleith (now East Dubuque) to Prairie du Chien] Up river,—the river, say sixty rods wide, or three-quarters of a mile between the bluffs. . . . The birds are kingfishers, small ducks, swallows, jays, etc. . . .

[At Prairie du Chien]   The redwing blackbird is the prevailing bird till the Mississippi River; on the river, pigeons, kingfishers, crows, jays, etc., with swallows (the white-bellied).

[The following selection is the most complete list of the birds Thoreau saw near the Mississippi and in Minnesota. Probably the "black-throated waxwing" was a slip of the pencil and Thoreau meant to list the black-throated bunting now called the Dickcissel.

Minnesota is flooded by migrating birds during May, and great flocks of shorebirds pass over the state then. No doubt Thoreau did see the Killdeer which nests in Minnesota, but he gives no clue to the second species of plover which he saw on the prairie near St. Anthony, now Minneapolis.]

[Undated. Perhaps June 1861]   [St. Anthony]   The redwing blackbird, which I found was the prevailing bird till I reached the Mississippi, is also common here. Here, too I see or hear the marsh hawk, on the prairie the nighthawk, swallows (in the bank), martins (?) a *sereepa* note, (the particolored warbler, Maryland yellow-throat and night warbler). The horned lark is here very tame,—white on the end of the tail, chestnut head and yellowish. The bluebird, the thrasher and cat-bird, and the robin; the bay-wing, white-throated sparrow, chewink, tanager, lark, black-throated waxwing, and tufted kingfisher; pigeons, and I heard the flicker, who is such a telltale when near. The phoebe was on Nicollet Island; also the wood pewee and humming-bird,—the pewee seen in coming up the Mississippi. The red-start, summer yellowbird, and thrasher, the latter in the oaks behind St. Anthony. This mocker or the cat-bird I heard along the Mississippi as I came up. The red-headed woodpecker is here, and also all along through the great West. The plover (?) killdeer (?) (as on Cape Cod). The wood thrush (or hermit?) Wilson's thrush; Fringilla *socialis* and *melodia*, gold-finch, oriole, yellowthroat and warbling vireo heard, cherry-bird heard also. The rice-bird was seen in a low place in the woods at St. Anthony; the cowbird on the prairie there, and the crossbill in the woods and swamps; the brown snipe on the prairie at St. Anthony. Saw the killdeer and another plover (?) on the prairie there. On May 29, at the Minnehaha Falls, a rose-breasted grosbeak was eating the seeds of the slippery elm. There I got the horned lark (Otociris alpestris), and saw the chestnut-sided warbler near the "laughing water." The slippery elm is very common here, and upright and often large,—half the size of a large white elm. The seringo bird on the prairie at St. Anthony.

These are the birds I have noticed since Chicago and some before; Saw the nighthawk over the prairie in Illinois, as at Cape Cod, at mid-day. Heard the whippoorwill at Dunleith (?). Saw a large hawk or eagle, a pair (black-ish) over the bluffs on the Mississippi; larks on the prairies in Illinois, and Michigan, and along the Mississippi; crows along that river, and the blue jay, kingfisher, and passenger pigeon,—the latter Horace Mann saw in Illinois. At St. Anthony I saw a red-headed woodpecker on a telegraph-post within a stone's throw of the post office.

JUNE 6. [1861] . . . a wild pigeon's nest in a young bass tree, ten feet from the ground, four or five rods south of Lake Calhoun; built over a broad fork of the tree, where a third slender twig divided it, and a fourth forked it. . . . Built of slender hard twigs only, so open that I could see the eggs from the ground, and also so slight I could scarcely get to it with-out upsetting it. The bulk of the nest was six inches over; the ring of the concavity three-quarters of an inch thick, but irregular. At first (seeing the bird fly off) I thought it an unfinished nest.

JUNE 9. [1861] [By Lake Harriet] By the lake in a scarlet oak, eight feet up, I found a pigeon's nest like the former one, but more stable, con-taining one young bird three inches long, of a dirty yellowish and leaden color, with pinfeathers, and with a great bill bare at the base and a blackish tip. Another young bird slipped to the ground, fluttering as if wounded, two or three times, as she went off amid the shrubs. . . .

I come upon a third, fourth, and fifth nest of pigeons, with young,—the fourth not so high up (on a hop-hornbeam) as in the former nests,—say seven and a half feet high, and all much more substantially built, but made of the same-sized twigs as the first one. The last two nests were placed against the tree-trunk above a low branch or two.

[Bank Swallows dig their nest holes in sand or clay banks using their feet to kick away the earth. They cannot make holes in sandstone. Rough-winged Swallows, however, often use natural holes and crevices in sandstone cliffs as nesting places.]

JUNE 15. [1861]   [Between St. Anthony (Minneapolis) and St. Paul] The little brake grew in clefts of the sandstone; and there were many bank swallows' nests in and under the pillared and turreted (coped?) sandstone, so hard that you could not make the hole with your hand—or would not.

[Thoreau's trip on the *Frank Steele* with the distinguished company which included the Governor on his way to distribute government money to the Sioux, took Thoreau far into the interior of Minnesota. Along the Minnesota River he saw more Passenger Pigeons than elsewhere on the entire journey from Concord to the west.]

JUNE 17. [1861]   At nine P.M. we are near Stanhope. At five A.M. we are said to be in the big woods; the woods all alive with pigeons, and they flying across our course. The river is often only eight rods wide, and quite snaggy. About 7:30 we pass a beautiful open interval of native grass on the right. Many large turtle-tracks on shore . . . Very crooked river; acres of roses in the intervale. Swallows, kingfishers, blue jays, and warbling vireos along the shores. Grape-vines in blossom climbing on a cottonwood. We often strike the shore with our stern, or stop and back to get round snags and bars. Muddy-looking water, with soft-shelled and snapping turtles in it. See a turkey-buzzard and blue herons, and in the river some young ducks.

[JUNE 19. 1861]   [Thoreau found three to five young pigeons in nests and said the pigeons fed on pea-vines, which were swelling and sprouting purple flowers.]

We see ducks, a rail? . . . The pigeons seem straggling here. The Illinois man once lived where he could hear them at their roost, four miles off.

[The prairie which Thoreau studied around Lake Calhoun and Lake Harriet has been engulfed by Minneapolis, but the lakes and the land around them are now a part of the city park system. Boating, fishing, and water skiing are enjoyed on the lakes while bridle paths, picnic areas, golf courses, and gardens provide for other interests.

The last authentic record of a Passenger Pigeon in Minnesota was in 1895. Sometimes they had nested in tremendous concentrations. One such nesting in southern Minnesota in the 1870s covered more than two thousand acres and held a population of several million birds. Even when large nestings did not occur in the state, single nests could be found in the vicinity of Minneapolis at any time from late April to September. It was such isolated nests that Thoreau found on June 6 and June 19, 1861.]

An Alphabetical List
of Thoreau's Birds

Thoreau's obsolete names are preceded by an asterisk. Whenever Thoreau's name for a species is so similar to the one used to-day that there can be no confusion, only the currently accepted name is listed. For instance, Thoreau wrote of the bluebird, now called Eastern Bluebird, of the woodcock now called American Woodcock, of the Maryland yellow-throat now simply called Yellowthroat, and so on. Many of the names used by Thoreau are still in popular use, though no longer recognized as correct by ornithologists. Therefore it seemed unnecessary to lengthen the list by noting every variation in nomenclature.]

*Auk, Little. *See* Dovekie
*Bay-wing. *See* Sparrow, Vesper
*Beach-bird. *See* Plover, Piping
*Belcher-squelcher. See Bittern, American
Bittern, America: *Botaurus lentiginosus*
    *Great. See Bittern, American
    *Green. See Heron, Green
    Least: *Ixobrychus exilis*
    *Small. *See* Heron, Green
Blackbird, *Cow. *See* Cowbird, Brown-headed
    *Crow. *See* Grackle, Common
    Red-winged: *Agelaius phoeniceus*

Rusty: *Euphagus carolinus*
Bluebird, Eastern: *Sialis sialis*
Bobolink: *Dolichonyx oryzivorus*
Bobwhite: *Colinus virginianus*
Brant: *Branta bernicla*
Bufflehead: *Bucephala albeola*
Bunting, *Black-throated. *See* Dickcissel
    Indigo: *Passerina cyanea*
    Snow: *Plectrophenax nivalis*
*Butcher-bird. *See* Shrike, Northern
*Buzzard, Red-shouldered. *See* Hawk, Red-shouldered
    Turkey. *See* Vulture, Turkey
*Cape eagle. *See* Goshawk
Catbird: *Dumetella carolinensis*
*Cherry-bird. *See* Waxwing, Cedar
*Chewink. *See* Towhee, Rufous-sided
Chickadee, Black-capped: *Parus atricapillus*
Chicken, Greater Prairie. *See* Prairie Chicken, Greater
*Chicken, Mother Carey's. *See* Petrel, Wilson's
*Chip-bird. *See* Sparrow, Chipping
*Cock, Heath (or Heath Hen). *See* Prairie Chicken, Greater (The subspecies
    of the Greater Prairie Chicken, called Heath Cock or Heath Hen, which
    occurred in New England, is now extinct.)
*Coot. *See* Scoter. (All three American species of Scoter; Common, Surf, and
    White-winged, occur in New England and are still popularly called
    "coots" by duck hunters.)
Coot, American: *Fulica americana*
    *cinereus. *See* Coot, American
Cormorant, Double-crested: *Phalacrocorax auritus*
Cowbird, Brown-headed: *Molothrus ater*
*Coween. See Oldsquaw
Creeper, *Black-and-white. *See* Warbler, Black-and-white
    Brown: *Certhia familiaris*
*Pine. *See* Warbler, Pine
Crossbill, Red: *Loxia curvirostra*
*Crow-blackbird. *See* Grackle, Common
Crow, Common: *Corvus brachyrhynchos*
Cuckoo, Black-billed: *Coccyzus erythropthalmus*
    *St. Domingo. *See* Cuckoo, Black-billed
    Yellow-billed: *Coccyzus americanus*
Dickcissel: *Spiza americana*

*Dipper, Little: *See* Grebe, Horned and Grebe, Pied-billed, also Merganser, Hooded

*Diver (or Great Northern Diver). *See* Loon, Common and Loon, Red-throated

Dove, Mourning: *Zenaidura macroura*
    *Turtle. *See* Dove, Mourning

Dovekie: *Plautus alle*

Duck, Black: *Anas rubripes*
    *Dusky. *See* Duck, Black
    *Buffle-head. *See* Bufflehead
    *Eider. *See* Eider, Common
    *Spindle-tail. *See* Pintail
    *Spirit. *See* Bufflehead
    *Surf. *See* Scoter, Surf
    *Velvet. *See* Scoter, White-winged
    Wood: *Aix sponsa*

Eagle, Bald: *Haliaeetus leucocephalus*
    *Cape. *See* Goshawk
    *Fish. *See* Osprey
   *White-headed. *See* Eagle, Bald

Eider, Common: *Somateria mollissima*

*Election-bird (or Election Day bird). *See* Tanager, Scarlet and Redstart, American

*Evergreen-forest bird. *See* Warbler, Black-throated Green

Finch, *Grass. *See* Sparrow, Vesper
    Purple: *Carpodacus purpureus*

*Fiery Hangbird. *See* Oriole, Baltimore

*Fire-never-redder. *See* Tanager, Scarlet

Flicker, Yellow-shafted: *Colaptes auratus*

Flycatcher, Least: *Empidonax minimus*
    Olive-sided: *Nuttallornis borealis*
    Traill's: *Empidonax traillii*

*Fringilla (or *F.*) hyemalis. *See* Junco, Slate-colored
    *juncorum. *See* Sparrow, Field
    *linaria. *See* Redpoll, Common
    *melodia. *See* Sparrow, Song
    *passerina. *See* Sparrow, Savannah
    *savanna. *See* Sparrow, Grasshopper

Goldeneye, Common: *Bucephala clangula*

Goldfinch, Common: *Spinus tristis*

*Gold robin (or Golden robin). *See* Oriole, Baltimore

*Goosander. *See* Merganser, Common

Goose, Canada: *Branta canadensis*
    wild. See Goose, Canada
Goshawk: *Accipter gentillis*
Grackle, Common: *Quiscalus quiscula*
    rusty. See Blackbird, Rusty
Grass-bird. See Sparrow, Vesper
Grebe, Horned: *Podiceps auritus*
    Pied-billed: *Podilymbus podiceps*
    Red-necked: *Podiceps grisegena*
Grosbeak, Pine: *Pinicola enucleator*
    Rose-breasted: *Pheucticus ludovicianus*
Ground-bird: See Towhee, Rufous-sided (Thoreau occasionally used this
    term for such ground-feeding birds as Savannah, Vesper, and Song
    Sparrows.)
Ground-robin. See Towhee, Rufous-sided
Grouse, *Black. See* Grouse, Spruce
    Pinnated. See Prairie Chicken, Greater
    Ruffed: *Bonasa umbellus*
    Spruce: *Canachites canadensis*
Gull, *Black-headed. See* Gull, Bonaparte's
    Bonaparte's: *Larus philadelphia*
    Great Black-backed: *Larus marinus*
    Herring: *Larus argentatus*
    Mackerel. See Tern, Common (Fishermen along the New England
        coast also call Arctic Terns and Roseate Terns "Mackerel Gulls.")
Hangbird. See Oriole, Baltimore
Hair-bird. See Sparrow, Chipping
Harrier. See Hawk, Marsh
Hawk, Cooper's: *Accipiter cooperii*
    Fish. See Osprey
    Frog. See Hawk, Marsh
    Hen. See Hawk, Red-tailed and Hawk, Red-shouldered
    Marsh: *Circus cyaneus*
    Partridge. See Goshawk
    Pigeon: *Falco columbarius*
    Red-shouldered: *Buteo lineatus*
    Red-tailed: *Buteo jamaicensis*
    Rough-legged: *Buteo lagopus*
    Sharp-shinned: *Accipter striatus*
    Sparrow: *Falco sparvarius*
Hen-harrier. See Hawk, Marsh
Heath-hen. See Prairie Chicken, Greater

*Hen, Marsh. *See* Coot, American
*Hen, Meadow. *See* Rail, Virginia
*Hen, Mud. *See* Rail, Clapper
Heron, *Blue. *See* Heron, Great Blue
    Great Blue: *Ardea herodias*
    Green: *Butorides virescens*
*Huckleberry-bird. *See* Sparrow, Field
*Humility (This was a general term used by early colonists for the larger
    shorebirds of New England, such as willets and yellow-legs.)
Hummingbird, Ruby-throated: *Archilochus colubris*
*Indigo-bird. *See* Bunting, Indigo (Thoreau's "indigo-bird" of May 4, 1853,
    was a Black-throated Blue Warbler.)
Jay, Blue: *Cyanocitta cristata*
    *Canada. *See* Jay, Gray
    Gray: *Perisoreus canadensis*
Junco, Slate-colored: *Junco hyemalis*
Killdeer: *Charadrius vociferus*
Kingbird, Eastern: *Tyrannus tyrannus*
Kingfisher, belted: *Megaceryle alcyon*
Kinglet, Golden-crowned: *Regulus satrapa*
    Ruby-crowned: *Regulus calendula*
Kittiwake, Black-legged: *Rissa tridactyla*
*Lark. *See* Meadowlark, Eastern
Lark, Horned: *Eremophila alpestris*
    *shore. *See* Lark, Horned
*Linaria. *See* Redpoll, Common
Loon, Common: *Gavia immer*
    Red-throated: *Gavia stellata*
Mallard: *Anas platyrhynchos*
*Marsh-hen. *See* Coot, American
*Maryland yellow-throat. *See* Yellowthroat
Martin, Purple: *Progna subis*
*Mavis, red. *See* Thrasher, Brown
*Meadow-hen. *See* Rail, Virginia
Meadowlark, Eastern: *Sturnella magna*
    Western: *Sturnella neglecta*
Merganser, Common: *Mergus merganser*
    Hooded: *Lophodytes cucullatus*
    Red-breasted: *Mergus serrator*
*Merlin. *See* Hawk, Pigeon
Mockingbird: *Mimus polyglottos*
*Mother-Carey's-chicken. *See* Petrel, Wilson's

*Mud-hen. *See* Rail, Clapper
*Myrtle-bird. *See* Warbler, Myrtle
Nighthawk, Common: *Chordeiles minor*
*Night-warbler. *See* Ovenbird; also Yellowthroat (Thoreau was never satis-
    fied about the identity of his night warbler. Though on August 5, 1858,
    he identified the Yellowthroat as his mysterious singer, on most occas-
    ions it was probably the Ovenbird giving its aerial song.)
Nuthatch, *Red-bellied. *See* Nuthatch, Red-breasted
    Red-breasted: *Sitta canadensis*
    *White-bellied. *See* Nuthatch, White-breasted
    White-breasted: *Sitta carolinensis*
Oldsquaw: *Clangula hyemalis*
Oriole, Baltimore: *Icterus galbula*
Osprey: *Pandion haliaetus*
Ovenbird: *Sieurus aurocapillus*
Owl, *Acadian. *See* Owl, Saw-whet
    Barred: *Strix varia*
    *Cat. *See* Owl, Great Horned
    Great Horned: *Bubo virginianus*
    *Hoot (or hooting). *See* Owl, Great Horned (Barred Owls which give
        eight hoots divided into two groups of four notes each are also
        commonly called hoot owls. But Thoreau, in describing the call
        of his hoot owls, stated that they gave five hoots. Therefore he
        referred to the Great Horned Owl.)
    Long-eared: *Asio otus*
    *Red: *See* Owl, Screech
    Saw-whet: *Aegolius acadicus*
    Screech: *Otus asio*
    Short-eared: *Asio flammeus*
    Long-eared: *Asio otus*
    Snowy: *Nyctea scandiaca*
    *White. *See* Owl, Snowy
*Parti-colored Warbler (or -bird). *See* Warbler, Parula
*Partridge. *See* Grouse, Ruffed
*Peawai. *See* Wood Pewee, Eastern
*Peetweet. *See* Sandpiper, Spotted
*Pe-pe. *See* Flycatcher, Olive-sided
*Petrel, Fork-tailed Stormy. *See* Petrel, Wilson's
*Pewee. *See* Phoebe, Eastern
*Pewee, bridge. *See* Phoebe, Eastern
*Pewee, Wood. *See* Wood Pewee, Eastern
    *Small. *See* Flycatcher, Least (Thoreau's small pewee, *Muscicapa acadica*

of the Maine Woods, was probably Traill's Flycatcher, *Empidonax traillii*.)

Phalarope (No clue to species given)

Phoebe, Eastern: *Sayornis phoebe*

Pigeon, Passenger: *Ectopistes migratorius* (Now extinct)
 *wild. *See* Pigeon, Passenger

*Pigeon Woodpecker. *See* Flicker, Yellow-shafted

Pintail: *Anas acuta*

Pipit, Water: *Anthus spinoletta*

Plover, American Golden: *Pluvialis dominica*
 Piping: *Charadrius melodus*
 Semipalmated: *Charadrius semipalmatus*
 Upland. *Bartramia longicauda*
 *Wilson's. *See* Plover, Semipalmated

Prairie Chicken, Greater: *Tympanuchus cupido*

*Quail. *See* Bobwhite

*Rail-bird. (May refer to any of the rails of Concord including the King Rail
 (*Rallus elegans*), which Thoreau never mentioned in his writings.)

Rail, *Carolina. *See* Sora
 Clapper: *Rallus longirostris*
 Virginia: *Rallus limicola*

Raven, Common: *Corvus corax*

*Red-bird. *See* Tanager, Scarlet

*Red-crown. *See* Redpoll, Common

*Red Election-bird. *See* Tanager, Scarlet

*Red-eye. *See* Vireo, Red-eyed

*Red mavis. *See* Thrasher, Brown

Redpoll, Common: *Acanthis flammea*
 *Lesser. *See* Redpoll, Common
 *Yellow. *See* Warbler, Palm

Redstart, American: *Setophaga ruticilla*

*Red-wing. *See* Blackbird, Redwinged

*Rice-bird. *See* Bobolink

Robin: *Turdus migratorius*

*Robin, Gold (or Golden). *See* Oriole, Baltimore

Sanderling: *Crocethia alba*

Sandpiper, Pectoral: *Erolia melanotos*
 Solitary: *Tringa solitaria*
 Spotted: *Actitis macularia*

Scaup, Greater: *Aythya marila*
 Lesser: *Aythya affinis*

Scoter, Common: *Oidemia nigra*

Surf: *Melanitta perspicillata*
*Velvet. *See* White-winged Scoter (The Velvet Scoter is a European
  species rather similar to the White-winged Scoter.)
White-winged: *Melanitta deglandi*
*Sea-swallow. *See* Tern, Common
*Seringo (Thoreau frequently called the Savannah Sparrow the seringo or
  seringo-bird, but he also applied the name to other small birds. At least
  once he spoke of the seringo (song) of the Cedar Waxwing.)
*Shecorway. *See* Merganser, Common (Shecorway was the Abenaki Indian
  name for mergansers.)
*Sheldrake. *See* Merganser (Both Common and Red-breasted Mergansers
  are often called sheldrakes, but when he used this name, Thoreau gen-
  erally referred to the Common Merganser.)
*Shorelark. *See* Lark, Horned
Shrike, Northern: *Lanius excubitor*
Snipe, *Brown. *See* Snipe, Common
  Common: *Capella gallinago*
  *Wilson's. *See* Snipe, Common
*Snow-bird. *See* Junco, Slate-colored
*Snow-bird, Arctic. *See* Bunting, Snow
Sora: *Porzana carolina*
Sparrow, *Bay-wing. *See* Sparrow, Vesper
  Chipping: *Spizella passerina*
  Field: *Spizella pusilla*
  Fox: *Passerella iliaca*
  *Fox-colored. *See* Sparrow, Fox
  Grasshopper: *Ammodramus savannarum*
  *Rush. *See* Sparrow, Field
  Savannah: *Passerculus sandwichensis*
  *savannarum. *See* Sparrow, Grasshopper
  *slate-colored. *See* Junco, Slate-colored
  Swamp: *Melospiza georgiana*
  Song: *Melospiza melodia*
  Tree: *Spizella arborea*
  Vesper: *Pooecetes gramineus*
  White-throated: *Zonotrichia albicollis*
  *Yellow-winged. *See* Sparrow, Grasshopper
*Stake-driver. *See* Bittern, American
*Storm Petrel. *See* Petrel, Wilson's
*Sylvia paradalina. *See* Warbler, Canada
*Sylvia striata. *See* Warbler, Blackpoll
Swallow, Bank: *Riparia riparia*

Barn: *Hirundo rustica*
*Chimney. *See* Swift, Chimney
Cliff: *Petrochelidon pyrrhonta*
*Republican. *See* Swallow, Cliff
Tree: Iridoprocne bicolor
*White-bellied. *See* Swallow, Tree
Swan, Whistling: *Olor columbianus*
Swift, Chimney: *Chaetura pelagica*
Tanager, Scarlet: *Piranga olivacea*
*Tattler, Solitary. *See* Sandpiper, Solitary
Teal, Blue-winged: *Anas discors*
Green-winged: *Anas carolinensis*
*Tell-tale. *See* Yellowlegs, Greater; also Yellowlegs, Lesser
Tern, Common: *Sterna hirundo*
Thrasher, Brown: *Toxostroma rufum*
Thrush, Golden-crowned. *See* Ovenbird
Gray-checked: *Hylocichla minima* (Thoreau is believed to have heard the Bicknell's Thrush, a subspecies of the Gray-cheeked Thrush, in the White Mountains.)
Thrush, Hermit: *Hylocichla guttata*
Swainson's: *Hylocichla ustulata*
*Wilson's. *See* Veery
Wood. *Hylocichla mustelina*
*Tinker. *See* Rail, Clapper
*Titlark. *See* Pipit, Water
*Titmouse (Titmice). *See* Chickadee, Black-capped
*Totamus flavipes. *See* Yellowlegs, Lesser
Towhee, Rufous-sided: *Pipilo erythrophthalmus*
*Finch. *See* Towhee, Rufous-sided
*Troopial, Cow. *See* Cowbird, Brown-headed
*Turdus aquaticus. *See* Water-thrush, Northern
*Tweezer-bird. *See* Warbler, Parula
Veery: *Hylocichla fuscescens*
Vireo, Red-eyed: *Vireo olivaceus*
Solitary: *Vireo solitarius*
Warbling: *Vireo gilvus*
White-eyed: *Vireo griseus*
Yellow-throated: *Vireo flavifrons*
Vulture, Turkey: *Cathartes aura*
Warbler, Black-and-white: *Mniotilta varia*
*Black-and-yellow. *See* Warbler, Magnolia
Blackburnian: *Dendroica fusca*

Blackpoll: *Dendroica striata*
Black-throatd Blue: *Dendroica caerulescens*
Black-throated Green: *Dendroica virens*
*Blue yellow-backed. *See* Warbler, Parula
Canada: *Wilsonia canadensis*
Chestnut-sided: *Dendroica pensylvanica*
Connecticut: *Oporornis agilis*
Golden-winged: *Vermivora chrysoptera*
Magnolia: *Dendroica magnolia*
Myrtle: *Dendroica coronata*
Nashville: *Vermivora ruficapilla*
*Night. *See* Ovenbird; also Yellowthroat
Palm: *Dendroica palmarum*
*Parti-colored. *See* Warbler, Parula
Parula: *Parula americana*
Pine: *Dendroica pinus*
Pine-creeping. *See* Warbler, Pine
Yellow: *Dendroica petechia*
*Yellow-rumped. *See* Warbler, Myrtle
Waterthrush, Louisiana: *Seiurus motacilla*
Waxwing, Black-throated (Thoreau probably referred to the Black-throated
    Bunting, now called Dickcissel)
Cedar: *Bombycilla cedrorum*
Whip-poor-will: *Caprimulgus vociferus*
*Whistler. *See* Goldeneye
Woodcock, American: *Philchela minor*
Woodpecker, *Arctic Three-toed. *See* Woodpecker, Black-backed Three-toed
    Black-backed Three-toed: *Picoides arcticus*
    Downy: *Dendrocopos pubescens*
    *Golden-winged. *See* Flicker, Yellow-shafted
    Hairy: *Dendrocopes villosus*
    *Pigeon. *See* Flicker, Yellow-shafted
    Pileated: *Dryocopos pileatus*
    Red-headed: *Melanerpes erythrocephalus*
Wood Pewee, Eastern: *Contopus virens*
*White-in-tail: *See* Sparrow, Vesper
Wren, *Golden-crested. *See* Kinglet, Golden-crowned
    Long-billed Marsh: *Telmatodytes palustris*
    *Ruby-crested. *See* Kinglet, Ruby-crowned
    Short-billed Marsh: *Cictothorus platensis*
    Winter: *Troglodytes troglodytes*
*Yellow-bird (or Summer Yellow-bird). *See* Warbler, Yellow

Yellowlegs, Greater : *Totamus melanoleucus*
    Lesser : *Totamus flavipes*
*Yellow-rump. *See* Warbler, Myrtle
Yellowthroat : *Geothlypis trichas*
*Yellow-throat, Maryland. *See* Yellowthroat
*Yorrick. *See* Veery

A Selected Bibliography

Canby, Henry Seidel, *The Works of Thoreau*, Houghton Mifflin Co., Boston, 1939.

Griscom, Ludlow, *Birds of Concord*, Harvard University Press, Boston, 1939.

Harding, Walter E., *Thoreau, Man of Concord*, New York University Press, New York, 1960.

Harding, Walter E., *A Thoreau Handbook*, New York University Press, 1959.

Krutch, Joseph Wood, *Great American Nature Writing*, Wm. Sloane Associates, New York, 1950.

Krutch, Joseph Wood, *Henry David Thoreau*, Wm. Sloane Associates, New York, 1948.

Meltzer, Milton, and Harding, Walter E., *A Thoreau Profile*, Thomas Y. Crowell Co., New York, 1962.

Salt, Henry S., *The Life of Henry David Thoreau*, London, 1890.

Sanborn, Franklin Benjamin, *The First and Last Journeys of Thoreau*, The Bibliophile Society, Boston, 1905.

Shepard, Odell, editor, *The Heart of Thoreau's Journals*, Houghton Mifflin Co., 1927.

Teale, Edwin Way, *The Thoughts of Thoreau*, Dodd, Mead and Co., New York, 1962.

Thoreau, Henry David, *Notes on New England Birds*, edited by Francis H. Allen, Houghton Mifflin Co., Boston, 1910.

Thoreau, Henry David, *The Writings of Henry David Thoreau*, edited by Bradford Torey and Francis H. Allen, Houghton Mifflin Co., Boston, 1906. (This is the Walden Edition and contains the major part of Thoreau's writings, including most of the *Journal* which fills fourteen volumes of the twenty-volume set. The *Journal* alone (fourteen volumes) was republished by Houghton Mifflin with a foreword by Henry Seidel Canby in 1951.)

Thoreau, Henry David, *The Journal of Henry David Thoreau*, edited by Bradford Torrey and Francis H. Allen, with a foreword by Walter E. Harding, in two volumes, Dover, New York, 1962.

Thoreau, Henry David, *Consciousness in Concord*, with a commentary by Perry Miller, Houghton Mifflin Co., Boston, 1958.

Thoreau, Henry David, *In Wilderness is the Preservation of the World*, edited and illustrated by Eliot Porter, The Sierra Club, San Francisco, 1962.

A Week on the Concord and Merrimack Rivers, Walden, Cape Cod, The Maine Woods, and *Excursions*, have appeared in many editions ranging from de luxe to paperbacks, and are generally available.

INDEX

(Roman numerals refer to plate numbers)

About the Author

Helen Cruickshank is one of America's foremost bird authorities. She is author of *Wonders of the Bird World* and *Wonders of the Reptile World,* editor of *John and William Bartram's America,* and winner of the John Burroughs award for excellence in nature writing. Mrs. Cruickshank is wife of the famous bird photographer, Allan Cruickshank, with whom she co-authored *1001 Questions Answered about Birds.*